M. Van Houten

D0614718

LEGAL RESEARCH IN A NUTSHELL

By

MORRIS L. COHEN
Professor of Law and Law Librarian,
Harvard University Law School

THIRD EDITION

ST. PAUL, MINN.
WEST PUBLISHING CO.
1978

Cohen Legal Research 3rd Ed.

PREFACE

The literature of American law is rich and varied and has a long and distinguished history. Its primary sources contain the rules of human behavior by which our society is governed; its ingenious finding tools provide access to the mass of chronologically published decisions and statutes; and its wide ranging secondary sources illuminate the law by study of its past, its present, and its future.

Legal literature, reflecting and shaping the continuing struggle for justice and order, is part of our total cultural heritage. But knowledge of its forms and skill in its use are even more certainly an essential part of the lawyer's basic training and equipment. This epitome of American legal bibliography is designed to assist the student in achieving such knowledge and skill. It is intended as an introduction where a fuller course of study, such as might be based on comprehensive texts like Price & Bitner's *Effective Legal Research,* Jacobstein & Mersky's *Fundamentals of Legal Research,* or Cohen's *How to Find the Law,* is not offered. Since it is not intended to be a reference tool in any sense, footnotes and most bibliographic detail have been omitted or relegated to the Appendices. This *Nutshell* is rather designed to offer limited instruction through a

simple, concise text and for best effect should be followed by some form of bibliographic exposure in a library setting. This can be done through the traditional legal research "finger exercises," through somewhat more analytical legal method problems, or through legal writing assignments.

Since the publication of the first edition of this manual, the nature of legal research and the forms of legal material have undergone some change and will undoubtedly continue to incorporate new developments in information technology. Computerized legal research and the use of microforms are becoming accepted in law libraries and are described herein where relevant. While the essential publications and processes remain familiar, bibliographic advances are significantly improving the nature and effectiveness of legal research. The maximum potential inherent in both traditional and modern research techniques can only be realized by an adequate understanding of the form and content of legal literature. This guide is designed to facilitate such an understanding.

For their permission to reproduce exhibits from their respective publications, the author acknowledges the kindness of the Bureau of National Affairs, Columbia University Legislative Drafting Research Fund, Commerce Clearing House, Inc., the Congressional Information Service, Congressional Quarterly, Lawyers Co-operative Publishing Company, Shepard's Citations, Sweet & Max-

well, the Edward Thompson Company, and the West Publishing Company.

The author wishes to express his gratitude to colleagues at the Harvard Law School Library and at many other law libraries for their contributions and support in the preparation of this new edition. And to the long-suffering law students who may be introduced to legal research through these pages, the book is dedicated.

MORRIS L. COHEN

Cambridge, Massachusetts
September, 1977

*

OUTLINE

†

LEGAL RESEARCH IN A NUTSHELL

CHAPTER I

INTRODUCTION

The forms and usages of law books are varied and, in their entirety, may appear at first view somewhat confusing. However, legal literature can be divided into three broad categories: (a) primary sources; (b) search books or finding-tools; and (c) secondary materials.

Primary Sources. We can define the primary sources as those recorded rules of human behavior which will be enforced by the state. They include statutes passed by legislatures, decisions of courts, decrees and orders of executives, and regulations and rulings of administrative agencies.

American law today, as so construed, has a number of characteristics which should be noted for their bibliographic significance.

It is subject to constant change through tens of thousands of new decisions and new stat-

utes each year, requiring regular and prompt supplementation and updating.

Its development is marked, however, by a quest for certainty and stability, as reflected in the doctrine of *stare decisis,* which gives most law books a continuing relevance long beyond their period of publication.

It derives from many governmental agencies (judicial, legislative and executive) and from a variety of jurisdictions (the federal government, fifty states, a host of local counties, cities and towns, and even some international agencies, whose rules are accepted by tribunals here). This variety of law-making bodies vastly multiples the bibliographic *sources* of law in this country.

Its judicial system embodies hierarchies of courts (typically including, in each jurisdiction, a series of trial courts, one or more intermediate appeal courts, and a high court, frequently of last resort). This system includes a process of appellate review whereby appeal courts may be called upon to review the decisions of lower courts and even the acts of the legislative and executive branches.

Its legal publications differ in their relative authority—some are binding, others only persuasive in various degrees, and some lack-

ing in any formal legal force—leading to a need for careful evaluation by the user.

Its forms are issued *chronologically* in either official or unofficial publications, requiring some means of access by subject to enable the researcher to find the law applicable to a particular factual situation.

Federal and state statutes and appellate court decisions are the most important primary authorities. Traditionally they were the only primary sources of law, administrative materials being considered secondary forms since their authority *derived* from the legislature. Only in the last generation, by virtue of their great impact on the legal system, have administrative regulations, orders, and decisions, been treated as primary sources.

The primary sources relevant to any problem may range in time from the first enactments of law-making bodies to the most recent decisions, statutes and rulings. A current decision may be based on a precedent many generations old; an executive order may stem from a statute of another century. Since primary sources retain legal effect until expressly overruled or repealed, access to even the earliest sources is a continuing necessity. The accessibility of the latest legal sources is also, as we have seen, an inherent necessity in legal research.

Finding-Tools. Because of the great number of decisions and statutes issued since the beginning of our legal history and because of their chronological method of publication, the researcher needs some means of subject access into this large body of law. The effective operation of the doctrine of precedent requires that prior decisions be easily available. In legal research as in other aspects of the lawyer's work one must employ what should be a highly developed sense of relevance—a keen appreciation of what is legally and factually relevant to a particular problem. Without a topical approach to legal sources, we could not find existing statutes or decided cases in point. A varied group of finding-tools, typically issued by specialized private publishers, provide such access. These include digests of decisions, citators, encyclopedias, phrasebooks, annotated statutory compilations, looseleaf services, and indexes. Such research books may themselves lack legal authority, but they provide the means of locating the primary sources of authority.

Secondary Materials. Finally, there is the last major component of legal bibliography, the secondary sources. These include textbooks, treatises, commentaries, restatements, and periodicals which explain and describe the law for the practitioner, the scholar and the student. They vary widely in quality, form and authority, ranging

from monumental treatises by great academic scholars to superficial tracts by hack writers. Encyclopedias are sometimes considered to be in this group, although some scholars prefer to treat them primarily as case finders and cast them with the finding-tools and search books.

Although these works lack legal authority in a formal sense, some may have a persuasive influence in the law-making process by virtue of the recognized prestige of their authors or the quality of their scholarship. Access to these materials is usually provided by their own internal subject indexes, although a variety of separate indexes have been developed for periodicals and some guides and bibliographies are available for texts and treatises.

LAW LIBRARIES

There are many types of law libraries, serving many kinds of readers who are engaged in legal research for different reasons and with different approaches. These collections range in size and purpose from the million volume libraries at the Harvard Law School and the Law Library of Congress to the law office library of a thousand volumes serving a few practicing lawyers. They are also found in court houses, government agencies, corporations, bar associations, and even within public libraries.

Regardless of differences in size, purpose and clientele, most law libraries have a great deal in common. The following are the usual components of the larger law libraries, arranged somewhat arbitrarily into the three main categories of legal material:

Primary Sources

    Administrative decisions and rulings
    Administrative rules and regulations
    Constitutions
    Executive documents
    Judicial reports
    Statutes—session laws and codes
    Treaties

Finding Tools

    Bibliographies and research guides
    Citators
    Computerized research services
    Digests of case law
    Indexes to statutes and legislative history
    Looseleaf services
    Periodical indexes
    Word and phrase books

Secondary Materials

    Administrative reports and studies
    Appellate records and briefs
    Attorneys General opinions
    Bar association reports and proceedings

Biographies of lawyers and judges
Commentaries, histories and surveys of law
Constitutional conventions and documents
Dictionaries
Directories of lawyers and law firms
Encyclopedias
Fiction and anecdotes relating to law
Foreign and comparative legal sources
Form books
International legal sources
Legislative history
Periodicals
Practice and procedure manuals
Reference books—legal and general
Restatements of the Law
Sourcebooks of historical documents
Texts, treatises and monographs
Trials

Access to the contents of law libraries may be facilitated in several ways: law librarians, who are often trained bibliographic specialists, offer expert direction; the specialized indexes and finding-tools described herein provide access to the primary sources of law; and the card catalog, that most neglected and ingenious tool of information retrieval, aids in identifying and locating most of the library's collection. The advent of the computer is already adding a new means of access to the contents of law libraries.

AIDS TO RESEARCH

Because legal bibliography differs from other bibliography, and legal research from research in general, several special aids are recommended. For an understanding and mastery of the language of the law, a good law dictionary is a necessity for the beginning student. See Chapter IX, Secondary Materials, at pages 304–305 below, for specific suggestions.

To cope with the complex shorthand of legal citations, guides to proper citation form and usage are available. *A Uniform System of Citation,* published by the Harvard Law Review Association (12th ed., 1976) and commonly referred to as the *bluebook,* is the generally accepted standard.

Abbreviations of many kinds are widely used in legal writing, and aids to their meanings are frequently needed. The *bluebook* contains many explanatory lists of abbreviations. *Black's Law Dictionary* includes the most extensive coverage of abbreviations, but lacks the references to current reporters, session laws and statutory compilations which are covered well in the *bluebook.* *Effective Legal Research* and *Fundamentals of Legal Research,* described below, also contain substantial lists of abbreviations.

Detailed information on the sources of American law can be found in such bibliographic treatis-

es as Price & Bitner, *Effective Legal Research*;
Jacobstein & Mersky, *Fundamentals of Legal Research*; and *How to Find the Law* (edited by Morris L. Cohen). The detailed appendices and historical notes in the first edition (1953) of Price & Bitner give it a permanent value beyond that of its current edition.

Legal sources have been more fully described and cataloged than perhaps any other literature. The bibliographic approaches of legal research are the most sophisticated in pre-computer documentation. The new developments of information science are already improving access to the law even more, particularly by microfacsimiles and computerized search services. However, the practitioners of legal research have never fully exploited the tools at hand. The widespread failure to use the many aids and shortcuts now available leads to that sad by-product of bibliographic ignorance—needless waste of valuable time and effort.

CHAPTER II
JUDICIAL REPORTS

Law reports, containing the decisions of courts, form one of the two great sources of legal authority. Although statutes are seemingly more direct and imperative, many say that they are ineffective until construed or interpreted by judges and actually applied to particular situations. The development of the recording of judicial decisions undoubtedly has been related to the quest for certainty in the law. In seeking to achieve regularity in the impact of legal rules, those concerned with the law soon came to realize the value of recording the decisions of particular legal controversies. Such records not only aid in preventing further disputes, but may also provide guidance to later tribunals when faced with similar cases.

Karl Llewellyn formulated the following reasons for the doctrine of precedent:

> " * * * laziness as to the re-working of a problem once solved; the time and energy saved by routine, especially under the pressure of business; the values of routine as a curb on arbitrariness and as a prop of weakness, inexperience and instability; and the

social value of predictability; the power of whatever exists to produce expectations and the power of expectations to become normative * * * that curious, almost universal sense of justice which urges that all men are properly to be treated alike in like circumstances." ("Case Law" in the *Encyclopedia of Social Sciences,* 1937)

From its beginnings, law reporting facilitated the achievement of those purposes and the search for predictability. Only by written records could the future impact of the law be evaluated and the conduct of individuals influenced thereby. Whether or not that was the original rationale of law reporting, it certainly has been its most important by-product.

In addition to their value as legal precedent and their importance in legal bibliography and research, the law reports constitute a literary form with other values as well. They describe human problems and predicaments—domestic crises, moral failings, economic troubles. They reflect the larger social, political and economic trends and conditions of life in particular periods and places. And they frequently have a unique literary quality which adds to the tone and body of the prose of their time. Sometimes brilliant and sometimes dull, legal writing has always been an influential part of general literature.

The earliest evidence of law reporting in England follows close on the Norman conquest of 1066; scattered records of judicial decisions exist from that period. The *Plea Rolls* beginning with Richard I in 1189 contain fragmentary reports, which have been republished and cited in later works. Many of the oldest cases, however, remain only in the synthesis of early legal texts, such as those by Glanville (c. 1190) and Bracton (1250).

The next collection of judicial reports is to be found in the *Yearbooks* which cover the long period from 1285 to 1537. These reports were actually written in court, by either law students or lawyers. Some represent verbatim transcripts of the proceedings; others are brief summaries of the decision. In their entirety they constitute a great body of legal literature, which has been edited and republished in scholarly series by the Selden Society and similar groups.

Following the *Yearbooks* came the *nominative* reporters, that is, court reports named for the particular individual who recorded or edited them. The earliest of these reporters was probably James Dyer whose reports were published around 1550 and covered cases from 1537. Plowden's *Reports,* which were first published in 1571, are considered to be among the finest and most accurate, while the reports of Sir Edward Coke were perhaps the most influential of that period.

The nominatives continued until modern English law reporting began in 1865 with the establishment of the *Law Reports,* a quasi-official series of annual reporters for each of the four major English courts. These and other current English reporters are discussed more fully in Chapter XI below.

Among all of the foreign legal systems, that of England still has a special relevance in this country by virtue of our common legal history. The American colonies inherited the English common law and a legal tradition of statutes, cases, customs, and attitudes. This inheritance was made express in many of the newly independent states by the enactment of laws adopting the English common law and statutes as part of the law of the state. These reception statutes excluded, however, those portions of English law which were considered repugnant to the American experience. Although we have increasingly gone our separate ways, English laws and legal scholarship have continued to exert a persuasive influence here. The development of English law reporting has similarly shaped our own experience in that regard.

The reporting of court decisions is affected by the hierarchical structure of the judicial system at both the federal and state levels in this country. Typically, litigation begins in one of a variety of trial courts. The jurisdiction of these courts may

be based on a geographical unit (e. g. the U. S. District Courts in the federal court system, or county courts in many states), on the type of case they hear (e. g. the U. S. Court of Claims, or, in the states, family courts, probate courts, criminal courts, etc.), or often on a combination of the two factors. The trend in modern court reform is toward more unified systems in which trial courts have broad subject coverage, rather than utilizing many different and separate specialized courts.

Appeals from the decisions of trial courts are generally taken to an intermediary appellate court (e. g., the U. S. Court of Appeals on the federal level and similar tribunals on the state level). The highest court in each jurisdiction (the Supreme Court of the United States and the supreme courts of the various states) will hear appeals from the intermediary appellate courts, but under certain circumstances may take cases directly from the trial court. In a few special situations the high court may function as a court of original jurisdiction, i. e., hear a case in the first instance. The rules of jurisdiction vary from state to state, but the federal courts and their rules are increasingly used as models in state court reorganizations. The chart on page 15 below illustrates the typical pattern of court structure.

Type of Courts	Federal Courts	Typical State Pattern
High Court	Supreme Court of the United States	Supreme Court of _____
Intermediary Appellate Court	U.S. Court of Appeals (See map on p. 34 for various circuits)	Appellate Court, District Court of Appeals, Superior Court, etc.
Trial Court	U.S. District Court (and courts with specialized jurisdictions: U.S. Court of Claims, U.S. Customs Court, etc.)	County Court, District Court, etc. (or specialized courts: e.g., Civil Court, Criminal Court, Family Court, Probate Court, etc.)

AMERICAN FEDERAL LAW REPORTING

Reports of the U. S. Supreme Court

The early development of American reports followed the pattern of the British reports of the same period. While nominative reporting was still the common practice in England, the first American reports were also issued by, and under the name of, individual reporters, beginning with Kirby's *Reports* in Connecticut in 1789.

Official court reporting, that is the publication of reports pursuant to statutory direction, began in 1790 with the inception of the *United States Reports,* which today is still the official edition of United States Supreme Court decisions. Alexander J. Dallas was the Court's first official reporter and issued the first four volumes of the *U.S. Reports,* covering the period from 1790 to 1800. Citations to cases in the early volumes of the *U.S. Reports* must include the name of the particular reporter, such as *Marbury v. Madison,* 5 U.S. (1 Cranch) 137 (1803). A list of the early official reporters for the Supreme Court follows.

Nominative Reports			**U. S. Reports**
Dallas	1–4	(1790–1800)	1–4
Cranch	1–9	(1801–1815)	5–13
Wheaton	1–12	(1816–1827)	14–25

Nominative Reports   **U. S. Reports**

Peters	1–16 (1828–1842)	26–41
Howard	1–24 (1843–1860)	42–65
Black	1–2 (1861–1862)	66–67
Wallace	1–23 (1863–1874)	68–90

After volume 90 (1874), cases are normally cited only by volume number of the *U.S. Reports.* Thus the official citation of *Roe v. Wade,* a 1973 decision on abortion, is 410 U.S. 113 (1973), meaning the case beginning on page 113 of volume 410 of the *U.S. Reports.* The opening page of the official report of *Roe v. Wade* appears below in Exhibit 1.

Syllabus

ROE ET AL. *v.* WADE, DISTRICT ATTORNEY OF DALLAS COUNTY

APPEAL FROM THE UNITED STATES DISTRICT COURT FOR THE NORTHERN DISTRICT OF TEXAS

No. 70–18.   Argued December 13, 1971—Reargued October 11, 1972—Decided January 22, 1973

A pregnant single woman (Roe) brought a class action challenging the constitutionality of the Texas criminal abortion laws, which proscribe procuring or attempting an abortion except on medical advice for the purpose of saving the mother's life. A licensed physician (Hallford), who had two state abortion prosecutions

---

and presented justiciable controversies. Ruling that declaratory, though not injunctive, relief was warranted, the court declared the abortion statutes void as vague and overbroadly infringing those plaintiffs' Ninth and Fourteenth Amendment rights. The court ruled the Does' complaint not justiciable. Appellants directly appealed to this Court on the injunctive rulings, and appellee cross-appealed from the District Court's grant of declaratory relief to Roe and Hallford. *Held:*

1. While 28 U. S. C. § 1253 authorizes no direct appeal to this Court from the grant or denial of declaratory relief alone, review is not foreclosed when the case is properly before the Court on appeal from specific denial of injunctive relief and the arguments as to both injunctive and declaratory relief are necessarily identical. P. 123.

2. Roe has standing to sue; the Does and Hallford do not. Pp. 123–129.

(a) Contrary to appellee's contention, the natural termination of Roe's pregnancy did not moot her suit. Litigation involving pregnancy, which is "capable of repetition, yet evading review," is an exception to the usual federal rule that an actual controversy

---

Exhibit 1: The official *U.S. Reports,* showing the beginning of the official syllabus.

A similar form of citation, including case name and date, is used for all court reports, whether state or federal, official or unofficial. In practice, most attorneys include in their citations parallel references to the unofficial reporters, although it is not necessary.

In addition to the official *U.S. Reports,* there are also two privately published editions of the Supreme Court's decisions which provide special research aids and supplementary material not in the official edition. These unofficial editions, described below, reproduce the same text of decisions as the official reports and often include more decisions than the official by picking up a few minor motion decisions or memorandum rulings, which may not have been reported officially. Since the unofficial reports usually include references to the citation of the official report, the researcher can cite directly to the official text. This is sometimes facilitated by a method called "star paging" which superimposes the official pagination on the text of the unofficial report by marginal references. See Exhibit 2.

nant view, following the great common-law scholars, has been that it was, at most, a lesser offense. In a frequently cited passage, Coke took the position that abortion of a woman "quick with childe" is "a great misprision, and no murder." [24] Blackstone followed, saying that while abortion after quickening had once been considered manslaughter (though not murder), "modern law" took a less severe view.[25] A recent review of the common-law precedents argues, however, that those precedents contradict Coke and that even post-quickening abortion was never established as a common-law crime.[26] This is of some importance because while most American courts ruled, in holding or dictum, that abortion of an unquickened fetus was not criminal under their received common law,[27] others followed Coke in stating that abortion of a quick fetus was a "misprision," a term they translated to mean "misdemeanor." [28] That their reliance on Coke on this aspect of the law was uncritical and, apparently in all the reported cases, dictum (due probably to the paucity of common-

law prosecutions for post-quickening abortion), makes it now appear doubtful that abortion was ever firmly established as a common-law crime even with respect to the destruction of a quick fetus.

4. *The English statutory law.* England's first criminal abortion statute, Lord Ellenborough's Act, 43 Geo. 3, c. 58, came in 1803. It made abortion of a quick fetus, § 1, a capital crime, but in § 2 it provided lesser penalties for the felony of abortion before quickening, and thus preserved the "quickening" distinction. This contrast was continued in the general revision of 1828, 9 Geo. 4, c. 31, § 13. It disappeared, however, together with the death penalty, in 1837, 7 Will. 4 & 1 Vict., c. 85, § 6, and did not reappear in the Offenses Against the Person Act of 1861, 24 & 25 Vict., c. 100, § 59, that formed the core of English anti-abortion law until the liberalizing reforms of 1967. In 1929, the Infant Life (Preservation) Act, 19 & 20 Geo. 5, c. 34, came into being. Its emphasis was upon the destruction of "the life of

---

24. E. Coke, Institutes III *50.

25. 1 W. Blackstone, Commentaries *129–130.

26. Means, The Phoenix of Abortional Freedom: Is a Penumbral or Ninth-Amendment Right About to Arise from the Nineteenth-Century Legislative Ashes of a Fourteenth-Century Common-Law Liberty?, 17 N.Y.L.F. 335 (1971) (hereinafter Means II). The author examines the two principal precedents cited marginally by Coke, both contrary to his dictum, and traces the treatment of these and other cases by earlier commentators. He concludes that Coke, who himself participated as an advocate in an abortion case in 1601, may have intentionally misstated the law. The author even suggests a reason: Coke's strong feelings against abortion, coupled with his determination to assert common-law (secular) jurisdiction to assess penalties for an offense that traditionally had been an exclusively ecclesiastical or canon-law crime. See also Lader 78–79, who notes that some scholars doubt that the common law ever was applied to abortion; that the English ecclesiastical courts seem to have lost interest in the problem after

1527; and that the preamble to the English legislation of 1803, 43 Geo. 3, c. 58, § 1, referred to in the text, *infra*, at 718, states that "no adequate means have been hitherto provided for the prevention and punishment of such offenses."

27. Commonwealth v. Bangs, 9 Mass. 387, 388 (1812); Commonwealth v. Parker, 50 Mass. (9 Metc.) 263, 265–266 (1845); State v. Cooper, 22 N.J.L. 52, 58 (1849); Abrams v. Foshee, 3 Iowa 274, 278–280 (1856); Smith v. Gaffard, 31 Ala. 45, 51 (1857); Mitchell v. Commonwealth, 78 Ky. 204, 210 (1879); Eggart v. State, 40 Fla. 527, 532, 25 So. 144, 145 (1898); State v. Alcorn, 7 Idaho 599, 606, 64 P. 1014, 1016 (1901); Edwards v. State, 79 Neb. 251, 252, 112 N.W. 611, 612 (1907); Gray v. State, 77 Tex.Cr.R. 221, 224, 178 S.W. 337, 338 (1915); Miller v. Bennett, 190 Va. 162, 169, 56 S.E.2d 217, 221 (1949). Contra, Mills v. Commonwealth, 13 Pa. 631, 633 (1850); State v. Slagle, 83 N.C. 630, 632 (1880).

28. See Smith v. State, 33 Me. 48, 55 (1851); Evans v. People, 49 N.Y. 86, 88 (1872); Lamb v. State, 67 Md. 524, 533, 10 A. 208 (1887).

<u>Exhibit 2:</u>   Star-paging, as illustrated in an unofficial report of *Roe v. Wade.*

Supreme Court Reporter begins with volume 106 of the *U.S. Reports* and incorporates West Publishing Company's key number digest system, which purports to index the significant points of law in all reported appellate decisions under 420 broad legal topics and thousands of detailed sub-topics. (The key number system will be more fully discussed in Chapter III below.) Thus decisions appearing in the *Supreme Court Reporter* and in all of West's other reporters are preceded by headnotes containing short abstracts of the legal issues in that case. Each headnote is classified by the name of the digest topic and sub-topic numbers (called *key* numbers) which are assigned to the points of law in that case. The opening page of *Roe v. Wade* as it appears in the *Supreme Court Reporter* at 93 S.Ct. 705 is shown in Exhibit 3 below and illustrates these headnotes.

410 U.S. 113   ROE v. WADE   **705**

Cite as 93 S.Ct. 705 (1973)

410 U.S. 113, 35 L.Ed.2d 147

Jane ROE, et al., Appellants,

v.

Henry WADE.

No. 70–18.

Argued Dec. 13, 1971.

Reargued Oct. 11, 1972.

Decided Jan. 22, 1973.

Rehearing Denied Feb. 26, 1973.

See 410 U.S. 959. 93 S.Ct. 1409.

Action was brought for a declaratory and injunctive relief respecting Texas criminal abortion laws which were claimed to be unconstitutional. A declaratory aspects of case attacking constitutionality of Texas criminal abortion statutes where case was properly before Supreme Court on direct appeal from decision of three-judge district court specifically denying injunctive relief and the arguments as to both aspects were necessarily identical. 28 U. S.C.A. § 1253.

2. Constitutional Law ⊂⇒42.1(3), 46(1)

With respect to single, pregnant female who alleged that she was unable to obtain a legal abortion in Texas, when viewed as of the time of filing of case and for several months thereafter, she had standing to challenge constitution-

unconstitutional; that prior to approximately the end of the first trimester the abortion decision and its effectuation must be left to the medical judgment of the pregnant woman's attending physician, subsequent to approximately the end of the first trimester the state may regulate abortion procedure in ways reasonably related to maternal health, and at the stage subsequent to viability the state may regulate and even proscribe abortion except where necessary in appropriate medical judgment for preservation of life or health of mother.

Affirmed in part and reversed in part.

Mr. Chief Justice Burger, Mr. Justice Douglas and Mr. Justice Stewart filed concurring opinions.

Mr. Justice White filed a dissenting opinion in which Mr. Justice Rehnquist joined.

Mr. Justice Rehnquist filed a dissenting opinion.

1. Courts ⊂⇒385(7)

Supreme Court was not foreclosed from review of both the injunctive and

93 S.Ct.—45

3. Courts ⊂⇒383(1), 385(1)

Usual rule in federal cases is that an actual controversy must exist at stages of appellate or certiorari review and not simply at date action is initiated.

4. Action ⊂⇒6

Where pregnancy of plaintiff was a significant fact in litigation and the normal human gestation period was so short that pregnancy would come to term before usual appellate process was complete, and pregnancy often came more than once to the same woman, fact of that pregnancy provided a classic justification for conclusion of nonmootness because of termination.

5. Federal Civil Procedure ⊂⇒331

Texas physician, against whom there were pending indictments charging him with violations of Texas abortion laws who made no allegation of any substantial and immediate threat to any federally protected right that could not be asserted in his defense against state prosecutions and who had not alleged

Exhibit 3:   The unofficial *Supreme Court Reporter,* showing the West Publishing Company's key number system of headnotes.

Lawyers' Edition of the U.S. Supreme Court Reports is published by Lawyers Co-operative Publishing Company as a companion publication to *American Law Reports* (*A.L.R.*) and *American Law Reports—Federal,* which are annotated reporters of selected state and federal cases. *Lawyers' Edition,* as it is called, contributes to the reporting of U.S. Supreme Court decisions by including legal analyses in the form of annotations to a few of the more important decisions. Indexes preceding the text of the annotation provide detailed access to the annotation by subject, court and jurisdiction. The annotations in volumes 1–31 of *Lawyers' Edition 2d* are supplemented with later citations and comments in a separate volume entitled *Lawyers' Edition (2d series) Later Case Service.* Beginning with volume 32, each volume of reports contains a supplementary pocket part in the back of the volume for this purpose.

Preceding these annotations is an insert entitled *Total Client-Service Library References* which refers users to coverage on the same topic in other Lawyers' Co-op tools, such as *A.L.R. Digests* and *American Jurisprudence.*

The texts of the Supreme Court's decisions are, of course, identical with those in the other two editions, but unlike the *Supreme Court Reporter, Lawyers' Edition* contains all Supreme Court decisions since 1791. Also, only this reporter carries summaries of the arguments of counsel.

Exhibits 4, 5, 6 and 7 show the opening page of *Roe v. Wade* in *Lawyers' Edition,* the beginning of the annotation, and the summary of the arguments of counsel.

147

[410 US 113]
JANE ROE et al., Appellants,

v

HENRY WADE

410 US 113, 35 L Ed 2d 147, 93 S Ct 705, reh den 410 US 959, 35 L Ed 2d 694, 93 S Ct 1409

[No. 70–18]

Argued December 13, 1971.   Reargued October 11, 1972.
Decided January 22, 1973.

SUMMARY

An unmarried pregnant woman who wished to terminate her pregnancy by abortion instituted an action in the United States District Court for the Northern District of Texas, seeking a declaratory judgment that the Texas criminal abortion statutes, which prohibited abortions except with

---

ment, (5) the Texas criminal abortion statutes were void on their face, because they were unconstitutionally vague and overbroad, and (6) the application for injunctive relief should be denied under the abstention doctrine (314 F Supp 1217).   All parties took protective appeals to the United States Court of Appeals for the Fifth Circuit, which court ordered the appeals held in abeyance pending decision on the appeal taken by all parties to the United States Supreme Court, pursuant to 28 USCS § 1253, from the District Court's denial of injunctive relief.

SUBJECT OF ANNOTATION

Beginning on page 735, infra

Validity, under Federal Constitution, of
abortion laws

Briefs of Counsel, p 730, infra.

Exhibit 4:   The *Lawyers' Edition* report, showing the first page of its summary of *Roe v. Wade.*

ABORTION LAWS—CONSTITUTIONALITY   **735**
35 L Ed 2d 735

ANNOTATION

**VALIDITY, UNDER FEDERAL CONSTITUTION,
OF ABORTION LAWS**

by

Sheldon R. Shapiro, J.D.

Exhibit 5: The opening page of the annotation in *Lawyers'
        Edition* on the validity of abortion laws, show-
        ing references to the subject in other Lawyers
        Co-op research tools.

736   ROE v WADE
                          Reported p 147, supra
§ 7. Regulation of requirements as to hospital or other facility in which
      abortion is to be performed:
      [a] Generally, 764
      [b] Requirement that abortion be performed only in accredited
          hospital, 765
§ 8. Prohibition of advertisements concerning abortions, 766
§ 9. Elimination of restrictions upon grounds for abortion, 769

                              INDEX

                  TABLE OF COURTS AND CIRCUITS
        Consult POCKET PART in this volume for later case service

Exhibit 6: Subject index and table of courts and jurisdic-
            tions for the *Lawyers' Edition* annotation on
            abortion.

I. Preliminary matters

§ 1. Introduction

[a] Scope

This annotation[1] collects and analyzes the federal and state cases determining[2] whether, as a matter of federal constitutional law,[3] abortion[4] laws[5] are valid.

[b] Related matters

Indefiniteness of language as affecting validity of criminal legislation or judicial definition of common-law crime—Supreme Court cases. 96 L Ed 374, 16 L Ed 2d 1231.

Homicide based on killing of unborn child. 40 ALR3d 444.

Right of action for injury to or death of woman who consented to illegal abortion. 36 ALR3d 630.

Woman upon whom abortion is committed or attempted as accomplice for purposes of rule requiring corroboration of accomplice testimony. 34 ALR 3d 858.

Action for death of unborn child. 15 ALR3d 992.

Entrapment to commit or attempt abortion. 53 ALR2d 1156.

Pregnancy as element of abortion or homicide based thereon. 46 ALR 2d 1393.

Necessity, to warrant conviction of abortion, that fetus be living at time of commission of acts. 16 ALR2d 949.

Admissibility, in prosecution based on abortion, of evidence of commission of similar crimes by accused. 15 ALR2d 1080.

---

1. The annotation at 28 L Ed 2d 1053 is hereby superseded.

2. Dealing solely with cases which purport to determine federal constitutional issues as to the validity of abortion laws, the annotation does not discuss cases which merely present such issues without determining them.

3. For purposes of this annotation, if a particular issue involving the constitutionality of an abortion law is the type of issue which could arise either under the Federal Constitution or under a state constitution, and if the court, in discussing its decision of such issue, does not specify whether the decision is based upon the Federal Constitution or upon a state constitution, it is assumed, in the absence of any indication by the court to the contrary, that the decision is based upon the Federal Constitution.

[35 L Ed 2d]—47

4. This annotation is concerned solely with laws expressly referring to "abortion" or "miscarriage," the two terms having been treated by the courts as synonymous. This annotation is not, however, concerned with laws dealing generally with contraception or birth control, without dealing specifically with abortion; moreover, even if a contraception or birth control law consists in part of a reference to abortion, but if a court determines the constitutionality of the law only insofar as it relates to contraception or birth control, without discussing that part of the law referring to abortion, such a case is not included herein.

5. For present purposes, the term "laws" includes municipal ordinances as well as state and federal statutes, but does not include mere administrative action.

Exhibit 6: Cont'd.

730 ROE v WADE
35 L Ed 2d 147

JANE ROE et al., Appellants,

v

HENRY WADE

Reported in this volume: p 147, supra.

Holding: Texas criminal abortion statutes held unconstitutional.

Annotation: p 735, infra.

BRIEFS AND APPEARANCES OF COUNSEL

Sarah Weddington, of Austin, Texas, reargued the cause and, with **James R. Weddington,** also of Austin, Texas, **Roy Lucas, Norman Dorsen,** both of New York City, **Linda N. Coffee, Fred Bruner,** and **Roy L. Merrill, Jr.,** all of Dallas, Texas, filed briefs for appellants:

Plaintiffs Doe have standing to challenge the Texas abortion law and they do present a case or controversy. The Does are complaining not of a future, anticipated injury resulting from the unavailability of legal abortions, but of the effect that unavailability is currently having upon their marital relationship. Flast v Cohen, 392 US 83, 20 L Ed 2d 947, 88 S Ct 1942; Investment Co. Institute v Camp, 401 US 617, 28 L Ed 2d 367, 91 S Ct 1091; Epperson v Arkansas, 393 US 97, 21 L Ed 2d 228, 89 S Ct 266.

The fact that plaintiff Roe was forced to continue her pregnancy pending determinat' ⌐ of her suit and could not then obtain a safe abortion does not moot the appeal, particularly in light of the class allegations. Southern Pacific Terminal Co. v ICC, 219 US 498, 515, 55 L Ed 310, 31 S Ct 279; Moore v Ogilvie, 394 US 814, 816, 23 L Ed 2d 1, 89 S Ct 1493; Gaddis v Wyman, 304 F Supp 713, 717, aff'd mem sub nom Wyman v Bowens, 397 US 49, 25 L Ed 2d 38, 90 S Ct 813; Kelly v Wyman, 294 F Supp 887, 890, 893, aff'd sub nom Goldberg v Kelly, 397 US 254, 257, 25 L Ed 2d 287, 90 S Ct 1011; United States v W. T. Grant Co. 345 US 629, 633, 97 L Ed 1303, 73 S Ct 894.

The abortion statute directly curtailed the physicians' interests in providing adequate medical advice and treatment for patients. These interests are aspects of liberty, property, and association directly protected by the Fourteenth and First Amendments.

The opportunity to pursue one's profession is encompassed within the concepts of liberty and property. Willner v Committee on Character and Fitness, 373 US 96, 102, 103, 10 L Ed 2d 224, 83 S Ct 1175, 2 ALR3d 1254; Slochower v Board of Higher Educ. 350 US 551, 100 L Ed 692, 76 S Ct 637; Greene v McElroy, 360 US 474, 492, 3 L Ed 2d 1377, 79 S Ct 1400; Birnbaum v Trussell, 371 F2d 672.

The physician class has standing to assert the rights of patients to seek the medical care of induced abortion. Griswold v Connecticut, 381 US 479, 14 L Ed 2d 510, 85 S Ct 1678; United States ex rel. Williams v Zelker, 445 F2d 451; Crossen v Breckenridge, 446 F2d 833; Truax v Raich, 239 US 33, 60 L Ed 131, 36 S Ct 7; Pierce v Society of Sisters, 268 US 510, 69 L Ed 1070, 45 S Ct 571, 39 ALR 468; Eisenstadt v Baird, 405 US 438, 31 L Ed 2d 349, 92 S Ct 1029; YWCA v Kugler, 342 F Supp 1048; Abele v Markle, 452 F2d 1121; Poe v Menghini, 339 F Supp 986.

Injunctions against future enforcement of state criminal statutes are proper even absent a showing of bad-faith enforcement for the purpose of discouraging protected rights. Ex parte Young, 209 US 123, 52 L Ed 714, 28 S Ct 441; Truax v Raich, 239 US 33, 60 L Ed 131, 36 S Ct 7; Terrace v Thompson, 263 US 197, 68 L Ed 255, 44 S Ct 15; Hygrade Provision Co. v Sherman, 266 US 497, 69 L Ed 402, 45 S Ct 141.

Plaintiffs Roe and Doe were not in any sense involved in the pending pros-

---

Exhibit 7: The page showing a portion of the briefs of counsel in *Lawyers' Edition.*

The complete citation of the abortion decision, reflecting all three texts, is *Roe v. Wade,* 410 U.S. 113, 93 S.Ct. 705, 35 L.Ed.2d 147 (1973). This form is widely used, although technically the official citation is sufficient. The "2d" in the citation of *Lawyers' Edition* indicates that those reports are now in a second series, an arbitrary numbering technique employed by most publishers of court reports. When the volumes of a reporter reach a certain number (usually volume 300, but in the case of *Lawyers' Edition,* volume 100), the publisher starts a second series and begins numbering from volume 1 again (usually for commercial reasons). If a reporter is in its second series, that must be indicated in its citation in order to distinguish it from the same volume number in the first series.

The bound volumes of these three reporters of Supreme Court decisions are usually the last form of publication. The following services, presented here chronologically, provide the text of such decisions much sooner:

Looseleaf Services. Two unofficial commercial publications, issued in looseleaf form, publish the Supreme Court's decisions on the day after they are announced, so that many of their subscribers have them within forty-eight hours. These looseleaf services are *U.S. Law Week,* published by the Bureau of National Affairs, and *Supreme Court Bulletin,* published by Commerce Clearing House.

Both of these publishers issue looseleaf services on other legal topics as well, which will be discussed in detail in Chapter VII below. In addition to the prompt publication and delivery of the text of the decisions themselves, *U.S. Law Week* and *Supreme Court Bulletin* provide information about court calendars, dockets, motions, arguments, and general court news. They are extremely valuable to practitioners before the Supreme Court and of interest to legal researchers generally as a source of current information about the business of the Court. *U.S. Law Week* also includes another volume called General Law, which summarizes important weekly legal developments of all kinds— state and federal; judicial, legislative and administrative.

Slip Decision. Shortly after the unofficial looseleaf services appear, the official slip decision of the Supreme Court is issued by the Court itself and usually reaches subscribers two or three weeks after decision date. This is the first official and authoritative text of the decisions, but its pages are not numbered in final form. Each slip decision is a separate pamphlet, paginated separately. Slip decisions are available individually or by subscription from the U. S. Government Printing Office. They are accumulated until there are enough for publication together as the advance sheet (or preliminary print, as it is officially called) of the official *U.S. Reports*.

Advance Sheets. Each of the reporters of the Supreme Court's decisions (and many other court reports) issues a preliminary booklet, which contains the Court's latest decisions in a temporary form during the term. These pamphlets are called "advance sheets" and are issued periodically so that attorneys may have the text of decisions without having to wait for the accumulation and publication of a complete bound volume. The pagination of the advance sheets is the same as that in the bound volume, so that cases can be cited from the advance sheet exactly as they will appear when finally published.

The advance sheets of *Supreme Court Reporter* and *Lawyers' Edition* are usually issued faster than the official preliminary print and all three include to some extent the unique features of the series to which they belong. The preliminary print is the authoritative text of the Court's decisions until the bound volume of the *U.S. Reports* appears; *Supreme Court Reporter* incorporates West's unique key number digest; the *Lawyers' Edition* advance sheet provides subscribers with a prompt text of Supreme Court decisions, but does not contain the annotations or the summaries of briefs and arguments found in the bound volume, since they cannot be prepared that rapidly.

Bound Volumes. Finally, at the end of each term, the bound volumes of the three series are published. The identical text of the Court's decisions is contained in each, and the two unofficial reporters also contain citations to the volume and page of the official report so that an attorney using them will be able to cite to the official report, as required by the Court.

Lower Federal Court Reporting

During most of the nineteenth century, decisions of the U. S. District Courts and the U. S. Circuit Courts of Appeals were issued in over 200 separate series of nominative reports. Virtually every federal court published its own series and bibliographic chaos resulted from the impossibility of locating the reports of many courts anywhere but in its own locale or in the largest law libraries. Finally, in 1880, the West Publishing Company published a thirty volume series which included many of these decisions under the title *Federal Cases*. This closed set incorporated the most important lower federal court decisions from 1789 to 1880. At the same time, West initiated its *Federal Reporter* which began publishing decisions of both the district and circuit courts in 1880 and has continued to date.

In 1932 with the increasing volume of litigation in the federal courts, West began another series of

federal reports called *Federal Supplement* which since that time has published selected U. S. District Court decisions, leaving the *Federal Reporter* to cover the decisions of the various U. S. Circuit Courts of Appeals, now called U. S. Courts of Appeals. (A map indicating the states that make up each circuit is set out as Exhibit 8 on page 34.)

Each reporter now also includes a number of specialized federal courts. The coverage of special courts by these reporters has changed several times, but presently the *Federal Reporter* includes decisions of the U.S. Court of Customs and Patent Appeals and the U.S. Court of Claims. The *Federal Supplement* includes decisions of the U. S. Customs Court.

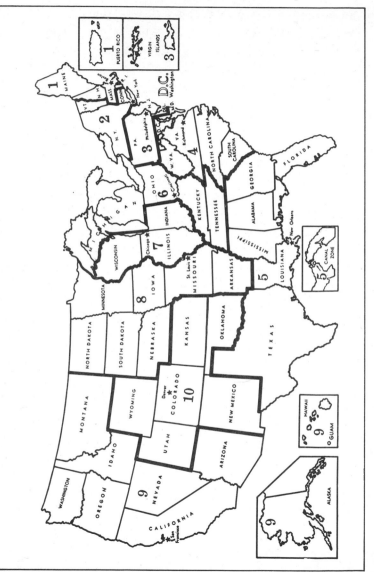

Exhibit 8:   The Eleven Federal Judicial Circuits.

In 1940 West began still another series, *Federal Rules Decisions,* which offers a limited number of decisions of the federal courts relating to procedural matters, as well as speeches and articles dealing with procedural law in the federal courts.

The decisions of the U. S. District Courts and the U. S. Courts of Appeals do not appear in an official edition, other than as slip decisions issued by some of the courts themselves. There are neither official advance sheets, nor official bound volumes for these courts. For access to lower federal court decisions, lawyers rely almost exclusively on *Federal Reporter, Federal Supplement* and *Federal Rules Decisions* and on the *American Law Reports-Federal,* a series begun by Lawyers Cooperative in 1969 to offer a selection of federal court decisions with annotations.

STATE REPORTS

American state reports are published in two forms: official reports, which are issued by the courts themselves as their authoritative text, and the unofficial reports. There are two general unofficial reporting systems—the West Publishing Company's comprehensive National Reporter System and Lawyers Co-operative Publishing Company's selective *American Law Reports.*

[*35*]

The official reports are important to the researcher because they are authoritative and must be cited in legal briefs and memoranda. Citation to the unofficial report is optional and, if given, should follow the official reference. The unofficial reports, however, are very widely used and usually cited, because of their superior research aids, fuller coverage and faster publication. In fact, they have become much more popular than the less imaginatively produced official editions.

National Reporter System. West's National Reporter System consists of a series of regional reporters which collectively publish most of the decisions issued by the appellate courts of the fifty states every year. It is the most comprehensive approach to law reporting ever devised and sometimes includes more decisions than the official reports. Although the system suffers to some extent from its huge scope and bulk, West's key number case-finding device has kept it fairly manageable. To simplify storage and preservation of the set in libraries, West has also produced an ultra-microfiche edition of the first series of the National Reporter System, and has begun gradual inclusion of the second series in this format.

The National Reporter System divides the country into seven regions: Atlantic, Pacific, North Eastern, South Eastern, North Western, South Western and Southern. The decisions of the ap-

pellate courts of the states in each of these regions are published together in one series of volumes. These series have been supplemented by West with separate reporters for the two most litigious states, *New York Supplement* and the *California Reporter,* which also include selected lower court decisions. These nine reporters, together with West's federal court reporters described above, comprise a uniform system which is tied together by the key number indexing and digesting scheme. A new *Military Law Reporter* has just been published as part of the system, covering the military courts of appeal. Exhibit 9 shows which states are included in each region of the reporter system. Appendix A gives a complete list of the contents of each reporter and their dates of inception.

The original rationale of the National Reporter System was that contiguous states shared similar legal development and therefore lawyers in one state would be interested in the law of adjacent states. Despite changes in the country which have tended to undermine this theory, the venture has flourished, largely because of the speed of publishing decisions of several states in groups, rather than individually; the greater number of decisions as compared with the official reports; and the case-finding advantages of the key number system. In addition, advance sheets for each of these reporters bring the decisions to the lawyer much faster than do the official reporters,

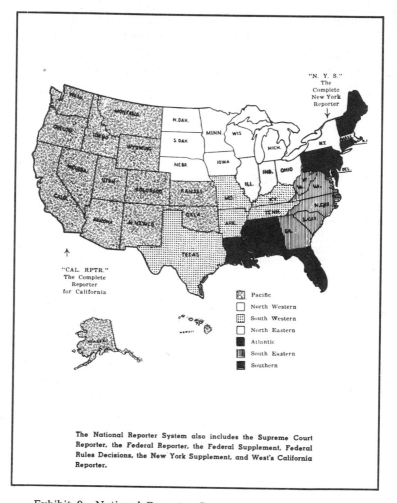

Exhibit 9: National Reporter System map, showing states included in each reporter.

which rarely offer such service. After four or five advance sheets appear, they are reissued on better paper in a bound volume with the same pagination. The superseded advance sheet can then be discarded.

By analyzing a single decision in one of the advance sheets, one can get a general idea of the make-up of an appellate decision, as well as of the special reporting aids which West provides for its subscribers. Such analysis would reveal the following items illustrated in Exhibit 10:

> Title or case name.
>
> Official citation if available.
>
> Other identifying data: docket number, date of decision, name of court and jurisdiction.
>
> Synopsis or brief descriptive paragraph of the case: its holding, how it arose, facts, etc.
>
> Brief statement of decision and notation of dissent or concurrence, if any.
>
> Headnotes summarizing the points of law discussed in the case with the identifying key numbers of the digest system.
>
> Syllabus by the Court, if provided.
>
> Names of counsel and judges.
>
> Full text of opinion, decision, and dissents or concurrences, if any.
>
> Reference, by number of headnote, to the section of the opinion which discusses the point of each headnote.

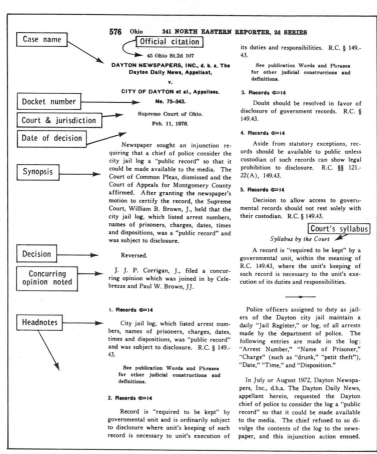

Case name

576   Ohio   **341 NORTH EASTERN REPORTER, 2d SERIES**

Official citation

45 Ohio St.2d 107

DAYTON NEWSPAPERS, INC., d. b. a. The Dayton Daily News, Appellant,

v.

CITY OF DAYTON et al., Appellees.

Docket number — **No. 75–343.**

Court & jurisdiction — Supreme Court of Ohio.

Date of decision — Feb. 11, 1976.

Synopsis — Newspaper sought an injunction requiring that a chief of police consider the city jail log a "public record" so that it could be made available to the media. The Court of Common Pleas, dismissed and the Court of Appeals for Montgomery County affirmed. After granting the newspaper's motion to certify the record, the Supreme Court, William B. Brown, J., held that the city jail log, which listed arrest numbers, names of prisoners, charges, dates, times and dispositions, was a "public record" and was subject to disclosure.

Decision — Reversed.

Concurring opinion noted — J. J. P. Corrigan, J., filed a concurring opinion which was joined in by Celebrezze and Paul W. Brown, JJ.

Headnotes —

1. Records ⟐14

City jail log, which listed arrest numbers, names of prisoners, charges, dates, times and dispositions, was "public record" and was subject to disclosure. R.C. § 149.-43.

See publication Words and Phrases for other judicial constructions and definitions.

2. Records ⟐14

Record is "required to be kept" by governmental unit and is ordinarily subject to disclosure where unit's keeping of such record is necessary to unit's execution of

its duties and responsibilities. R.C. § 149.-43.

See publication Words and Phrases for other judicial constructions and definitions.

3. Records ⟐14

Doubt should be resolved in favor of disclosure of government records. R.C. § 149.43.

4. Records ⟐14

Aside from statutory exceptions, records should be available to public unless custodian of such records can show legal prohibition to disclosure. R.C. §§ 121.-22(A), 149.43.

5. Records ⟐14

Decision to allow access to governmental records should not rest solely with their custodian. R.C. § 149.43.

Court's syllabus

Syllabus by the Court

A record is "required to be kept" by a governmental unit, within the meaning of R.C. 149.43, where the unit's keeping of such record is necessary to the unit's execution of its duties and responsibilities.

Police officers assigned to duty as jailers of the Dayton city jail maintain a daily "Jail Register," or log, of all arrests made by the department of police. The following entries are made in the log: "Arrest Number," "Name of Prisoner," "Charge" (such as "drunk," "petit theft"), "Date," "Time," and "Disposition."

In July or August 1972, Dayton Newspapers, Inc., d.b.a. The Dayton Daily News, appellant herein, requested the Dayton chief of police to consider the log a "public record" so that it could be made available to the media. The chief refused to so divulge the contents of the log to the newspaper, and this injunction action ensued.

Exhibit 10: A decision of the Supreme Court of Ohio as reported in the advance sheet of *North Eastern Reporter*.

DAYTON NEWSPAPERS, INC. v. CITY OF DAYTON   Ohio   **577**

Cite as 341 N.E.2d 576

The newspaper's complaint alleged that the log is a public record required to be kept by the city, and that access to the log is therefore authorized by R.C. 149.43, which reads:

"As used in this section, 'public record' means any record required to be kept by any governmental unit, including, but not limited to, state, county, city, village, township, and school district units, except records pertaining to physical or psychiatric examinations, adoption, probation, and parole proceedings, and records the release of which is prohibited by state or federal law.

"All public records shall be open at all reasonable times for inspection. Upon request, a person responsible for public records shall make copies available at cost, within a reasonable period of time."

Upon the city's motion to dismiss the action for failure to state a claim upon which relief can be granted (Civ.R. 12[B][6]), the Court of Common Pleas held that the log was not a "public record" and entered judgment of dismissal. That judgment was affirmed by the Court of Appeals, and we granted the newspaper's motion to certify the record.

Counsel

Estabrook, Finn & McKee, Robert P. Bartlett, Jr., and Thomas L. Czechowski, Dayton, for appellant.

James W. Drake, City Atty., and Edward B. Neuman, Dayton, for appellees.

Stanley K. Laughlin, Jr., Columbus, for other interested parties.

WILLIAM B. BROWN, Justice.

Speaking for a unanimous court in *State ex rel. White v. Cleveland* (1973), 34 Ohio St.2d 37, 40, 295 N.E.2d 665, 668, Justice Corrigan states " * * * that R.C. 149.43 establishes a public right to the inspection and copying of public records and imposes upon municipal corporations the mandatory duty to permit same." The Dayton jail log is certainly a "record." If it is "required to be kept" by the city, appellees must grant access to appellant because the log

341 N.E.2d—37

does not come within any of the exceptions set forth in R.C. 149.43.

Discussion of headnotes 1 and 2

[1, 2] This court has not directly considered the "required to be kept" element of R.C. 149.43. That element is ambiguous, and the reason for its insertion in the statute is not readily apparent. Appellees urge that we construe it to mean required by statute (or at least, by the official policy of a unit of government) to be kept. We would be more readily inclined to follow appellees' argument if the statute stated "required *by law* to be kept." Cf. *State ex rel. Grosser v. Boy* (1975), 42 Ohio St. 2d 498, 330 N.E.2d 442.

On the other hand, appellant would have the statutory phrase describe any record which but for its keeping the governmental unit could not carry out its duties and responsibilities; that the *raison d'etre* of such record is to assure the proper functioning of the unit. We accept the interpretation suggested by appellant, and, in so doing, we reject the holdings of the courts below that the Dayton jail log is not a "public record" subject to disclosure.

Prior to the enactment of R.C. 149.43 in 1963 (130 Ohio Laws 155), this court, in *State ex rel. Patterson v. Ayers* (1960), 171 Ohio St. 369, 171 N.E.2d 508, affirmed the issuance of a writ of mandamus to allow inspection of Bureau of Motor Vehicles records. Although the statute therein declared that *all* records of the bureau were "public records," we find instructive the approach taken by the court on the question of access. Judge Zimmerman, at page 371, 171 N.E.2d at page 509, quoted with approval the following passage from Ohio Jurisprudence:

"The rule in Ohio is that public records are the people's records and that the officials in whose custody they happen to be are merely trustees for the people; therefore anyone may inspect such records at any time, subject only to the limitation that such inspection does not endanger the safe-

Exhibit 10: Cont'd.

ty of the record, or unreasonably interfere with the discharge of the duties of the officer having custody of the same." And then he stated, at page 372, 171 N.E.2d at page 510:

"How far the General Assembly might go in limiting access to and inspection of public records is not now before us. Suffice it to say, such body has not *denied* the right to inspect the records in the office of the Registrar of Motor Vehicles in the respect demanded by relator. We do not doubt that the registrar may establish and enforce reasonable rules and regulations covering the examination of the records in his custody and control to insure the orderly and efficient operation of his department, but under the statutes in their present wording he may not arbitrarily and wholly close those records to public view." (Emphasis *sic*.)

See, also, *State ex rel. Louisville Title Ins. Co. v. Brewer* (1946), 147 Ohio St. 161, 164, 70 N.E.2d 265, which involved a similar mandamus action wherein a title research company requested access to a special card index for land records kept by the Probate Court of Cuyahoga County. (The writ was denied, but the court failed to indicate which of numerous valid grounds were determinative in refusing relief.)

Discussion of headnotes 3 and 4 ▶ **[3, 4]** On the basis of *Ayers, supra* (171 Ohio St. 369, 171 N.E.2d 508), we believe that doubt should be resolved in favor of disclosure of records * held by governmental units. Aside from the exceptions mentioned in R.C. 149.43, records should be available to the public *unless* the custodian of such records can show a legal prohibition to disclosure. Cf. R.C. 121.22(A), as amended November 28, 1975.

Discussion of headnote 5 ▶ **[5]** The decision to allow access to governmental records should not rest solely

---

* "A public record has be defined as a record required by law to be kept, *or necessary to be kept*, in the discharge of a duty imposed by law, or directed by law to serve as a memorial

with the custodian. "Law has reached its finest moments when it has freed man from the unlimited discretion of some ruler, some civil or military official, some bureaucrat. Where discretion is absolute, man has always suffered." *United States v. Wunderlich* (1951), 342 U.S. 98, 101, 72 S.Ct. 154, 156, 96 L.Ed. 113, Douglas, J., dissenting.

We hold that information contained in the Dayton jail log is required to be kept in the operation of the jail. Accordingly, the judgment of the Court of Appeals is reversed, and the cause its remanded to the Court of Common Pleas for further proceedings consistent with this opinion.

Judgment reversed. **Judges**

C. WILLIAM O'NEILL, C. J., and HERBERT, J. J. P. CORRIGAN, STERN, CELEBREZZE and PAUL W. BROWN, JJ., concur.

J. J. P. CORRIGAN, Justice (concurring). **Concurring opinion**

Unreservedly, I join in the judgment and opinion of Justice William B. Brown. An additament occurs to me in connection with the constitutional requirement of due process.

The Fifth Amendment to the United States Constitution mandates that no person shall "be deprived of * * * liberty * * * without due process of law," thereby securing this right against invasion by the federal government. The right is safeguarded against state action by the Fourteenth Amendment. As the United States Supreme Court said, in *Betts v. Brady* (1942), 316 U.S. 455, 462, 62 S.Ct. 1252, 1256, 86 L.Ed. 1595: "* * * The phrase formulates a concept less rigid and more fluid than those envisaged in other specific and particular provisions of the

an evidence of something written, said, or done. * * *'" (Emphasis added.) *State v. Brooks* (1971), 27 Ohio St.2d 144, 147, 271 N.E.2d 869, 871.

Exhibit 10: Cont'd.

FIRST NATIONAL BANK OF WILMINGTON v. KOSYDAR   Ohio   **579**

Cite as 341 N.E.2d 579

Bill of Rights. Its application is less a matter of rule. Asserted denial is to be tested by an appraisal of the totality of the facts in a given case. That which may, in one setting, constitute a denial of fundamental fairness, shocking the universal sense of justice, may, in other circumstances, and in the light of other considerations, fall short of such a denial. * * *"

Due process then is measured by that whole community sense of decency and fairness that has been woven into the fabric of acceptable conduct. " * * * It is on this bedrock that this Court has established the concept of due process," said the United States Supreme Court in *Breithaupt v. Abram* (1957), 352 U.S. 432, 436, 77 S. Ct. 408, 410, 1 L.Ed.2d 448.

The city of Dayton assumes that the "Jail Register" is kept only for a "convenience" of the jailer, and, as such, is exempt from the state open-records law because no official record of who is in the jail is required by statute, ordinance or court rule. If a person is arrested on a warrant, of course there is a record of that arrest. But, if a person is arrested without a warrant having been issued, then, according to the city of Dayton, it is not necessary to keep a record, although the "Jail Register" is kept. During oral argument of this case before us, counsel for the city of Dayton was asked, "What is the record of an arrest when no warrant is issued?" "There is none" he answered, "but there is no requirement for such a record."

Such an attitude on the part of an arresting authority does not comport with due process in my opinion. The right of a person to due process begins when he is arrested. If a warrant has not been issued, he has a right, under Crim.R. 4(E)(2), to have the arresting officer without unnecessary delay bring him before a court having jurisdiction of the offense for which he was arrested; he has a right to release after arrest, as provided by Crim.R. 4(F), under certain circumstances by the arresting officer or his superior without unnecessary delay; and, at the time of his arrest, he has a right to be informed of the cause of his arrest, a right to certain warnings if he is to be interrogated and a right to counsel. If there is no official arrest record at the jail, except the private log of the jailer, how is it to be determined if there was unnecessary delay in according the person arrested his rights? How is his family or a friend going to learn of his arrest if, on inquiry, they are advised there is no official record? The constitutional foundation underlying these rights is the respect a state or city must accord to the dignity and worth of its citizens. It is an integral part of constitutional due process that a public record of such arrests be maintained.

CELEBREZZE and PAUL W. BROWN, JJ., concur in the foregoing concurring opinion.

45 Ohio St.2d 101

The FIRST NATIONAL BANK OF WILMINGTON, Appellant,

v.

KOSYDAR, Tax Commr., Appellee.

No. 75–385.

Supreme Court of Ohio.

Feb. 11, 1976.

Appeal was taken as of right from decision of Board of Tax Appeals affirming Tax Commissioner's assessment of partial-year prorated personal property tax against bank which in May of 1972 purchased truck wash and related equipment and entered into five-year lease. The Supreme Court, Celebrezze, J., held that since the bank had been continuously engaged in

Similarly by examining the opening pages of a typical West advance sheet one can observe the features which make these reporters so useful in legal research: (See Exhibits 11 to 19).

Judicial highlights from recent state and federal decisions.

Parallel reference tables from official citations of recent decisions to unofficial citations, and vice versa.

Table of cases reported.

Table of statutes construed.

Table of words and phrases.

Key number digest for cases in that issue.

Table of procedural rules construed.

Table of *ABA Standards for Criminal Justice* cited in that issue.

cause of errors in the information-gathering process, the release would not assist consumers to better evaluate the safety of television receivers, and thus would not further the purposes of the Consumer Product Safety Act. GTE Sylvania Inc. v. Consumer Product Safety Commission, 404 F.Supp. 352 (opinion by Chief Judge James L. Latchum).

ARREST—Use of Deadly Force to Prevent Escape. The United States District Court for the Eastern District of Missouri has upheld against constitutional attack a Missouri statute, similar to statutes in some thirty-three other United States jurisdictions, making it justifiable homicide for a policeman to kill a fleeing felon. Plaintiff, the father of an 18-year-old who was slain while resisting arrest for robbery, argued that the statute was void as violating his rights to raise a family and to retain his parental rights until terminated by due process of law; that equal protection was violated by the law's exclusion of misdemeanors which are more "serious" than some felonies; and that the use of deadly force constituted cruel and unusual punishment. Mattis v. Schnarr, 404 F.Supp. 643 (opinion by District Judge John F. Nangle).

COLLEGES AND UNIVERSITIES—Use of Dormitory Commons Rooms for Religious Services. In a case of apparent first impression, the Supreme Court of Delaware has held that it is permissible under the Establishment Clause of the Constitution for a state university to permit the use of dormitory commons rooms for religious services, and that university regulations to the contrary constitute an impermissible burden on students' constitutional rights to free exercise of religion. Keegan v. University of Delaware, 349 A.2d 14 (opinion by Justice John J. McNeilly).

PRISONS—Law Libraries. The United States District Court for the Middle District of Georgia has upheld a claim by a state prison inmate that, other adequate means of legal assistance not being made available to Georgia prisoners, the State is obligated to furnish access to a law library containing relevant annotated state and federal laws and modern state and federal cases, so as to permit the inmate himself to perform research necessary to prepare petitions for post-conviction relief, habeas corpus, or redress for deprivation of civil rights. Nothing less, the court felt, would adequately protect the prisoners' right to free access to the courts. Wilson v. Zarhadnick, December 3, 1975 (opinion by District Judge Wilbur D. Owens, Jr.).

Exhibit 11: Judicial highlights from recent state and federal decisions as summarized in the *North Eastern Reporter* advance sheet.

PARALLEL CITATION TABLES

45 OHIO STATE REPORTS, SECOND SERIES
Partial Table

Ohio St. 2d Pg.	N.E.2d Vol.	Pg.	Ohio St. 2d Pg.	N.E.2d Vol.	Pg.	Ohio St. 2d Pg.	N.E.2d Vol.	Pg.	Ohio St. 2d Pg.	N.E.2d Vol.	Pg.	Ohio St. 2d Pg.	N.E.2d Vol.	Pg.	Ohio St. 2d Pg.	N.E.2d Vol.	Pg.
1	340	840	27	340	395	57	341	302	85	341	575	107	341	576	137	341	843
11	340	411	28	340	403	59	340	847	86	341	585	112	341	594	143	341	851
13	340	407	34	340	392	63	341	847	93	341	600	117	341	589	146	341	835
16	340	396	39	340	398	66	341	597	96	341	592	121	341	826	151	341	839
19	340	838	47	341	298	71	341	304	98	341	583	130	341	849	154	341	832
23	340	408	53	341	296	81	341	573	101	341	579	134	341	841			

41 OHIO APPELLATE REPORTS, SECOND SERIES
Complete Table

Ohio App. 2d Pg.	N.E.2d Vol.	Pg.	Ohio App. 2d Pg.	N.E.2d Vol.	Pg.	Ohio App. 2d Pg.	N.E.2d Vol.	Pg.	Ohio App. 2d Pg.	N.E.2d Vol.	Pg.	Ohio App. 2d Pg.	N.E.2d Vol.	Pg.	Ohio App. 2d Pg.	N.E.2d Vol.	Pg.
1	321	897	65	322	146	107	322	333	144	324	182	181	324	755	228	325	255
17	321	890	69	322	149	113	322	693	147	324	301	186	324	759	231	325	257
27	322	133	76	322	127	118	322	690	150	324	583	191	324	779	240	325	249
37	322	139	81	322	348	124	322	688	160	324	594	201	324	774	244	325	252
48	322	311	90	322	283	127	322	897	165	324	589	209	325	901	248	325	267
60	322	130	98	322	291	141	324	578	171	324	762	219	325	243	251	325	901

42 OHIO APPELLATE REPORTS, SECOND SERIES
Complete Table

Ohio App. 2d Pg.	N.E.2d Vol.	Pg.	Ohio App. 2d Pg.	N.E.2d Vol.	Pg.	Ohio App. 2d Pg.	N.E.2d Vol.	Pg.	Ohio App. 2d Pg.	N.E.2d Vol.	Pg.	Ohio App. 2d Pg.	N.E.2d Vol.	Pg.	Ohio App. 2d Pg.	N.E.2d Vol.	Pg.
1	325	910	19	326	696	41	327	796	56	327	789	63	329	702	83	330	726
8	325	899	26	326	691	45	328	409	59	329	699	69	330	454	89	330	452
11	326	701	35	327	791	53	328	414									

43 OHIO APPELLATE REPORTS, SECOND SERIES
Complete Table

Ohio App. 2d Pg.	N.E.2d Vol.	Pg.	Ohio App. 2d Pg.	N.E.2d Vol.	Pg.	Ohio App. 2d Pg.	N.E.2d Vol.	Pg.	Ohio App. 2d Pg.	N.E.2d Vol.	Pg.	Ohio App. 2d Pg.	N.E.2d Vol.	Pg.	Ohio App. 2d Pg.	N.E.2d Vol.	Pg.
1	331	737	38	332	376	79	334	478	119	334	488	137	334	511	163	335	373
3	332	69	44	332	366	89	334	5	126	322	679	141	334	530	171	334	520
10	332	73	53	333	147	93	334	503	129	334	514	154	334	492	176	334	523
18	332	79	63	332	770	98	334	545	134	334	518	157	334	484	187	334	538
31	332	371	73	334	1	105	334	494									

44 OHIO APPELLATE REPORTS, SECOND SERIES
Partial Table

Ohio App. 2d Pg.	N.E.2d Vol.	Pg.	Ohio App. 2d Pg.	N.E.2d Vol.	Pg.	Ohio App. 2d Pg.	N.E.2d Vol.	Pg.	Ohio App. 2d Pg.	N.E.2d Vol.	Pg.	Ohio App. 2d Pg.	N.E.2d Vol.	Pg.	Ohio App. 2d Pg.	N.E.2d Vol.	Pg.
1	335	741	55	335	735	115	335	868	186	337	158	293	338	531	325	338	547
5	335	708	63	335	722	121	336	453	199	337	181	303	338	539	383	324	576
10	335	751	69	335	743	130	336	442	201	337	627	315	338	544	387	339	668
13	336	637	74	335	746	140	336	439	209	337	167	318	338	767	389	339	666
22	335	712	82	335	734	143	336	464	217	337	660	335	338	793	393	339	840
29	335	883	85	335	727	146	336	460	223	337	655	351	338	784	402	339	856
37	335	717	89	335	706	152	336	458	230	337	666	359	338	789	410	339	835
40	335	729	92	335	731	155	336	448	233	337	664	365	338	780	419	339	851
43	336	466	95	335	874	161	336	851	236	337	646	370	338	772	422	339	846
45	335	753	108	335	887	163	337	173	248	337	642	375	338	775	428	-339	853
50	335	719	113	335	872	177	337	633	256	337	639						

341 N.E.2d No.4

342 N.E.2d No.1

II

Exhibit 12:　Parallel citation table in *North Eastern Reporter* advance sheet: official citation to unofficial citation. The Dayton Newspaper Case indicated by the arrow.

PARALLEL CITATION TABLES

339 NORTH EASTERN REPORTER, SECOND SERIES

N.E.2d Page	State Report	N.E.2d Page	State Report	N.E.2d Page	State Report	N.E.2d Page	State Report
249...44	Ohio St.2d 119	633...44	Ohio St.2d 132	668...44	Ohio App.2d 387	830...44	Ohio St.2d 219
252...44	Ohio St.2d 123	641...44	Ohio St.2d 163	670...44	Ohio Misc. 97	835...44	Ohio App.2d 410
253...44	Ohio Misc. 102	648...44	Ohio St.2d 172	673.——	Ohio Misc. ——	840...44	Ohio App.2d 393
622...44	Ohio St.2d 155	652...44	Ohio St.2d 186	814. 44	Ohio St.2d 199	846...44	Ohio App.2d 422
624...44	Ohio St.2d 159	654...44	Ohio St.2d 188	817...44	Ohio St.2d 225	851...44	Ohio App.2d 419
626...44	Ohio St.2d 128	658...44	Ohio St.2d 178	820...44	Ohio St.2d 208	853...44	Ohio App.2d 428
628...44	Ohio St.2d 125	663...44	Ohio St.2d 151	826...44	Ohio St.2d 229	856...44	Ohio App.2d 402
630...44	Ohio St.2d 195	666...44	Ohio App.2d 389	828...44	Ohio St.2d 204		

340 NORTH EASTERN REPORTER, SECOND SERIES

N.E.2d Page	State Report	N.E.2d Page	State Report	N.E.2d Page	State Report	N.E.2d Page	State Report
392...45	Ohio St.2d 34	408...45	Ohio St.2d 23	427...45	Ohio App.2d 38	838...45	Ohio St.2d 19
395...45	Ohio St.2d 27	411...45	Ohio St.2d 11	430...45	Ohio App.2d 1	840...45	Ohio St.2d 1
396...45	Ohio St.2d 16	413...45	Ohio App.2d 24	433...45	Ohio App.2d 5	847...45	Ohio St.2d 59
398...45	Ohio St.2d 39	418...45	Ohio App.2d 20	436...45	Ohio App.2d 9	849...45	Ohio App.2d 13
403...45	Ohio St.2d 28	421...45	Ohio App.2d 43	439...45	Ohio Misc. 5	854...45	Ohio Misc. 9
407...45	Ohio St.2d 13	423...45	Ohio App.2d 32	441...45	Ohio Misc. 1		

341 NORTH EASTERN REPORTER, SECOND SERIES

N.E.2d Page	State Report	N.E.2d Page	State Report	N.E.2d Page	State Report	N.E.2d Page	State Report
296...45	Ohio St.2d 53	337...45	Ohio App.2d 69	583...45	Ohio St.2d 98	606...45	Ohio App.2d 155
298...45	Ohio St.2d 47	341...45	Ohio App.2d 57	585...45	Ohio St.2d 86	611...45	Ohio App.2d 176
302...45	Ohio St.2d 57	349...45	Ohio App.2d 137	589...45	Ohio St.2d 117	616...45	Ohio App.2d 97
304...45	Ohio St.2d 71	356...45	Ohio Misc. 15	592...45	Ohio St.2d 96	622...45	Ohio App.2d 127
311...45	Ohio App.2d 83	573...45	Ohio St.2d 81	594...45	Ohio St.2d 112	626...45	Ohio App.2d 107
320...45	Ohio App.2d 147	575...45	Ohio St.2d 85	597...45	Ohio St.2d 66	635...45	Ohio App.2d 183
325...45	Ohio App.2d 76	576...45	Ohio St.2d 107	600...45	Ohio St.2d 93	638...45	Ohio App.2d 197
329...45	Ohio App.2d 45	579...45	Ohio St.2d 101	602...45	Ohio App.2d 122	641...45	Ohio App.2d 132

Exhibit 13: Parallel citation table in *North Eastern Reporter* advance sheet: unofficial citation to official citation.

CASES REPORTED

Exhibit 14: Table of cases reported in a *North Eastern Reporter* advance sheet.

STATUTES CONSTRUED

Rules of Probate Courts

Rule
45[1959]—341 N.E.2d 691

Rules of Appellate Procedure

3(a)—341 N.E.2d 655
9—341 N.E.2d 655
9(c)—341 N.E.2d 655
10(c)—341 N.E.2d 655

Rules of Appellate Tax Board

25—341 N.E.2d 649

Laws

1934, ch. 181, § 1—341 N.E.2d 691
1934, ch. 181, § 1—341 N.E.2d 702
1953, ch. 372—341 N.E.2d 684
1956, ch. 75—341 N.E.2d 651
1956, ch. 132, § 1—341 N.E.2d 684
1960, ch. 374, § 1—341 N.E.2d 682
1965, ch. 208, § 1—341 N.E.2d 684
1968, ch. 292—341 N.E.2d 649
1970, ch. 118—341 N.E.2d 649
1971, ch. 976, § 2B—341 N.E.2d 662
1972, ch. 614, § 2—341 N.E.2d 645
1973, ch. 939—341 N.E.2d 645

NEW YORK

Constitution

Art.
6, § 6—405 F.Supp. 326
13, § 13—405 F.Supp. 326

Civil Practice Law and Rules

Sec. or
Rule
4404—341 N.E.2d 557
5501(b)—341 N.E.2d 532

Civil Service Law

Sec.
204—341 N.E.2d 532

County Law

702—405 F.Supp. 326

Criminal Procedure Law

290.10—341 N.E.2d 546

Domestic Relations Law

115-b—341 N.E.2d 526
115-b, subd. 2—341 N.E.2d 526

Education Law

3102, subd. 6. See Laws 1956, ch. 710, § 2—341 N.E.2d 532

Partnership Law

91(1)(a)—527 F.2d 445
91(1)(b)—527 F.2d 445

Penal Law

220.25—341 N.E.2d 546
265.02, subd. 4—341 N.E.2d 540

Public Service Law

120 et seq.—341 N.E.2d 544

Sec.
121, subd. 1—341 N.E.2d 544
122, subd. 1—341 N.E.2d 544
122, subd. 1(c)—341 N.E.2d 544
126, subd. 1(c)—341 N.E.2d 544
126, subd. 2—341 N.E.2d 544

Workmen's Compensation Law

2, subd. 7—341 N.E.2d 527
21, subd. 5—341 N.E.2d 527
23—341 N.E.2d 527
48—341 N.E.2d 527

Commercial Code

8-315—527 F.2d 445

Laws

1956, ch. 719, § 2—341 N.E.2d 532
1973, ch. 276. Amended by Laws 1973, ch. 278—341 N.E.2d 546
1973, ch. 278—341 N.E.2d 546
1974, ch. 1041—341 N.E.2d 540

OHIO

Revised Code

Sec.
111.15—341 N.E.2d 585
121.22(A)—341 N.E.2d 576
149.43—341 N.E.2d 576
2311.38—341 N.E.2d 594
2505.02—341 N.E.2d 641
2903.11–2903.13—341 N.E.2d 622
2903.21—341 N.E.2d 622
2923.11—341 N.E.2d 622
2945.71—341 N.E.2d 635
2945.71(B)—341 N.E.2d 635
2945.72—341 N.E.2d 635
3107.06(D)—341 N.E.2d 616
3107.09—341 N.E.2d 616
3311.06—341 N.E.2d 589
3719.41—341 N.E.2d 635
3937.18—341 N.E.2d 597
4509.01 et seq.—341 N.E.2d 600
4909.16—341 N.E.2d 585
4509.20—341 N.E.2d 597
4509.45—341 N.E.2d 600
4511.19—341 N.E.2d 606
4511.20—341 N.E.2d 635
4511.191—341 N.E.2d 606
4511.191(A)—341 N.E.2d 606
5701.02—341 N.E.2d 573
5703.05(B)—341 N.E.2d 626
5711.01(B)—341 N.E.2d 579
5711.03—341 N.E.2d 579
5711.04—341 N.E.2d 579
5711.16—341 N.E.2d 573
5711.22(E)—341 N.E.2d 573
5711.24—341 N.E.2d 626
5711.25—341 N.E.2d 626
5711.26—341 N.E.2d 626
5711.31—341 N.E.2d 626
5717.02—341 N.E.2d 626
5717.04—341 N.E.2d 573
5725.26—341 N.E.2d 579
5747.01 et seq.—341 N.E.2d 611

Exhibit 15: Table of statutes construed in a *North Eastern Reporter* advance sheet.

WORDS AND PHRASES

For other definitions of Words and Phrases listed below, see publication **WORDS AND PHRASES**, comprising judicial definitions of Words and Phrases by the Courts, State and Federal, in paragraph form.

ALFORD,
Tempo Trucking & Transfer Corp. v. Dickson, D.C.N.Y., 405 F.Supp. 506, 516.
CONSEQUENCE,
Faulisi v. Daggett, C.A.Ind., 527 F.2d 305, 309.
CONTINGENCY THE NON-OCCURRENCE OF WHICH,
Center Garment Co., Inc. v. United Refrigerator Co., Mass., 341 N.E.2d 669, 673.
CONVICTION,
Tempo Trucking & Transfer Corp. v. Dickson, D.C.N.Y., 405 F.Supp. 506, 518.
EXHAUSTION,
Brown v. Genakos, D.C.Mass., 405 F.Supp. 381, 382.
EXPENSE OF PROSECUTION,
People v. Goss, Ill.App., 341 N.E.2d 437, 439.
FINAL DETERMINATION,
Michelin Tire Corp. v. Kosydar, Ohio App., 341 N.E.2d 626, 631, 632.
FINANCIAL RESPONSIBILITY BOND,
Republic-Franklin Ins. Co. v. Progressive Cas. Ins. Co., Ohio, 341 N.E.2d 600, 602.
INSURANCE,
Republic-Franklin Ins. Co. v. Progressive Cas. Ins. Co., Ohio, 341 N.E.2d 600, 602.
INVESTMENT CONTRACT,
Swank Federal Credit Union v. C. H. Wagner & Co., Inc., D.C.Mass., 405 F.Supp. 385, 388.
LIABILITY INSURANCE POLICY,
Republic-Franklin Ins. Co. v. Progressive Cas. Ins. Co., Ohio, 341 N.E.2d 600, 602.
MATERIALITY,
U. S. v. Natelli, C.A.N.Y., 527 F.2d 311, 319.
NOLO CONTENDERE,
Tempo Trucking & Transfer Corp. v. Dickson, D.C.N.Y., 405 F.Supp. 506, 516.
PERSON,
Gresham v. City of Chicago, D.C.Ill., 405 F.Supp. 410, 411.
Naprstek v. City of Norwich, D.C.N.Y., 405 F.Supp. 521, 522.
PUBLIC RECORD,
Dayton Newspapers, Inc. v. City of Dayton, Ohio, 341 N.E.2d 576, 577.
RECKLESSNESS,
People v. Parr, Ill.App., 341 N.E.2d 439, 441.
REQUIRED TO BE KEPT,
Dayton Newspapers, Inc. v. City of Dayton, Ohio, 341 N.E.2d 576, 577.
SERRANO,
Tempo Trucking & Transfer Corp., v. Dickson, D.C.N.Y., 405 F.Supp. 506, 515.
STATUTORY PRESUMPTION,
People v. Leyva, 341 N.E.2d 546, 551, 38 N.Y.2d 160.
UNINSURED AUTOMOBILE,
Shelby Mutual Ins. Co. v. Smith, Ohio, 341 N.E.2d 597, 599.
UPON ITS OWN MOTION,
State ex rel. Dunbar v. Ham, Ohio, 341 N.E.2d 594, 596.
UNREASONABLY DANGEROUS,
Becker v. Aquaslide 'N' Dive Corp., Ill.App., 341 N.E.2d 369, 377.
WILLFUL AND WANTON,
Turner v. Commonwealth Edison Co., Ill.App., 341 N.E.2d 488, 493.

341 N.E.2d   XXXII

Exhibit 16: Table of words and phrases in a *North Eastern Reporter* advance sheet.

PLEADING—Cont'd.

provision in its employment contract to allow defendant to remain in the house for a definite term, affirmative defense that district had wrongfully discharged him did not state a legally sufficient defense to the action and was correctly stricken.—Joppa High School Dist. No. 21, Massac County v. Jones, 341 N.E.2d 419.

PRINCIPAL AND SURETY.

⛧185
Ohio 1976. If surety of a financial responsibility bond is compelled to make payments for damages caused by the principal the surety has the right to seek reimbursement from the principal.—Republic-Franklin Ins. Co. v. Progressive Cas. Ins. Co., 341 N.E.2d 600, 45 Ohio St.2d 93.

PRODUCTS LIABILITY.

⛧88
Ill.App. 1975. Testimony by persons who were at party at which plaintiff was injured while using swimming pool slide to the effect that there were floating chairs in the water was sufficient to permit jury, which was considering plaintiff's products liability action against slide manufacturer, to determine if there were in fact chairs in the water and to consider expert testimony that plaintiff's injuries could have resulted from his striking one of the floating chairs rather than from striking the bottom of the pool.—Becker v. Aquaslide 'N' Dive Corp., 341 N.E.2d 309.

⛧96
Ill.App. 1975. Instruction, given in products liability case, which informed jury that "unreasonably dangerous" meant a hazard of which the user of the product was not aware or any danger beyond the expectation of the ordinary user with the ordinary knowledge common to the community was proper.—Becker v. Aquaslide 'N' Dive Corp., 341 N.E.2d 309.

In the context of products liability cases, the concept of "unreasonably dangerous" is neither generally understood by jurors nor within their common experience and an instruction defining the term is necessary.—Id.

⛧97
Ill.App. 1975. Instructions which informed jury that plaintiff claimed that swimming pool slide was unreasonably dangerous in certain respects and which stated that the plaintiff had the burden of proving that the slide was defective and unreasonably dangerous and that the unreasonably dangerous condition was a proximate cause of the injuries suffered by the plaintiff was proper.—Becker v. Aquaslide 'N' Dive Corp., 341 N.E.2d 309.

PUBLIC SERVICE COMMISSIONS.

⛧19(1)
Ohio 1976. Public Utilities Commission had the statutory authority to temporarily alter or amend an existing order affecting a public utility in case of emergency without following the statutory procedures for amendment of rules. R.C. §§ 111.15, 4909.16.—East Ohio Gas Co. v. Public Utilities Commission, 341 N.E.2d 585, 45 Ohio St.2d 86.

RECORDS.

⛧14
Ohio 1976. City jail log, which listed arrest numbers, names of prisoners, charges, dates, times and dispositions, was "public record" and was subject to disclosure. R.C. § 149.43.—Dayton Newspapers, Inc. v. City of Dayton, 341 N.E.2d 576, 45 Ohio St.2d 107.

RECORDS—Cont'd.

Record is "required to be kept" by governmental unit and is ordinarily subject to disclosure where unit's keeping of such record is necessary to unit's execution of its duties and responsibilities. R.C. § 149.43.—Id.

Doubt should be resolved in favor of disclosure of government records. R.C. § 149.43.—Id.

Aside from statutory exceptions, records should be available to public unless custodian of such records can show legal prohibition to disclosure. R.C. §§ 121.22(A), 149.43.—Id.

Decision to allow access to governmental records should not rest solely with their custodian. R.C. § 149.43.—Id.

REFERENCE.

⛧47
Ohio App. 1975. Provisions of rule allowing referral of cases to referees are not to be construed as granting referees right to render judgment which has not received independent analysis by the court. Civ.R. 53.—Logue v. Wilson, 341 N.E.2d 641, 45 Ohio App.2d 132.

⛧86
Ohio App. 1975. Report of referee to which case has been referred must contain statement of basis for his findings and recommendations. Civ.R. 53.—Logue v. Wilson, 341 N.E.2d 641, 45 Ohio App.2d 132.

Referee's entry of "report" which did not contain statement of basis for his findings and recommendations and which was worded as a judgment rather than merely recommending proposed judgment to reviewing court was improper. Civ.R. 53.—Id.

⛧102(3)
Ohio App. 1975. Entry of judgment by court on same day it received "report" of referee was improper under rule which provides for referring of cases to referee and which gives parties 14 days to serve written objections concerning report on other parties and to apply to court for action upon report. Civ.R. 53, 53(E).—Logue v. Wilson, 341 N.E. 2d 641, 45 Ohio App.2d 132.

REFORMATION OF INSTRUMENTS.

⛧16
Mass. 1976. Supreme Judicial Court will not decree a reformation of an instrument unless it is convinced that the parties expressed agreement and expressed an intention to be bound in accordance with the terms that the Court has been asked to establish and enforce. —Sancta Maria Hospital v City of Cambridge, 341 N.E.2d 674.

⛧19(1)
Mass. 1976. Where a party's acquiescence in an agreement is induced by his own mistake alone, rescission and restitution may be proper remedies, but reformation will not be granted. —Sancta Maria Hospital v. City of Cambridge, 341 N.E.2d 674.

ROBBERY.

⛧24.1(4)
Mass.App. 1976. Evidence that police officers, responding to robbery-in-progress call, noticed white automobile traveling in opposite direction, that police officer recognized defendant as driver, that object, later identified as pistol used in robbery, was thrown from automobile, and that two passengers who jumped from automobile during police pursuit were subsequently identified by victim as robbers, was sufficient to give rise to jury question as to whether defendant was involved in robbery, and was sufficient to support defend-

For Earlier Cases, See Same Topic and Key Number in Any West Key Number Digest

Exhibit 17: Key number digest for cases reported in a *North Eastern Reporter* advance sheet.

COURT OF CLAIMS RULES

Rule
40 ....527 F.2d   613

FEDERAL RULES OF CIVIL PROCEDURE

Supplementing

Wright and Miller, Federal Practice and Procedure: Civil

Barron and Holtzoff, Federal Practice and Procedure

Rule			Rule			Rule		
6(a)	527 F.2d	416	15(a)	405 F.Supp.	435	54(b)	527 F.2d	469
7(b)(1)	405 F.Supp.	435	19	527 F.2d	216	54(d)	527 F.2d	269
9(c)	405 F.Supp.	562	19(a)	527 F.2d	216	56	527 F.2d	486
10(c)	405 F.Supp.	370	23	527 F.2d	204	56(b)	405 F.Supp.	406
12(b)(1)	405 F.Supp.	435	23	527 F.2d	532	56(c)	527 F.2d	161
12(b)(6)	405 F.Supp.	326	23(c)	527 F.2d	532	56(e)	405 F.Supp.	370
12(b)(6)	405 F.Supp.	338	30(e)	527 F.2d	473	57	405 F.Supp.	482
12(b)(6)	405 F.Supp.	370	32(a)(4)	527 F.2d	473	60(a)	527 F.2d	592
12(b)(6)	405 F.Supp.	435	32(d)	527 F.2d	473	60(b)	527 F.2d	592
12(b)(6)	405 F.Supp.	482	42(a)	527 F.2d	216	60(b)(1)	527 F.2d	592
12(f)	405 F.Supp.	482	52(a)	527 F.2d	394	60(b)(6)	527 F.2d	592
13(a)	527 F.2d	216	52(a)	527 F.2d	465	65	405 F.Supp.	482
14	527 F.2d	296	54(b)	527 F.2d	257	77(a)	527 F.2d	416
15	405 F.Supp.	435						

FEDERAL RULES OF CRIMINAL PROCEDURE

Supplementing

Wright, Federal Practice and Procedure: Criminal

Rule			Rule			Rule		
7(c)	527 F.2d	289	14	527 F.2d	586	30	527 F.2d	165
7(c)(1)	527 F.2d	311	15	405 F.Supp.	578	30	527 F.2d	311
8(a)	527 F.2d	586	15(a)	527 F.2d	473	32(d)	405 F.Supp.	473
11	527 F.2d	305	15(d)	527 F.2d	473	32(d)	405 F.Supp.	583
11	405 F.Supp.	583	17(a)	405 F.Supp.	578	35	527 F.2d	491
11(b)	405 F.Supp.	506	17(b)	405 F.Supp.	578	48(b)	527 F.2d	562
11(f)	405 F.Supp.	506	29(a)	527 F.2d	311	52(b)	527 F.2d	311
14	527 F.2d	423	29(c)	527 F.2d	586	52(b)	527 F.2d	386

341 N.E.2d   IX

Exhibit 18: Tables of procedural rules in a *North Eastern Reporter* advance sheet.

AMERICAN BAR ASSOCIATION

STANDARDS FOR CRIMINAL JUSTICE

TABLE OF STANDARDS CITED

     XI

Exhibit 19: Table of ABA Standards for Criminal Justice in a *North Eastern Reporter* advance sheet.

[*53*]

Official State Reports.   Once one is familiar
with case reporting in the National Reporter System, there is little more that can be learned from
the official reports, despite their continuing importance.   However, it should be noted that the
National Reporter System was created in the late
nineteenth century.   Therefore, only the official
report may exist for earlier state cases.   To facilitate access to these reports, Trans-Media Publishing Company has issued a microfilm edition
of the official state reports which antedate the
National Reporter System.   It should also be remembered that the official report is still the authoritative text and must be cited in briefs or
memoranda.   It is customary to give the official
report before the unofficial in citing the case, for
example, *Dayton Newspapers, Inc. v. City of
Dayton,* 45 Ohio St.2d 107, 341 N.E.2d 576 (1976).
The citation to the official Ohio State Reports
precedes the unofficial *North Eastern Reporter.*
Note that both the official and unofficial reporters in this citation are in their second series.

Because of the success of the West system and
for reasons of economy, a number of states have
abandoned their official reporters and some of
these have adopted the West reporter as official.
West, in turn, issues separate editions of the decisions of approximately 35 states by reproducing
the pages of these decisions as they appear in the
West regional reporter and cumulating them into

bound volumes with their original page numbering. The following states have given up their official reports and the list will undoubtedly continue to grow: Alaska, Delaware, Florida, Iowa,
Kentucky, Louisiana, Maine, Mississippi, Missouri, North Dakota, Oklahoma, Tennessee, Texas
and Wyoming. In addition, West now publishes the
official reports for Alabama, Arizona, Idaho, New
Jersey, New Mexico and Utah. Iowa has adopted
the West regional reporter (*North Western Reporter*) as its official reporter, and the following
states have adopted a separately published state
edition of their West regional reporter as the official reporter for that state: Alaska, Delaware,
Florida, Kentucky, Maine, Mississippi, Missouri,
Oklahoma, Tennessee and Wyoming. Appendix
B gives fuller information on the current status
of court reporting in each state at the present
time, but bear in mind that these designations
are subject to change.

Most official reporters include only the reports
of the high court for that state, usually called the
supreme court. A few states (e. g., New York,
California, Illinois and Pennsylvania) issue more
than one series of official reports, because they
have an intermediate appellate court and a heavy
volume of litigation. It is interesting to note
that in New York where there are three official
series of reports (*New York Reports,* covering
the Court of Appeals; *Appellate Division Re-*

ports covering the Appellate Divisions of the Supreme Court; and *Miscellaneous Reports* covering a selection of the decisions of the various lower courts) one single West series, *New York Supplement*, publishes as many cases as the three official reporters. In addition, the *North Eastern Reporter* also publishes the decisions of the N.Y. Court of Appeals, that state's highest court.

Official slip decisions and advance sheets are not commonly published on the state level.

Annotated Reports. While West purports to publish virtually all of the appellate decisions in the United States, Lawyers Co-operative Publishing Company approaches case reporting from a different point of view. Its series, *American Law Reports*, is based on the annotated reporting of a small selection of significant cases. *A.L.R.*, as it is called, includes only a few hundred carefully chosen state court decisions annually, each of which is annotated with an editorial discussion of the law of that case. Before 1969, *A.L.R.* also included some annotated *federal* decisions, but since 1969 these appear in *A.L.R.-Federal*. The annotation includes past developments, the current law in most states on that problem, and probable future trends. The annotations are not prepared by independent scholars, but by editorial writers employed by the publisher. *A.L.R.* is favored by many legal researchers for the exhaustive coverage in many of its annotations. Even

though the leading decision may be from another state, its annotation provides a well-indexed survey of the law in all states. By focusing on those decisions which significantly affect legal development or facilitate the detailed editorial development of an important area of law, the *A.L.R.* annotation frequently offers quicker access to the leading cases than other tools. It should be noted that advance sheets are not issued for *A.L.R.*, since the annotations require time for preparation and there would be little value in issuing a temporary edition of the decisions alone.

Before *A.L.R.* was developed in its present form, various predecessors were published with annotations of varying frequency and quality. These include the following: (1) Trinity series (*American Decisions*, *American Reports* and *American State Reports*), 1760–1911; (2) *American and English Annotated Cases*, 1906–1911; (3) *American Annotated Cases*, 1912–1918; (4) *Lawyers Reports Annotated*, 1888–1918; (5) *American Law Reports*, 1st series: 1918–1947; 2nd series: 1948–1965. *A.L.R.* is currently in its third series.

Access to the decisions and annotations of *A.L.R.* is provided by tables of cases, by word indexes and by digests similar to the West's key number digest, but somewhat more limited. In addition, supplemental services and, in the third series, pocket parts provide access to later deci-

sions and annotations and permit the researcher to up-date any relevant decisions or annotations with later citations. The methods of access and supplementation are explained more fully in Chapter III below.

Special Subject Reporters. There is another significant type of unofficial court reporting, which brings together cases in a particular subject area. Examples of such series are the *American Maritime Cases, Public Utilities Reports Annotated,* and *U.S. Patents Quarterly.* Some of these, like CCH's *Labor Cases* and Prentice-Hall's *American Federal Tax Reports,* are published as adjuncts to looseleaf services on those topics. Some of these reporters also contain decisions of administrative agencies in the same field, such as *Federal Carrier Cases* which includes Interstate Commerce Commission decisions on the regulation of carriers.

LOCATING PARALLEL CITATIONS
OF CASE REPORTS

Since there are several reporting systems publishing simultaneously, the same decision often appears both in the official reports and in the National Reporter System—occasionally it may also be in the *American Law Reports.* Frequently the researcher will have a citation to only one of these reports and will want to obtain citations to the others, either to complete the citation in a brief or to examine the other report.

For that purpose parallel citation tables, such as the following, are used:

1. Case Name. If the case name is known, the Table of Cases volume of the West digest for the appropriate jurisdiction or period will include both the official and unofficial citation. Note the *Roe v. Wade* citations (with digest topics and key numbers) appearing in the following exhibit from the West *U. S. Supreme Court Digest*:

Rockton & R B R v. Walling, SC, 65 SCt 1026, 324 US 880, 89 LEd 1431, den'g cert 146 F2d 111.

Rockwell Mfg Co v. Stanley Works, Pa, 74 SCt 30, 346 US 818, 98 LEd 345, den'g cert Stanley Works v. Rockwell Mfg Co, 203 F2d 846.

Rodgers v. U S, Tenn, 67 SCt 1309, 331 US 799, 91 LEd 1824. Mem.

Rodgers v. U S, Tenn, 68 SCt 5, 332 US 371, 92 LEd 3—Agric 1; Interest 1.

Rodney v. Paramount Pictures, NY, 71 SCt 572, 340 US 953, 95 LEd 687, den'g cert, Paramount Pictures v. Rodney, 186 F2d 111.

Rodrigue v. Aetna Cas & Sur Co, La, 80 SCt 1825, 295 US 352, 23 LEd2d 360—Adm 1.10, 1.20(1), 21, 22.

Rodriquez v. U S, Cal, 89 SCt 1715, 395 US 327, 23 LEd2d 340—Crim Law 997.5, 1004, 1072, 1077.3, 1188.

Roe v. Wade, Tex, 93 SCt 705, 410 US 113, 35 LEd2d 147, reh den 93 SCt 1409, 410 US 959, 35 LEd2d 694—Abort 1; Action 6; Const Law 42.1(3), 46(1), 82, 210, 252, 258(3); Courts 383(1), 385(1, 7), 508(7); Fed Civ Proc 321, 331; Statut 64(6).

Roebling v. C I R 65 SCt 131, 323 US 773, 89 LEd 618, den'g cert 143 F2d 810.

Rogalski, People of State of New York ex rel v. Martin, NY, 64 SCt 53, 320 US 767, 88 LEd 458, reh den 64 SCt 258, 320 US 814, 88 LEd 492. Mem.

Rogers v. Squier, Wash, 67 SCt 1346, 331 US 866, 91 LEd 1870. Mem.

Rogers v. State of Conn, Conn, 76 US 809, 100 LEd 726, rev'g Rogers, 143 Conn 167, 120 A2d 409.

Rogers v. Teets, Cal, 76 SCt 98, 350 US 809, 100 LEd 726, rev'g Rogers, Application of, 229 F2d 754.

Rogers v. U S, Colo, 70 SCt 978, 339 US 956, 94 LEd 1368, gr'g cert Rogers v. U S, 179 F2d 559.

Rogers v. U S, Colo, 70 SCt 979, 339 US 958, 94 LEd 1369, den'g cert Rogers v. U S, 180 F2d 103.

Rogers v. U S, Colo, 71 SCt 438, 340 US 367, 95 LEd 344, 19 ALR2d 378, reh den 71 SCt 619, 341 US 912, 95 LEd 1348—Consp 24, 47(1); Insurrect 2; With 297(1, 12), 298, 305(1), 306, 307, 308.

Rogers' Estate v. C I R 65 SCt 269, 323 US 780, 89 LEd 623, den'g cert 143 F2d 695, 156 ALR 1239.

Rogers' Estate v. Helvering, US, 64 SCt 172, 320 US 410, 88 LEd 134 Int Rev 20.2, 992, 1004.

Rogers v. U S, USLa, 95 SCt 2091, on remand 519 F2d 1084—Courts 383 (8); Crim Law 636(1), 641.12(2), 863(1), 885, 1174(1).

Rogoff v. U S, NY, 65 SCt 553, 323 US 799, 89 LEd 638, den'g cert 145 F2d 82.

Rohde v. O'Donnell, Ill, 70 SCt 1015, 339 US 990, 94 LEd 1390, den'g cert People v. Rohde, 403 Ill 41, 85 NE 2d 24.

Exhibit 20: Table of cases in the *U.S. Supreme Court Digest*, showing the listing for *Roe v. Wade*.

2. Popular Name. If the case has acquired through common usage a popular name, it can be traced through that designation in popular name tables published by Shepard's. Originally published by Shepard's in pamphlet form, a separate Shepard's volume was issued in 1968 entitled *Shepard's Acts and Cases by Popular Names— Federal and State.* That volume is updated by pamphlet supplements. The following exhibit illustrates entries in the case section of that volume:

FEDERAL AND STATE CASES CITED BY POPULAR NAMES	Bus

A	B
Abortion Cases 410 US 113, 35 LE2d 147, 93 SC 705; 410 US 179, 35 LE2d 147, 35 LE2d 201, 93 SC 739, 93 SC 755, 93 SC 756, 93 SC 762	**Baby Lenore Case** 28 NY2d 185, 269 NE2d 787, 321 NYSupp2d 65
Admission Tickets Case 302 FS 1339	**Baby Scarpetta Case** 28 NY2d 185, 269 NE2d 787, 321 NYSupp2d 65
Adulterated Food Case 95 SC 1903	**Banana Cases** 237 Miss 141, 112 So2d 529 252 Miss 693, 173 So2d 603

Angeline Case 401 US 715, 28 LE2d 434, 91 SC 1041	**Black and White Scotch Case** 390 F2d 117
Antibiotic Drug Cases 404 US 548, 30 LE2d 721, 92 SC 731; 426 F2d 32; 281 FS 837 295 FS 1402; 297 FS 1126; 299 FS 1403; 301 FS 1158 314 FS 710 320 FS 586 333 FS 267 333 FS 274 333 FS 278 333 FS 291 333 FS 299 333 FS 310 52 FRD 131	**Bloody Shorts Case** 386 US 1, 17 LE2d 690, 87 SC 785 **Bootstrap Cases** 305 US 165, 83 LE 104, 59 SC 134 308 US 371, 84 LE 329, 60 SC 317 330 US 258, 91 LE 884, 67 SC 677 **Border Patrol Cases** 422 US 873, 45 LE2d 607, 95 SC 2574 422 US 891, 45 LE2d 623, 95 SC 2585 422 US 916, 45 LE2d 641, 95 SC 2569, 95 SC 2590

Exhibit 21:   The case table in *Shepard's Acts and Cases by Popular Names,* showing the popular name of *Roe v. Wade.*

Popular names of cases are also listed separately in the main table of cases of many digests.

3. From Official to Unofficial Report, that is, where the official citation is known and the unofficial is sought, one can use either of the following:

(a) *National Reporter Blue Book* which is issued by West for this purpose and updated annually:

43 OHIO STATE REPORTS, SECOND SERIES

Ohio St. 2d Pg.	N.E.2d Vol.	Pg.	Ohio St. 2d Pg.	N.E.2d Vol.	Pg.	Ohio St. 2d Pg.	N.E.2d Vol.	Pg.	Ohio St. 2d Pg.	N.E.2d Vol.	Pg.	Ohio St. 2d Pg.	N.E.2d Vol.	Pg.	Ohio St. 2d Pg.	N.E.2d Vol.	Pg.
1	330	697	34	330	686	75	330	924	109	330	899	155	331	410	186	331	440
5	330	699	40	330	660	79	330	908	114	330	904	157	331	710	195	331	723
11	330	662	43	330	671	88	330	891	119	330	913	161	331	407	205	331	408
14	330	659	48	330	694	95	330	902	126	330	921	163	331	411	209	331	702
17	330	690	53	330	678	98	330	896	131	331	424	171	331	445	224	331	416
23	330	667	62	330	684	103	330	917	148	331	435	175	331	730	237	331	713
28	330	674	66	330	720												

44 OHIO STATE REPORTS, SECOND SERIES

Ohio St. 2d Pg.	N.E.2d Vol.	Pg.	Ohio St. 2d Pg.	N.E.2d Vol.	Pg.	Ohio St. 2d Pg.	N.E.2d Vol.	Pg.	Ohio St. 2d Pg.	N.E.2d Vol.	Pg.	Ohio St. 2d Pg.	N.E.2d Vol.	Pg.	Ohio St. 2d Pg.	N.E.2d Vol.	Pg.
1	335	703	36	336	835	72	337	776	107	338	570	144	338	783	188	339	854
3	335	700	39	337	622	73	337	777	109	338	762	151	339	663	195	339	630
5	335	703	43	337	788	78	337	783	111	338	757	155	339	622	199	339	814
8	335	701	46	337	782	83	337	786	119	339	249	159	339	624	204	339	828
11	335	867	49	337	625	86	338	522	123	339	252	163	339	641	208	339	820
13	336	433	53	337	780	89	338	530	125	339	628	172	339	648	219	339	830
23	336	429	56	337	790	90	338	526	120	339	626	178	339	638	225	339	817
28	336	426	58	337	773	96	338	366	132	339	633	186	339	652	229	339	826
33	336	849	62	337	766	104	338	524									

45 OHIO STATE REPORTS, SECOND SERIES

Ohio St. 2d Pg.	N.E.2d Vol.	Pg.	Ohio St. 2d Pg.	N.E.2d Vol.	Pg.	Ohio St. 2d Pg.	N.E.2d Vol.	Pg.	Ohio St. 2d Pg.	N.E.2d Vol.	Pg.	Ohio St. 2d Pg.	N.E.2d Vol.	Pg.	Ohio St. 2d Pg.	N.E.2d Vol.	Pg.
1	340	840	57	341	302	107	341	576	159	342	688	234	344	138	292	345	71
11	340	411	59	340	847	112	341	594	165	343	100	236	344	129	295	345	58
13	340	407	63	341	847	117	341	589	178	343	121	238	344	133	298	345	75
16	340	396	66	341	597	121	341	826	187	343	94	245	344	126	300	345	66
19	340	838	71	341	304	130	341	849	196	342	691	249	344	118	308	345	61
23	340	408	81	341	573	134	341	841	207	343	93	262	344	327	316	345	57
27	340	395	85	341	575	137	341	843	210	343	110	267	344	132	351	345	390
28	340	403	86	341	585	143	341	851	216	343	114	270	344	137	366	345	399
34	340	392	93	341	600	146	341	835	228	343	109	271	344	334	319	345	407
39	340	398	96	341	592	151	341	839	231	344	130	283	344	330	351	345	390
47	341	298	98	341	583	154	341	832	233	344	125	289	345	73	366	345	399
53	341	296	101	341	579												

Exhibit 22:   Part of an entry in the *National Reporter Blue Book*, showing reference from official to unofficial citation of the Ohio case, previously noted.

(b) Shepard's state citations—the first citation in the listing of each case refers to the alternate report of the case in the regional reporter. That parallel citation is usually in parentheses.

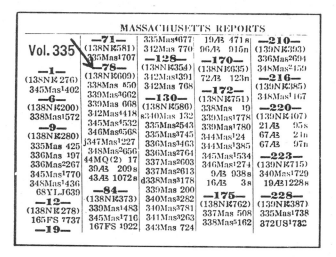

Exhibit 23: From *Shepard's Massachusetts Citations.*

4. From Unofficial to Official Report:

(a) State Blue and White books, issued by West for twenty-four states to provide parallel citations from the official reports to the *National Reporter System.* White pages also carry citation tables from the unofficial to the official report. These books are available to law libraries only for the state in which they are located.

Their arrangement is similar to that in the *National Reporter Blue Book.* (Exhibit 22).

(b) Shepard's regional reporter citations—the first entry, in parentheses, is to the *official* report.

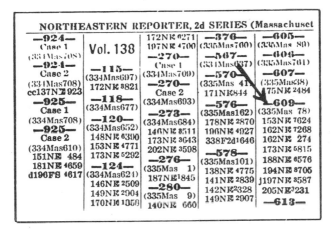

Exhibit 24: From *Shepard's Northeastern Reporter Citations.*

(c) The official citation is also supplied at the beginning of the case in the regional reporter, if it is available at the time of printing.

CHAPTER III
CASE–FINDING

Under the modern view of law as a dynamic process rather than a mechanical search for and application of fixed rules, legal authority can be viewed as including any material which may persuade a tribunal or influence its deliberations. So regarded, primary sources of law may be more authoritative than secondary materials, but the difference is not absolute. Legal research thus can be seen as a wide-ranging and creative inquiry, but still must begin with the primary rules found in appellate decisions and statutes.

The doctrine of precedent can operate effectively only if judicial decisions are published and made easily available, so that they can be cited by lawyers and used by courts in deciding later cases. In order to discover what is the applicable law, lawyers must have some means of locating "cases in point," that is, earlier decisions which are factually and legally relevant to the cases on which they are working. They must be able to locate precedents with which they can support their positions and persuade a court to accept their arguments. However, as we have seen, judicial decisions are published in chronological order, both in their official and unofficial reports. This body of law, consisting of over 3,000,000

decisions to which are added over 30,000 new decisions every year, could hardly be searched for relevant precedents, unless there were some means of subject access.

Such access is, in fact, provided by various finding tools, such as case digests, encyclopedias, citators, annotated law reports, statutory codes, looseleaf services, legal treatises, periodicals, and, in recent years, computerized search services. Of these, the traditional beginning point and certainly the one most specifically designed as a case finder has been the case digest. Bear in mind, however, that for some searches one of the other case finders may be preferred, and that individual preference can always lead you to another tool.

A digest to judicial decisions superimposes a subject classification upon chronologically published cases. The classification scheme consists of an alphabetically arranged scheme of legal topics and subtopics which can be approached through a detailed index. Brief abstracts of the points of law in decided cases are classified by subject and set out in the digests under appropriate topical headings. They are then located and retrieved by the researcher through the index to the digest.

As soon as comprehensive case reporting began to develop in England, finding tools were published to provide a topical approach. Initially this function was performed by texts, but then abridgments and digests were devised to enable lawyers

to find relevant prior cases on particular topics. These finding tools were alphabetical arrangements of brief abstracts of important court decisions set out under broad legal topics. One of the earliest of these was Statham's Abridgment, printed around 1490. Later important abridgments were made by Fitzherbert (1514); Brooke (1568); Rolle (1668); Jacobs (1713); Bacon (1736); and Viner (1742). The early abridgments and digests were prototypes of the modern digests, but used only a few broad topics and included a relatively small number of decisions. Gradually these finding tools grew more and more intensive, employing finer internal subdivisions, and more and more extensive, covering more areas of law and a larger number of cases.

WEST DIGESTS

Today the digests of the West Publishing Company constitute the most comprehensive subject approach to case law, although computerized search systems are rapidly developing more effective approaches. The basic unit of the West digest system is the "squib" or one sentence summary of each principle of law dealt with in each of the cases found in the West reporters. As shown in Exhibit 25, the digest as a whole consists of a series of squibs, arranged by topic name and key number (here *Abortion* ☞1, relating to *Roe v. Wade*) derived from West's key number classification scheme.

⇔1 ABORTION

For later cases see same Topic and Key Number in Pocket Part

U.S.Tex. 1973. Prior to approximately the end of the first trimester of pregnancy the attending physician in consultation with his patient is free to determine, without regulation by state, that in his medical judgment the patient's pregnancy should be terminated, and if that decision is reached such judgment may be effectuated by an abortion without interference by the state.

Roe v. Wade, 93 S.Ct. 705, 410 U.S. 113, 35 L.Ed.2d 147, rehearing denied 93 S.Ct. 1409, 410 U.S. 959, 35 L.Ed.2d 694.

From and after approximately the end of the first trimester of pregnancy a state may regulate abortion procedure to extent that the regulation reasonably relates to preservation and protection of maternal health.

Roe v. Wade, 93 S.Ct. 705, 410 U.S. 113, 35 L.Ed.2d 147, rehearing denied 93 S.Ct. 1409, 410 U.S. 959, 35 L.Ed.2d 694.

If state is interested in protecting fetal life after viability it may go so far as to proscribe abortion during that period except when necessary to preserve the life or the health of the mother.

Roe v. Wade, 93 S.Ct. 705, 410 U.S. 113, 35 L.Ed.2d 147, rehearing denied 93 S.Ct. 1409, 410 U.S. 959, 35 L.Ed.2d 694.

State criminal abortion laws like Texas statutes making it a crime to procure or attempt an abortion except an abortion on medical advice for purpose of saving life of the mother regardless of stage of pregnancy violate due process clause of Fourteenth Amendment protecting right to privacy against state action. U.S.C.A.Const. Amend. 14; Vernon's Ann.Tex.P.C. arts. 1191–1194, 1196.

Roe v. Wade, 93 S.Ct. 705, 410 U.S. 113, 35 L.Ed.2d 147, rehearing denied 93 S.Ct. 1409, 410 U.S. 959, 35 L.Ed.2d 694.

State in regulating abortion procedures may define "physician" as a physician currently licensed by State and may proscribe any abortion by a person who is not a physician as so defined.

Roe v. Wade, 93 S.Ct. 705, 410 U.S. 113, 35 L.Ed.2d 147, rehearing denied 93 S.Ct. 1409, 410 U.S. 959, 35 L.Ed.2d 694.

C.A.Fla. 1975. The fundamental right to an abortion applies to minors as well as adults. U.S.C.A.Const. Amends. 1, 14.

Poe v. Gerstein, 517 F.2d 787.

Portion of Florida abortion statute requiring consent of parent, custodian or legal guardian if pregnant woman is under 18 years of age and unmarried could not be justified by state interests in preventing illicit sexual conduct among minors, protecting minors from

their own improvidence, fostering parental control, and supporting the family as a social unit, and thus such consent requirement was unconstitutional. West's F.S.A. §§ 381.382, 458.22(3), 744.13, 827.06; U.S.C.A.Const. Amends. 1, 14.

Poe v. Gerstein, 517 F.2d 787.

Fundamental right to abortion could not be abridged on the basis of compelling state interests, where, inter alia, the statute in question was not "necessary" to achievement of such interests or was unlikely to achieve them. West's F.S.A. § 458.22(3).

Poe v. Gerstein, 517 F.2d 787.

State's societal interest in marriage relationship was not sufficiently "compelling" to justify Florida statute precluding abortion without the written consent of husband if pregnant woman was married, unless husband was voluntarily living apart from his wife. West's F.S.A. § 458.22(3).

Poe v. Gerstein, 517 F.2d 787.

Florida statute precluding abortion without consent of husband if pregnant woman was married and husband was not voluntarily living apart from her could not be justified by state's interest in protecting the husband's rights with respect to the fetus and with respect to the procreation potential of his marriage, and said statute was unconstitutional as infringement on woman's fundamental right to abortion. West's F.S.A. § 458.22(3).

Poe v. Gerstein, 517 F.2d 787.

C.A.Ill. 1974. It is not until from and after the first trimester of pregnancy that a state may regulate abortions by regulations reasonably related to the preservation and protection of maternal health.

Friendship Medical Center, Ltd. v. Chicago Bd. of Health, 505 F.2d 1141, certiorari denied 95 S.Ct. 1438.

Any general health regulations which would apply to first trimester abortions must be limited so as to give effect to a woman's fundamental right of privacy.

Friendship Medical Center, Ltd. v. Chicago Bd. of Health, 505 F.2d 1141, certiorari denied 95 S.Ct. 1438.

C.A.Minn. 1974. Absent compelling circumstances of state interest, regulation of certain fundamental rights, including abortion, is unconstitutional.

Nyberg v. City of Virginia, 495 F.2d 1342, certiorari denied 95 S.Ct. 169, 419 U.S. 891, 42 L.Ed.2d 136.

Where state fails to take cognizance of separate trimesters of pregnancy in its regulation of abortion procedures, the regulation is overbroad and invalid.

Nyberg v. City of Virginia, 495 F.2d 1342, certiorari denied 95 S.Ct. 169, 419 U.S. 891, 42 L.Ed.2d 136.

For cited U.S.C.A. sections and legislative history

Exhibit 25: A page from *Federal Practice Digest 2d*, showing *Roe v. Wade* under key number Abortion 1.

As illustrated in Exhibits 26 and 27, this key number system, consisting of over 400 digest topics, divides the entire field of American law into seven main divisions and thirty-two subheadings. Within each West digest, the 400 topics are arranged alphabetically from "Abandonment" to "Zoning." Each topic acts as a chapter in the digest, covering generally the legal issues to be found within that chapter. Each of the 400 topics is further divided into subtopics which bear the name of the broader topic and a key number designating its specific subdivision. Some short topics like *Lotteries* or *Obscenity* employ relatively few subdivisions and key numbers, while broader ones like *Constitutional Law* or *Criminal Law* may have thousands. See Exhibit 28 for an analysis of *Abortion,* a relatively small topic.

KEY NUMBER SYSTEM LAW CHART

*Digest Topics arranged by subject matter in the
Key Number classification system.*

1. **PERSONS**
2. **PROPERTY**
3. **CONTRACTS**
4. **TORTS**
5. **CRIMES**
6. **REMEDIES**
7. **GOVERNMENT**

---

1. PERSONS

**RELATING TO NATURAL
PERSONS IN
GENERAL**

Civil Rights
Dead Bodies
Death
Domicile
Food
Health
Holidays
Intoxicating Liquors
Names
Poisons
Seals
Signatures
Sunday
Time
Weapons

**PARTICULAR CLASSES
OF NATURAL
PERSONS**

Absentees
Aliens
Bastards
Citizens
Convicts
Drunkards
Indians
Infants
Mental Health
Paupers
Slaves
Spendthrifts

PERSONAL RELATIONS

Adoption
Apprentices
Attorney and Client
Executors and Administra-
tors
Guardian and Ward
Husband and Wife
Labor Relations
Marriage
Master and Servant
Parent and Child
Principal and Agent
Workmen's Compensation

**ASSOCIATED AND ARTI-
FICIAL PERSONS**

Associations
Beneficial Associations
Building and Loan Associa-
tions
Clubs
Colleges and Universities
Corporations
Exchanges
Joint-Stock Companies and
Business Trusts
Partnership
Religious Societies

**PARTICULAR OCCU-
PATIONS**

Agriculture
Auctions and Auctioneers
Banks and Banking
Bridges
Brokers
Canals
Carriers
Commerce
Detectives
Druggists
Electricity
Explosives
Factors
Ferries
Gas
Hawkers and Peddlers
Innkeepers
Insurance
Licenses
Livery Stable Keepers
Manufactures
Mercantile Agencies
Monopolies
Pawnbrokers and Money
Lenders
Physicians and Surgeons
Pilots
Railroads
Seamen
Shipping
Steam
Street Railroads
Telecommunications
Theaters and Shows
Towage
Turnpikes and Toll Roads
Warehousemen
Wharves

2. PROPERTY

**NATURE, SUBJECTS, AND
INCIDENTS OF OWN-
ERSHIP IN GENERAL**

Abandonment
Accession
Adjoining Landowners
Confusion of Goods
Improvements
Property

**PARTICULAR SUBJECTS
AND INCIDENTS OF
OWNERSHIP**

Animals
Annuities

Automobiles
Boundaries
Cemeteries
Common Lands
Copyrights
Crops
Fences
Fish
Fixtures
Franchises
Game
Good Will
Literary Property
Logs and Logging
Mines and Minerals
Navigable Waters
Party Walls
Patents
Public Lands
Trade Regulation
Waters and Water Courses
Woods and Forests

**PARTICULAR CLASSES
OF ESTATES, OR
INTERESTS IN
PROPERTY**

Charities
Curtesy
Dower
Easements
Estates
Estates Tail
Ground Rents
Joint Tenancy
Landlord and Tenant
Life Estates
Perpetuities
Powers
Remainders
Reversions
Tenancy in Common
Trusts

**PARTICULAR MODES
OF ACQUIRING OR
TRANSFERRING
PROPERTY**

Abstracts of Title
Adverse Possession
Alteration of Instruments
Assignments
Assignments for Benefit of
Creditors
Chattel Mortgages
Conversion
Dedication
Deeds
Descent and Distribution
Escheat
Escrows
Finding Lost Goods
Fraudulent Conveyances
Gifts
Lost Instruments
Mortgages
Pledges
Secured Transactions
Wills

3. CONTRACTS

**NATURE, REQUISITES,
AND INCIDENTS OF
AGREEMENTS IN
GENERAL**

Contracts
Customs and Usages
Frauds, Statute of
Interest
Usury

**PARTICULAR CLASSES
OF AGREEMENTS**

Bailment
Bills and Notes
Bonds
Breach of Marriage Promise
Champerty and Maintenance
Compositions with Creditors
Compromise and Settlement
Covenants
Depositaries
Exchange of Property
Gaming
Guaranty
Indemnity
Joint Adventures
Lotteries
Principal and Surety
Rewards
Sales
Subscriptions
Vendor and Purchaser

**PARTICULAR CLASSES
OF IMPLIED OR CON-
STRUCTIVE CON-
TRACTS OR QUASI
CONTRACTS**

Account Stated
Contribution
Money Lent
Money Paid
Money Received
Use and Occupation
Work and Labor

**PARTICULAR MODES
OF DISCHARGING
CONTRACTS**

Novation
Payment
Release
Subrogation
Tender

4. TORTS

Assault and Battery
Collision
Conspiracy
False Imprisonment
Forcible Entry and Detainer

Exhibit 26: West's key number classification system,
arranged by subject categories.

Fraud
Libel and Slander
Malicious Prosecution
Negligence
Nuisance
Seduction
Torts
Trespass
Trover and Conversion
Waste

5. CRIMES

Abduction
Abortion
Adulteration
Adultery
Affray
Arson
Bigamy
Blasphemy
Breach of the Peace
Bribery
Burglary
Common Scold
Compounding Offenses
Counterfeiting
Criminal Law
Disorderly Conduct
Disorderly House
Disturbance of Public As-
  semblage
Dueling
Embezzlement
Embracery
Escape
Extortion
False Personation
False Pretenses
Fires
Forgery
Fornication
Homicide
Incest
Insurrection and Sedition
Kidnapping
Larceny
Lewdness
Malicious Mischief
Mayhem
Miscegenation
Neutrality Laws
Obscenity
Obstructing Justice
Perjury
Piracy
Prize Fighting
Prostitution
Rape
Receiving Stolen Goods
Rescue
Riot
Robbery
Sodomy
Suicide
Threats
Treason
Unlawful Assembly
Vagrancy

6. REMEDIES

**REMEDIES BY ACT OR
AGREEMENT OF
PARTIES**

Accord and Satisfaction
Arbitration and Award
Submission of Controversy

**REMEDIES BY POS-
SESSION OR
NOTICE**

Liens
Lis Pendens
Maritime Liens
Mechanics' Liens
Notice
Salvage

**MEANS AND METHODS
OF PROOF**

Acknowledgment
Affidavits
Depositions
Estoppel
Evidence
Oath
Records
Witnesses

**CIVIL ACTIONS IN
GENERAL**

Action
Declaratory Judgment
Election of Remedies
Limitation of Actions
Parties
Set-Off and Counterclaim
Venue

**PARTICULAR PROCEED-
INGS IN CIVIL
ACTIONS**

Abatement and Revival
Appearance
Continuance
Costs
Damages
Dismissal and Nonsuit
Execution
Exemptions
Homestead
Judgment
Jury
Motions
Pleading
Process
Reference
Stipulations
Trial

**PARTICULAR REMEDIES
INCIDENT TO CIVIL
ACTIONS**

Arrest
Assistance, Writ of
Attachment
Bail
Deposits in Court
Discovery
Garnishment
Injunction
Judicial Sales
Ne Exeat
Receivers
Recognizances
Sequestration
Undertakings

**PARTICULAR MODES OF
REVIEW IN CIVIL
ACTIONS**

Appeal and Error
Audita Querela
Certiorari
Exceptions, Bill of
New Trial
Review

**ACTIONS TO ESTABLISH
OWNERSHIP OR RE-
COVER POSSESSION
OF SPECIFIC
PROPERTY**

Detinue
Ejectment
Entry, Writ of
Interpleader
Possessory Warrant
Quieting Title
Real Actions
Replevin
Trespass to Try Title

**FORMS OF ACTIONS
FOR DEBTS OR
DAMAGES**

Account, Action on
Action on the Case
Assumpsit, Action of
Covenant, Action of
Debt, Action of

**ACTIONS FOR PARTIC-
ULAR FORMS OR
SPECIAL RELIEF**

Account
Cancellation of Instruments
Creditors' Suit
Divorce
Marshaling Assets and Se-
  curities
Partition
Reformation of Instruments
Specific Performance

**CIVIL PROCEEDINGS
OTHER THAN
ACTIONS**

Habeas Corpus
Mandamus
Prohibition
Quo Warranto
Scire Facias
Supersedeas

**SPECIAL CIVIL JURIS-
DICTIONS AND PRO-
CEDURE THEREIN**

Admiralty
Bankruptcy
Equity
Federal Civil Procedure
Insolvency

**PROCEEDINGS PECUL-
IAR TO CRIMINAL
CASES**

Extradition
Fines
Forfeitures
Grand Jury
Indictment and Information
Pardon and Parole
Penalties
Searches and Seizures

7. GOVERNMENT

**POLITICAL BODIES AND
DIVISIONS**

Counties
District of Columbia
Municipal Corporations
States
Territories
Towns
United States

**SYSTEMS AND
SOURCES OF
LAW**

Administrative Law and
  Procedure
Common Law
Constitutional Law
International Law
Parliamentary Law
Statutes
Treaties

**LEGISLATIVE AND EX-
ECUTIVE POWERS
AND FUNCTIONS**

Bounties
Census
Customs Duties
Eminent Domain
Highways
Inspection
Internal Revenue
Levees and Flood Control
Pensions
Post Office
Private Roads
Public Service Commissions
Schools and School Districts
Social Security and Public
  Welfare
Taxation
Weights and Measures
Zoning

**JUDICIAL POWERS AND
FUNCTIONS, AND
COURTS AND
THEIR OFFI-
CERS**

Amicus Curiæ
Clerks of Courts
Contempt
Court Commissioners
Courts
Judges
Justices of the Peace
Removal of Cases
Reports
United States Commission-
  ers

**CIVIL SERVICE, OFFI-
CERS, AND INSTI-
TUTIONS**

Ambassadors and Consuls
Asylums
Attorney General
Coroners
District and Prosecuting
  Attorneys
Elections
Hospitals
Newspapers
Notaries
Officers
Prisons
Reformatories
Registers of Deeds
Sheriffs and Constables
United States Marshals

**MILITARY AND NAVAL
SERVICE AND WAR**

Armed Services
Militia
War and National Defense

Exhibit 26: Cont'd.

LIST OF DIGEST TOPICS

The digest topics used in this digest conform to the
American Digest System

———

Abandonment
Abatement and Revival
Abduction
Abortion
Absentees
Abstracts of Title
Accession
Accord and Satisfaction
Account
Account, Action on
Account Stated
Acknowledgment
Action
Action on the Case
Adjoining Landowners
Administrative Law and
    Procedure
Admiralty
Adoption
Adulteration
Adultery
Adverse Possession
Affidavits
Affray
Agriculture
Aliens
Alteration of Instruments
Ambassadors and Consuls
Amicus Curiae
Animals
Annuities
Appeal and Error
Appearance
Apprentices
Arbitration
Armed Services
Arrest
Arson
· Assault and Battery
Assignments
Assignments for Benefit of
    Creditors

Assistance, Writ of
Associations
Assumpsit, Action of
Asylums
Attachment
Attorney and Client
Attorney General
Auctions and Auctioneers
Audita Querela
Automobiles
Aviation
Bail
Bailment
Bankruptcy
Banks and Banking
Bastards
Beneficial Associations
Bigamy
Bills and Notes
Blasphemy
Bonds
Boundaries
Bounties
Breach of Marriage Promise
Breach of the Peace
Bribery
Bridges
Brokers
Building and Loan Associ-
    ations
Burglary
Canals
Cancellation of Instruments
Carriers
Cemeteries
Census
Certiorari
Champerty and Maintenance
Charities
Chattel Mortgages
Citizens
Civil Rights
Clerks of Courts

Clubs
Colleges and Universities
Collision
Commerce
Common Lands
Common Law
Common Scold
Compositions with Creditors
Compounding Offenses
Compromise and Settlement
Confusion of Goods
Conspiracy
Constitutional Law
Contempt
Continuance
Contracts
Contribution
Conversion
Convicts
Copyrights
Coroners
Corporations
Costs
Counterfeiting
Counties
Court Commissioners
Courts
Covenant, Action of
Covenants
Creditors' Suit
Criminal Law
Crops
Curtesy
Customs and Usages
Customs Duties
Damages
Dead Bodies
Death
Debt, Action of
Declaratory Judgment
Dedication
Deeds
Depositaries

6—8th Dec. VI

Exhibit 27: A list of the digest topics used in West's key
number classification system, arranged
alphabetically.

[71]

VII   **LIST OF DIGEST TOPICS**

Depositions
Deposits in Court
Descent and Distribution
Detectives
Detinue
Discovery
Dismissal and Nonsuit
Disorderly Conduct
Disorderly House
District and Prosecuting
    Attorneys
District of Columbia
Disturbance of Public
    Assemblage
Divorce
Domicile
Dower
Drains
Drugs and Narcotics
Drunkards
Dueling
Easements
Ejectment
Election of Remedies
Elections
Electricity
Embezzlement
Embracery
Eminent Domain
Entry, Writ of
Equity
Escape
Escheat
Escrows
Estates
Estates Tail
Estoppel
Evidence
Exceptions, Bill of
Exchange of Property
Exchanges
Execution
Executors and Administra-
    tors
Exemptions
Explosives
Extortion
Extradition
Factors
False Imprisonment
False Personation
False Pretenses
Federal Civil Procedure

Federal Courts
Fences
Ferries
Finding Lost Goods
Fines
Fires
Fish
Fixtures
Food
Forcible Entry and Detainer
Forfeitures
Forgery
Fornication
Franchises
Fraud
Frauds, Statute of
Fraudulent Conveyances
Game
Gaming
Garnishment
Gas
Gifts
Good Will
Grand Jury
Ground Rents
Guaranty
Guardian and Ward
Habeas Corpus
Hawkers and Peddlers
Health and Environment
Highways
Holidays
Homestead
Homicide
Hospitals
Husband and Wife
Improvements
Incest
Indemnity
Indians
Indictment and Information
Infants
Injunction
Innkeepers
Insane Persons, *See*
    Mental Health
Insolvency
Inspection
Insurance
Insurrection and Sedition
Interest
Internal Revenue
International Law

Interpleader
Intoxicating Liquors
Joint Adventures
Joint-Stock Companies and
    Business Trusts
Joint Tenancy
Judges
Judgment
Judicial Sales
Jury
Justices of the Peace
Kidnapping
Labor Relations
Landlord and Tenant
Larceny
Levees and Flood Control
Lewdness
Libel and Slander
Licenses
Liens
Life Estates
Limitation of Actions
Lis Pendens
Literary Property
Livery Stable Keepers
Logs and Logging
Lost Instruments
Lotteries
Malicious Mischief
Malicious Prosecution
Mandamus
Manufactures
Maritime Liens
Marriage
Marshaling Assets and
    Securities
Master and Servant
Mayhem
Mechanics' Liens
Mental Health
Mercantile Agencies
Militia
Mines and Minerals
Miscegenation
Money Lent
Money Paid
Money Received
Monopolies
Mortgages
Motions
Municipal Corporations
Names
Navigable Waters

Exhibit 27:   Cont'd.

LIST OF DIGEST TOPICS

Ne Exeat
Negligence
Neutrality Laws
Newspapers
New Trial
Notaries
Notice
Novation
Nuisance
Oath
Obscenity
Obstructing Justice
Officers
Pardon and Parole
Parent and Child
Parliamentary Law
Parties
Partition
Partnership
Party Walls
Patents
Paupers
Pawnbrokers and Money
    Lenders
Payment
Penalties
Pensions
Perjury
Perpetuities
Physicians and Surgeons
Pilots
Piracy
Pleading
Pledges
Poisons
Possessory Warrant
Post Office
Powers
Pretrial Procedure
Principal and Agent
Principal and Surety
Prisons
Private Roads
Prize Fighting
Process
Products Liability
Prohibition
Property
Prostitution
Public Contracts
Public Lands
Public Service Commissions

Quieting Title
Quo Warranto
Railroads
Rape
Real Actions
Receivers
Receiving Stolen Goods
Recognizances
Records
Reference
Reformation of Instruments
Reformatories
Registers of Deeds
Release
Religious Societies
Remainders
Removal of Cases
Replevin
Reports
Rescue
Reversions
Review
Rewards
Riot
Robbery
Sales
Salvage
Schools and School Districts
Scire Facias
Seals
Seamen
Searches and Seizures
Secured Transactions
Securities Regulation
Seduction
Sequestration
Set-Off and Counterclaim
Sheriffs and Constables
Shipping
Signatures
Slaves
Social Security and Public
    Welfare
Sodomy
Specific Performance
Spendthrifts
States
Statutes
Steam
Stipulations
Street Railroads
Submission of Controversy

Subrogation
Subscriptions
Suicide
Sunday
Supersedeas
Taxation
Telecommunications
Tenancy in Common
Tender
Territories
Theaters and Shows
Threats
Time
Torts
Towage
Towns
Trade Regulation
Trade Unions, *See Labor
    Relations*
Treason
Treaties
Trespass
Trespass to Try Title
Trial
Trover and Conversion
Trusts
Turnpikes and Toll Roads
Undertakings
United States
United States Magistrates
United States Marshals
Unlawful Assembly
Use and Occupation
Usury
Vagrancy
Vendor and Purchaser
Venue
War and National
    Emergency
Warehousemen
Waste
Waters and Water Courses
Weapons
Weights and Measures
Wharves
Wills
Witnesses
Woods and Forests
Work and Labor
Workmen's Compensation
Zoning

Exhibit 27: Cont'd.

1–7th D—57

ABORTION

SUBJECTS INCLUDED

Causing or procuring miscarriage or premature delivery of a pregnant woman, and acts done for or in aid of such purpose

Nature and extent of criminal responsibility therefor, and grounds of defense

Prosecution and punishment of such acts as public offenses

Civil liability therefor

SUBJECTS EXCLUDED AND COVERED BY OTHER TOPICS

Death, civil liability for causing, see DEATH

Homicide committed in attempting to procure abortion, see HOMICIDE

Malpractice, civil liability for, see PHYSICIANS AND SURGEONS

For detailed references to other topics, see Descriptive-Word Index

---

Analysis.

⟸1. Nature and elements of offenses.
  2. Defenses.
  3. Persons liable.
  4. Indictment and information.
  5. —— Requisites and sufficiency.
  6. —— Issues, proof, and variance.
  7. Evidence.
  8. —— Presumptions and burden of proof.
  9. —— Admissibility in general.
 10. —— Dying declarations.
 11. —— Weight and sufficiency.
 12. Trial.
 13. —— Instructions.
 14. —— Verdict.
 15. Sentence and punishment.
 16. Civil liability.

⟸**1. Nature and elements of offenses.**
  U.S.Conn. 1965. Connecticut law forbidding use of contraceptives unconstitutionally intrudes upon the right of marital privacy. C.G. S.A. § 53–32; U.S.C.A.Const. Amends. 1, 3, 4, 5, 9, 14.—Griswold v. State of Conn., 85 S.Ct. 1678.
  Ariz. 1962. Under the statute prohibiting advertising to produce abortion or prevent conception and the rule of noscitur a sociis, the words "writes, composes or publishes" may limit the meaning of "notice" and "advertisement," and the words "write" and "compose" connote a more or less formal announcement as contrasted to a person to person referral, and the word "publish" implies the utilization of newspaper or some similar mass media and hence the word "advertising" is not used in a broad sense but has a limited meaning. A.R.S. § 13–213.—Planned Parenthood Committee of Phoenix, Inc. v. Maricopa County, 375 P.2d 719.

  Articles and press releases in newspapers and periodicals including editorials, commentaries and informational articles on matters of general public interest are not "advertising" within the proscription of the statute prohibit-

For subsequent case history information, see Table of Cases

<u>Exhibit 28:</u> Scope-Note and Analysis of the topic *Abortion* in a West digest.

Use of this key number classification system begins early in the West reporting process. As mentioned previously, editors at West create squibs or abstracts for every significant point of law discussed in each case appearing in the West reporters. Each squib is assigned a topic name and key number which designates its subject content. These squibs first appear as headnotes preceding the text of the opinion in the West reporter advance sheet. (See Exhibit 10, at p. 40). All headnotes within each advance sheet are also arranged by topic and key number in the Key Number Digest which appears in the front of the advance sheet of every West reporter, and then in bound reporter volumes. (See Exhibit 17, at p. 51). By bringing together all headnotes bearing the same topic and key number, the digest provides in one place summaries and citations to all cases in that advance sheet which deal with the same legal principle.

As the advance sheets are replaced by bound volumes, the squibs from the Key Number Digests in all West advance sheets are collected and published in monthly and then quarterly cumulations. These cumulations constitute the *General Digest*, the most current component of West's comprehensive digest, the American Digest System.

The American Digest System covers all decisions published in all of West's reporters. Thus the coverage is primarily of appellate court de-

cisions, though selected lower court opinions from some jurisdictions are also included (e. g., those reported in *Federal Supplement* and *New York Supplement*). Since the accumulation into one set of all appellate decisions in the history of the United States would be unmanageable and would require frequent revision, the System is divided into separate units, each of which covers a ten year period. These ten year units are called *decennial digests,* the last one of which, the *Eighth Decennial,* includes cases decided between 1966 and 1976. The first unit of the system, called the *Century Digest,* covers 1658 to 1896, when the volume of litigation was, of course, relatively small. The following are the various units of the American Digest System:

Years	Digest Unit
1658 to 1896	Century Digest
1897 to 1906	First Decennial
1907 to 1916	Second Decennial
1916 to 1926	Third Decennial
1926 to 1936	Fourth Decennial
1936 to 1946	Fifth Decennial
1946 to 1956	Sixth Decennial
1956 to 1966	Seventh Decennial
1966 to 1976	Eighth Decennial
1976 +	General Digest, Fifth Series

The *General Digest, Fifth Series* will provide subject access to cases through its quarterly cumu-

lations until 1986 when the *Ninth Decennial* will be compiled and a new *General Digest* begun, unless the present pattern is changed.

The topics and key numbers used for points of law and types of cases are the same in each of the component parts of the digest system, from the most recent all the way back to the *First Decennial* covering 1897–1906. The original unit, the *Century Digest* (1658–1896), employs a slightly different numbering system, but a table in volume 21 of the *First Decennial* bridges this discrepancy by providing references from the *Century Digest* key numbers to those in the *First Decennial*. In order to go back from the numbers of the *First Decennial* to those of the *Century Digest*, reverse cross references appear under each key number in the volumes of the *First* and *Second Decennials*. Thus research under the same topic may turn up cases from the seventeenth century down to those decided a few weeks ago.

Each of the American Digest System units includes cases appearing in all of West's reporters— in the National Reporter System, the various federal reporters, and West's individual state reporters. In addition, West also publishes smaller digests which cover in a single set (or sometimes in two or three) all of the decisions of smaller geographical or jurisdictional units. For example, there are such digests for each of the regional reporter series except the *South Western*

Reporter and the *North Eastern Reporter,* the latter having been discontinued in 1972.

For each state, except Delaware, Nevada and Utah, West publishes individual digests. Although they are the publisher of these digests, West in some cases has retained the name of the former publisher or compiler of the digest, such as the *Vale Pennsylvania Digest* or *Abbott's New York Digest*. Each state digest is devoted to only one state except for the *Dakota Digest* and the *Virginia-West Virginia Digest*. These digests include references to all cases decided in the state's courts which are reported in the National Reporter System, as well as references to federal cases which began in or were appealed from the state. (Only the digest for New York *excludes* references to federal cases.) The state digests contain some features that make them especially beneficial to practitioners and researchers in the particular state, such as references to opinions of that state's attorney general as well as to important legal periodicals and bar association journals published in that state.

For the federal courts, there is also a separate digest. This digest, originally called the *Federal Digest,* includes references to reported federal cases prior to 1939. Two supplementary series have been added—the *Modern Federal Practice Digest* which covers cases from 1939–1961 and *Federal Practice Digest, 2d,* begun in 1976 and

covering cases from 1962 to the present. These series abstract cases found primarily in the *Supreme Court Reporter, Federal Reporter, Federal Supplement,* and *Federal Rules Decisions.*

Finally, the Supreme Court has a West digest devoted solely to its decisions, the *United States Supreme Court Digest.* (Note that Lawyers Co-op also has a digest for the Supreme Court with a similar name, *Digest of United States Supreme Court Reports.*)

All of the cases which are digested in these publications also appear in the all-inclusive American Digest System. The same key numbers and topics are used in the local digests as are used in the main one, and the researcher can move between them easily.

Despite its unquestioned value as a case finder, the digest has the following shortcomings:

> It contains no explanatory text or comment, but merely a series of separate unevaluated case digests.

> It does not conveniently indicate change in the law, whether by statute or later decision.

> It reflects much dicta and over-abstracts every case, so that the researcher must wade through a great deal of irrelevant material in order to get citations to significant authorities.

It does not contain the texts of primary authority, but only provides the means of finding such authority.

It does not introduce contemporary terminology for its topics or establish separate headings for burgeoning areas of the law as fast as the need is felt by researchers. However, West attempts to stay abreast of new developments by revising and expanding old topics and establishing new topics as the need arises. For example, in recent years, the topics *Securities Regulations, Civil Rights,* and *Drugs and Narcotics* have been added to the digest. When new topics are introduced, they are accompanied by a scope-note and analysis similar to that shown for the topic *Abortion* in Exhibit 28 at p. 74. The new section includes all cases on the subject under the new key number despite the fact that they have appeared in earlier digests under other key numbers. Tables provide a means of converting previously used topics and key numbers into those newly adopted and vice versa. See Exhibits 29 and 30, below.

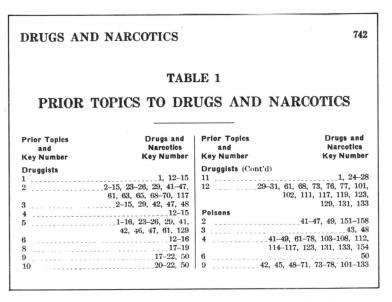

DRUGS AND NARCOTICS   742

TABLE 1

PRIOR TOPICS TO DRUGS AND NARCOTICS

Prior Topics and Key Number	Drugs and Narcotics Key Number	Prior Topics and Key Number	Drugs and Narcotics Key Number
Druggists		**Druggists** (Cont'd)	
1	1, 12–15	11	1, 24–28
2	2–15, 23–26, 29, 41–47, 61, 63, 65, 68–70, 117	12	29–31, 61, 68, 73, 76, 77, 101, 102, 111, 117, 119, 123, 129, 131, 133
3	2–15, 29, 42, 47, 48	**Poisons**	
4	12–15	2	41–47, 49, 151–158
5	1–16, 23–26, 29, 41, 42, 46, 47, 61, 129	3	43, 48
6	12–16	4	41–49, 61–78, 103–108, 112, 114–117, 123, 131, 133, 154
8	17–19	6	50
9	17–22, 50	9	42, 45, 48–71, 73–78, 101–133
10	20–22, 50		

Exhibit 29: Conversion table for new topic in the West digest system.

743   **DRUGS AND NARCOTICS**

ˉ TABLE 2

DRUGS AND NARCOTICS TO PRIOR TOPICS

Drugs and Nar-cotics Key Number	Prior Topic and Key Number	Drugs and Nar-cotics Key Number	Prior Topic and Key Number
1	Druggists ☞1, 5, 11	73	Druggists ☞12;
2–11	Druggists ☞2, 3, 5		Internal Revenue ☞2401;
12–15	Druggists ☞1–6		Poisons ☞2, 4, 9
16	Druggists ☞5, 6	74	Customs Duties ☞125,
17–19	Druggists ☞8, 9		134;
20–22	Druggists ☞9, 10		Poisons ☞4, 9
23	Druggists ☞2, 5	75	Poisons ☞4, 9
24–26	Druggists ☞2, 5, 11	76	Customs Duties ☞125;
27, 28	Druggists ☞11		Druggists ☞12;
29	Druggists ☞2, 3, 5, 12		Internal Revenue ☞2401,
30, 31	Druggists ☞12		2447;
41	Druggists ☞2, 5;		Poisons ☞4, 9
	Physicians and Surgeons ☞10;	77	Customs Duties ☞125;
	Poisons ☞2, 4		Druggists ☞12;
42	Druggists ☞2, 3, 5;		Poisons ☞2, 4, 9
	Poisons ☞2, 4, 9	78	Poisons ☞2, 4, 9
43	Druggists ☞2;	101, 102	Druggists ☞12;
	Internal Revenue ☞2401;		Poisons ☞2, 9
	Poisons ☞2, 4	103	Customs Duties ☞134;
44	Poisons ☞2, 4, 9		Internal Revenue ☞2433,
45	Druggists ☞2;		2441;
	Poisons ☞2–4, 9		Poisons ☞2, 4, 9
46	Druggists ☞2, 5;	104	Poisons ☞4, 9
	Poisons ☞2, 4	105	Internal Revenue ☞2433;
47	Druggists ☞2, 3, 5;		Poisons ☞4, 9
		106	Customs Duties ☞134;

Exhibit 30:   Conversion table for new topic in West digest system.

Occasionally the squibs do not accurately state
the points of law they purport to contain. Thus,
the attorney using a digest for case finding must
locate and choose the relevant line of cases for
study. One must then read the apparently rele-

vant cases and synthesize those which appear *most* relevant, to arrive at an understanding or statement of the applicable law. Finally, the search must be updated and the current status and authority of the cases determined, by using the appropriate volumes of Shepard's citators.

The researcher who wants to use the digest must have some convenient way of locating the topic and key number relevant to the problem being researched. Access to the digest is through one of the following approaches: (1) by the name of a particular case which is known to be in point (or through its headnotes); (2) by the relevant legal concept; or (3) by an analysis of the factual make-up of the problem.

1. Via Tables of Cases or Case Headnotes. If the researcher already knows of a case in point, its citation and the key numbers assigned to it can be located by using the table of cases volume or volumes for the appropriate unit of the West digest system. Every unit of the system, except the *Century Digest* and the *First Decennial,* has its own table of cases volume. A combined table of cases for the *Century Digest* and *First Decennial* is contained in volumes 21–25 of the *First Decennial.*

Even if the researcher knows only the name of the defendant in the case, it is still possible to use the table of cases approach since the *U. S.*

Supreme Court Digest, the *Federal Digest* series, and all state digests have tables of cases arranged by defendant as well as by plaintiff.

If the jurisdiction in which the case was decided is known, one can go to the local digest for that state or region. Otherwise, it is necessary to know in which decennial digest the case appears, since there is no overall table of cases for the entire American Digest System. From that decennial's table a direct reference to the appropriate key numbers under which the points of law of that case have been indexed can be obtained. With the relevant key numbers, it is easy to locate other earlier or later cases on the same topic in the body of the digest. If the table of cases does not contain those references, the report of the case can be located by its citation in the table of cases. The headnotes in the reported decision can then be examined, and the appropriate key numbers for further search obtained from them.

If the complete citation of a case known to be relevant is already in hand, one can of course go directly to its report and obtain the relevant key numbers from its headnotes. By using the table of cases, however, one can also obtain parallel citations to the official report of the same case, the later history of the case (whether it was affirmed, reversed, or modified), and possibly a reference to an *A.L.R.* annotated report. Exhibit 20, at page 59 above, illustrates a typical case name

table in a West digest. It is difficult, however, to use the table of cases approach to the digest unless one knows the approximate date or jurisdiction of the case in question, since, as we have seen, there is no single table of cases covering the entire digest system.

2. Topic Approach. This method requires the researcher to select the legal topic used in the West digests which is most relevant to the problem at hand. There is a list of these topics in front of each volume of the digest system and the searcher can run through the list, select the appropriate topic, turn to it in the digest and, by inspecting the detailed table of contents at the beginning of each particular topic (as in Exhibit 28 at page 74 above), find the appropriate key number. With that key number, one can then proceed to locate other cases in point in the digest proper. This is a chancy method and obviously less desirable than the factual approach described below. It is also inefficient to search through the list of topics and then to examine the content analysis of the chosen topic in order to obtain the appropriate key number. A great deal of time and effort can be wasted through the use of this method, particularly where the relevant topic is a broad one like *Constitutional Law* or *Criminal Law*.

3. Descriptive Word Method. The most efficient procedure for case finding in the digest re-

lies on the use of specific factual catch words derived from an analysis of the problem in question. This approach allows common words rather than more difficult legal concepts to be used as access points. These words are searched in the Descriptive Word Indexes of the West digests in order to find the appropriate key number and topic for that problem. Exhibit 31 below illustrates such an index in the *Modern Federal Practice Digest* covering the subject matter of *Roe v. Wade*.

It is usually much faster to use these alphabetical indexes, which contain many thousands of legally significant catchwords and phrases, rather than the less precise conceptual approach.

ABORTION

1 F Pr D D W I—4

References are to Digest Topics and Key Numbers

ABORTION (Cont'd)
CONSENT—
  Minor's parent—
    Custodian or guardian, validity of statutory prerequisite. **Abort 1**
    Validity of statute forbidding operation without. **Abort 1**
  Parent of minor or husband, validity of statute requiring. **Abort 1**
  Written consent of husband, validity of provision taking prerequisite—
    Abort 1
    Const Law 82
CONSPIRACY, EVIDENCE. **Consp 47(8)**
CONSTITUTIONAL LAW—
  Abort 1
  Const Law 82
COUNTY general hosptial, validity of forbidding elective abortions in first trimester. **Hosp 6**
CRIMES, validity of statutes limiting abortion to saving mother's life—
  Abort 1
  Const Law 258(3)
DOCTOR'S certificate, suspension or revocation for abetting procuring abortion. **Phys 2**
EVIDENCE—
  Admissibility, harmless error. **Crim Law 1169.1(3)**
  Conspiracy. **Consp 47(8)**
FEDERAL judgment declaring statute invalid, state prosecution of nonparties. **Decl Judgm 390**
HABEAS CORPUS, doctor, state abortion statute invalid. **Hab Corp 32**
HOSPITALS—
  Accreditation, validity of limiting abortions to accredited hospitals—
    Abort 1
    Const Law 208(1)
  Federal aid, staff privileges renewal conditioned on not performing abortions. **Civil R 13.5(1)**
  Private hospital accepting federal funds, refusal of abortion patients. **Hosp 5**
  Ban on nontherapeutic abortions in municipal hospitals, permissibility. **Abort 1**
  Reimbursement by state, elective abortions of indigent persons. **Social S 241**
HUSBAND'S written consent, validity of statute requiring. **Abort 1**
INDIGENT PERSONS—
  Informal policy precluding payment for operations with welfare funds. **Const Law 253(2)**
INFANTS, parent's written consent, validity of statute requiring. **Abort 1**
INJUNCTION—
  Federal court refusing to issue after invalidating state statute. **Decl Judgm 387**
INJUNCTION, state court enjoining following federal injunction permitting, representative in federal class action, standing. **Inj 114(2), 158**
LAWFUL justification requirement, vagueness—
  Abort 1
  Const Law 82, 275(1)
LECTURER, warrantless and unjustified arrest. **Civil R 13.5(3)**
LIFE of mother—
  Conditioning of abortions on preserving, validity of statutes. **Abort 1**
  Or fetus, limiting abortion to preservation, permissibility—
    Abort 1
    Const Law 82
  Preservation, validity of penal statute excepting only abortions necessary for—
    Abort 1
    Const Law 258(3)
  Validity of statute forbidding abortion except to save—
    Abort 1
    Const Law 82, 274(2)

ABORTION (Cont'd)
MAILING matter concerning—
  Corruption of public morals, validity of statute forbidding mailing. **Const Law 82, 90.1(1)**
MEDICAID—
  Certification of necessity, validity of forbidding payment without. **Social S 241**
  Consent of patient before first trimester, validity of state requirement for presenting. **Const Law 242.3(1)**
  Discrimination between therapeutic and non-therapeutic abortions, permissibility. **Social S 241**
  Limit therapeutic abortions, validity of state regulation excluding. **Social S 241**
  Statute forbidding elective abortion, consistency with federal statute. **Social S 241**
  Validity of state regulations excluding payment for elective abortions. **Social S 241**
  Validity of withholding benefits for non-therapeutic abortion—
    Const Law 211
    Social S 241
MEDICAL ASSISTANCE—
  State policy denying not applied when litigation threatened. **Social S 241**
  Validity of forbidding for operation not medically indicated—
    Const Law 208(3)
    Social S 241
MEDICAL services, indigent women, state reimbursement of hospitals. **Social S 241**
MENTAL HEALTH, validity of statute forbidding abortion to preserve for mother. **Abort 1**
MOOTNESS, hospital rule forbidding elective abortions, challengers terminating own pregnancies. **Inj 22**
MUNICIPAL hospitals, power to forbid staff physicians from using facilities for abortions. **Hosp 6**
NONPHYSICIANS, validity of statute forbidding operation by. **Abort 1**
NOTICE to husband, statute requiring physicians to give before operation, self-incrimination. **Inj 85(1)**
ORDINANCE, validity of sweeping clinic regulation. **Mun Corp 594(1)**
OVERBREADTH of coverage, statute forbidding abortions unless by duly licensed physician. **Crim Law 13.1(13)**
PARENTAL consent for performing on woman under 18, validity of statute requiring. **Abort 1**
PARTIES, concealment of identity, challenge to state statutes. **Fed Civ Proc 101**
PHYSICIANS, confirmation of recommendation by two physicians, validity of requirement. **Phys 2**
POSTQUICKENING abortions necessary to preserve health of pregnant women, failure of statute to except from statutory prohibition. **Const Law 70.1(10)**
PRIVACY, right of including abortion. **Const Law 82**
PUBLIC hospital, policy of forbidding elective abortions, inadequate facilities. **Hosp 6**
QUICK child, validity of statute proscribing killing and destruction. **Abort 1**
REGULATIONS—
  Place or facility for performing operations, privacy. **Const Law 82**
  Vagueness, physician having common knowledge of procedures. **Health & E 21**
RESIDENCE, validity of requirement—
  Abort 1
  Const Law 207(1)
RETROACTIVITY, decision invalidating statutes forbidding abortions in first trimester. **Courts 100(1)**

Exhibit 31: A page from the Descriptive Word Index in the *Modern Federal Practice Digest.*

There is a Descriptive Word Index for each decennial digest and for each state and regional digest. West recommends that in using this method the researcher obtain relevant search words by analyzing the problem into these components: (a) Parties; (b) Places and things; (c) Basis of action or issue; (d) Defenses; and (e) Relief sought. A sample case used by West involves a professional wrestling match in which the referee was thrown from the ring in such a way that he struck and injured plaintiff who was a front row spectator. West offers the following analysis of that problem to provide appropriate search words for the index:

(a) Parties—Spectator, Patron, Arena Owner, Wrestler, Referee, Promoter

(b) Places and Things—Wrestling Match, Amusement Place, Theater, Show

(c) Basis of Action or Issue—Negligence, Personal Injury to Spectator, Liability

(d) Defense—Assumption of Risk

(e) Relief Sought—Damages

With that analysis, the researcher can look up the most specific words and phrases in the Descriptive Word Index and thereby locate relevant key numbers and their cases covering that problem.

CASE–FINDING IN A.L.R.

American Law Reports and its companion, *American Law Reports-Federal,* also provide subject access to their chronologically published reports and annotations by a variety of digests and indexes.

A.L.R. 1st and *2nd* each have a separate multi-volume digest which gives references to cases in much the same way as the West digests, though using a different classification scheme. Additionally, both series also have a Word Index, similar to West's Descriptive Word Index, which refers to the annotations in those two series.

With *A.L.R. 3rd* and *A.L.R. Federal,* a new method of access, the Quick Index, was developed. This index combines both the digest approach and the factual word approach in one alphabet. It is now the standard means of access to the annotations in the *A.L.R.* series, Quick Indexes having been created to cover the entire *A.L.R.* system.

A.L.R. also provides access to cases reported in full by means of a table of cases in the digests for *A.L.R. 1st* and *2nd* and in the back of the *A.L.R. 2nd and 3rd Quick Index* and its *Supplement.*

A.L.R. annotations are kept up to date by collecting all the cases in point which have been decided since the annotation was written. The later cases for each annotation in *A.L.R. 1st* are found

[*89*]

in a five volume set entitled *A.L.R. 1st Blue Book of Supplemental Decisions.* For *A.L.R. 2d,* the supplementing service is *A.L.R. Later Case Service.* *A.L.R. 3rd* and *A.L.R. Federal* are kept current by cumulative pocket supplements in each volume.

When the effect of later cases is to change substantially the existing law on a particular subject, a new annotation may be written that will supplement or completely supersede a previous annotation. To determine the existence of an annotation supplementing or superseding one in *A.L.R. 1st,* the researcher should consult the *A.L.R. 1st Blue Book* and its supplements. For updates of annotations in *A.L.R. 2d* and *3rd,* one should check the Annotation History Table located in the Quick Index. Exhibit 32, of a similar table appearing in *Lawyers' Edition,* shows that the annotation on abortion at 28 L Ed 2d 1053 has been superseded by a new annotation at 35 L Ed 2d 735.

ANNOTATION HISTORY TABLE

48 L Ed 860–870
Superseded 32 L Ed 2d 869

50 L Ed 428
Superseded 42 L Ed 2d 870

64 L Ed 141–157
Superseded 11 ALR Fed 606

65 L Ed 138–142
Superseded 32 L Ed 2d 869

84 L Ed 137–151
Partially superseded in 34 L Ed 2d 805
(state regulatory power)

84 L Ed 383
Supplemented 9 L Ed 2d 1260 and
18 L Ed 2d 1420

88 L Ed 614–635
Partially superseded in 34 L Ed 2d 805
(state regulatory power)

89 L Ed 1336–1338
Superseded 24 ALR Fed 9

94 L Ed 806–810
Superseded 38 L Ed 2d 796

94 L Ed 856–864
Superseded 33 L Ed 2d 783

96 L Ed 968–977
Superseded 37 L Ed 2d

97 L Ed 145–146
Superseded 37 L Ed 2d

7 L Ed 2d 994–1009
Superseded in part in 15 ALR Fed 665

9 L Ed 2d 998–1067
Supplemented 20 L Ed 2d 1528

10 L Ed 2d 1243–1306
Superseded 22 ALR Fed 556

98 L Ed 73–76
Superseded 18 ALR Fed 489

98 L Ed 982–987
Superseded 31 L Ed 2d 975

99 L Ed 241–246
Superseded 11 ALR Fed 640

99 L Ed 301–302
Superseded 18 ALR Fed 489

100 L Ed 533–544
Superseded 32 L Ed 2d 869

1 L Ed 2d 1596–1599
Superseded 38 L Ed 2d 796

1 L Ed 2d 1647–1668
Superseded in part in 15 ALR Fed 665

1 L Ed 2d 1918–1926
Superseded 24 ALR Fed 162

2 L Ed 2d 2040–2045
Superseded 33 L Ed 2d 783

3 L Ed 2d 1787–1791
§ 3 Superseded in 34 L Ed 2d 749

5 L Ed 2d 950–951
Superseded 32 L Ed 2d 869

6 L Ed 2d 1394–1400
Superseded 37 L Ed 2d

21 L Ed 2d 928–935
Superseded 37 L Ed 2d

28 L Ed 2d 1053–1087 ✓
Superseded 35 L Ed 2d 735

Exhibit 32: Annotation History Table in *Lawyers' Edition,*
showing the new annotation on abortion.

ENCYCLOPEDIAS

Conditioned by the use of scholarly general encyclopedias, one tends to expect American legal encyclopedias to be equally scholarly reference works. However, legal encyclopedias are generally less highly reputed, particularly in academic circles, and really function best as case-finders. Since the leading encyclopedias do not cover statutes to any significant extent, they tend to give a somewhat distorted view of the law in many areas. In addition they have a tendency to over-simplify and over-generalize which often does not accurately reflect the complexity of our changing law. Their pocket part supplementation, although useful for references to later cases, does not completely cure this shortcoming.

The two major encyclopedias of national scope are *Corpus Juris Secundum* (published by West) and *American Jurisprudence* (published by Lawyers Co-operative Publishing Co.), now in its second series. Since the voluminous footnotes to the articles in *Corpus Juris Secundum* and *American Jurisprudence 2d* contain thousands of case references, they can be used directly as finding tools for that purpose. Each has general index volumes, as well as separate topical indexes, to help the researcher locate relevant articles and the most applicable sections thereof. The encyclopedias do not, however, contain tables of cases, presumably because of the large number of cases

cited. Not surprisingly, West's *C.J.S.* purports to carry in its footnotes virtually all of the decisions listed in the various West digests, while Lawyers Co-op's *Am.Jur.* provides similar access to the relevant annotations of *A.L.R.* and *A.L.R. Federal.*

Illustrating an encyclopedia are the following pages from *Corpus Juris Secundum* and its pocket part in Exhibits 33 and 34:

---

1 C.J.S.   *ABORTION*   § 4

§ 2. Statutory Provisions

Abortion is a statutory crime in practically all jurisdictions under statutes that vary to some extent in their respective provisions.

Although abortion has been made a crime by statute in practically all jurisdictions, the statutes vary to some extent, and hence reference should be made to the statute of particular jurisdiction in which the crime is alleged to have been committed.[8] Where the crime of abortion is defined by statute, it has been held that decisions from courts of last resort in other states whose statutes are different from those of the forum cannot control the construction of the statute,[9] and the legislative intent as expressed in the statute of the forum furnishes the only rule and guide.[10] The power to penalize or to legalize the act of producing an abortion is a matter for the states, and not for congress.[11]

§ 3. Nature and Elements in General

The material element of the crime of abortion is an overt act to use means with the necessary intent to procure an unlawful expulsion of the fetus.

nothing to do with the guilt or innocence of the person prosecuted as an accessory to such abortion.[15] A statute making it a crime to "counsel any person" to procure a miscarriage has been held to mean some person other than the pregnant woman.[16]

Overt act. A mere guilty intention to procure an abortion is not sufficient to constitute the crime; there must be an overt act tending to the perpetration of the crime.[17] Under a statute making it a crime to advise a woman to take a noxious thing with intent to cause a miscarriage, it has been held that the giving of the advice is the only overt act necessary for the completion of the crime, and it is immaterial whether the advice be followed or not.[18]

Trap to catch accused. Where accused was not a passive instrument in the hands of the trapping parties and where he did the act with which he was charged voluntarily, with full knowledge of the subject, the mere fact that he was detected by means of a trap set for him is not a defense to the crime.[19]

Assault. The procuring of an unlawful abortion

---

crimes of abortion resulting in death and attempts to procure a miscarriage, but simple abortion is a common law offense in this state.—Commonwealth v. Kelsea, 157 A. 42, 103 Pa.Super. 399.

In Texas Pen.Code (1895) arts. 641,

mother's life, to remove the unborn fœtus. To such highly honorable and proper acts, in accord with the highest ethics of the medical profession, the dictates of humanity, and all legal precepts, the statute has, and can have, no application. But to the destruction of unborn life for reasons,

20. State v. Farnam, 161 P. 417, 82 Or. 211.

21. In Pennsylvania the Act of May 12, 1897 (P.L. p 63), has been held to prohibit the use of drugs which will cause a miscarriage, regardless of the intent accompanying the same.

313

<u>Exhibit 33:</u> A sample page from *Corpus Juris Secundum*, showing its treatment of abortion in the bound volume.

Page 313

sions requiring certification of circumstances justifying an abortion by several physicians,[11.40] and limiting performance of the procedure to designated hospitals,[11.45] must be shown to bear a necessary and reasonable relationship to a compelling state interest, and their scope must be restricted to furthering that interest.

11.35 U.S.—Doe v. Woodahl, D.C.Mont., 360 F.Supp. 20.
Cal.—People v. Orser, 107 Cal.Rptr. 458, 31 C.A.3d 528.
Md.—State v. Ingel, 308 A.2d 223, 18 Md.App. 514.
Miss.—Spears v. State, 278 So.2d 443.
Part of conditions held invalid
Cal.—People v. Barksdale, 96 Cal.Rptr. 265, 18 C.A.3d 813.
Putative father's consent not required
Fla.—Jones v. Smith, App., 278 So.2d 339, cert. den. 94 S.Ct. 1486, 415 U.S. 958, 39 L.Ed.2d 573.
Life or health of female
Fla.—Jones v. Smith, App., 278 So.2d 339, cert. den. 94 S.Ct. 1486, 415 U.S. 958, 39 L.Ed.2d 573.
Nonphysician
Mich.—People v. Bricker, 208 N.W.2d 172, 389 Mich. 524.
Miss.—Spears v. State, 278 So.2d 443.
Statute requiring written consent of husband or parents unconstitutional
U.S.—Doe v. Gerstein, D.C.Fla., 376 F.Supp. 695, app. dism., 94 S.Ct. 2246, 417 U.S. 279, 41 L.Ed.2d 68, affd. in part, 94 S.Ct. 2247, 417 U.S. 281, 41 L.Ed.2d 70—Planned Parenthood of Central Missouri v. Danforth, Mo., 96 S.Ct. 2831.
Written consent of woman required
U.S.—Planned Parenthood of Central Missouri v. Danforth, Mo., 96 S.Ct. 2831.
11.40 U.S.—Poe v. Menghini, D.C.Kan., 339 F.Supp. 986.
11.45 U.S.—Poe v. Menghini, D.C.Kan., 339 F.Supp. 986.
Record keeping requirements
U.S.—Planned Parenthood of Central Missouri v. Danforth, Mo., 96 S.Ct. 2831.

The United States Supreme Court has held that a pregnant woman does not have an absolute constitutional right to abortion on her demand.[11.50] The United States Supreme Court has further declared that for the stage prior to approximately the end of the first trimester, the abortion decision and its effectuation must be left to the medical judgment of the pregnant woman's attending physician; for the stage subsequent to approximately the end of the first trimester, the State, in promoting its interest in the health of the mother, may, if it chooses, regulate the abortion procedure in ways that are reasonably related to maternal health; and for the stage subsequent to viability the State, in promoting its interest in the potentiality of human life, may, if it chooses, regulate, and even proscribe, abortion except where it is necessary, in appropriate medical

1 C.J.S.—5
1977 P.P.

judgment, for the preservation of the life or health of the mother.[11.55]

11.50 U.S.—Doe v. Bolton, Ga., 93 S.Ct. 739, 410 U.S. 179, 35 L.Ed.2d 201, reh. den. 93 S.Ct. 1410, 410 U.S. 959, 35 L.Ed.2d 694—Nyberg v. City of Virginia, C.A.Minn., 495 F.2d 1342, cert. den. 95 S.Ct. 169, 419 U.S. 891, 42 L.Ed.2d 136—Word v. Poelker, C.A.Mo., 495 F.2d 1349.
N.J.—State v. Norflett, 337 A.2d 609, 67 N.J. 268.
Interest of husband
U.S.—Roe v. Rampton, D.C.Utah, 394 F.Supp. 677, affd., C.A., 535 F.2d 1219.
11.55 U.S.—Roe v. Wade, Tex., 93 S.Ct. 705, 410 U.S. 113, 35 L.Ed.2d 147, reh. den. 93 S.Ct. 1409, 410 U.S. 959, 35 L.Ed.2d 694—Nyberg v. City of Virginia, C.A.Minn., 495 F.2d 1342, cert. den. 95 S.Ct. 169, 419 U.S. 891, 42 L.Ed.2d 136.
Word v. Poelker, C.A.Mo., 495 F.2d 1349—Doe v. Rose, C.A.Utah, 499 F.2d 1112—Friendship Medical Center, Ltd. v. Chicago Bd. of Health, C.A.Ill., 505 F.2d 1141, cert. den. 95 S.Ct. 1438, 420 U.S. 997, 43 L.Ed. 2d 650—Doe v. Mundy, D.C.Wis., 378 F.Supp. 731, stay den. 95 S.Ct. 28, 419 U.S. 813, 42 L.Ed.2d 40, affd., 514 F.2d 1179—Hodgson v. Anderson, D.C.Minn., 378 F.Supp. 1008, app. dism., 95 S.Ct. 819, 420 U.S. 903, 42 L.Ed.2d 833—Foe v. Vanderhoof, D.C.Colo., 389 F.Supp. 947.
Mich.—People v. Nixon, 212 N.W.2d 797, 50 Mich.App. 38.
Pa.—Com. v. Jackson, 312 A.2d 13, 454 Pa. 429.
Regulation required for first trimester
U.S.—Doe v. Bolton, Ga., 93 S.Ct. 739, 410 U.S. 179, 35 L.Ed.2d 201, reh. den. 93 S.Ct. 1410, 410 U.S. 959, 35 L.Ed.2d 694—Doe v. Wohlgemuth, D.C.Pa., 376 F.Supp. 173, mod. on oth. grds., cause remd., C.A., 523 F.2d 611, cert. gr. 96 S.Ct. 3220—Hodgson v. Anderson, D.C.Minn., 378 F.Supp. 1008, app. dism. 95 S.Ct. 819, 420 U.S. 903, 42 L.Ed.2d 833—Wolfe v. Schroering, D.C.Ky., 388 F.Supp. 631.
Statute invalid for being applicable to any trimester
U.S.—Doe v. Rampton, D.C.Utah, 366 F.Supp. 189.
Exempt from licensing requirements
U.S.—Hallmark Clinic v. North Carolina Dept. of Human Resources, D.C.N.C., 380 F.Supp. 1153, affd., C.A., 519 F.2d 1315.
After second trimester abortion may be completely proscribed
N.J.—State v. Norflett, 337 A.2d 609 67 N.J. 268.
Statute unconstitutional
U.S.—Planned Parenthood of Central Missouri v. Danforth, Mo., 96 S.Ct. 2831.
Definition of viability constitutional
U.S.—Connecticut v. Menillo, 96 S.Ct. 170, 423 U.S. 9, 46 L.Ed.2d 152.
State intervention on behalf of husband not permitted until fetus becomes "viable"
U.S.—Doe v. Zimmerman, D.C.Pa., 405 F.Supp. 534.
Definition of "viable" vague
U.S.—Doe v. Zimmerman, D.C.Pa., 405 F.Supp. 534.
Portion of statute constitutional
U.S.—Spears v. Circuit Court, Ninth Judicial Dist., Warren County, State of Miss., C.A.Miss., 517 F.2d 360.
Woman less than 24 weeks pregnant entitled to abortion under statute
N.Y.—Chapman v. Schultz, 383 N.Y.S. 2d 512, 86 Misc.2d 543.

In regulating abortion procedures, a state may proscribe any abortion

by a physician not currently licensed by the state,[11.60] and may preserve the right of hospitals to refuse to admit a patient for an abortion and the right of physicians and other employees to refrain from participating in abortion procedures on moral or religious grounds.[11.65]

11.60 U.S.—Roe v. Wade, Tex., 93 S.Ct. 705, 410 U.S. 113, 35 L.Ed.2d 147, reh. den. 93 S.Ct. 1409, 410 U.S. 959, 35 L.Ed.2d 694—Spears v. Ellis, D.C. Miss., 386 F.Supp. 653, affd. 96 S.Ct. 9, 423 U.S. 802, 46 L.Ed.2d 23.
Nonmedically trained person subject to conviction
N.J.—State v. Norflett, 337 A.2d 609, 67 N.J. 268.
Midwife not authorized
U.S.—Spears v. Circuit Court, Ninth Judicial Dist., Warren County, State of Miss., C.A.Miss., 517 F.2d 360.
11.65 U.S.—Doe v. Bolton, Ga., 93 S.Ct. 739, 410 U.S. 179, 35 L.Ed.2d 201, reh. den. 93 S.Ct. 1410, 410 U.S. 959, 35 L.Ed.2d 694.

Residency requirements for patients seeking abortions are invalid, where they are not based on a policy of preserving state supported facilities for residents of the state.[11.70]

11.70 U.S.—Doe v. Bolton, Ga., 93 S.Ct. 739, 410 U.S. 179, 35 L.Ed.2d 201, reh. den. 93 S.Ct. 1410, 410 U.S. 959, 35 L.Ed.2d 694.

Procedural requirements not reasonably related to the purpose of an abortion statute are invalid.[11.75]

11.75 Accreditation of hospital
U.S.—Doe v. Bolton, Ga., 93 S.Ct. 739, 410 U.S. 179, 35 L.Ed.2d 201, reh. den. 93 S.Ct. 1410, 410 U.S. 959, 35 L.Ed.2d 694.
Approval by hospital abortion committee
U.S.—Doe v. Bolton, Ga., 93 S.Ct. 739, 410 U.S. 179, 35 L.Ed.2d 201, reh. den. 93 S.Ct. 1410, 410 U.S. 959, 35 L.Ed.2d 694.

§ 3. Nature and Elements in General

12. Va.—Coffman v. Com., supra, n. 2.
13. Cal.—People v. Root, 55 Cal.Rptr. 89, 246 C.A.2d 600.
Mass.—Commonwealth v. Wood, 19 N.E. 2d 1220, 302 Mass. 265.
Mo.—C.J.S. cited in State v. Fitzgerald, 174 S.W.2d 211, 216.
Wis.—State v. Mac Greens, 161 N.W.2d 245, 40 Wis.2d 179.
Good health of woman not essential element of offense
Mo.—State v. Hacker, 291 S.W.2d 155.
14. **Determination involving professional judgment of physician**
D.C.—Doe v. General Hospital of District of Columbia, D.C., 313 F.Supp. 1170, motion den. 434 F.2d 423, 140 U.S. App.D.C. 149, and 434 F.2d 427, 140 U.S.App.D.C. 153, op. supp., 434 F.2d 427, 140 U.S.App.D.C. 153.
Performance by unlicensed physician
Mass.—Com. v. Brunelle, 277 N.E.2d 826, 361 Mass. 6.
Right to abortion
Fla.—Jones v. Smith, App., 278 So.2d 339, cert. den. 94 S.Ct. 1486, 415 U.S. 958, 39 L.Ed.2d 573.
17. Cal.—People v. Cummings, 296 P.2d 610, 141 C.A.2d 193.

Exhibit 34: A sample page from the pocket part of volume 1 of *Corpus Juris Secundum*, showing reference to *Roe v. Wade*.

WORDS AND PHRASES

Another useful case-finding tool is *Words and Phrases,* an encyclopedia of definitions and interpretations of legally significant words and phrases, published in forty-six volumes by West. This set consists of an alphabetical arrangement of thousands of words and phrases followed by abstracts of judicial decisions which have interpreted, defined or construed them. The abstracts are in the same form as the West digest squibs, containing a one sentence summary of the legal interpretation and the citation to the decision from which it is taken. A typical page looks like the sample in Exhibit 35 below.

Words and Phrases is supplemented by annual pocket parts inserted in the back of each volume and by tables of words and phrases which appear in every West advance sheet and bound reporter for the cases therein. *Words and Phrases* entries also appear in the various West digests.

Civil Rights Act and thus was not liable to suit thereunder. Educational Equality League v. Tate, C.A.Pa., 472 F.2d 612, 614.

Term "person" as used in statute prohibiting person from denying an individual the full and equal enjoyment of facilities of a place of public accommodation because of race, color, religion or national origin includes every legal, commercial and governmental entity. Oklahoma Human Rights Commission v. Hotie, Inc., Okl., 505 P.2d 1320, 1322.

Even those who have been convicted remained "persons" under Constitution and a fortiori that is true of persons in county jails most of whom are awaiting trial and presumed to be innocent. U. S. ex rel. Manicone v. Corso, D.C.N.Y., 365 F.Supp. 576, 577.

Unborn child is a "person" for purpose of remedies given for personal injuries, and child may sue after his birth. Weaks v. Mounter, Nev., 493 P.2d 1307, 1309.

"Person" is defined as a human being. Bale v. Ryder, Me., 290 A.2d 359, 360.

Word "person" as used in the Fourteenth Amendment does not include the unborn. Roe v. Wade, U.S.Tex., 93 S.Ct. 705, 729, 410 U.S. 113, 35 L.Ed.2d 147.

An unborn child is not a "person" within meaning of wrongful death statute. Bayer v. Suttle, 100 Cal.Rptr. 212, 214, 23 C.A.3d 361.

Federal courts sit not to supervise prisons but to enforce constitutional rights of all "persons," which includes prisoners. Cruz v. Beto, U.S.Tex., 92 S.Ct. 1079, 1081, 405 U.S. 319, 31 L.Ed.2d 263.

A housing authority is a "person" within Fourteenth Amendment and therefore has standing to challenge constitutionality of state statute under due process and equal protection clauses. Housing Authority of City of Woonsocket v. Fetzik, R.I., 289 A.2d 658, 662.

Political subdivision is not a "person" within the meaning of the Civil Rights Act when pecuniary damages are sought. Reed v. Nebraska School Activities Ass'n, D.C.Neb., 341 F. Supp. 258, 260.

Sale of a security to a husband and wife so denominated is a sale made to one "person" within meaning of the Securities Law provision exempting seller from registration so long as total number of holders does not exceed 25 and during a period of 12 consecutive months, sales are made to not more than an additional 15 "persons". Cann v. M & B Drilling Co., Mo.App., 480 S.W.2d 81, 85.

Legislature, in enacting Administrative Procedure and Review Act section providing that any "person" who is aggrieved by a final decision shall be entitled to judicial review, intended that such right be available to any person, party or not, who can show himself to be aggrieved by the decision. State ex rel. Pruitt-Igoe Dist. Community Corp. v. Burks, Mo.App., 482 S.W.2d 75, 77.

If a foetus is born alive it becomes a "person" with at least theoretical possibility of survival and of enduring consequences of prenatal injury throughout its life but a foetus not born alive incurs no such risk of continuing injury and is not a "person" within meaning of the wrongful death statute. Leccese v. McDonough, Mass., 279 N.E.2d 339, 341.

Viable fetus born dead as result of prenatal injuries is not "person" within Wrongful Death Act, and no cause of action therefore existed for death of fetus, notwithstanding fetus would have been able to maintain cause of action for his injuries incurred prior to birth had he survived to be born alive. Chrisafogeorgis v. Brandenberg, 279 N.E.2d 440, 442, 3 Ill.App.3d 422.

A "person" is generally understood as denoting a natural person and word ordinarily will be taken in that sense unless, from statu-

tory context or elsewhere, it appears that artificial persons are intended to be embraced. People v. McGreal, 278 N.E.2d 504, 510, 4 Ill. App.3d 312.

Where suit under 1871 civil rights statute sought no damages but only equitable relief and where University of Alaska by Alaskan statute had power to sue and be sued in its own name, university, its president and Board of Regents were "persons" within the statute. Wolfe v. O'Neill, D.C.Alaska, 336 F.Supp. 1255, 1258.

A fetus is not a "person" or "citizen" within contemplation of the Fourteenth Amendment and the Civil Rights Act. McGarvey v. Magee-Womens Hospital, D.C.Pa., 340 F.Supp. 751, 754; Abele v. Markle, D.C.Conn., 351 F. Supp. 224, 228.

A viable fetus is a "person" within statute governing actions for wrongful death. Rice v. Rizk, Ky., 453 S.W.2d 732, 735.

Where signatures on check gave no indication that check was signed in representative capacity, fact that check, underneath date, contained statement "Food for Love Acc't" did not indicate a "person" so as to alert payee to any representational capacity in which signature was executed. Star Dairy, Inc. v. Roberts, 326 N.Y.S.2d 85, 87, 37 A.D.2d 1038.

Employer who borrowed truck for use by his employee was a "person" under statute which provides that no person shall operate any motor truck after dark unless truck is equipped with flares or other warning devices and the employer's failure to so equip a ¾ ton pickup truck constituted independent actionable negligence as to motorist and passenger injured in a collision after dark with the unlighted truck. Taylor v. Purifoy, 445 S.W. 2d 485, 487, 247 Ark. 368.

Unborn viable child was not a "person" within meaning of wrongful death statute. Lawrence v. Craven Tire Co., 169 S.E.2d 440, 442, 210 Va. 138.

Viable fetus is "person" within intendment of West Virginia's Wrongful Death Statute. Panagopoulous v. Martin, D.C.W.Va., 295 F. Supp. 220, 226.

Viable unborn child is entity in meaning of general word "person" within wrongful death statute. City of Louisville v. Stuckenborg, Ky., 438 S.W.2d 94, 95.

"Person" liable for withholding, F.I.C.A., and other taxes includes but is not restricted to persons designated by statute. Lawrence v. U. S., D.C.Tex., 299 F.Supp. 187, 190.

Stillborn child is not "person" under Massachusetts Wrongful Death statute, and action is not maintainable for wrongful death based upon injury-caused stillbirths of viable fetuses. Henry v. Jones, D.C.Mass., 306 F.Supp. 726, 727.

In sense intended by legislature in enacting statute limiting crime of vehicular homicide to death of a "person", quoted word means a living individual, and a seven-month, viable, unborn child could be considered such a "person". State v. Dickinson, Ohio Com.Pl., 248 N.E.2d 458, 461, 18 Ohio Misc. 151.

Once the stage of viability is reached the fetus is regarded as a legal "person" with separate existence of its own, as respects issue whether there is a cause of action on behalf of unborn fetus for tort injury. Orange v. State Farm Mut. Auto. Ins. Co., Ky., 443 S.W. 2d 650, 651, 652.

A viable unborn child of insured was a legal "person" with a separate existence of its own, and, hence, was member of class excluded from coverage by a "family" or "household" exclusion clause of automobile liability policy. Id.

Word "person" has no fixed and rigid signification. U. S. v. Merchants Mut. Bonding Co., D.C.Iowa., 220 F.Supp. 163, 182.

Exhibit 35: A sample page from *Words and Phrases.*

CASE CITATORS

Case citators provide access to the judicial history and interpretation of reported decisions. Shepard's Citations, Inc., publisher of the most comprehensive system of case citators in the United States, accomplishes this function by listing in separate sets virtually every published case by citation in both its official and unofficial reporter and then by listing under that citation every subsequent case that has cited the case in question.

Thus, the use of Shepard's citators aids a lawyer in accomplishing the following three purposes:

1. Tracing the judicial history of each case appearing in an official or West reporter, by providing parallel citations to that case in the other reporter (as shown above in Exhibits 23 and 24 at pages 62–63) and citations to all later proceedings in that same case.

2. Verifying the current status of each case in order to establish whether it is still effective law, or has been reversed, overruled, or its authority otherwise diminished.

3. Finding later cases which have cited the main case, as well as providing research leads to periodical articles, attorney general opinions, *A.L.R.* annotations, etc.

Shepard's citators exist for the reports of every state, the District of Columbia and Puerto Rico, every region of the National Reporter System, the lower federal courts, the Supreme Court, and some administrative agencies. The formats for each series of citators are similar. However, the types of citing materials included for the cited cases may vary among the series. Therefore, to be certain that one is obtaining all available citations to a particular case, it is wise to consult the fuller explanations of each set of citators in *How to Use Shepard's Citations,* a teaching pamphlet issued by Shepard's and available in most law school libraries. The preliminary pages in each citator will list the cited material and the citing sources contained in that citator.

For an example of variation in citing material, note the differences between *Shepard's North Eastern Reporter Citations* and *Shepard's Ohio Citations*. Both citators provide the parallel citation to the case in the other reporter, the judicial history of the case, and citations to other Ohio cases which have cited the case. However, citations to the case by *other* state courts can be found only in *Shepard's North Eastern Reporter Citations*, while references to the case in the opinions of the attorney general of Ohio and in local law reviews can be found only in the Ohio Shepard's.

To give the most up-to-date information on the status of a particular case, Shepard's citators are supplemented frequently. For each citator there is usually one or more bound volumes, a red paperback supplement, and a white advance sheet. To insure that the researcher has at hand all the parts necessary to shepardize a specific case, Shepard's prints in a box on the cover of the pamphlets a list of all the issues needed for a complete search in that particular citator. See Exhibit 36.

What Your Library Should Contain

1945 Bound Volume   1945–1974 Bound Volume
1974 Bound Volume
Supplemented with
April, 1977 Cumulative Supplement Vol. 69 No. 2

Destroy All Other Issues

Exhibit 36: Listing on the face of a Shepard's advance sheet of all issues of a particular citator.

As an example of how a Shepard's citator functions, let us refer to its treatment of *Roe v. Wade,* 410 U.S. 113 (1973).

To clarify the following explanations, Exhibit 37 below has been marked with numbers to illustrate the various ways in which a cited case is treated. These different treatments include the following:

(1) When the case is *first* listed in *Shepard's U. S. Citations,* parallel citations are given to the alternative unofficial reports of *Roe v. Wade* in the *Supreme Court Reporter* and *Lawyers' Edition.* These citations appear in parentheses.

(2) Next are listed the citations of the case in the U. S. Supreme Court and the lower federal courts with appropriate symbols to show the history of *Roe v. Wade* in its earlier stages.

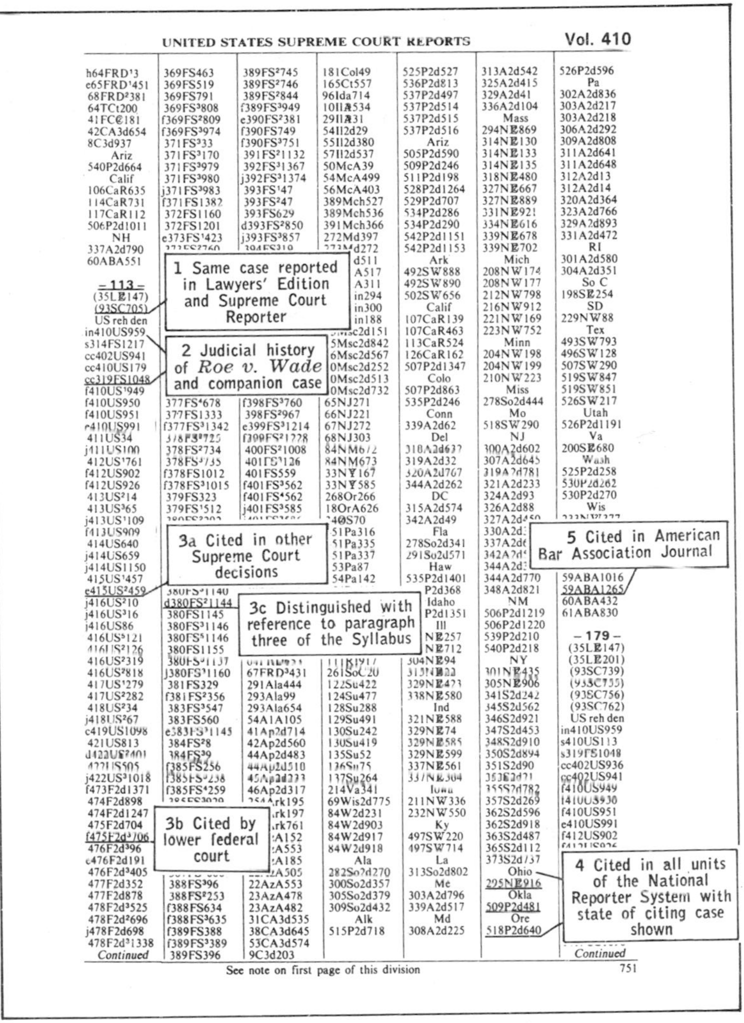

UNITED STATES SUPREME COURT REPORTS   Vol. 410

Column 1

h64FRD¹3
c65FRD⁴451
68FRD²381
64TC1200
41FCℂℰ181
42CA3d654
8C3d937
Ariz
540P2d664
Calif
106CaR635
114CaR731
117CaR112
506P2d1011
NH
337A2d790
60ABA551

[Box 1] 1 Same case reported in Lawyers' Edition and Supreme Court Reporter

=113=
(35Lℰ147)
(93SC705)
US reh den
in410US959
s314FS1217
cc402US941
cc410US179
cc319FS1048
f410US⁵949
f410US950
f410US951
r410US991
411US34
j411US100
412US⁵761
f412US902
f412US926
413US²14
413US³65
j413US³109
f413US909
414US640
j414US659
j414US1150
415US⁴457
e415US²459
j416US⁵710
j416US⁵716
416US86
416US⁵121
416US²126
416US²319
416US⁵818
417US¹279
417US²282
418US³34
j418US⁵767
c419US1098
421US813
j422US⁵1018
f473F2d1371
474F2d898
474F2d1247
475F2d704
[475F2d³706]
476F2d⁴96
e476F2d1191
476F2d³405
477F2d352
477F2d878
478F2d⁴525
478F2d⁴696
j478F2d698
478F2d³1338
Continued

Column 2

369FS463
369FS519
369FS791
369FS⁴808
f369FS⁴809
f369FS⁵974
371FS³33
371FS⁵170
371FS⁵979
371FS⁵980
j371FS⁵983
f371FS1382
372FS1160
372FS1201
e373FS³423

[Box 2] 2 Judicial history of Roe v. Wade and companion case

377FS⁴678
377FS1333
f377FS³1342
j378FS³725
378FS²734
378FS⁴735
f378FS1012
f378FS³1015
379FS323
379FS⁵512

[Box 3a] 3a Cited in other Supreme Court decisions

380FS²1140
d380FS²1144
380FS¹1145
380FS⁵1146
380FS⁵1146
380FS1155

[Box 3c] 3c Distinguished with reference to paragraph three of the Syllabus

380FS⁵1155
380FS⁵1137
j380FS³1160
381FS329
f381FS356
383FS⁵547
383FS560
54A1A105
e383FS³1145
384FS⁵8
384FS⁵9
f385FS⁴256
44Ap2d483
44Ap2d510
45Ap2d333
46Ap2d317
254Ark195

[Box 3b] 3b Cited by lower federal court

rk197
:rk197
:A152
:A553
:A185
:A505
388FS²96
388FS²253
388FS634
f388FS635
f389FS388
389FS⁵389
389FS396

Column 3

389FS²745
389FS²746
389FS⁷844
961da714
101Iℰ534
291IℰA31
54Iℰ2d29
55Iℰ2d380
57Iℰ2d537
50McA39
54McA499
56McA403
389Mch527
389Mch536
391Mch366
272Md397
272Md272
104Fℰ310

5Msc2d842
6Msc2d567
0Msc2d252
0Msc2d513
0Msc2d732
65NJ271
66NJ221
67NJ272
68NJ303
84NMb72
84NM673
33Nℰ167
33NℰT585
268Or266
180rA626
240S70

Column 4

181Col49
165Ct557
d511
A517
A311
in294
in300
in188
msc2d151
525P2d527
536P2d813
537P2d497
537P2d514
537P2d515
537P2d516
Ariz
505P2d590
509P2d246
511P2d198
528P2d1264
529P2d707
534P2d286
534P2d290
542P2d1151
542P2d1153
Ark
492SW888
492SW890
502SW656
Calif
107CaR139
107CaR463
113CaR524
126CaR162
507P2d1347
Colo
507P2d863
535P2d246
Conn
339A2d62
Del
318A2d637
319A2d32
320A2d767
344A2d262
DC
315A2d574
342A2d49
Fla
278So2d341
291So2d571
Haw
535P2d1401
P2d368
Idaho
P2d1351
Ill
Nℰ257
Nℰ712
304Nℰ94
315Nℰ32
329Nℰ473
338Nℰ580
Ind
321Nℰ588
329Nℰ74
329Nℰ585
329Nℰ599
337Nℰ561
337Nℰ304
Iowa
211NW336
232NW550
Ky
495SW220
497SW714
La
313So2d802
Me
300So2d357
305So2d379
309So2d432
Md
308A2d225

Column 5

313A2d542
325A2d415
329A2d41
336A2d104
Mass
294Nℰ869
314Nℰ130
314Nℰ33
314Nℰ135
318Nℰ480
327Nℰ667
327Nℰ889
331Nℰ921
334Nℰ616
339Nℰ678
339Nℰ702
Mich
208NW174
208NW177
212NW798
216NW912
221NW169
223NW752
Minn
204NW198
204NW199
210NW223
Mo
278So2d444
518SW290
NJ
300A2d602
307A2d645
319A2d781
321A2d233
324A2d93
326A2d88
327A2d450

[Box 5] 5 Cited in American Bar Association Journal

330A2d
337A2d
342A2d
344A2d
344A2d770
348A2d821
NM
506P2d1219
506P2d1220
539P2d210
540P2d218
NY
301Nℰ435
305Nℰ906
341S2d242
345S2d562
346S2d921
347S2d453
348S2d910
350S2d894
351S2d690
352S2d871
355S2d782
357S2d269
362S2d596
362S2d918
363S2d487
365S2d112
373S2d737
Ohio
295Nℰ916
Okla
509P2d481
Ore
518P2d640

Column 6

526P2d596
Pa
302A2d836
303A2d217
303A2d218
306A2d292
309A2d808
311A2d641
311A2d648
312A2d13
312A2d14
320A2d364
323A2d766
329A2d893
331A2d472
RI
301A2d580
304A2d351
So C
198Sℰ254
229NW88
Tex
493SW793
496SW128
507SW290
519SW847
519SW851
526SW217
Utah
519SW851
526P2d1191
Va
200Sℰ680
Wash
525P2d258
530P2d262
530P2d270
Wis
222NW277

59ABA1016
59ABA1265
60ABA432
61ABA830
-179-
(35Lℰ147)
(35Lℰ201)
(93SC739)
(93SC755)
(93SC756)
(93SC762)
US reh den
in410US959
s410US113

[Box 4] 4 Cited in all units of the National Reporter System with state of citing case shown

373S2d737
Ohio
295Nℰ916
Okla
509P2d481
Ore
518P2d640

Continued
751

See note on first page of this division

(3) Then follow citations to other decisions in federal tribunals: (a) U. S. Supreme Court and (b) lower federal courts. Symbols, such as "e" for explained, "d" for distinguished, or "f" for followed, indicate the nature of the citing court's treatment of *Roe v. Wade*. Explanation of all the symbols so used are set forth in Exhibit 38.

ABBREVIATIONS – ANALYSIS

History of Case

a (affirmed)	Same case affirmed on rehearing.
cc (connected case)	Different case from case cited but arising out of same subject matter or intimately connected therewith.
m (modified)	Same case modified on rehearing.
r (reversed)	Same case reversed on rehearing.
s (same case)	Same case as case cited.
S (superseded)	Substitution for former opinion.
v (vacated)	Same case vacated.
US reh den	Rehearing denied by U. S. Supreme Court.
US reh dis	Rehearing dismissed by U.S. Supreme Court.

Treatment of Case

c (criticised)	Soundness of decision or reasoning in cited case criticised for reasons given.
d (distinguished)	Case at bar different either in law or fact from case cited for reasons given.
e (explained)	Statement of import of decision in cited case. Not merely a restatement of the facts.
f (followed)	Cited as controlling.
h (harmonized)	Apparent inconsistency explained and shown not to exist.
j (dissenting opinion)	Citation in dissenting opinion.
L (limited)	Refusal to extend decision of cited case beyond precise issues involved.
o (overruled)	Ruling in cited case expressly overruled.
p (parallel)	Citing case substantially alike or on all fours with cited case in its law or facts.
q (questioned)	Soundness of decision or reasoning in cited case questioned.

Exhibit 38: Shepard's case symbols with explanatory notes.

Small raised numbers to the left of the page numbers of the citing cases correspond to the number of the paragraph of the syllabus or head-note of *Roe v. Wade* which states the legal principle involved in the citing case. Attention to (c), the symbols and superior numbers, can improve the use of Shepard's as a case finder by reducing the number of citing cases to be consulted by focusing on those dealing specifically with the aspect of *Roe v. Wade* in which the lawyer or researcher is interested.

(4) Next are lists of citations to decisions in state reporters and units of the National Reporter System.

(5) We find here that *Roe v. Wade* has been cited in a periodical article in the *American Bar Association Journal*.

In using any of the above citations in Shepard's, it should be remembered that each reference to a citing case is to the *page* of that case on which the cited case is found. Therefore, the citation usually will not be to the beginning page of the citing decision.

COMPUTERIZED CASE–FINDING

In recent years, computerized legal research has developed as an important addition to traditional finding tools and is rapidly achieving acceptance among lawyers and legal scholars. Two systems,

LEXIS, owned by Mead Data Central Corporation, and WESTLAW, a West Publishing Company offering, have emerged after years of experimentation as the major commercial services of this type. Several other legal services are operating successfully in the federal government, particularly JURIS, at the U.S. Department of Justice, and FLITE, at the Judge Advocate General's office of the U. S. Air Force. A computerized citation service of Lawyers Co-op called AUTOCITE seems more limited in coverage than the Shepard's citators and has not offered the versatility of LEXIS and WESTLAW. Various projects of the Aspen Systems Corporation, one of the pioneers in this field, have unfortunately not achieved wide commercial success.

LEXIS is a computer system which enables one to search the full text of recent cases and statutes from the federal level and from approximately ten states. Through its search logic, references to cases, statutes and regulatory material can be retrieved by matching relevant words and phrases to their occurrence in the primary sources. Citations, abstracts and even the text itself can be called up on a cathode ray tube similar to a T.V. screen or recorded on a hard copy printer. LEXIS also includes specialized "libraries" of material on federal taxation, trade regulation, securities law, and legal ethics, and has been constantly expanding its data base by adding new states, subject fields, and earlier time periods.

WESTLAW utilizes a different approach to that of LEXIS and has so far focused its search technique on the material in the West digest system (covering a limited period of recent years), rather than on the full text of the original documents. Like LEXIS, it employs a simple keyboard for making search requests, a cathode ray tube for displaying the results of the search, and a printer for quick prints of the material located. Although WESTLAW is basically a computerization of West's digests, its speed and coverage give it distinct advantages over the traditional search in the many volumes of the digest system. West has recently announced plans to add a full-text search capability as well.

Although LEXIS and WESTLAW are competitive systems, both have unique capabilities and in some respects complement each other. As these services expand their respective coverages, their usefulness will increase and old habits of research will be changed for a more efficient and effective access to legal materials. Unfortunately, the high cost of these systems now limit their availability, but as they achieve a wider acceptance, it is to be hoped that that obstacle will be reduced.

OTHER CASE–FINDING TOOLS

Brief mention should be made of other research tools, discussed in later chapters, which can be used as case-finders.

Annotated editions of the statutes of a jurisdiction include under each section of the statute squibs or abstracts of cases which have applied or construed the statute. When researching a problem which focuses on a statutory provision, the annotated code for that jurisdiction may be the most effective case-finder. See Chapter IV below for further details. Looseleaf services provide prompt notation of new cases which relate to the subject of the service. Their frequent supplementation, detailed indexing and publication of varied sources in the subject field make them very useful research aids. (See Chapter VII.) Treatises and periodical articles cite cases both in their texts and in their footnotes and should not be overlooked as case-finders. (See Chapter IX.) The annotations to judicial decisions published in conjunction with the *Restatements of the Law* are another useful case-finding approach, when a Restatement rule is relevant to a particular problem. (See Chapter IX.)

No single case-finder can be designated as the "best." Selection of the most useful case-finder for any particular search will depend upon the nature of the problem at hand. The availability of a computer search service might lead one to that sophisticated tool. A problem involving a statute would begin most profitably in an annotated statutory code, a problem involving the definition of a word in *Words and Phrases,* a problem

requiring general background knowledge of a topic in an encyclopedia. Each research problem must be analysed separately, the available tools evaluated, and the most compatible approach chosen. Inevitably personal preference will play a part when two or more tools seem equally useful as case-finders.

CHAPTER IV

STATUTES

Statutory material appears very early in recorded history, as evidenced by the legal codes of the ancient Near East, many of which are well known to us today (e. g., those of the Assyrians, Babylonians, Hittites, and particularly the Hebrew codes of the Bible). Legal codes were used throughout the ages to formulate new rules of kings or priests, as well as to codify existing custom and judicial pronouncements. There are fundamental differences between the decisional material of case law and the directive texts of statutory enactments: differences of purpose and source, of language and style, and of bibliographic form and reference.

There are also very significant differences between the statutory forms of different ages and legal systems. In modern times, Anglo-American laws have developed very differently from the Napoleonic codes in Europe. The Continental codes legislate in general terms, using provisions which are quite broad and yet concise and simple in language. American statutes, on the other hand, have sought to meet every future situation specifically, using many words and considerable detail to do so. The multiplicity of American statutes is in part due to our optimistic striving

for a solution of all social and economic problems by legislation; the prolixity results from our desire to anticipate every conceivable violation. Although our compilations are often called codes, they are as different from the European codes as the Penal Law of Pennsylvania is from the Ten Commandments.

American statutes are published in three forms. The first published official text of a statute is the *slip law*. Each law is issued as a pamphlet with separate pagination, or as a single sheet. Slip laws of the U.S. Congress are available shortly after enactment, but on the state level are often quite difficult to obtain.

Next are the *session laws,* which are published in separate volumes for each year or session of the legislature. Within each volume, the statutes are arranged by date of passage. *Statutes at Large* is the name of the session laws of the U. S. Congress. Examples of state session laws are the *Laws of New York* and *Acts and Resolves of Massachusetts*. All states issue official editions of their session laws, the titles varying from state to state, and a few also have commercial editions.

Access to laws on a specific subject is very difficult through this chronological form of publication. Subject access is required by the lawyer who must find all of the statutes which are currently applicable to a particular problem. Such access is provided by statutory compilations

known generally as *codes*. They collect those statutes of a jurisdiction which have general application, and are in force, and arrange them by broad topics. Each topic is given a descriptive title and frequently a title number. The statutes collected under each title are arranged in numbered sections. Frequently a single law, as enacted in the session laws, will be broken up and listed under several different titles, or in different sections of the same title of the code. A more or less detailed index enables the researcher to find the sections dealing with particular problems or topics. Many editions of codes, particularly unofficial editions, also include annotations to relevant court decisions from the same jurisdiction, which interpret, construe, or apply each statutory section. Such annotations consist of a one sentence squib of the applicable legal principle and a citation to the case from which it was taken, similar to the West reporter headnote and digest abstracts.

Codes or statutory compilations must be updated promptly to include the output of the latest legislative session. Because of the numerous changes which are made in statutory law every time a legislature meets and because of the frequency of legislative sessions in this country (by 1974, thirty-five state legislatures were meeting annually and fifteen biennially), it is necessary to provide some form of prompt and convenient

supplementation.   Failure to do so would render a legislative compilation virtually useless.   Supplementation is usually provided by pocket parts in the back of the bound volumes or by looseleaf additions.   Some official editions of the codes are updated only by the publication of revised editions every few years.

With statutes, as with case law, there are both official and unofficial editions and the *unofficial* texts usually provide additional research material which make them more useful than the official edition.   For example, most of the *annotated* codes are published unofficially by commercial publishers.   These usually provide faster and more convenient supplementation than the official editions, fuller editorial notes, historical comments, analyses of statutes, and other interpretative material.   The *U. S. Code* is the official edition of the federal statutory code, and there are also two unofficial, annotated editions—*U. S. Code Annotated* and *U. S. Code Service*.

The official text is, as always, the authoritative one and must be cited in every legal reference. The citation problem for statutes is also somewhat complicated by the fact that there may be *two* official sources: the *chronologically* published session laws and a *subject* compilation or code of statutes in force.   Usually only one of these forms is the *authoritative* text, which should always be cited, although both may be official.

While the session law is generally the authoritative text, the researcher may have difficulty in determining this. In a few states, unofficial codes have been recognized as authoritative to some extent or for some purpose, because of the absence of convenient official editions.

There are also jurisdictional problems of statutory coverage and authority which arise in part from our federal system and in part from the multiplicity of state laws. We have both a federal legislature and fifty state legislatures. Sometimes there is conflict between enactments of the United States Congress and those of the states and sometimes uncertainty as to which law applies in a particular situation. There are also problems of interpretation and application arising from the variety of laws on the same subject in the fifty states. This has given rise to a movement for uniform state laws, which is reflected in the work of the National Conference of Commissioners on Uniform State Laws. The publication of these laws is described below at pages 138–139.

It is also relevant to note that legislation comes not only from traditional legislative bodies like the Congress and the state legislatures, but also from subordinate legislative units. These lawmaking bodies, generally operating under a statutory delegation of authority from the legislature, include administrative agencies and executive de-

partments; courts which issue their own rules; towns, municipalities and other local units of government.

The nature of legal authority assigned to legislation is different from that of case law. Statutes have binding or mandatory authority in the jurisdiction in which they are enacted or promulgated. Outside of that jurisdiction they have no effect and are not even persuasive authority, except of course as evidence of the law of the state which enacted them. If, however, a state is contemplating the adoption of a law already passed by another state, the latter's experience under that law may be persuasive to the deliberating legislature or to later courts which may have to construe the statute.

Finally, it should be pointed out that statutes are often marked by ambiguities or vagueness which give rise to legal controversy by making their interpretation and application difficult. This has led to a considerable concern with ascertaining the lawmakers' intent through the collection and study of documents of legislative history. This statutory ambiguity may stem from linguistic uncertainty or poor draftsmanship, but frequently is the inevitable result of negotiation and compromise in the legislative process. Research in legislative history is discussed in Chapter V below.

TYPES OF LEGISLATION

Legislative materials can be divided into the following important classes, which have been briefly described above:

1. Conventional legislation and subordinate or delegated legislation.

2. Federal and state legislation.

3. Statutory compilations and session laws.

4. Official and unofficial publications.

5. Authoritative and non-authoritative texts.

6. Annotated and unannotated editions.

There are other descriptive categories of legislation which should be mentioned. Among them are the following forms which legislation can take in this country:

1. Constitutions are the organic laws of particular jurisdictions. They define political relationships, enumerate the rights and liberties of citizens, and create the necessary governmental framework. Constitutions are published in the statutory code of each jurisdiction, as well as in separate editions.

2. Resolutions (joint, concurrent and simple) and **Acts** are the forms by which a legislature carries on its work and promulgates laws. In the United States Congress, laws in the usual sense

are passed by either a *joint resolution* or an *act*. Simple and concurrent resolutions are used for expressing the sentiment or intent of Congress or for performing housekeeping functions short of actual legislation. A simple resolution is the action of one house of Congress, while a concurrent resolution stems from both houses.

3. Treaties are the instruments by which sovereign nations can act or agree to act with other nations. Treaties are considered a legislative form, but are discussed separately in Chapter VIII below.

4. Interstate Compacts are agreements between two or more states, which are legislative in nature and somewhat like treaties in form and effect. Compacts require the consent of Congress before the states can enter into them, so they often appear in both federal and state legislative publications.

5. Reorganization Plans are presidential proposals to reorganize executive agencies below the departmental level which are submitted to Congress pursuant to a general authorizing statute. If Congress does not veto the plan, it becomes law automatically in a reversal of the usual legislative process—that is, enactment by the President, subject to veto by the Congress, instead of vice versa.

6. **Executive Legislation** includes presidential proclamations, orders and messages, all of which belong more properly in the area of administrative law and will be discussed in Chapter VI below.

7. **Administrative Regulations** (substantive and procedural) consist of rules adopted by executive and regulatory agencies, pursuant to congressional authorization, which are clearly legislative in nature. These will also be discussed in detail in Chapter VI below.

8. **Court Rules** are enactments for the regulation of proceedings in the courts. They are promulgated by the courts themselves, or by conferences of judges, usually under authority specifically granted by statute.

9. **Local Laws and Ordinances** are delegated legislation in that the power to legislate has been delegated by the state legislature to some law-making agency of local government. Publication is generally very poor in this area, although a tremendous number of such laws are enacted regularly by municipalities and counties.

In addition to the foregoing legislative categories, the distinction between *public laws* and *private laws* must also be mentioned. Public laws are those which are designed to affect the general public, as distinguished from private laws which are passed to meet a special need of an individual

[*116*]

or small group. In some cases, the distinction is hard to justify, as when a special interest group promotes legislation, which, although general in tone, actually affects very few people. Both types are passed in the same way and both usually appear in the session law publication, but only *public* laws become part of the statutory code.

FEDERAL STATUTORY FORMS

1. The Quick Text. Many laws take effect upon enactment or soon thereafter and, whether immediately effective or not, lawyers and researchers need the text of such new laws as soon as possible. Congress itself is the best source for the text of new laws immediately after enactment.

As we have seen, the first *official* text is the *slip law*, which can be requested from the appropriate congressional clerk or an individual congressman, or ordered from the Superintendent of Documents, U. S. Government Printing Office, on an individual basis or by subscription. There is often, however, a frustrating time lag between enactment and distribution of slip laws to subscribers.

Commercially published specialized looseleaf services provide a quick text of federal enactments in particular subject fields. Since these publications are usually supplemented on a weekly basis, they are an excellent source for new legislation. Such services are commonly published in public

law fields like taxation, labor law, trade regulation, etc. and will be discussed below in Chapter VII. Their publishers will also frequently supply copies of new laws at the request of subscribers, even though they do not appear in full in the service itself.

One of the most popular sources of new federal *public* laws is the *U.S. Code Congressional and Administrative News*, published fortnightly by West during the congressional session and monthly when Congress is not in session. It appears initially in an advance sheet edition containing the complete text of all public laws along with some legislative history (in the form of committee reports) on the more important enactments. *U.S. C.C.A.N.* also contains congressional news notes, selected administrative regulations, executive documents, and rather useful tables and indexes.

2. Session Law Form. At the end of each session of Congress, the public and private slip laws are accumulated and corrected. Together with Presidential proclamations, reorganization plans, and proposed and ratified Constitutional amendments, they are then issued in bound volumes as the official *Statutes at Large* for that session. These are cited by volume and page, for example, 84 Stat. 1590 (referring to volume 84 of the *Statutes at Large,* page 1590). The *Statutes at Large* supersede the slip laws as the authoritative text of

federal laws and remain the authoritative text for all but those nineteen titles of the *U. S. Code* which have been reenacted as positive law. The *Statutes at Large* contain an index for each session, but since these indexes do not cumulate the researcher must use the topical arrangement of the *U. S. Code* and *its* general index in order to locate the current law on a particular subject.

Public Law 91-596

December 29, 1970
[S. 2193]

AN ACT

To assure safe and healthful working conditions for working men and women; by authorizing enforcement of the standards developed under the Act; by assisting and encouraging the States in their efforts to assure safe and healthful working conditions; by providing for research, information, education, and training in the field of occupational safety and health; and for other purposes.

Occupational
Safety and Health
Act of 1970.

Be it enacted by the Senate and House of Representatives of the United States of America in Congress assembled, That this Act may be cited as the "Occupational Safety and Health Act of 1970".

CONGRESSIONAL FINDINGS AND PURPOSE

SEC. (2) The Congress finds that personal injuries and illnesses arising out of work situations impose a substantial burden upon, and are a hindrance to, interstate commerce in terms of lost production, wage loss, medical expenses, and disability compensation payments.

DUTIES

SEC. 5. (a) Each employer—
　　(1) shall furnish to each of his employees employment and a place of employment which are free from recognized hazards that are causing or are likely to cause death or serious physical harm to his employees;
　　(2) shall comply with occupational safety and health standards promulgated under this Act.
(b) Each employee shall comply with occupational safety and health standards and all rules, regulations, and orders issued pursuant to this Act which are applicable to his own actions and conduct.

APPROPRIATIONS

SEC. 33. There are authorized to be appropriated to carry out this Act for each fiscal year such sums as the Congress shall deem necessary.

EFFECTIVE DATE

SEC. 34. This Act shall take effect one hundred and twenty days after the date of its enactment.
Approved December 29, 1970.

Exhibit 39:　The beginning, a middle section, and the end of a statute from the *U.S. Statutes at Large,* the Occupational Safety and Health Act of 1970. This act will be the focus of most of the exhibits in this chapter and in chapters V and VI.

There are also two unofficial session law texts of public laws. *U. S. Code Congressional and Administrative News,* mentioned above, is published by the West Publishing Company separately and as a supplement to its *United States Code Annotated.* *U.S.C.C.A.N.* cumulates at the end of each session into bound volumes which provide a permanent record of public legislation, with a selection of legislative history in the form of congressional committee reports.

U. S. Code Service, published by Lawyers Co-op, is another subject compilation of federal statutes. Formerly known as *Federal Code Annotated,* it is now in the process of changing over, volume by volume, to its new *U.S.C.S.* format. It is supplemented by a monthly advance sheet service, called *U.S.C.S. Advance,* which provides the texts of public laws, summaries of the legislative history of each public law, texts of new court rules, executive orders and Presidential proclamations. In the past, these advance sheets were cumulated into bound volumes, but this feature of the service has apparently been discontinued. These monthly advance sheets provide subscribers to the *U.S.C.S.* with a session law service similar to that of *U.S.C.C.A.N.,* but without the actual documents of legislative history. Neither *U.S.C.C.A.N.* nor *U.S.C.S. Advance* include *private* laws; these are only available in the official *Statutes at Large.*

3.   Subject compilations. The first official subject compilations of federal statutes designed
to provide such access were the *U.S. Revised
Statutes* of 1873 and its second edition of 1878.
These one volume compilations arranged all *public, general* and *permanent* federal statutes into
some seventy-five titles or subject categories with
consecutive section numbering and a general index.   The *Revised Statutes* of 1873 were more
than just a subject compilation, however. It actually reenacted as positive law the statutes it contained and expressly repealed their original *Statutes at Large* texts.   Therefore, for those public
laws which predate 1873 and are included in the
Revised Statutes, that compilation has become
their authoritative text.   The second edition, however, did not have that status, although little distinction is made between them today.

Although it soon became apparent that the *Revised Statutes* were not adequate to provide a convenient subject arrangement of current federal
statutes, no other official compilation was prepared for almost fifty years.   Then in 1926, the
first edition of the *United States Code* was published, arranging the public, general, permanent
laws by subject into some fifty titles.   The *Code*
is published in a completely revised edition every
six years with bound cumulative supplements in
the intervening years.   As previously noted, the
statutes contained in approximately one-third of

the titles of the *Code* have been reenacted and for them the *Code* has become the authoritative text. For the others, the *Statutes at Large* retain that status. The congressional plan of reenactment is described in the preface of the *Code* as follows:

> "Inasmuch as many of the general and permanent laws which are required to be incorporated in this Code are inconsistent, redundant, and obsolete, the Committee on the Judiciary is engaged in a comprehensive project of revising and enacting the Code into law, title by title. In furtherance of this plan bills have been enacted to revise, codify and enact into law Titles 1, 3, 4, 5, 6, 9, 10, 13, 14, 17, 18, 23, 28, 32, 35, 37, 38, 39, 44. In addition, bills relating to other titles are being prepared for introduction at an early date. When this work is completed all the titles of the Code will be legal evidence of the general and permanent law and recourse to the numerous volumes of the Statutes at Large for this purpose will be unnecessary."

Citations to the *Code* refer to title and section, rather than to volume and page, as in the *Statutes at Large*. For example, 18 U.S.C. § 1621 describes Title 18 of the *U. S. Code,* section 1621. If the title is one of those reenacted into positive law, it is technically unnecessary to cite its *Statutes at Large* source, but the general practice varies.

In addition to the actual text of statutes, the *Code* also includes historical and editorial notes, parallel tables and other research aids. Each section of the *Code* is followed by a citation to the *Statutes at Large* provision which originally enacted it. These alternative citations are particularly important where the *Statutes at Large* is still the authoritative source and must be cited. In the edition of the *U. S. Code* issued in 1977, cross references are provided at the beginning of each title to citations of sections in that title made elsewhere in the *Code*.

(4) Nothing in this chapter shall be construed to supersede or in any manner affect any workmen's compensation law or to enlarge or diminish or affect in any other manner the common law or statutory rights, duties, or liabilities of employers and employees under any law with respect to injuries, diseases, or death of employees arising out of, or in the course of, employment. (Pub. L. 91–596, § 4, Dec. 29, 1970, 84 Stat. 1592.)

REFERENCES IN TEXT

The Outer Continental Shelf Lands Act, referred to in subsec. (a), is classified to section 1331 et seq. of Title 43, Public Lands.

The Act of June 30, 1936, commonly known as the Walsh-Healey Act, referred to in subsec. (b)(2), is classified to sections 35 to 45 of Title 41, Public Contracts.

The Service Contract Act of 1965, referred to in subsec. (b)(2), is classified to chapter 6 of Title 41.

Public Law 91–54, Act of August 9, 1969, referred to in subsec. (b)(2), is classified to section 333 of Title 40, Public Buildings, Property, and Works.

Public Law 85–742, Act of August 23, 1958, referred to in subsec. (b)(2), is classified to section 941 of Title 33, Navigation and Navigable Waters.

The National Foundation on Arts and Humanities Act, referred to in subsec. (b)(2), is classified to section 951 et seq. of Title 20, Education.

The effective date of this chapter, referred to in subsec. (b)(2), (3), is the effective date of Pub. L. 91–596, which is 120 days after Dec. 29, 1970.

EFFECTIVE DATE

Section effective 120 days after Dec. 29, 1970, see section 34 of Pub. L. 91–596, set out as a note under section 651 of this title.

SECTION REFERRED TO IN OTHER SECTIONS

This section is referred to in section 673 of this title.

§ 654. Duties of employers and employees.

(a) Each employer—

(1) shall furnish to each of his employees employment and a place of employment which are free from recognized hazards that are causing or are likely to cause death or serious physical harm to his employees;

(2) shall comply with occupational safety and health standards promulgated under this chapter.

(b) Each employee shall comply with occupational safety and health standards and all rules, regulations, and orders issued pursuant to this chapter which are applicable to his own actions and conduct. (Pub. L. 91–596, § 5, Dec. 29, 1970, 84 Stat. 1593.)

EFFECTIVE DATE

Section effective 120 days after Dec. 29, 1970, see section 34 of Pub. L. 91–596, set out as a note under section 651 of this title.

SECTION REFERRED TO IN OTHER SECTIONS

This section is referred to in sections 658, 666 of this title.

§ 655. Standards.

(a) Promulgation by Secretary of national consensus standards and established Federal standards; time for promulgation; conflicting standards.

Without regard to chapter 5 of Title 5 or to the other subsections of this section, the Secretary shall, as soon as practicable during the period beginning with the effective date of this chapter and ending two years after such date, by rule promulgate as an occupational safety or health standard any national consensus standard, and any established Federal standard, unless he determines that the promulgation of such a standard would not result in improved safety or health for specifically designated employees. In the event of conflict among any such standards, the Secretary shall promulgate the standard which assures the greatest protection of the safety or health of the affected employees.

(b) Procedure for promulgation, modification, or revocation of standards.

The Secretary may by rule promulgate, modify, or revoke any occupational safety or health standard in the following manner:

(1) Whenever the Secretary, upon the basis of information submitted to him in writing by an interested person, a representative of any organization of employers or employees, a nationally recognized standards-producing organization, the Secretary of Health, Education, and Welfare, the National Institute for Occupational Safety and Health, or a State or political subdivision, or on the basis of information developed by the Secretary or otherwise available to him, determines that a rule should be promulgated in order to serve the objectives of this chapter, the Secretary may request the recommendations of an advisory committee appointed under section 656 of this title. The Secretary shall provide such an advisory committee with any proposals of his own or of the Secretary of Health, Education, and Welfare, together with all pertinent factual information developed by the Secretary or the Secretary of Health, Education, and Welfare, or otherwise available, including the results of research, demonstrations, and experiments. An advisory committee shall submit to the Secretary its recommendations regarding the rule to be promulgated within ninety days from the date of its appointment or within such longer or shorter period as may be prescribed by the Secretary, but in no event for a period which is longer than two hundred and seventy days.

(2) The Secretary shall publish a proposed rule promulgating, modifying, or revoking an occupational safety or health standard in the Federal Register and shall afford interested persons a period of thirty days after publication to submit written data or comments. Where an advisory committee is appointed and the Secretary determines that a rule should be issued, he shall publish the proposed rule within sixty days after the submission of the advisory committee's recommendations or the expiration of the period prescribed by the Secretary for such submission.

(3) On or before the last day of the period provided for the submission of written data or comments under paragraph (2), any interested person may file with the Secretary written objections to the proposed rule, stating the grounds therefore and requesting a public hearing on such objections. Within thirty days after the last day for filing such objections, the Secretary shall publish in the Federal Register a notice specifying the occupational safety or health standard to which objections have been filed and a hearing requested, and specifying a time and place for such hearing.

(4) Within sixty days after the expiration of the period provided for the submission of written data

Exhibit 40:   A page from the *U.S. Code*, showing the codification of part of the Occupational Safety and Health Act of 1970.

[*125*]

In order to get from the *Statutes at Large* citation to the *Code* citation, tables are provided at the end of the *U. S. Code* itself, which give such parallel references. The form of these tables, as revised in the 1970 edition of the *Code,* is shown in Exhibit 41. Similar tables also appear in the two unofficial editions of the *Code.*

		STATUTES AT LARGE				Page 13448
91st Cong.					**U.S.C.**	
84 Stat.	**Pub. L.**	**Section**	**Page**	**Title**	**Section**	**Status**
1970—Dec. 24........	91–588	10..	1585	38	521 nt.............................	
	91–589	1..	1586	2	168..............................	
		2..	1586	2	168a..............................	
		3..	1586	2	168b..............................	
		4..	1587	2	168c..............................	
		5..	1587	2	168d..............................	
28........	91–590	1..	1587	49	903...............................	
		2..	1587	49	903 nt...........................	
	91–591	2..	1588	7	2284.............................	
		3..	1588	7	2285.............................	
29........	91–596	1..	1590	29	651 nt...........................	
		2..	1590	29	651..............................	
		3..	1591	29	652..............................	
		4..	1592	29	653..............................	
		5..	1593	29	654..............................	
		6..	1593	29	655..............................	

Exhibit 41: A parallel reference table in the 1970 edition of *U.S. Code,* showing the codification of the Occupational Safety and Health Act of 1970.

4. Annotated Subject Compilations. In addition to the *U. S. Code,* which is the official subject compilation, there are also two privately published, annotated editions of the *Code.* As noted above, these are the *U. S. Code Annotated* (*U.S. C.A.*), published by West, and the *U. S. Code Service* (*U.S.C.S.*), published by Lawyers Co-op. Both compilations follow the same title and section numbering as the official edition and contain the

same statutory text, but add the following features:

> (a) Annotations of court decisions, interpret-
> ing, construing, and applying each sec-
> tion.
>
> (b) Editorial notes and analytical discussions
> on particular statutes or provisions.
>
> (c) References to attorney general opinions
> and legislative history.
>
> (d) Supplementation by annual pocket parts,
> quarterly pamphlets, and revised vol-
> umes as necessary.

U.S.C.S. also contains annotations of uncodified
laws and treaties, and preserves the original *Statutes at Large* text in which the law was enacted.
Both the *U.S.C.* and *U.S.C.A.*, on the other hand,
may make minor changes in integrating particular provisions into the *Code* format.

Their special research aids have made the annotated statutes very popular with attorneys and
scholars and they are therefore used widely in
preference to the official text. Exhibit 42 shows
the *U.S.C.A.* version of the same section of Title
29 as was shown in Exhibit 40. Exhibit 43 shows
a page of annotations to court decisions following
that section in *U.S.C.A.*; it also illustrates the
summary indexing of such annotations. Exhibits
44 and 45 show the corresponding section and annotations in *U.S.C.S.* Note the Research Guide in
that edition, citing to relevant secondary sources.

ly to make a new statute applicable to Puerto Rico. Caribtow Corp. v. Occupational Safety and Health Review Commission, C.A.1, 1974, 493 F.2d 1064.

2. Workmen's compensation laws

Since intestate's death, which resulted from injuries sustained in accident arising out of and in the course of his employment with defendant, was covered under the North Carolina Workmen's Compensation Act, subsec. (b)(4) of this section providing that nothing in this chapter should be construed to supersede any workmen's compensation law or to enlarge or diminish liability of employer precluded a private remedy, and plaintiff was not entitled to recover from employer for alleged negligence in violation of this chapter. Byrd v. Fieldcrest Mills, Inc., C.A.N.C.1974, 496 F.2d 1323.

3. Common law or statutory rights, duties or liabilities

Federal safety and health regulations did not enlarge responsibility of the property owner who hired prime contractor or of the prime contractor who hired independent sewer line subcontractor whose employee was killed during excavation of sewer line trench in view of provision in this section stating that this chapter does not enlarge or diminish the common law or statutory rights, duties, or liabilities of employers and employees with respect to injuries, diseases or death of employees arising out of employment. Hare v. Federal Compress & Warehouse Co., D.C.Miss.1973, 359 F.Supp. 214.

This chapter was not applicable in situation where employee was injured while voluntarily complying with his employer's request during a two man repair job on a farm roof, inasmuch as its provisions do not enlarge or diminish or affect in any other manner the common law or statutory rights, duties, or liabilities of employers and employees under the law with respect to injuries, diseases, or death of employees arising out of, or in course of, employment. Dekle v. Todd, Ga.App.1974, 207 S.E.2d 654.

§ 654.   Duties of employers and employees

(a) Each employer—

(1) shall furnish to each of his employees employment and a place of employment which are free from recognized hazards that are causing or are likely to cause death or serious physical harm to his employees;

(2) shall comply with occupational safety and health standards promulgated under this chapter.

(b) Each employee shall comply with occupational safety and health standards and all rules, regulations, and orders issued pursuant to this chapter which are applicable to his own actions and conduct.

Pub.L. 91–596, § 5, Dec. 29, 1970, 84 Stat. 1593.

Historical Note

Effective Date. Section effective 120 days after Dec. 29, 1970, see section 34 of Pub.L. 91–596, set out as a note under section 651 of this title.

Legislative History. For legislative history and purpose of Pub.L. 91–596, see 1970 U.S.Code Cong. and Adm.News, p. 5177.

Notes of Decisions

Accident or injury, prerequisites to violation 10
Defenses 13
Employees to whom duty is owed 1
Hazardous conduct
  Prerequisites to violation 11
  Prevention of 7

Injury, prerequisites to violation 10
Knowledge of employer, recognized hazards 4
Likelihood of hazard to cause death or injury 6
Persons liable 12

Exhibit 42: The *U.S.C.A.* version of 29 *U.S.C.* sec. 654.

29 § 654   LABOR   Ch. 15
Note I

---

1. Employees to whom duty is owed

Employer does not owe a lesser duty of care to its supervisory personnel under this section than is owed to the rank-and-file employees. National Realty & Const. Co., Inc. v. Occupational Safety and Health Review Commission, 1973, 489 F.2d 1257, 160 U.S.App.D.C. 133.

2. Places of employment where duty is owed

Fact that circuit breaker power room was not open to all employees but only to certain authorized personnel did not render it immune from coverage of this chapter. REA Exp., Inc. v. Brennan, C.A.2, 1974, 495 F.2d 822.

3. Recognized hazards—Generally

Within this section, a "recognized hazard" is not limited to one which can be recognized directly by human senses without assistance of any technical instruments. American Smelting & Refining Co. v. Occupational Safety and Health Review Commission, C.A.8, 1974, 501 F.2d 504.

4. ——— Knowledge of employer

Employer's obligation under this section is to maintain a work place free from "recognized hazards" which are causing or likely to cause death or serious physical harm to employees; a "recognized hazard" is a condition that is known to be hazardous, and is known not necessarily by each and every individual employer, but is known by taking into account the standard of knowledge in the industry. Brennan v. Occupational Safety and Health Review Commission, C.A.7, 1974, 501 F.2d 1196.

This section requires that, for a serious violation citation to be sustained, danger must be one of which employer knew or, with reasonable diligence, could have known. Id.

A hazard is "recognized" for purposes of this section, if an employer has actual knowledge of a hazard. Brennan v. Occupational Safety and Health Review Commission, C.A.8, 1974, 494 F.2d 460.

5. ——— Unpreventable hazards

This section does not impose an absolute liability on the employer, since it may be that some hazards are unpreventable, particularly if employee's conduct is wilfully reckless or so unusual that employer cannot reasonably prevent the existence of the hazard which such behavior creates. REA Exp. Inc. v. Brennan, C.A.2, 1974, 495 F.2d 822.

Standard imposed by this section is not intended to impose strict liability but to require elimination only of preventable hazards, and unpreventable hazards are not to be considered "recognized" under this section. National Realty & Const. Co., Inc. v. Occupational Safety and Health Review Commission, 1973, 489 F.2d 1257, 160 U.S.App.D.C. 133.

6. Likelihood of hazard to cause death or injury

Although act of employee in cutting band which held packaged railroad ties together prior to time unloader was in place gave rise to a substantial probability that death or serious physical harm would result, a serious violation of this section did not occur in respect to employee's death, where instruction given employee to stay away from trucks because the unloader did all the unloading was sufficient to satisfy employer's duty, and employer, using reasonable diligence, would not have foreseen danger. Brennan v. Occupational Safety and Health Review Commission, C.A.7, 1974, 501 F.2d 1196.

Where it was reasonably foreseeable that awkward and uncomfortable respirators would not be properly worn by employees, furnishing of such respirators could not be relied on by employer to establish that its protective measures prevented the likelihood of harm to employees from airborne lead, for purposes of this section. American Smelting and Refining Co. v. Occupational Safety and Health Review Commission, C.A.8, 1974, 501 F.2d 504.

No mathematical test as to probability of serious mishap is proper in construing the "likely to cause death or serious physical harm" element of this section. National Realty & Const. Co., Inc. v. Occupational Safety and Health Review Commission, 1973, 489 F.2d 1257, 160 U.S. App.D.C. 133.

Exhibit 43: Annotations under 29 *U.S.C.A.* sec. 654.

[*129*]

§ 654. Duties of employer and employee

(a) Each employer—

(1) shall furnish to each of his employees employment and a place of employment which are free from recognized hazards that are causing or are likely to cause death or serious physical harm to his employees;

(2) shall comply with occupational safety and health standards promulgated under this Act.

(b) Each employee shall comply with occupational safety and health standards and all rules, regulations, and orders issued pursuant to this Act which are applicable to his own actions and conduct.

(Dec. 29, 1970, P. L. 91-596 § 5, 84 Stat 1593.)

HISTORY; ANCILLARY LAWS AND DIRECTIVES

References in text:

"This Act", referred to in this section, is the Occupational Safety and Health Act of 1970, and appears as 29 USCS §§ 651–678; 42 USCS

---

29 USCS § 654   LABOR

§ 3142-1, and as amendments to 5 USCS §§ 5108, 5314, 5315, 7902; 15 USCS §§ 633, 636; 18 USCS § 1114; 29 USCS § 533; 49 USCS § 1421.

Effective dates:

For effective date of this section, see effective date note to 29 USCS § 651.

CROSS REFERENCE

This section is referred to in 29 USCS §§ 658, 666.

RESEARCH GUIDE

Am Jur:

Am Jur 2d New Topic Service, Occupational Safety and Health Acts § 6.

Law Review Articles:

Morey, The General Duty Clause of the Occupational Safety & Health Act of 1970. 86 Harvard L Rev 988, April 1973.

OSHA: Employer beware. 10 Houston L Rev 426 (January, 1973).

Occupational Health and the Federal Government: The Wages are Still Bitter. 38 L and Contemporary Problems 651 (Summer-Autumn, 1974).

On the Economics of Industrial Safety. 38 L and Contemporary Problems 669 (Summer-Autumn, 1974).

The Control of Industrial Accidents: Economic Theory and Empirical Evidence. 38 L and Contemporary Problems 700 (Summer-Autumn, 1974).

The Feasibility of an "Injury Tax" Approach to Occupational Safety. 38 L and Contemporary Problems 730 (Summer-Autumn, 1974).

The Occupational Safety and Health Act of 1970 and the Law of Torts. 38 L and Contemporary Problems 612 (Summer-Autumn, 1974).

Exhibit 44: Section 654 of Title 29 in *U.S.C.S.* with Research Guide.

INTERPRETIVE NOTES AND DECISIONS

I. IN GENERAL

1. Effect of promulgation of standards
2. Reservation of place for additional regulations
3. Constitutionality of standards
4. Inspection methods
5. Persons responsible—Employer generally
6. —Joint enterprise
7. —Lessee of equipment
8. —Principal contractor
9. —Subcontractor
10. —Imputation of knowledge
11. Number of citations
12. Effect of accident to establish violation
13. Necessity of accident to establish violation
14. Necessity of employee exposure to establish violation
15. Duty as to safety training
16. Duty as to record keeping
17. Amendment of citation

II. GENERAL DUTY CLAUSE

18. Purpose
19. Construction
20. "Recognized hazard" defined
21. —Required tests
22. When hazard is "likely" to cause harm
23. Application following promulgation of specific standard
24. Evidence supporting violation
25. Serious violations

III. COMPLIANCE WITH PRESCRIBED STANDARDS

A. Generally

26. Employer notice of standards

27. Necessity that employees be affected
28. Effect of conflicting ruling by Secretary
29. Effect of difficulty of compliance
30. Justification for noncompliance

B. Standards Relative to Specific Hazards

31. Air pollution
32. Noise pollution
33. Electrical shock
34. —Clearance between crane boom and high voltage line
35. Prevention of falls   Safety nets
36. —Guard rails
37. —Safety lines
38. —Access ladders
39. Safety shoes
40. Maintenance of equipment
41. Guards on moving machinery
42. Building load limits
43. Fire hazards
44. Explosions
45. Cleanliness of site
46. Means of access
47. Protection from mobile equipment
48. Maritime employment generally
49. Drowning
50. Falling objects
51. Chemical hazards
52. Toilet facilities
53. Cave-in of excavation
54. Safety glasses and face shields

IV. EMPLOYEE DUTY

55. Generally

I. IN GENERAL

1. Effect of promulgation of standards

lations, since content of those reserved titles are unknown, and furthermore, 29 USCS § 654(a)(2) provides that each employer shall comply with Occupational Safety and Health Standards promulgated. Delmarva Power & Light Co. (1974) OSHRC Docket No. 1416, 1973–1974 CCH OSHD ¶ 17904.

3. Constitutionality of standards

As long as safety and health regulations, adopted under 29 USCS § 654(a)(2), afford reasonable warning of proscribed conduct in light of common understanding and practices, they will pass constitutional muster. Ryder Truck Lines, Inc. v Brennan (1974, CA5) 497 F2d 230.

29 CFR § 1910.132(a) requiring certain safety equipment "wherever it is necessary by reason of hazards or processes or environment," is not unconstitutionally vague. Ryder Truck Lines, Inc. v Brennan (1974, CA5) 497 F2d 230.

4. Inspection methods

Efficient air sampling method for detecting airborne lead in industrial plant is reasonable method of inspection by Secretary of Labor where biological monitoring system had been proved ineffective. American Smelting & Refining Co. v Occupational Safety & Health Review Com. (1974, CA8) 501 F2d 504.

5. Persons responsible—Employer generally

Employer violates 29 USCS § 654(a) when his employees are affected by violative condition, and it is no defense that others created condition, were responsible for its existence, or had control of site or equipment where such condition existed. California Stevedore & Ballast Co. (1974) OSHRC Docket No. 1132, 1973–1974

Exhibit 45:   Annotations to Section 654 of Title 29 in *U.S. C.S.*

5. Constitutional Texts and Sources. The United States Constitution appears in numerous publications ranging from simple pamphlets put out by patriotic organizations to large annotated texts with full scholarly apparatus. It is also included in most subject compilations of federal and state statutes. The best separate edition had been that edited by Edward Corwin and published by the Library of Congress in 1953. Revised editions of this work by Lester Jayson were published in 1964 and 1973 with the title: *The Constitution of the United States of America, Analysis and Interpretation.* It includes the text of the Constitution along with case annotations and detailed discussions of each provision, its history and interpretation. Although pocket part supplementation (unfortunately lacking in the previous editions) is provided in the current edition, it is not sufficiently frequent. Recourse to other updating services is therefore essential.

The Constitution appears in the *U. S. Code,* the *U.S.C.A.* and the *U.S.C.S.,* although it is not an integral part of the *Code* itself. The *U.S.C.A.* and *U.S.C.S.* versions are, of course, heavily annotated with thousands of case abstracts, in the typical format of those code editions.

There is also a great historical literature concerning the original drafting and adoption of the Constitution. Among the most useful of these publications are *Documents Illustrative of the For-*

mation of the Union of American States (U.S.G.
P.O.1927); *Documentary History of the Consti-
stitution of the U.S.A., 1786–1870* (U.S.Dept. of
State, 1894–1905) in five volumes; and Max Far-
rand's *Records of the Federal Convention of 1787*
in four volumes (Yale Univ. Press 1937, reprinted
in paperback 1967). A new multi-volume series,
*The Documentary History of the Ratification of
the Constitution* (State Historical Society of Wisconsin, 1976—   ), edited by Merrill Jensen, provides invaluable background material on constitutional ratification.

6. Other Statutory Sources. Looseleaf services which collect legal source material in certain
subject areas and are kept up-to-date by weekly
supplementation, offer another practical means of
access to statutes, as noted above. There are also
subject compilations of statutes put out by various
groups in the areas of their interest. These include government agencies (e. g., *Federal Labor
Laws and Agencies,* issued by the Department of
Labor); Congress itself (e. g., *Radio Laws of the
U. S.* and *Laws Relating to Veterans*); trade associations (e. g., *Credit Manual of Commercial Laws,*
published by the National Association of Credit
Men); and private publishers (e. g., Schneider's
Workmen's Compensation Laws). These collections are often quite helpful to people working in
fields of law which are not serviced by looseleaf
publications. However, they are never kept up-to-

date with the same regularity as looseleaf services (in fact many are never supplemented at all) and thus must be used with considerable caution and updated by some other means.

STATE STATUTES

Most of the significant forms encountered in federal statutes also appear in state statutes. There are official and unofficial editions of state statutes; annotated and unannotated texts; slip laws, session laws, and codes; acts and resolutions; public and private laws. There are also the universal problems of providing for subject access to chronologically published laws and keeping up-to-date an everchanging mass of legislation. In fact, the publication of state laws reproduces many of the achievements, difficulties and short-comings of federal statutory publication.

1. State Constitutions. State constitutions have developed a bibliography of their own because of their variety and legal importance. There is an excellent looseleaf compilation of state constitutions called *Constitutions of the U. S.: National and State* (Oceana, 2d ed., 1974–75) in five volumes, and a companion volume, the *Index-Digest of State Constitutions* (Columbia University Legislative Drafting Research Fund, 2nd ed. 1959), which provides subject access to all of the constitutions. A typical entry is set forth in Exhibit 46.

CIVIL RIGHTS

See ALIENS; CIVIL SERVICE — IN-SERVICE PROVISIONS — DISCRIMINATION; CITIZEN-SHIP; COLORED PERSONS; EDUCATION — PUBLIC SCHOOLS—SEGREGATION; ELECTIONS —QUALIFICATIONS OF ELECTORS—RACIAL; PUBLIC OFFICERS — QUALIFICATIONS — RACIAL; PARKS AND RECREATION — RACIAL SEGREGATION; WOMEN; RELIGION — DIS-CRIMINATION;—FREEDOM OF OPINION AND CONSCIENCE.

All persons equal and entitled to equal rights, opportunities and protection under law; all persons have corresponding obligations to people and state. **Alas I 1.**

No person to be denied enjoyment of civil or political rights because of race, color, creed or national origin. **Alas I 3.**

Right of all persons to fair and just treatment in course of executive investigations not to be infringed. **Alas I 7.**

No citizen to be deprived of right, privilege or immunity, or exempted from burden or duty on account of race, color, or previous condition of servitude. **Ark II 3.**

No person to be denied enjoyment of civil rights or be discriminated against because of race, religion, sex or ancestry. **H I 4.**

Exhibit 16: An entry in the *Index-Digest of State Constitutions.*

The best sources for individual state constitutions, however, are still the annotated statutes of the individual states, where one can usually find the latest text of the constitution, along with annotations of court decisions interpreting and construing it. Popular pamphlet texts are also available in many states. Shepard's citators for the

various states are useful in developing both legislative and judicial histories of state constitutions.

2. State Session Laws. Slip laws are issued in many of the states, but are rarely distributed to the public. However, every state has a session law publication which cumulates on a chronological basis the laws enacted at each sitting of its legislature usually with a non-cumulative index for each volume or session. These chronological collections are similar to the *U. S. Statutes at Large* in form and purpose. They are initially the authoritative text of each state's laws and in most states never lose that status, since only rarely does the subject compilation acquire positive law status. In citing session laws, one must always include the year of the session, e. g., *Laws of New York, 1964.* Without the year, the citation is meaningless.

There is a considerable time lag in the publication of most state session laws and they are often delayed until long after the end of the session.   In some states, the commercial publisher of the statutory compilation provides a "session law service" which gives access to new session laws even while the legislature is still sitting, very much as the *U. S. Code Congressional and Administrative News* and *U.S.C.S. Advance* do for congressional enactments.

3. State Codes. Since the indexes to state session laws do not cumulate, there is need for

some means of subject access to relevant laws in force. Most states now have a subject compilation of their statutes, similar to the *U. S. Code,* which serves that function. These are usually commercially published, unofficial collections, which typically include annotations of court decisions on those statutes. For a few states, there is no unofficial edition and the state itself publishes an official subject compilation, usually without annotations. A few other states have both an official and an unofficial edition of the code. As one might suspect, the better edited and more useful unofficial editions are gradually driving out the less elaborate (but usually less expensive) official sets. The *bluebook* contains a useful table of the current codes for each state, with session law information as well.

The authority of the unofficial editions varies from state to state. These editions are usually accepted as at least *prima facie* evidence of the statutory law. They are rarely considered the "positive law" or authoritative text of statutes, but that distinction is becoming increasingly a matter of form rather than substance. One can usually determine the status of a subject compilation by looking for a certificate which indicates its authority in the front of each volume. Sometimes such information is supplied in the preface.

State statutes are annotated and supplemented in much the same way as federal statutes. The

West Publishing Company's state codes are usually similar to *U.S.C.A.* in format and coverage. The best of them contain analytical notes, reference to historical sources, parallel tables, citations to attorney general opinions, and other useful research material, in addition to the usual judicial annotations. Supplementation is generally by pocket part or looseleaf insertions, although West also provides quarterly pamphlet supplements and session law services for most of its codes.

4. Uniform Laws. As noted above, there has been a movement in this country for some years to secure enactment by the states of various uniform laws. It has been felt that in many fields there is unnecessary confusion and conflict because of widely different state statutes. Sometimes this is a necessary reflection of the peculiar history, customs, economics or geography of the region, but in many cases there is no reasonable justification for these differences. The National Conference of Commissioners on the Uniform State Laws is a quasi-official body with representatives from every state, which meets annually to propose, draft, and promote uniform legislation. There are now almost 100 such acts which have been passed by at least one state. Among the most widely known is the *Uniform Commercial Code* which has been adopted by virtually every state.

All of the uniform laws are compiled and published by West in one annotated set called *Uni-*

form Laws Annotated (Master edition, 1968–1975). Not only does this set contain every uniform law adopted by at least one state, along with the commissioners' notes on these laws, but it also includes annotations to the court decisions of *every* state which has adopted and then litigated each law. These annotations are particularly useful in giving enacting states the benefit of the case law developed in those states having the same uniform law. The *U.L.A.* also contains tables indicating which states have adopted each law, variations in their adoptions, and other useful information. The set is kept up-to-date annually by pocket parts and is supplemented by the annual *Handbook of the National Conference of Commissioners on the Uniform State Laws* which provides current information about new laws, discussions of pending and proposed laws, and recent adoptions.

The text of each uniform law can, of course, also be found in the statutes of each state which has adopted that law, usually with annotations on the law from the courts of that particular state. This source is particularly valuable since the uniform laws are frequently enacted in a form different from that proposed by the Commissioners.

5. Procedural Legislation and Court Rules. There are legal and bibliographic distinctions between procedural and substantive legislation. Procedural laws describe the procedures to be followed in the courts in effectuating one's legal

rights and remedies. They concern the forms of action and defense, motion practice, time limitations, service of papers, hearing and trial arrangements, and all of the thousands of other details relating to the administration of legal business. In many states these procedural requirements are statutory in form, as in the Civil Practice Acts; in some states, they appear as non-statutory rules promulgated by the judiciary. In others, the procedural law is a combination of both statutes and rules.

Most statutory subject compilations include both substantive and procedural law, but in many states the procedural law is also separately published in unofficial services or manuals. These are typically annotated with court decisions and sometimes with sample forms to guide the practicing attorney. Such practice manuals are generally well supplemented or frequently revised.

Every state also has local court rules which govern the operation of its courts. These tend to be even more specific than the civil practice acts or rules, including such things as hours of court, make-up of court calendars, place and times for filing legal papers, etc. Court rules are published in the following forms: (a) as issued, in the official state reports (sometimes indicated by a notation on the spine of the particular volume that it contains new rules); (b) in the state statutory compilations; and (c) in separate pamphlets issued by the particular court.

6. Local Law Sources. As we have seen, our legal system encompasses many different levels of jurisdiction—federal, state, county, town, city. Legislation is passed by all of these units and there is a large literature of local ordinances, charters, and codes, which is usually poorly published, rarely annotated and infrequently supplemented. Many of the larger cities in the United States now publish collections of their ordinances with some attempt at supplementation (e. g. *Philadelphia Code of Ordinances, New York City Charter and Administrative Code,* etc.), but for the rest, very little effort is made for proper publication. As some legal publishers begin to see profit in these publications, more and more local law compilations are appearing. On the whole, however, the situation is still very bad and in many cities there is no accessible, up-to-date compilation of ordinances. Generally, individual ordinances may be obtained at the county, city or town clerk's office, which may also be the only depository for all of the ordinances of that jurisdiction. The astute lawyer must become familiar with what is generally available in the area and then take steps to locate sources of further information. With the increasing importance of local law in many fields, such as environmental protection, welfare, housing, transportation, etc., better access to these sources is badly needed. The unavailability of local ordinances is a serious impediment to the proper administration of justice.

FINDING–TOOLS FOR STATUTES

In addition to the subject compilations of statutes, there are other aids to statutory research. Among these are indexes of various kinds, which provide a direct topical approach to statutes, and tables which permit the researcher to convert citations from one form to another.

1. Indexes to Federal Statutes. Among the useful retrospective indexes to federal laws are Beaman and MacNamara, *Index Analysis of the Federal Statutes, 1789–1873* and McClenon and Gilbert, *Index to the Federal Statutes, 1874–1931.* The indexes to the *Revised Statutes* (1873 and 1878 editions) and to the various editions of the *U. S. Code* permit searching of those compilations as well.

There are indexes to current statutes by their legislative session in the volumes of the *Statutes at Large* and its unofficial edition, *U.S.C.C.A.N.,* described above. Indexes for the entire body of currently effective, public, general and permanent federal statutes can be found in the *U.S. Code, U.S. Code Annotated* and *U.S. Code Service.* These are probably the most frequently used of all statutory indexes, since most research is done in the latest subject compilations. The page of the *U. S. Code* index shown in Exhibit 47 below is typical of this group.

Page 16333 GENERAL INDEX

OBSTRUCTING JUSTICE—Continued

Mississippi—Continued
- Military assistance for removal of unlawful obstructions in, 10 § 332 note, Ex. Ord. No. 11053

Obstruction of proceedings before departments, agencies, and committees, 18 § 1505
Picketing or parading near courthouse or residence of judicial officer, witness, etc., 18 § 1507
Resistance to extradition agent, 18 § 1502
Sentence and punishment,
- Assault on process server, 18 § 1501
- False bail, 18 § 1506
- Influencing juror by writing, 18 § 1504
- Influencing or injuring officer, juror or witness, 18 §§ 1503 to 1505
- Obstruction of,
  - Court orders, 18 § 1509
  - Criminal investigations, 18 § 1510
  - Proceedings before departments, agencies, and committees, 18 § 1505
- Picketing or parading, 18 § 1507
- Recording, listening to, or observing proceedings of grand or petite juries while deliberating or voting, 18 § 1508
- Resistance to extradition agent, 18 § 1502
- Theft or alteration of record or process, 18 § 1506

Sound-truck or similar device to impede or obstruct justice, 18 § 1507
Theft or alteration of record or process, 18 § 1506

OBSTRUCTION

Capitol buildings or grounds, unlawful to obstruct passage through, 40 §§ 193f, 193h
Criminal investigations of U.S., penalties, 18 § 1510
Federal authority, use of militia and armed forces to enforce during unlawful obstruction, 10 § 332
Internal revenue law administration, 26 § 7212
Mail or Mailing, this index
Navigable waters. Obstructions in Navigable Waters, generally, this index
President of U.S., temporary residences or offices, obstructing ingress or egress to or from buildings, etc., designated as, penalties, 18 § 1752
Public lands,
- Entry on, 43 §§ 1062, 1064
- Passage or transit over, 43 §§ 1063, 1064

Revenue officer by master of vessel, 19 § 70

OBSTRUCTIONS IN NAVIGABLE WATERS

Anchoring vessels prohibited, 33 § 409
Bridges, 33 § 494
- Criminal liability for failure to alter, 33 § 502
- Removal, 33 § 494

Consent of Congress necessary to creation of obstruction, 33 § 403
Crimes and offenses, 33 §§ 403, 410, 411
Floating timber prohibited, 33 § 409
- Exception, 33 § 410

Grounded vessels, summary removal of obstruction, 33 § 415
Logs, prohibition against floating, 33 § 409
- Exception, 33 § 410

Marking, 14 § 86
Master of vessel, liability, 33 § 412
Mississippi River, removal from, 33 § 604
New York City, consent of Congress, 33 § 454
Ohio River, removal, appropriations, 33 § 606
Penalties and punishment, 33 § 411
Pilots, liability, 33 § 412
Removal, snags, debris, etc., 33 § 701g
Sack rafts, prohibition against floating, 33 § 409
- Exception, 33 § 410

Sale of vessel obstructing navigation, 33 § 415
Summary removal of water craft obstructing navigation, 33 § 415
Sunken vessels,
- Appropriation for removal, 31 § 725a(b)(14)
- Marking, 14 § 86; 33 § 409
- Removal, 33 § 409
  - Secretary of Army, 33 § 414

OCALA, FLA.

District court held at, 28 § 89

OCALA NATIONAL FOREST

Game preserves, hunting and killing in, 16 § 692a
Refuge, creation, 16 § 692

OCCUPATIONAL DISEASES

Coal Mines, this index
Metal and nonmetallic mine safety,
- Inspections, 30 §§ 723, 733
- Reports, 30 § 732

OCCUPATIONAL SAFETY AND HEALTH

Text of Act of 1970. See Popular Name Table
Analysis of statistics, 29 § 673
Applicability of Act, 29 § 653
Appropriations, 29 § 678
- National Commission on State Workmen's Compensation Laws, 29 § 676

Assistant Secretary of Labor, rate of pay, 5 § 5315
Attorney General, civil litigation subject to direction and control of, 29 § 663
Audits, 29 § 674
Citations for violations, 29 § 658
- Enforcement, 29 § 659
- Penalties, 29 § 666

Civil defense workers, protection and incentives, emergency preparedness functions of Secretary of Labor, 50 App. § 2292 note, Ex. Ord. No. 11490
Civil litigation, representation of Secretary in, 29 § 663
Civil service, classification of positions, placement by Secretary of Labor and Review Commission, 5 § 5108
Commerce, defined, 29 § 652
Compensation, chairman and members of Review Commission, 5 §§ 5314, 5315
Confidentiality of trade secrets, 29 § 664
Congressional findings, 29 § 651
Contracts,
- National Commission on State Workmen's Compensation Laws, 29 § 676
- National Institute, 29 § 671
- Studies, 29 § 669

Exhibit 47: A page from the index to the *U.S. Code.*

For federal statutes which have become commonly known by a popular name, there are popular name tables (similar to those described above for cases) which provide citations to their actual text. Such tables can be found in the *Shepard's Acts and Cases by Popular Names—Federal and State,* and in the designated volumes of the *U.S.C., U.S.C.A.* and *U.S.C.S.* Exhibit 48 illustrates the Shepard's table:

FEDERAL AND STATE ACTS CITED BY POPULAR NAMES   Off

O

Obscene Literature Commission Act
Okla. Stat. 1961, Title 21, §1040.1 et seq.

Obscene Publications Act
R. I. Gen. Laws 1956, 11-31.1-1 et seq.

Obscenity Act
Colo. Rev. Stat. 1963, 40-28-1 et seq.
Ida. Code 1947, 18-1513 et seq.
Mis. Code 1972, §99-33-1 et seq.
Okla. Stat. 1971, Title 21, §1040.11 et seq.
S. D. Comp. Laws 1967, 22-24-11 et seq.
Va. Code 1950, §18.1-227 et seq.

Occupational Safety and Health Acts
Az. Rev. Stat. 1956, §23-401 et seq.
Colo. Rev. Stat. 1973, 8-11-100.1 et seq.
Haw. Rev. Stat. 1968, §396-1 et seq.
Ind. Code 1971, 22-8-1.1-1 et seq.
Mich. Comp. Laws 1970, 408.1001 et seq.
Mich. Comp. Laws 1970, 498.851 et seq.
Min. Stat. 1974, 182.65 et seq.
N. C. Gen. Stat. 1943, §95-126 et seq.
Nev. Rev. Stat. 1973 Reprint, 618.005 et seq.
Ten. Code Anno. 1955, 50-501 et seq.
Utah Code Anno. 1953, 35-9-1 et seq.

Occupational Therapy Practice Act
Fla. Laws 1975, Ch. 179

Occupational Disease Disability Act
Colo. Rev. Stat. 1973, 8-60-101 et seq.
S. D. Comp. Laws 1967, 62-8-1 et seq.

Occupational Education Act
Colo. Rev. Stat. 1973, 23-60-101 et seq.

Occupational Health Act
Mont. Rev. Code 1947, 69-4206 et seq.

Occupational Health and Safety Act
N. M. Stat. Anno. 1953, 59-14-1 et seq.
Okla. Stat. 1971, Title 40, §401 et seq.
Wyo. Stat. 1957, §27-274 et seq.

Occupational License Act
N. C. Gen. Stat. 1943, §105-33 et seq.

Occupational Safety and Health Act of 1970
U. S. Code 1970 Title 29, §651 et seq.
Dec. 29, 1970, P. L. 91-596, 84 Stat. 1590

Office of Education and Related Agencies Appropriation Act, 1972
U. S., July 9, 1971, P. L. 92-48, 85 Stat. 103

Office of Education Appropriation Act, 1971
U. S., Aug. 18, 1970, P. L. 91-380, 84 Stat. 800

Office of Federal Procurement Policy Act
U. S. Code 1970 Title 41, §401 et seq.
Aug. 30, 1974, P. L. 93-400, 88 Stat. 796

Office of Fiscal Affairs Act
N. J. Rev. Stat. 1937, 52:11-43 et seq.

Office of the Town Clerk Law
N. Y. Local Laws 1972 Town of Oyster Bay, p. 2471

Official Lottery Act
P. R. Laws Anno. 1954, Title 15, §111 et seq.

Exhibit 48: Shepard's table showing federal acts by popular name.

2. Parallel Conversion and Transfer Tables. In view of the varied forms which statutes take, it is necessary to provide parallel reference tables from one form or stage of a law to another form or a later stage of the same law. The following is a list of the most commonly used tables or aids and where they can be found:

(a) **Bill number to public law number:**

    (1) In legislative status tables which include enactments (e. g., CCH *Congressional Index, Congressional Calendars, Digest of Public General Bills, Congressional Monitor, Congressional Information Service/Index,* and *Congressional Record*).

    (2) *U.S.C.C.A.N.*: Table of Enacted Bills.

    (3) *Statutes at Large*: List of Bills Enacted into Public Law (beginning with 88th Congress, 1st Sess., 1963).

(b) **Public law number to bill number:**

    (1) Slip laws and *Statutes at Large* at the head of the text.

    (2) Public Law Table of *Digest of Public General Bills*.

    (3) *Daily Digest* of *Congressional Record*: History of Bills Enacted into Public Law (see Exhibit 62 below).

[145]

    (4) *U.S.C.C.A.N.*: Table of Public Laws.

    (5) CCH *Congressional Index*: Table of Enactments.

    (6) *Congressional Information Service/ Index*.

(c) **Bill number or public law number to Statutes at Large:**

    (1) Text of Slip Law (since 1951).

    (2) *Statutes at Large:* List of Public Laws.

    (3) *U.S.C.C.A.N.*: Slip Law and Table of Public Laws.

    (4) *U.S. Code: Statutes at Large* table (see Exhibit 41 above).

(d) **Bill number or public law number to Code:**

    (1) *U.S.C.C.A.N.*: Table of Classifications.

    (2) *U.S. Code: Statutes at Large* table, which also lists statutes by their public law number (Exhibit 41 above).

(e) To go from *U.S. Code* sections to *Statutes at Large* citations—use parenthetical references following text of *Code* section.

3. State Statutory Finding Tools. Research in state statutes involves very much the same techniques as in federal statutes, although the indexes, tables and other research aids are frequently less sophisticated in state materials.

State statutes can be searched in the following ways:

(a) By subject—via the general index of the various annotated codes and by the annual indexes in the session law volumes;

(b) By retrospective, cumulative statutory indexes which have been published from time to time in a few of the states;

(c) By indexes to the laws of more than one state (e. g., with the *State Law Index* during the period 1925 to 1948, and the computer-produced, *Monthly Digest of Current Legislation*, and its several predecessors, from 1963 to 1972. Unfortunately, both of these services have been discontinued and complete multistate statutory access will have to wait on further development of the computerized research services.);

(d) By popular name tables which are provided by Shepard's citators and in the annotated codes of some states.

Cross references for state statutes, similar to those for federal, are provided in the following ways:

(a) **From session law citation to that of the code:** in the tables of the annotated codes.

(b) **From code to session law:** usually following the text of the code section in a footnote or parenthetical reference.

(c) **From an earlier code edition to a later revision or vice-versa:** by parallel conversion tables in the tables volume or individual title volumes of the annotated codes.

4. Supplementation and Updating of Statutes. As we have noted, laws are being passed by Congress every year and by the various state legislatures in annual or biennial sessions. Hence there is need for constant supplementation to be sure that the statutory texts reflect the latest changes. A compilation of statutes which does not have internal supplementation is almost useless, unless it can be easily updated by some other means. Statutory supplementation is ordinarily provided by pocket parts inserted annually in the back of each volume; by pamphlets, such as the quarterly supplements to the *U.S.C.A.*; or by looseleaf, as in those few states which issue their codes in that form (e. g. Alaska and Oregon). Statutes

of some of the states are also updated by *session law services* which provide advance sheet pamphlets while the legislature is in session.

Shepard's state citators enable the researcher to determine whether there have been any changes in a statutory text, thereby updating the statute, but, of course, not providing the actual text of any changes recorded therein.

5. Methods of Access to Statutory Material. Judicial decisions, as noted previously, can be located by their case name, by the legal concept involved or by descriptive factual catchwords. Statutes can be approached in the same three ways, that is (a) by a citation table or popular name table; (b) through the relevant legal concept, by selecting the apparently pertinent title of the code and using its analytical breakdowns to find the appropriate section; or (c) using the statutory word indexes to get directly to the relevant sections. The circuitous approach (b) suffers from the same disadvantage as approaching a case digest by its broad legal divisions rather than through the descriptive word index. It is almost always faster to use method (c) based on indexes which provide quick reference to relevant sections by specific catchwords and phrases.

Future research in statutory materials will undoubtedly be vastly improved by new computerized services. The LEXIS service already in-

cludes the provisions of the U.S.Code and the codes of several states, and offers the same full-text search capability as described for case-finding on page 104 above. The LEXIS data base also contains slip laws of enactments during the current legislative session. It thereby updates the codes rapidly and provides access by very specific words, phrases and concepts, more effectively than by traditional indexes. Hopefully, the service will be adding many more state codes in the future.

CITATORS FOR STATUTORY MATERIALS

Shepard's publishes statutory citators which perform much the same function as their case citators, although the former are somewhat more difficult to use because of the different statutory forms. There is a statutory citator for every state and for federal laws, with the usual advance sheet supplementation to keep them up to date.

On the federal level, *Shepard's United States Citations* includes entries for every section of the *U.S.Code* and for every provision in the *Statutes at Large* which has not been incorporated into the *Code*. Exhibits 49 and 50 explain those two types of coverage.

United
States
Code, 1970
Edition
and
Supple-
ment, 1972

TITLE 18

§ 700
Ad82St291 |1
C302FS1112 |2
394US604
22LE592
89SC1372
445F2d226
462F2d96
479F2d1177 3
313FS49
317FS138
322FS593
324FS1278
343FS165
41/3504n |5

Subsec. a
C454F2d972
C462F2d96
445F2d226
479F2d1179
321FS1278

Subsec. b 6
C462F2d96
445F2d226

Subsec. c
394US598
22LE588
89SC1369
322FS585

UNITED STATES CODE
(Illustrative Statute)

Citations to section "§" 700 of Title 18 of the United States Code, 1970 Edition and Supplement 2, 1972 are shown in the left margin of this page in the same form in which they appear in this volume. In Shepard's United States Citations, Statute Edition any citation to a section of the United States Code presently in effect is shown as is illustrated here and any citation to a section of the United States Code no longer in effect is shown as referring to the section number of the United States Code of the year when that section number last appeared.

Citations to each cited statutory provision are grouped as follows:

1. amendments, repeals, etc. by acts of Congress subsequent to 1962;
2. citations by the United States Supreme Court and the lower federal courts analyzed as to constitutionality or validity;
3. other citations by the United States Supreme Court and the lower federal courts;
4. citations in articles in the American Bar Association Journal;
5. citations in annotations of the Lawyers' Edition, United States Supreme Court Reports and of the American Law Reports;
6. citations to specific subdivisions.

For the purpose of illustration only, this grouping has been indicated by bracketing the citations accordingly. It will be noted that as yet there are no citations in group four.

The first citation shown indicates that section 700 of Title 18 was added "Ad" ·by an act of Congress printed in 82 United States Statutes at Large "St" at page 291. The section is next shown to have been held constitutional "C" by a lower federal court in a case reported in 302 Federal Supplement "FS" 1112 and cited without particular comment by the United States Supreme Court in a case reported in 394 United States Supreme Court Reports "US" 604 as well as in 22 Lawyers' Edition, United States Supreme Court Reports, Second Series "LE" 592 and 89 Supreme Court Reporter "SC" 1372. These references are followed by eight citations in lower federal court opinions reported in either the Federal Reporter, Second Series "F2d" or Federal Supplement. The section was also cited in an annotation "n" of the American Law Reports, Third Series " A3 "

Exhibit 49: Explanation on the *U.S.Code* in Shepard's *United States Citations.*

United
States
Statutes
at Large
(Not in
United
States
Code)

1968

May 29
P. L. 90-321
82 St. 146

§ 201
465F2d41
310FS355
323FS231
327FS256   3

7ARF961n   5

Subd. a
402US147
28LE688
91SC1358
7ARF951n   6
¶ 1
C422F2d586   2
309FS465
¶ 3
C422F2d586
309FS465
¶ 4   6
C422F2d586
309FS466
Subd. b
7ARF952n
§ 401
et seq.
55ABA27   4
§ 404
Subd. b
A84St440
A86St382   1
§ 406
Subd. e
A86St382
§ 407
A86St382
§ 501
et seq.
55ABA27
§ 503
Subd. 3
326FS430
§ 504
Subd. b
332FS407
Subd. d
Ad84St1114   1

UNITED STATES STATUTES AT LARGE
(Illustrative Statute)

———

Citations to an act of the Congress of the United States of May 29, 1968, Public Law "P.L." 90–321, Volume 82 of the United States Statutes at Large "St." at page 146 are shown in the left margin of this page in the same form in which they appear in this volume. This act has not been included in the United States Code.

Citations to each cited statutory provision are grouped as follows:

1. amendments, repeals, etc. by acts of Congress;

2. citations by the United States Supreme Court and the lower federal courts analyzed as to constitutionality or validity;

3. other citations by the United States Supreme Court and the lower federal courts;

4. citations in articles in the American Bar Association Journal;

5. citations in annotations of the Lawyers' Edition, United States Supreme Court Reports and of the American Law Reports;

6. citations to specific subdivisions.

For the purpose of illustration only, this grouping has been indicated by bracketing the citations accordingly.

In indicating the legislative and judicial operation of a cited statute, the letter-form abbreviations shown on page 16 are used.

The first citations shown indicate that section "§" 201 of the act has been cited by the lower federal courts in cases reported in 465 Federal Reporter, Second Series "F2d" 41, 310 Federal Supplement "FS" 355, 323 FS 231 and 327 FS 256 and that the section has been referred to in an annotation "n" in 7 American Law Reports, Federal "ARF" 961.

Citing references to specific subdivisions are then shown. Subdivision "Subd." a of section 201 has been cited by the United States Supreme Court in a case reported in 402 United States Supreme Court Reports "US" 147 as well as in 28 Lawyers' Edition, United States Supreme Court Reports, Second Series "LE" 688 and 91 Supreme Court Reporter "SC" 1358 and subdivision a was cited also in 7 ARF 951n. Paragraph "¶" 1 and paragraphs 3 and 4 of subdivision a were held constitutional "C" in 422 F2d 586 and cited in 309 FS 465 and 466. Subdivision b was cited in an American Law Reports, Federal, annotation.

Exhibit 50: Explanation on the *Statutes at Large* in Shepard's *United States Citations.*

In the Shepard's state citators, statutes are usually listed by their citations in the latest code edition. Where the code is completely lacking in authority, as in Pennsylvania, they may use the session law approach. Even if the code is used as the basis of listing, there will still be many statutes not in the code which will be listed in Shepard's by their *session law* citation. Citators for state legislation are similar in format to those for federal statutes, as illustrated in Exhibits 49 and 50 above.

Shepard's citators can be used and, in fact, often *must* be used for the following purposes: to verify the current status of particular laws; to trace the legislative and judicial history of particular laws to determine whether they have been changed or affected by later enactments or judicial interpretations; and to develop further research leads to court decisions, attorney general opinions or legal periodical articles.

Shepard's statutory citators typically cover the following classes of cited and citing materials:

Cited Material	Citing Material
Constitutions	Later statutes and legislative changes
Codes	
Session laws	Cases
Treaties	Legal periodicals
Administrative regulations	Opinions of the Attorney General
Municipal charters	*A.L.R.* annotations
Local ordinances	
Court rules	
Jury instructions	

Shepard's also publishes *U.S. Patents and Trademark Citations*, which lists citations to patents, copyrights and trademarks.

Shepard's uses the following symbols to indicate significant actions which have been taken with respect to a particular statute either by later legislative changes or court decisions:

ABBREVIATIONS—ANALYSIS

Form of Statute

Amend.	Amendment	¶	Paragraph	Subch.	Subchapter
Art.	Article	P.L.	Public Law	Subcl.	Subclause
Ch.	Chapter	Pr.L.	Private Law	Subd.	Subdivision
Cl.	Clause	Proc.	Proclamation	Sub ¶	Subparagraph
Ex. Ord.	Executive Order	Pt.	Part	Subsec.	Subsection
H.C.R.	House Concurrent Resolution	Res.	Resolution	Vet. Reg.	Veterans' Regulations
No.	Number	§	Section		
		St.	Statutes at Large		

Operation of Statute
  Legislative

A	(amended)	Statute amended.
Ad	(added)	New section added.
E	(extended)	Provisions of an existing statute extended in their application to a later statute, or allowance of additional time for performance of duties required by a statute within a limited time.
L	(limited)	Provisions of an existing statute declared not to be extended in their application to a later statute.
R	(repealed)	Abrogation of an existing statute.
Re-en	(re-enacted)	Statute re-enacted.
Rn	(renumbered)	Renumbering of existing sections.
Rp	(repealed in part)	Abrogation of part of an existing statute.
Rs	(repealed and superseded)	Abrogation of an existing statute and substitution of new legislation therefor.
Rv	(revised)	Statute revised.
S	(superseded)	Substitution of new legislation for an existing statute not expressly abrogated.
Sd	(suspended)	Statute suspended.
Sdp	(suspended in part)	Statute suspended in part.
Sg	(supplementing)	New matter added to an existing statute.
Sp	(superseded in part)	Substitution of new legislation for part of an existing statute not expressly abrogated.
Va	(validated)	

Judicial			
C	Constitutional.	V	Void or invalid.
U	Unconstitutional.	Va	Valid.
Up	Unconstitutional in part.	Vp	Void or invalid in part.

Exhibit 51: Shepard's abbreviations for statutory material in its *United States Citations*.

Although Shepard's is the primary and indispensable citator in American legal research, there are other citators which may be useful for limited purposes. Looseleaf services frequently provide a citator of sorts for statutes in their fields. Because of the prompt supplementation of these services, they often inform the subscribers of changes in particular laws more quickly than that information is conveyed by Shepard's. In addition, the looseleaf services provide the text of the statute itself which can not be found in Shepard's. However, looseleaf services exist for only some subjects and even in those areas do not offer as complete coverage of citations to cases and other materials as does Shepard's.

For local ordinances, Shepard's offers its *Ordinance Law Annotations* (1969–1970, 6 vols.), which digests leading American state decisions that interpret or apply city and county ordinances. These annotations are arranged alphabetically by 157 broad topics and then subdivided by more specific subjects. It provides a unique research tool which is closer to a digest than to the usual Shepard's citator and is kept up to date by annual pocket parts. (See Exhibit 52.)

§ 16. Prohibiting Most Businesses

A Sunday closing ordinance prohibiting most businesses from operating on Sunday is not unconstitutional as violating any provision of the 1st Amendment of the U.S. Constitution, or as impinging on freedom of conscience or compelling or denying the observance of any religious duty.

> **NC**   State v McGee (1953) 237 NC 633, 75 SE2d 783.

D. Invalid Sunday Closing

§ 17. When Enabling Statute Is Void

An ordinance restricting or regulating the carrying on of business on Sunday, which derives its legislative grant from an invalid statute, is itself void.

> **NC**   High Point Surplus v Pleasants (1965) 264 NC 650, 142 SE2d 697.

§ 18. Discriminatory Closing

An ordinance making it unlawful to carry on certain businesses on Sunday is invalid where it prohibits the exercise of businesses or occupations legitimate and lawful within themselves, which do not carry inherent reasons for special discrimination, while allowing general privileges to similar occupations.

> **Ariz**   Elliott v State (1926) 29 Ariz 389, 242 P 340, 46 ALR 284.

An ordinance may prohibit the conducting of businesses or occupations on Sunday, except those of necessity or charity, on the ground that the peace, good order, good government, and welfare of the inhabitants will be promoted. But if such an ordinance is discriminatory or amounts to class or special legislation, it is not authorized.

> **Colo**   Allen v Colorado Springs (1937) 101 Colo 498, 75 P2d 141.

An ordinance prohibiting the operation of any business on Sunday, but excepting motels, restaurants, eating places, drug, tobacco and confectionery stores, news dealers, ice dealers, shoe shine parlors, garages, gasoline filling stations, telephone exchanges, telegraph offices, and moving picture theaters, is invalid as arbitrary and discriminatory,

931

Exhibit 52:   Shepard's *Ordinance Law Annotations,* showing cases digested under the topic "Sunday Laws."

Shepard's also provides coverage of local ordinances in two ways in its various state statutory citators. The ordinances of the municipalities of each state are included as cited material in the statutory citator for that state, with judicial citations, legislative references, attorney general opinions and legal periodical articles listed as citing material where appropriate. (See Exhibit 53.) In addition, subject indexes to local ordinances are included in the statutory citators. (See Exhibit 54 below.) These indexes enable the researcher to identify the relevant ordinance, which can then be located in the citator section for ordinances and shepardized there.

REVISED ORDINANCES OF BOSTON, 1961 (As Amended, 1963)　　Ch. 29

Exhibit 53:　Local ordinances (of the City of Boston) listed as cited material in *Shepard's Massachusetts Citations,* illustrating such coverage in various state statutory citators.

[*158*]

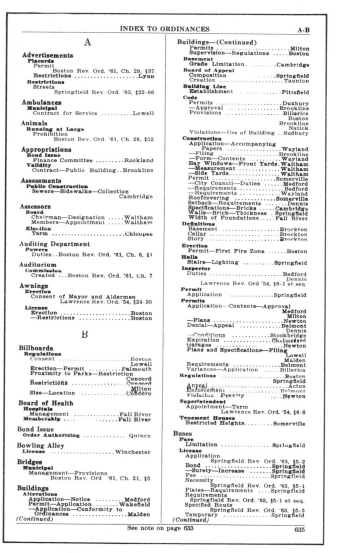

See note on page 633

Exhibit 54: Subject index to local ordinances (from *Shepard's Massachusetts Citations*), appearing in Shepard's various state statutory citators.

[*159*]

CHAPTER V
LEGISLATIVE HISTORY

Statutory research often involves the investigation of the pre-enactment history of an existing statute or the current status of a proposed law which is then under consideration in the legislature. Both of these inquiries require the study of what we call "legislative history". The ambiguities which occur so frequently in the language of our laws also require lawyers and scholars to locate legislative documents from which they can learn the intent of Congress or a state legislature. There are thus two main purposes in this area of research: (a) to determine the meaning or intent of a particular *enactment* from the documents of its consideration by the legislature; and (b) to ascertain the status of a pending *bill* during the legislative session, or to follow the steps in its legislative progress.

SOURCES OF LEGISLATIVE HISTORY

The principal sources in which evidence of congressional intent may be sought are the following:

1. Presidential Messages. Although not legislative in origin, these documents accompany legislation proposed to Congress by the executive

and often explain the purpose and intent of the draftsmen. Messages are also frequently issued when the President signs or vetoes proposed legislation. They are printed and indexed in the *Congressional Record,* appear in the *Weekly Compilation of Presidential Documents*, and the *House* and *Senate Journals*, and are also issued as *House* and *Senate Documents*. Important messages are reproduced in the advance sheets of the *U. S. Code Congressional and Administrative News*. While only indirect evidence of congressional intent, they provide helpful background information for that purpose. For an example of a presidential message, see Exhibit 55.

WEEKLY COMPILATION OF PRESIDENTIAL DOCUMENTS

OCCUPATIONAL SAFETY AND HEALTH

The President's Message to the Congress.   August 6, 1969

To the Congress of the United States:

   Technological progress can be a mixed blessing. The same new method or new product which improves our lives can also be the source of unpleasantness and pain. For man's lively capacity to innovate is not always matched by his ability to understand his innovations fully, to use them properly, or to protect himself against the unforeseen consequences of the changes he creates.

   The side effects of progress present special dangers in the workplaces of our country. For the working man and woman, the byproducts of change constitute an especially serious threat. Some efforts to protect the safety and health of the American worker have been made in the past both by private industry and by all levels of government. But new technologies have moved even faster to create newer dangers. Today we are asking our workers to perform far different tasks from those they performed five or fifteen or fifty years ago. It is only right that the protection we give them is also up-to-date.

   There has been much discussion in recent months about the quality of the environment in which Americans live. It is important to note in this regard that during their working years most American workers spend

---

Exhibit 55: A presidential message on the subject of occupational safety and health.

2. Congressional Bills. Differences between the several bills leading to a particular enactment may aid in determining legislative intent, since deletions, additions, or other variations in the bill at different stages of the legislative process imply deliberate choices of language by the legislators. The bills of each house are individually numbered in series and retain their identifying number through both sessions of a Congress. At the end of a term, a bill lapses and must be reintroduced and renumbered if it is to be considered. (The term of a Congress is two years, consisting of two one-year sessions.) The bill number is used in all status tables and on most legislative documents to identify the proposed legislation. It also appears on the law after enactment, both in its slip form and in the bound volumes of the *Statutes at Large.*

Bills are received in the larger research law libraries in a slip form and can also be obtained individually from the clerk of the House or Senate, their sponsor, or the appropriate congressional committee, if requested promptly after their introduction. Commerce Clearing House through its expensive *Legislative Reporting Service* also regularly supplies subscribers with bills on particular subjects. Microform editions of bills and most other legislative documents referred to in this chapter are commercially available.

The form of a bill is shown in Exhibit 56 below. (Note that the exhibits that follow in this chapter illustrate various stages in the progress of this bill through Congress and its treatment in several legislative guides.)

91ST CONGRESS
1ST SESSION

S. 2193

IN THE SENATE OF THE UNITED STATES

MAY 16, 1969

Mr. WILLIAMS of New Jersey (for himself, Mr. KENNEDY, Mr. MONDALE, and Mr. YARBOROUGH) introduced the following bill; which was read twice and referred to the Committee on Labor and Public Welfare

A BILL

To authorize the Secretary of Labor to set standards to assure safe and healthful working conditions for working men and women; to assist and encourage States to participate in efforts to assure such working conditions; to provide for research, information, education, and training in the field of occupational safety and health, and for other purposes.

1   *Be it enacted by the Senate and House of Representa-*

2   *tives of the United States of America in Congress assembled,*

3   That this Act may be cited as the "Occupational Safety and

4   Health Act of 1969".

VII—O

Exhibit 56: A congressional bill on occupational safety and health.

3. Hearings. These are transcripts of testimony before Senate and House committees on proposed legislation or on a particular subject under congressional investigation. In addition to such testimony, exhibits contributed by interested individuals or groups are also included (e. g. letters, statements, statistical material, newspaper articles, etc.). The purpose of a hearing is to determine the need for new legislation or to bring before Congress information relevant to its preparation and enactment. Hearings are not, however, held for all legislation, nor are all hearings published.

In using hearings to explore the background of a particular piece of legislation, one should keep in mind that the quality of the testimony given at hearings will vary depending on the bias of the testifying witness and his or her degree of expertise on the subject under investigation. Thus, as a source of legislative intent, hearings are less authoritative than committee reports and must be used with discrimination.

A search for relevant hearings should not be limited to the session in which the particular law is enacted, since hearings may extend over more than one session and be issued in multiple parts and volumes. There is no uniformity in the numbering of the various series of hearings issued by the committees of Congress, but they are generally identified by the *name of the committee* hold-

ing them, the *session* and *Congress* during which they are held, the *title* which appears on the cover, the *bill* on which they are being held, and the *date span* of the testimony.

Hearings are available from the committee conducting them, from the Government Printing Office, or occasionally from members of the committee. They are listed in the *Monthly Catalog of U. S. Government Publications* by committee and subject, though not by bill number. Since 1970, the difficulty in locating hearings has been eased by *Congressional Information Service/Index,* a finding aid described below, which provides indexing to congressional hearings by subject, bill number, committee, title, and witness.

The U. S. Senate Library publishes an extremely useful retrospective index to the hearings of both houses entitled *Cumulative Index of Congressional Committee Hearings* (formerly *Index of Congressional Committee Hearings*). It is arranged in three parts—by subject, bill number and committee. The first index, published in 1929, covered hearings prior to March 4, 1929. Its various supplements extend the coverage to 1971 and additional updating is planned.

Exhibit 57 below shows the title page of a typical hearing.

OCCUPATIONAL SAFETY AND HEALTH ACT, 1970

HEARINGS

BEFORE THE

SUBCOMMITTEE ON LABOR

OF THE

COMMITTEE ON LABOR AND PUBLIC WELFARE UNITED STATES SENATE

NINETY-FIRST CONGRESS

FIRST AND SECOND SESSIONS

ON

S. 2193 and S. 2788

BILLS ON OCCUPATIONAL SAFETY AND HEALTH

SEPTEMBER 30, NOVEMBER 4, 21, 24, 26, DECEMBER 9, 15, 16, 1969 ; MARCH 7, AND APRIL 10, 28, 1970

PART 1

Printed for the use of the Committee on Labor and Public Welfare

U.S. GOVERNMENT PRINTING OFFICE

42-537 O   WASHINGTON : 1970

Exhibit 57: Title page of a hearing on various bills related to occupational safety and health.

The *Monthly Catalog,* incidentally, is the most complete listing of U. S. Government documents and includes many documents of legal significance.   It is issued monthly with a detailed subject and author index and its December issue contains a cumulative index of the entire year.   It is a particularly important finding tool for legislative material, since it lists each individual committee report, document, published hearing, message and enactment, as it is published.   There is often, however, a substantial time lag between publication and listing, during which the supply of documents may be exhausted.   The *Catalog* also lists some publications which are not on sale or publicly available, although its statements as to availability and source are not always accurate. Exhibit 58 below illustrates a typical page from the *Monthly Catalog.*

GOVERNMENT PUBLICATIONS

Judiciary Committee, Senate
Washington, DC 20510

11132 Federal Trade Commission procedures, hearings before Subcommittee on
Administrative Practices and Procedures, 91st Congress, 1st session, on
Agency responsiveness to public needs, Federal Trade Commission.
pt. 1. Sept. 12 and 16, 1969. 1970. iii+244 p. † ● Item 1042
L.C. card 77–607946   Y 4.J 89/2 : F 31/12/pt.1

11133 Increasing Sherman act criminal penalties, hearings before Subcommittee
on Antitrust and Monopoly, 91st Congress, 2d session, on S. 3036, Mar. 4
and 5, 1970. 1970. iii+57 p. il. † ● Item 1042
L.C. card 70–608053   Y 4.J 89/2 : Sh 5/3

11134 Threat of U.S. security posed by stepped-up Sino-Soviet hostilities (testi-
mony of Stefan T. Possony), hearing before Subcommittee to Investigate
Administration of Internal Security Act and Other Internal Security
Laws, 91st Congress, 2d session, Mar. 17, 1970. 1970. ii+140+vii p. il.
2 maps. * Paper, $1.00. ● Item 1042
L.C. card 74–608046   Y 4.J 89/2 : Si 6

Labor and Public Welfare Committee, Senate
Washington, DC 20510

11135 Alcoholism and narcotics, hearings before Special Subcommittee on Alcoholism and Narcotics, 91st Congress, 2d session, on inquiry into problem of alcoholism and narcotics.
pt. 5. Des Moines, Iowa, Feb. 14, 1970. 1970. iv+895–1014 p. † ● Item 1043
L.C. card 77–606161   Y 4.L 11/2 : Al 1/4/pt.5

11136 American folklife foundation act, hearing before Subcommittee on Education, 91st Congress, 2d session, on S. 1591, May 18, 1970. 1970. iv+96 p.
il. † ● Item 1043
L.C. card 74–608054   Y 4.L 11/2 : Am 3/2

11137 Federal drug abuse and drug dependence prevention, treatment, and rehabilitation act of 1970, hearings before Special Subcommittee on Alcoholism and Narcotics, 91st Congress, 2d session. † ● Item 1043
L.C. card 70–607770   Y 4.L 11/2 : D 84/2/pt.(nos.)
pt. 1. Mar. 1625, 1970. 1970. v+1–305 p.
pt. 2. Mar. 26–Apr. 15, 1970. 1970. v+397–666 p. il.
pt. 3. Apr 10–11, 1970. 1970. iv+667–817 p. il. [Hearings held in Winchester
and Lynn, Mass.]

11138 Manpower development and training legislation, 1970, hearings before Subcommittee on Employment, Manpower, and Poverty, 91st Congress, 1st
and 2d sessions, on S. 3867, S. 2838, [and] S. 3878.
pt. 2. Feb. 20–Mar. 18, 1970. 1970. vi+743–1091 p. il. [Hearings held in Cleveland, Ohio, and Washington, D.C.] † ● Item 1043
L.C. card 71–606926   Y 4.L 11/2 : M 31/7/970/pt.2

11139 Migrant and seasonal farmworker powerlessness, hearings before Subcommittee on Migratory Labor, 91st Congress, 1st and 2d sessions. †
● Item 1043
L.C. card 77–607666   Y 4.L 11/2 : M 58/8/pt.(nos.)
pt. 2.   Migrant subculture, July 28 ,1970. 1970. v+333–548 p. il.
pt. 3–A. Efforts to organize, July 15, 1970. 1970. vi+549–870 p.

11140 Occupational safety and health act, 1970, hearings before Subcommittee
on Labor, 91st Congress, 1st and 2d sessions, on S. 2193 and S. 2788. †
● Item 1043
L.C. card 71–608099   Y 4.L 11/2 : Sa 1/3/970/pt.(nos.)
pt. 1. Sept. 30, 1969–Apr. 28, 1970. 1970. xI+1–1006 p. il.
pt. 2. May 5, 1970. vi+1007–1790 p. il.

11141 Prescription drug legislation, hearings before Subcommittee on Health,
91st Congress, 2d session, on S. 3096, S. 3651, S. 3652, S. 3297, and related
bills. Apr. 28 and 29, 1970. 1970. v+258 p. † ● Item 1043
L.C. card 73–607823   Y 4.L 11/2 : D 84/3

Exhibit 58: *Monthly Catalog of U.S. Government Publications*, showing entries for congressional hearings.

Most publications listed in the *Monthly Catalog* are available at federal depository libraries, one of which is located in each congressional district. Libraries designated as Regional Depositories are required to retain one copy of every government publication reviewed; other depositories may be selective. The September issue of the *Catalog* includes a list of these libraries and their locations.

4. Committee Reports. Reports are the most important source of legislative history. They are issued by the congressional committees of both houses (and by conference committees of the two houses) on each bill reported out of committee for action. Reports frequently include the text of the bill, describe its contents and purposes, and give reasons for the committee's recommendations (sometimes including a minority view). They are also issued by committees on various investigations, studies and hearings not related to a particular bill under consideration. Committee reports are published in a numbered series which indicates house, Congress, and report number, e. g., Senate Report No. 91–1282. Conference committee reports are included in the numbered series of House reports. Like all congressional documents, reports are listed in the *Monthly Catalog* and in many of the finding tools, described below.

Reports are sometimes available from the committee issuing them or from the clerk of the House or Senate, as the case may be. Many are placed on sale and can be purchased from the Government Printing Office. Reports on the most important enactments are also published selectively in the *U. S. Code Congressional and Administrative News* and all appear, along with House and Senate Documents, in the bound official compilation called the *Serial Set*. A typical report is illustrated in Exhibit 59 below.

Calendar No. 1300

| 91ST CONGRESS
2d Session | SENATE | REPORT
No. 91–1282 |

OCCUPATIONAL SAFETY AND HEALTH ACT OF 1970

OCTOBER 6–(legislative day, OCTOBER 5), 1970.—Ordered to be printed

Mr. WILLIAMS of New Jersey, from the Committee on Labor and Public Welfare, submitted the following

REPORT

together with

INDIVIDUAL AND MINORITY VIEWS

[To accompany S. 2193]

The Committee on Labor and Public Welfare, to which was referred the bill (S. 2193) to authorize the Secretary of Labor to set standards to assure safe and healthful working conditions for working men and women, to assist and encourage States to participate in efforts to assure such working conditions, to provide for research, information, education, and training in the field of occupational safety and health, and for other purposes, having considered the same, reports favorably thereon with an amendment (in the nature of a substitute) and recommends that the bill (as amended) do pass.

PURPOSE

The purpose of S. 2193 is to reduce the number and severity of work-related injuries and illnesses which, despite current efforts of employers and government, are resulting in ever-increasing human misery and economic loss.

The bill would achieve its purpose through programs of research, education and training, and through the development and administration, by the Secretary of Labor, of uniformly applied occupational safety and health standards. Such standards would be developed with the assistance of the Secretary of Health, Education and Welfare, and both their promulgation and their enforcement would be judicially reviewable. Encouragement is given to Federal-state cooperation, and financial assistance is authorized to enable states, under approved plans, to take over entirely and administer their own programs for achieving safe and healthful jobsites for the Nation's workers.

48–010—70——1

Exhibit 59: A congressional report, accompanying the proposed Occupational Safety and Health Act of 1970.

5. Debates. The *Congressional Record* is a nearly verbatim transcript of legislative debates and proceedings, published each day that one or both houses are in session. It is subject to revision only by members of Congress who wish to amend their own remarks. In addition, the Appendix to the *Congressional Record* includes extensions of floor remarks, exhibits from legislators, communications on pending legislation and almost any other material a congressman wishes to get into the *Record*. Beginning with the Eightieth Congress, each issue contains a Daily Digest which summarizes the day's activities, including news of legislation introduced, reported on or passed and actions taken within various committees. There is a fortnightly index, and at the end of the session, a bound edition usually consisting of over thirty volumes. That compilation includes a cumulative index (with entries by subject, title and member of Congress), a cumulation of the Daily Digest, and a complete status table for that session entitled History of Bills and Resolutions. (For a description of this status table, see page 178 below.) Since the Eighty-Third Congress, second session, the Appendix has not been included in the bound set, although the Index still cites to it. It is available on microfilm, however.

The *Congressional Record* differs from the *House* and *Senate Journals* in that the journals

do not include the verbatim debates. The journals merely record the proceedings, indicate whether there was debate, and report the resulting action and votes taken. The *Congressional Record* never contains hearings and only on rare occasions reports. <u>Some bills are read into the *Record*, but it is not to be considered a major source for bills.</u> Its importance is primarily as a report of debates and actions taken. For an excerpt from the *Record,* see Exhibit 60 below.

36508   CONGRESSIONAL RECORD — SENATE   *October 13, 1970*

ought not be dispersed throughout the Office of Education, not administered by bureaus which are also responsible for other programs involving greater amounts of grant money.

The Committee believes that the environment education program should have viability and that its Director should have sufficient stature as to have direct access to the Commissioner. Moreover, the administrative unit charged with responsibility for the program ought to be staffed with a sufficient number of specialists. If the environmental education program is placed in one of the present bureaus, its Director would be at least three degrees removed from the office of the Commissioner and would have to compete with other programs for personnel, at a time when adequate staffing and proper administrative direction are difficult problems for the Office of Education.

It is for these reasons that the committee recommends the establishment of the Office of Environmental Education by law. Further, the committee recommends, in section 3(d), language which permits appropriations to be used for the administration of the program.

The intent of Congress to establish an independent office in the Office of the Commissioner is unequivocally clear.

OCCUPATIONAL SAFETY AND HEALTH ACT OF 1970

Mr. MANSFIELD. Mr. President, I ask unanimous consent that the pending

A bill (S. 2193) to authorize the Secretary of Labor to set standards to assure safe and healthful working conditions for working men and women; to assist and encourage States to participate in efforts to assure such working conditions; to provide for research, information, education, and training in the field of occupational safety and health; and for other purposes.

The PRESIDING OFFICER. The question is on agreeing to the motion to proceed to the consideration of the bill.

The Senator from New York is recognized.

Mr. JAVITS. Mr. President, a parliamentary inquiry.

The PRESIDING OFFICER. The Senator will state it.

Mr. JAVITS. Mr. President, am I correct in assuming that the motion is debatable?

The PRESIDING OFFICER. The motion is debatable.

Mr. JAVITS. Mr. President, I would like to be recognized, if I may, for a moment. Will the Senator from Montana yield to me?

Mr. MANSFIELD. I yield the floor.

The PRESIDING OFFICER. The Senator will be in order. Senators and staff members will take their seats.

Mr. JAVITS. Mr. President, I am the

the disagreement. But the fundamental point is that the bill is extremely important and extremely desirable for all the workers.

I doubt very much that the bill could be finished in the 24 or 36 hours we have remaining. The Senator from Colorado (Mr. DOMINICK)—whether he does so by a substitute or by amendment—he has some 19 amendments, I understand. Every one of them is substantive and is not a facade or an effort to delay the matter.

However, Mr. President, I hope the Senate will proceed to the consideration of the bill. At the very least, if we cannot finish it by tomorrow night, it will be the pending business when we return.

We can pass the bill, and it should be passed. It is a critically important piece of legislation.

I hope that Senators will not be confused and believe that the amendments represent management-labor differences. In all honesty, most of them do not.

The bill should be passed.

Mr. President, I think it is important and fair to rebut any idea that any Senators have sought to stall the bill and not come to grips with it. The idea that this should be challenged and debated and that it should have the deliberate consideration of the Senate is only fair.

The PRESIDING OFFICER. The bill will be reported.

The assistant legislative clerk read as follows:

deal of difference of opinion on certain matters. Although I have my views—and I tried to work them out on the committee—I think there is some substance to

that feel the same way. That was why objection was made to the unanimous-consent request that had been propounded on two other occasions.

Exhibit 60:   An excerpt from the debates on the Occupational Safety and Health Act of 1970, as reported in the *Congressional Record.*

The predecessors of the *Congressional Record,* which began in 1873, are: the *Annals of Congress* (1789–1824); the *Register of Debates* (1824–1837); and the *Congressional Globe* (1833–1873).

6. House and Senate Documents. Only occasionally useful as sources of legislative history, House and Senate Documents include reports of some congressional investigations not in the regular committee reports. They also contain presidential messages, special studies or exhibits prepared by or at the request of Congress, and communications to Congress from executive departments or agencies. They are listed in the *Monthly Catalog* and in the *Congressional Information Service/Index,* described below, and are published by the Government Printing Office in a numbered series for each house and Congress. Identification is by house, Congress, and document number, similar to the identification scheme for the Report series.

7. Senate Executive Documents and Reports. These are restricted or confidential publications of the Senate forming an essential part of the legislative histories of treaties. The Senate Executive Documents contain the texts of treaties before the Senate for its advice and consent and related correspondence from the President and Secretary of State. Senate Executive Reports are issued by the Foreign Relations Committee after

its consideration of individual treaties. Only
when released by the Senate are they listed in the
Monthly Catalog and made available to the public.
They are not, however, routinely sent to depository libraries. The Senate Executive Reports are
numbered, while the Documents receive an alphabetical designation. Both also require the Congress and session number for identification.

OUTLINE OF LEGISLATIVE STEPS
AND RELEVANT DOCUMENTS

An understanding of the legislative process is
essential for one compiling a legislative history.
Each of the relevant documents of legislative history can be associated with the stage of law-making at which it is issued. The following are the
most significant steps and their related documents:

Action	Document
Preliminary Inquiry	Hearings on the general sub- ject of the proposed legislation. (N. B. Relevant hearings may have been held in a previous Congressional session or may run through several sessions.)
Executive Recommendation	Presidential Message proposing an administration bill.
Introduction of Bill	Original text—Slip Bill as in- troduced.
Referred to Committee	Committee Print of Bill.

Action	Document
Hearings on Bill	Hearings—published transcript and exhibits, sometimes including a Hearing Print of Bill.
Executive Agency Recommendations	House or Senate Document or in *Congressional Record Appendix*.
Reported out of Committee	Committee Report including Committee's version or Reported Print of Bill.
Legislative Debates	*Congressional Record,* sometimes including texts of bill in amended forms.
Passage or defeat	Final House or Senate version of bill.
Other House	Generally same procedure and documents as above.
Referred to Conference Committee (if texts passed by each House differ)	Conference Committee version of bill; Conference Committee Report.
Passage by 2nd House	Enrolled Bill signed by Speaker of House or President of Senate and then sent to President (not available to public).
If vetoed	Presidential Veto Message.
If approved by President	Slip law (also *U.S.C.C.A.N.* & *U.S.C.S.* advance sheet). Subsequently bound into *Statutes at Large* and annual volumes of *U.S.C.C.A.N.* and *U.S.C.S.* Then classified in the appropriate titles of the *U. S. Code* and its unofficial, annotated editions. Presidential Message may also be issued on signing of the law.

FINDING TOOLS

The essential finding tools for locating and tracing congressional bills and their legislative history are status tables, which are published in a variety of forms. Status tables are lists of pending bills and resolutions, with statements of the actions taken thereon and references to the documents which reflect such actions. They are arranged by bill numbers and often include a short digest of each bill. Status tables enable the researcher to trace the history of a bill or locate legislative documents which may aid in ascertaining its congressional intent.

Some finding tools are official publications, while others are produced by commercial publishers. The latter are often more useful since they usually include other research aids in addition to status tables, are updated more frequently, and/or contain more comprehensive indexing. The following publications are themselves status tables or contain status tables and additional references to legislative information.

1. Congressional Record-History of Bills and Resolutions. Arranged by bill and resolution number, this table includes a brief summary of each bill and resolution, the committee investigating the proposed legislation, and the action taken on the legislation to date, including amendments and passage. It is the best source of page references to debates within the *Record,* includes House and

Senate Report numbers, if any, and public law number if the measure has been enacted.

This table is published fortnightly in the Index to the *Record* and then cumulated for each session in the bound Index volume. The final cumulative History is very useful for retrospective research and is weak only in lacking references to hearings. The fortnightly listing is less helpful since it lists only those bills and resolutions acted upon within the preceding two week period. However, the information supplied on each bill is complete from date of introduction to the present. This table is illustrated in Exhibit 61 below.

2176–2362   **SENATE BILLS**

S. 2176—To implement the Convention on Offenses and Certain Other Acts Committed on Board Aircraft, and for other purposes.
From Committee on Commerce, 27879.—Reported (S. Rept. 91–1083), 27879.—Passed Senate, 20040.—Referred to House Committee on Interstate and Foreign Commerce, 28990.—Rules suspended. Passed House (in lieu of 14301), 34808.—Examined and signed, 35398, 35595.—Presented to the President, 35597.—Approved [Public Law 91–449], 37264.

S. 2193—To amend the title so as to read: "to assure safe and healthful working conditions for working men and women; by authorizing enforcement of the standards developed under the act; by assisting and encouraging the States in their efforts to assure safe and healthful working conditions; by providing for research, information, education, and training in the field of occupational safety and health; and for other purposes."
Cosponsor, 4266.—Cosponsors added, 14296, 37546.—Reported with amendment (S.

Rept. 91–1282), 35087.—Debated, 35968, 36369, 36508, 36511, 36520, 36529, 36534, 37317, 37601, 37605, 37613, 37615.—Amended and passed Senate, 37632.—Amended and passed House (in lieu of H.R. 16785), 38724.—Title amended, 38722.—House insists on its amendments and asks for a conference, 38733.—Conferees appointed, 38733.—Senate disagrees to amendments of House and agrees to a conference, 39193.—Conferees appointed, 39193. Conference report (H. Rept. 91–1765), submitted in Senate and agreed to 41760. Conference report (H Rept. 91–1765) submitted in House and agreed to, 41965, 42199.—Examined and signed, 42666, 43257.—Presented to the President, 43258.—Approved [Public Law 91–596], 44064.

S. 2208—To authorize the Secretary of the Interior to study the feasibility and desirability of a national lakeshore on Lake Tahoe in the States of Nevada and California, and for other purposes.
Cosponsor added, 12706.—From Committee on Interior and Insular Affairs, 14816.—

Exhibit 61: History of Bills and Resolutions table in the *Congressional Record,* providing a brief summary of S.2193 and actions taken thereon.

2. Congressional Record-Daily Digest. This daily summary of congressional activity is published in each issue of the *Record* and includes a subject index which serves as a status table for bills acted upon that day. The Daily Digest cumulates at the end of each session into a separate bound volume of the *Record* which contains the final History of Bills Enacted into Public Law. This table is a useful one, although it lacks the debate references found in the History of Bills and Resolutions. It is illustrated in Exhibit 62 below.

3. Digest of Public General Bills and Resolutions. This publication of the Congressional Research Service of the Library of Congress is primarily useful for its synopses of all public bills and resolutions introduced in each session of Congress. These digests are arranged by bill or resolution number for each house, with somewhat fuller coverage for those measures which have been reported. A two-part status table provides lengthy abstracts and brief legislative histories first for measures that have been enacted into law (arranged by public law number) and then for all other measures upon which action has been taken (arranged by bill and resolution number). The legislative history for each item includes the date reported, the report number, date of consideration and passage, and conference or presidential action taken. No information on hearings is included.

HISTORY OF BILLS ENACTED INTO PUBLIC LAW (91ST CONG., 2D SESS.)

(Cross-reference of bill number to public law number may be found on pp. D741–D742)

Title	Bill No.	Date introduced	Committee House	Committee Senate	Date reported House	Date reported Senate	Report No. House	Report No. Senate	Page House	Page Senate	Date of passage House	Date of passage Senate	PL Date approved	PL No.
Designating the first week in May of each year as National Employ the Older Worker Week.	S.J. Res. 74	Mar. 10, 1969	Jud	Jud		Sept. 21		91-1207	40917	33349	Dec. 10	Sept. 23	Dec. 28	91-593
To authorize the President to proclaim the first full calendar week in May of each year as "Clean Water for America Week."	S.J. Res. 172	Feb. 10	Jud	Jud		Feb. 16		91-703	40917	3496	Dec. 10	Feb. 17	Dec. 28	91-594
Authorizing President to designate the third Sunday in June of each year as Father's Day.	S.J. Res. 187	Mar. 25	Jud	Jud		Sept. 21		91-1209	40916	33150	Dec. 10	Sept. 23	Dec. 28	91-595
To establish comprehensive safety and health standards for the American worker.	S. 2193 (H.R. 19375)	May	E&L	LPW	July 9	Oct. 6	91-1291	91-1282	38724	37632	Nov. 24	Nov. 17	Dec. 29	91-596
Providing for inspection of certain egg products by the Department of Agriculture.	H.R. 19888 (S. 2116)	Dec. 8	Agr	Agr	Dec. 3	Jan. 28	91-1670	91-659	41116	41338, 2089	Dec. 11	Dec. 14, Feb. 2	Dec. 29	91-597
To establish a Federal Broker-Dealer Insurance Corporation.	H.R. 19331 (S. 2348)	Sept. 1	IFC	BC	Oct. 21	Sept. 21	91-1613	91-1218	39370	40907	Dec. 1	Dec. 16	Dec. 30	91-598
To authorize U.S. participation in increase in the resources of certain international financial institutions.	H.R. 18306	July 8	IFC	FR	July 14	Sept. 24	91-1300	91-1241	31477	42913	Sept. 14	Dec. 21	Dec. 30	91-599
To extend and improve programs under the Library Services and Construction Act.	(H.R. 3318) 3365	Jan. 2	E&L	LPW	Dec. 3	Sept. 9	91-1659	91-1162	40181	32871	Dec. 7	Sept. 2	Dec. 30	91-600
To authorize the establishment of standards for the child-resistant packaging of hazardous substances.	(H.R. 2162)	May 1, 1969	IFC	Com	Dec. 1	May 6	91-1642	91-845	40193	14797	Dec. 7	May 1	Dec. 30	91-601
To provide that the President transmit his Economic Report to the Congress not later than Feb. 1, 1971, and that the Joint Economic Committee file its report thereon with the House not later than Mar. 1, 1971.	H.J. Res. 1417	Dec. 1	MMF	Com	Aug. 11	Dec. 9	91-1404	91-1424	41480	41765	Dec. 15	Dec. 16	Dec. 31	91-602
To authorize regulations to assist the United Seamen's Service to provide facilities and services to U.S. merchant seamen.	H.R. 15549	Jan. 2	IFC	PW	June 3	Sept. 17	91-1146	91-1196	31441	41166	Sept. 14	Dec. 11	Dec. 31	91-603
Providing establishment of air quality standards.	H.R. 17255 (S. 4358)	Apr. 2	PW	PW	Oct. 2	Sept. 30	91-1534	91-1254	19244	33120	June 10	Sept. 22	Dec. 31	91-604
Federal-Aid Highway Amendments of 1970.	H.R. 19504 (S. 4415)	Sep. 29	PW	PW	Sept. 29	Aug. 31	91-1524	91-1157	38997	40095, 34995	Nov. 25	Dec. 7, Dec. 2	Dec. 31	91-605
To establish a comprehensive Federal program for disaster relief and assistance.	H.R. 3619	Mar. 20	BC	BC	July 23	Aug. 10	91-387	91-1084	34798	31058	Oct. 5	Sept. 9	Dec. 31	91-606
To amend the Bank Holding Company Act of 1956.	H.R. 6778	Feb. 12, 1969	BC	BC	Dec. 9	Dec. 18	91-1697	91-1497	33154	32136	Nov. 5, Dec. 10	Dec. 29	Dec. 31	91-607
To name a lock of the Cross-Florida Barge Canal as the "Henry Holland Buckman Lock."	H.R. 956 (S. 4368)	Jan. 3, 1969	BC	PW	Oct. 5	Sept. 21	91-1556	91-1216	40921	42773	Dec. 10	Dec. 8	Dec. 31	91-608
Housing and Urban Development Act of 1970.	H.R. 19436, H.R. 19401	Sept. 23, Sept. 22	BC, E&L	LPW	Dec. 3	Dec. 14	91-1660	91-1433	39842, 40184	40459, 42118	Dec. 3	Dec. 8, Dec. 27	Dec. 31	91-609, 91-610
To extend for 1 year the authorization for various programs under the Vocational Rehabilitation Act.	H.R. 19877 (S. 4572)	Nov. 0	PW	PW	Dec. 3	Dec. 8	91-1665	91-1422	40152	40620	Dec. 7	Dec. 9	Dec. 31	91-611
Omnibus rivers and harbors and flood control authorizations bill.	H.R. 6114	Feb. 4, 1969	Jud	Jud	Oct. 1	Oct. 8	91-1550	91-1295	35164	36316	Oct. 6	Oct. 12	Dec. 31	91-612
Private relief bill, and providing 3-year extension of exemption from marine safety standards of the vessel *Delta Queen*.	H.R. 6049	Feb. 4, 1969	WM	Fin	May 18	Dec. 16	91-1102	91-1465	20626	42354	June 22	Dec. 18	Dec. 31	91-613
To revise the definition of "metal bearing ores" in the tariff schedules. Establishing working capital fund for the Treasury Department, to continue certain excise taxes, and to accelerate the collection of estate and gift taxes.	H.R. 16199	Feb. 6	WM	Fin	May 13	Dec. 15	91-1078	91-1444	16131	43891	May 19	Dec. 29	Dec. 31	91-614

Exhibit 62: Daily Digest: History of Bills Enacted into Public Law, recording the steps in the passage of the Occupational Safety and Health Act of 1970.

During each congressional session, the *Digest* is issued in five or more cumulations with bi-weekly supplementation. The final cumulation in two volumes is helpful for retrospective searches.

Exhibit 63 illustrates the synopsis and legislative history of Public Law 91–596, the Occupational Safety and Health Act of 1970.

Considered in House 12/10/70.
Passed House (amend.) 12/10/70.
Senate agreed to House (amend.)
12/15/70.

Authorizes the President to designate the third Sunday in June, 1971 as "Fathers' Day".

Pub. L. 91–596.   Approved 12/29/70. S. 2193.
Reported in Senate 10/6/70,
S. Rept. 91–1282.
Considered in Senate 10/13/70;
11/16/70–11/17/70.
Passed Senate 11/17/70.
Brought to House floor by
unanimous consent 11/24/70.
Considered in House 11/24/70.
Passed House (amend.) 11/24/70.
Senate agreed to Conf. Rept.
12/16/70.
House agreed to Conf. Rept.
12/17/70. H. Rept. 91–1765.

Occupational Safety and Health Act – Makes it a finding of Congress that personal injuries and illnesses arising out of work impose a substantial burden upon interstate commerce; and declares a Congressional policy to assure as far as possible every working man and woman safe and healthful working conditions and to preserve our human resources.

Procedure Act) as an occupational safety or health standard any national consensus standard or any established Federal standard unless he determines promulgation would not result in improved safety or health for specifically designated employees.

Provides that the Secretary may request the recommendations of an advisory committee whenever he determines from information submitted in writing by an interested person, a representative of an employer or employee organization, a nationally recognized standard producing organization, the Secretary of Health, Education, and Welfare, the National Institute of Occupational Health and Safety, a State or political subdivision, or on the basis of his own information, that a rule (standard) should be promulgated.

Requires the Secretary to publish a proposed rule promulgating, modifying or revoking an occupational safety or health standard in the Federal Register and afford interested persons a period of 30 days after publication to submit written comments.

Permits any interested person to file with the Secretary written objections to the proposed rule and requesting a public hearing on or before the last day of the period.

Provides that where the Secretary determines that employees are being exposed to grave dangers from exposure to substances or agents determined to be toxic or physically harmful or from new hazards and that an emergency standard is necessary to

---

of employment free from recognized hazards so as to provide safe and healthful working conditions; and (2) must comply with occupational health and safety standards and rules, regulations and orders promulgated under this act, except as provided in section 16 (relating to State jurisdiction and State plans).

Directs the Secretary as soon as practicable after the effective date of the act, and until two years from such date, to promulgate (without regard to the rule making provisions of the Administrative

consent of any Federal agency, the services, facilities, or personnel of such Federal agency, with or without reimbursement, or of a State or its political subdivision with reimbursement; and (2) employ experts and consultants.

Provides that each committee is to include one or more designees of the Secretary of Health, Education, and Welfare, and may include employer and employee representatives in equal numbers, representatives of State and local safety agencies,

196

Exhibit 63:   Summary and legislative history of the Occupational Safety and Health Act of 1970, as it appears in the *Digest of Public General Bills and Resolutions.*

4. Legislative Calendars (for the House, Senate and various committees). Each house and most committees issue calendars of pending business for the use of their members. These calendars, occasionally available in law libraries, contain very useful status tables, including the House of Representatives' *Numerical Order of Bills and Resolutions Which Have Passed Either or Both Houses, and Bills Now Pending on the Calendar*. This status table is particularly valuable because of its frequency. It appears daily, is cumulative, and includes reported bills of both the House and Senate. The final issue comes out *before* the bound volumes of the *Congressional Record* and includes actions during both sessions of Congress. However, unlike the History of Bills and Resolutions, it does not include all bills introduced, but only those on which action was taken. Note that committee calendars are usually excellent sources of information on hearings.

5. Congressional Information Service/Index. This service, begun in 1970, attempts to index and abstract nearly all congressional publications, except the *Congressional Record*. Its indexing is extremely detailed, providing access to hearings, reports, and documents, by subject, title (both official and popular), name (corporate and individual), number if any, and, in case of hearings by witness. See Exhibits 64 and 65. The reference in the index is to the abstract por-

tion of the service. Exhibit 66 shows the abstract of the hearing on the Occupational Safety and Health Act.

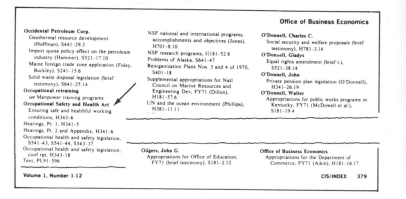

Office of Business Economics

Occidental Petroleum Corp.
Geothermal resource development (Hoffman), S441–29.3
Import quota policy effect on the petroleum industry (Hammer), S521–17.10
Maine foreign trade zone application (Foley, Buckley), S241–15.6
Solid waste disposal legislation (brief testimony), S641–25.14
Occupational retraining
see Manpower training programs
Occupational Safety and Health Act
Ensuring safe and healthful working conditions, H343–6
Hearings, Pt. 1, H341–5
Hearings, Pt. 2 and Appendix, H341–6
Occupational health and safety legislation, S541–43, S541–44, S543–37
Occupational health and safety legislation, conf rpt, H343–18
Text, PL91–596

NSF national and international programs, accomplishments and objectives (Jones), H701–8.10
NSF research programs, H181–52.8
Problems of Alaska, S641–47
Reorganization Plans Nos. 3 and 4 of 1970, S401–18
Supplemental appropriations for Natl Council on Marine Resources and Engineering Dev, FY71 (Dillon), H181–57.6
UN and the ocean environment (Phillips), H381–11.11

O'Donnell, Charles C.
Social security and welfare proposals (brief testimony), H781–3.14
O'Donnell, Gladys
Equal rights amendment (brief t.), S521–38.14
O'Donnell, John
Private pension plan legislation (O'Donnell), H341–26.19
O'Donnell, Walter
Appropriations for public works programs in Kentucky, FY71 (McDowell et al.), S181–19.4

Odgers, John G.
Appropriations for Office of Education, FY71 (brief testimony), S181–2.12

Office of Business Economics
Appropriations for the Department of Commerce, FY71 (Aikin), H181–16.17

Volume 1, Number 1-12

CIS/INDEX   379

Exhibit 64: References in the *CIS/Index* to documents related to the OSHA of 1970.

Educational exchanges

Educational exchanges
Appropriations for the Fogarty International Center for Advanced Study in the Health Sciences, FY71 (Leavitt), H181–47.14
Appropriations, FY71, PL91–472
Departments of State, Justice, and

U.S. Foreign Service Corps scholarship program (Davis), S541–29.7
Educational tests
Basic skills in Detroit Public Schools, S341–1.7
Genetic differences in educational

Social security and welfare proposals (brief testimony), H781–3.14
Edwards, Robert L.
Appropriations for the Bureau of Commercial Fisheries, FY71 (Glasgow et al.), S181–7.16

testimony), H341–12.9
Public broadcasting financing, H501–23, S261–20
see also Public broadcasting
Educational Testing Service
Preschool education and day-care services (brief testimony), H341–13.21

(brief testimony), S541–20.10
Edwards, Nelson Jack
Economics of aging: pension aspects (Edwards, Solenberger), S141–12.3
Edwards, Ozzie
Family Assistance Act of 1970 (brief t.), S361–17.22

Egeberg, Roger O.

Narcotic and dangerous drug abuse control (Egeberg), S521–3.23
Occupational health and safety legislation (Egeberg), S541–43.2

156   CIS/INDEX

January-December 1970

Exhibit 65: Indexing by witness to hearings on the Occupational Safety and Health Act of 1970 in *CIS/Index*.

recommendations for action, including replacement of paternalism by community action; possible role of guaranteed income in affecting power structure.

Insertions: Excerpt from the Colorado Migrant Council Annual Report, Mar. 1967 to Feb. 1968, describing migrant life-style (p. 916-920).

"M.A.Y.O. Del Campo," an article describing the Mexican American Youth Organization and its goals (p. 921-922).

S541—42.4: July 16, 1969. p. 922-1072.

Witness: **KRUEGER, Edgar A. (Rev.),** Rio Grande Valley, Tex.

Statement and Discussion: Oversupply of labor on Texas border and its effect on wages, working conditions, and employer-employee relations; criticism of Texas Employment Commission; lack of migrant education and political power; alleged failure of Government programs, including the Farmers Home Administration, to reach people at the grass roots level; allegedly biased law enforcement; emergence, problems, and effect of indigenous groups (list, p. 943-944) including Colonias del Valle, Inc.; recommendations for legislative action.

Insertions: U.S. Commission on Civil Rights staff reports:

a. "Demographic, Economic and Social Characteristics of the Spanish-Surname Population of Five Southwestern States": Arizona, California, Colorado, New Mexico, Texas (p. 945-951).

b. "The Mexican American Population of Texas" (p. 952-981).

c. "Farm Workers." Describes problems of farm labor force originating in Texas (p. 982-1011).

d. "Employment." Describes and presents statistics on the employment status of Mexican Americans in Texas (p. 1013-1024).

e. Excerpts from report on administration of justice concerning treatment of Mexican Americans (p. 1047-1057).

Information and statistics on the population of South Texas counties, including the role of the migrant in the Lower Rio Grande Valley economy, from an OEO Grant Application by Colonias Del Valle, Inc. (p. 1030-1035).

"La Huelga-In Starr County, Tex." by Irving L. Cohen, from Farm Labor Developments, USDA. Describes efforts to organize field workers in the Lower Rio Grande Valley, Tex. (p. 1025-1028).

"Housing of Migrant Agricultural Workers" by Richard B. Brann, from the Texas Law Review, July 1968 (p. 1036-1047).

S541—42.5: July 17, 1969. p. 1073-1093.

Witness: **GODWIN, James L.,** executive director, Coastal Progress, Inc., New Bern, N.C.

Statement and Discussion: Problems facing the rural poor in Jones, Pamlico, and Craven Counties, N.C., with particular emphasis on the lack of transportation; recommendations including funding of transportation for rural peoples and service to poor as alternative to military service; strike by Eastern Farm Workers Association blueberry pickers against Jason Morris Farms, Inc. and role of Coastal Progress, Inc.

S541—42.6: July 17, 1969. p. 1094-1099.

Witness: **MORRIS, Jason,** Jason Morris Farms, Inc., Bridgeton, N.C.

Statement and Discussion: Describes strike by blueberry pickers and wages and labor conditions on his farms.

S541—42.7: July 17, 1969. p. 1099-1109.

Witnesses: **KEYS, Emma Jean,** Trenton, N.C.

SMITH, Lena, cochairman, Eastern Farm Workers Association, New Bern, N.C.

Statements and Discussion: Participants' description of North Carolina blueberry strike, including allegedly biased law enforcement during strike; working conditions in blueberry fields.

S541—42.8: July 17, 1969. p. 1109-1141.

Witnesses: **RICE, Ken,** law student, Duke University, appearing on behalf of:

WALLACE, Thomas B., deputy director, Coastal Progress, Inc.

Statement and Discussion: Alleged denial of justice to blacks in Craven County, N.C.; arrests during blueberry workers' strike.

Insertion: Selected newspaper articles and supplementary documentation dealing with the blueberry workers' strike and farmworker powerlessness (p. 1111-1141).

S541—42.9: July 17, 1969. p. 1141-1150.

Witness: **PARKER, T. W.,** deputy sheriff, Craven County, N.C.

Statement and Discussion: Alleged violations of law by blueberry workers and others during strike; alleged role of Coastal Progress, Inc. in strike.

S541—42.10: July 17, 1969. p. 1150-1157.

Witness: **GAVIN, James F.,** cochairman, Craven County Good Neighbor Council; accompanied by **Burley, Delores,** and **Brown, Ernestine,** Trenton, N.C.

Statement and Discussion: Activities of Craven County Good Neighbor Council, N.C., alleged hostility between law enforcement officials and black community in Craven County.

▶ **S541—43   OCCUPATIONAL SAFETY AND HEALTH ACT, 1970. Part 1.**

Sept. 30, Nov. 4, 21, 24, 26, Dec. 9, 15, 16, 1969, Mar. 7, Apr. 10, 28, 1970. 91-1; 91-2.

† eltem 1043. xi+1006 p.

†4.L11/2:Sa11/3/970/pt.1

11140(70).   71-608000

Hearings before the *Subcommittee on Labor* on the following bills:

S. 2193 (text, p. 2-31), the Occupational Safety and Health Act of 1969, to authorize the Secretary of Labor to set standards to ensure safe and healthful working conditions, to assist and encourage States to participate in efforts to ensure such working conditions, and to provide for research, information, education, and training in occupational safety and health; and

S. 1788 (text, p. 32-73), the Administration's Occupational Safety and Health Act of 1969, to provide a program for safe and healthful working conditions by creating a National Occupational Safety and Health Board, appointed by the President, to set mandatory safety and health standards; by

authorizing enforcement; assisting State efforts; and by providing for research, information, education, and training.

Supplementary material includes submitted statements and correspondence (p. 872-878, 1004-1006).

Hearings held Mar. 7, 1970 in Jersey City, N.J.; Apr. 10, 1970 in Duquesne, Pa.; and Apr. 28, 1970 in Greenville, S.C.

(For summary of brief items of testimony, see S541-43.25.)

S541—43.1: Sept. 30, 1969. p. 76-95.

Witness: **SHULTZ, George P.,** Secretary of Labor; accompanied by **Hodgson, James D.,** Under Secretary; and **Silberman, Laurence H.,** Solicitor.

Statement: Support for S. 2788; need for comprehensive safety legislation; analysis of existing Federal, State, and private section safety and health activities. Analysis of S. 2788. (p. 76-87)

Discussion: Review of penalty provisions in S. 2788; reasons for extending coverage to large farms; operations of the proposed Board. (p. 87-95)

S541—43.2: Nov. 4, 1969. p. 98-163.

Witness: **EGEBERG, Roger O. (Dr.),** Assistant Secretary of HEW for Health and Scientific Affairs; accompanied by **Johnson, Charles C., Jr.,** Administrator Consumer Protection and Environmental Health Service; **Key, Marcus M.,** Director, Bureau of Occupational Health and Safety; and **Meyer, Alvin,** Special Assistant for Legislative Affairs.

Statement and Discussion: Support for S. 2788; extent of occupational health hazards; support for consensus method for determining standards, and explanation of methodology in setting standards. Extent and nature of occupational diseases from pesticides in agriculture, and byssinosis or "brown lung" in the textile industry. Anticipated funding and personnel requirements.

Insertions: Status of State and local government occupational health programs, Jan. 1969 (p. 103-109).

"A Review of State Occupational Health Legislation," by Andrew D. Hosey and Lorice Ede (p. 110-137).

S541—43.3: Nov. 21, 1969. p. 165-181.

Witnesses: **CLAYTON, George D.,** executive secretary, American Industrial Hygiene Association.

ZAPP, John A., Jr., vice president and director, Haskell Laboratories, E. I. du Pont de Nemours & Co.

Statements and Discussion: Support for S. 2788 and consensus method for arriving at standards; changing social attitudes toward occupational health hazards; need for emphasis on industrial hygiene.

S541—43.4: Nov. 21, 1969. p. 198-255.

Witness: **GORDON, Jerome D.,** president, Delphic Systems and Research Corp.

Statement and Discussion: Extent of air pollution in industrial buildings; inadequacy of occupational safety and health statistical reporting systems; and present Federal and State health and safety programs. Suggestions to reorganize executive responsibilities in occupational safety and health by forming a President's Occupational Safety and Health Advisory Committee.

Exhibit 66: Abstract of the hearing held on the Occupational Safety and Health Act of 1970 in *Congressional Information Service/Index.*

[*185*]

CIS/Index is published monthly with a cumulative index each quarter, covering documents indexed and abstracted during the previous three months.

An annual volume, *CIS/Annual,* cumulates all the abstracts published during the year and provides a cumulative index "to the entire congressional output for the year."   (A five year cumulative index now covers 1970–1974.)   In addition, the annual volumes contain excellent legislative histories of enacted laws.   See Exhibit 67.

Microfiche copies of all publications listed in the *CIS/Index* are available by subscription from the CIS/Microfiche Library.

Legislative History (H.J. Res. 1413 and related bills):

House Hearings: *See 1971 CIS/Annual: H501-4.*

Senate Hearings: *See 1971 CIS/Annual: S541-2.*

House Reports: H503-69 (No. 91-1686); H503-70 (No. 91-1714, Conference Report).

Senate Report: S543-41 (No. 91-1426).

Congressional Record Vol. 116 (1970):

Dec. 9, considered and passed House; considered and passed Senate, amended, in lieu of S.J. Res. 248.

Dec. 10, House and Senate agreed to conference report.

PL91-548 MINUTE MAN NATIONAL HISTORICAL PARK, boundary revision.
Dec. 14, 1970. 91-2. *
●Item 575. 1 p.
84 STAT. 1436.

"To amend the Act of September 21, 1959 (73 Stat. 590), to authorize the Secretary of the Interior to revise the boundaries of Minute Man National Historical Park, and for other purposes."

Also increases authorization.

Legislative History (H.R. 13934).

Senate Hearings: *See 1971 CIS/Annual: S441-5.*

House Report: H443-60 (No. 91-1398).

Senate Report: S443-97 (No. 91-1390).

Congressional Record Vol. 116 (1970):

Sept. 14, considered and passed House.

Dec. 4, considered and passed Senate.

PL91-554 WILSON'S CREEK BATTLEFIELD NATIONAL PARK, name change.
Dec. 16, 1970. 91-2. *
●Item 575. 1 p.
84 STAT. 1441.

"To amend the Act of April 22, 1960, providing for the establishment of the Wilson's Creek Battlefield National Park."

Legislative History (H.R. 1160 and related bill):

Senate Hearings: *See 1971 CIS/Annual: S441-5.*

House Report: H443-54 (No. 91-1395).

Senate Report: S443-96 (No. 91-1389).

Congressional Record Vol. 116 (1970):

Sept. 14, considered and passed House.

Dec. 4, considered and passed Senate.

Congressional Record Vol. 115 (1969):

Sept. 5, considered and passed Senate.

Congressional Record Vol. 116 (1970):

Dec. 10, considered and passed House.

PL91-574 WILLIAM G. STONE NAVIGATION LOCK, CALIF., designation.
Dec. 24, 1970. 91-2. *
●Item 575. 1 p.
84 STAT. 1508.

"To designate the navigation lock on the Sacramento deepwater ship channel in the State of California as the William G. Stone navigation lock."

Legislative History (S. 3192 and related bill):

House Hearings: *See 1971 CIS/Annual: H641-2.*

House Report: [Public Works]RB (No. 91-1703, accompanying H.R. 15205).

Senate Report: [Public Works] (No. 91-1032).

Congressional Record Vol. 116 (1970):

July 21, considered and passed Senate.

Dec. 10, considered and passed House, in lieu of H.R. 15205.

PL91-576 PICK-SLOAN MISSOURI BASIN PROGRAM, designation.
Dec. 24, 1970. 91-2. *
●Item 575. 1 p.
84 STAT. 1541.

"To designate the comprehensive Missouri River Basin development program as the Pick-Sloan Missouri Basin program."

Legislative History (S. 1100):

House Hearings: *See 1971 CIS/Annual: H641-2.*

House Report: [Public Works] (No. 91-1710).

Senate Report: [Public Works] (No. 91-891).

Congressional Record Vol. 116 (1970):

May 25, considered and passed Senate.

Dec. 10, considered and passed House.

PL91-583 WILLIAM "BILL" DANNELLY RESERVOIR, ALA., designation.
Dec. 24, 1970. 91-2. *
●Item 575. 1 p.
84 STAT. 1574.

PL91-590 INTERSTATE COMMERCE ACT, amendment.
Dec. 28, 1970. 91-2. *
●Item 575. 2 p.
84 STAT. 1587.

"To amend section 308(b) of the Interstate Commerce Act to modernize certain restrictions upon the application and scope of the exemption provided therein, and for other purposes."

Applies to water carriers transporting bulk and non-bulk commodities

Legislative History (H.R. 8298):

Senate Hearings: *See 1971 CIS/Annual: S261-3.*

House Reports: [Interstate and Foreign Commerce] (No. 91-520); H563-71 (No. 91-1744, Conference Report).

Senate Report: S263-34 (No. 91-1330).

Congressional Record Vol. 116 (1970):

Aug. 12, considered and passed House.

Nov. 23, considered and passed Senate, amended

Dec. 16, Senate and House agreed to conference report.

PL91-596 OCCUPATIONAL SAFETY AND HEALTH ACT OF 1970.
Dec. 29, 1970. 91-2. *
●Item 575. 31 p.
84 STAT. 1590.

"To assure safe and healthful working conditions for working men and women; by authorizing enforcement of the standards developed under the Act; by assisting and encouraging the States in their efforts to assure safe and healthful working conditions; by providing for research, information, education, and training in the field of occupational safety and health; and for other purposes."

Legislative History (S. 2193 and related bill):

Senate Hearings: S541-43; S541-44.

Senate Committee Print: *See 1971 CIS/Annual: S542-17.*

House Reports: H343-6 (No. 91-1291, accompanying H.R. 16785); H343-18 (No. 91-1765, Conference Report).

Senate Report: S543-37 (No. 91-1282).

Congressional Record Vol. 116 (1970):

Oct. 13, Nov. 16, 17, considered and passed Senate.

Nov. 23, 24, considered and passed House, amended, in lieu of H.R. 16785.

Dec. 16, Senate agreed to conference report.

Dec. 17, House agreed to conference report.

Senate Report: [Public Works] (No. 91-391).   Dec. 10, considered and passed House.   House Hearings: H561-15.

Exhibit 67: Legislative history of the Occupational Safety and Health Act of 1970, in the *Congressional Information Service/Annual.*

6. Congressional Index (Commerce Clearing House, Inc.). This commercial service is a very popular guide to current legislative information. Although it does not contain the actual texts of bills, debates or reports, it does provide extensive indexes, including an index of public general bills by subject and author, a digest of each bill and a status table of actions taken thereon. This status table contains references to hearings, a characteristic lacking in many of the research aids described here.

In addition, *Congressional Index* contains an index of enactments, a table of companion bills, a list of pending treaties, a table of voting records on each bill and resolution, and a weekly newsletter on the highlights of the week in Congress.

Issued in two volumes for each Congress, the *Index* has a looseleaf format which permits convenient weekly supplementation of all its indexes and tables.

2462 Current Senate Status Table Number 114–130
For digest, see "Senate Bills" Division.
See also Senate Status Table.

2116
Reptd., no amend., S. Rept. 91-639 ..
.... 1/28/70
Amended on S. Floor [Voice] 2/2/70
Passed S., with amend. [Voice] 2/2/70
To H. Agriculture 2/3/70

2143
S. hearing available 3/13/70

★2162
Reptd., with amend., S. Rept. 91-845
.... 5/6/70
Passed S. as reported [Voice] 5/11/70
To H. Interstate and Foreign Com-
merce 5/12/70
H. hearing available 9/18/70
Reptd., with amend., H. Rept. 91-1642
.... 12/1/70
Passed H., without amend., [Voice]
.... 12/7/70
H. appoints conferees 12/8/70
S. appoints conferees 12/10/70
Conf. Rept. submitted to H., H. Rept.
91-1755 .... 12/15/70
Conf. Rept. agreed to by S. 12/16/70
Conf. Rept. agreed to by H. 12/16/70
Approved [Public Law 91-601].... 12/30/70

★2176
S. hearing available 7/7/70
Reptd., no amend., S. Rept. 91-1083 ...
.... 8/10/70
Passed S., without amend., [Voice] .....
.... 8/13/70
To H. Interstate and Foreign Com-
merce 8/14/70
Passed H., without amend., [Voice]
.... 10/5/70
Approved [Public Law 91-449] 10/14/70

★2193
S. hearing available (Parts 1 & 2) ......
.... 8/13/70
Reptd., with amend., S. Rept. 91-1282
.... 10/6/70
Amended on S. Floor [Voice] 11/19/70
Amended on S. Floor [Roll-call]
.... 11/19/70
Passed S., with amend., [Roll-call]
.... 11/17/70
Amended on H. Floor [Voice] 11/24/70
Passed H., with amend., in lieu of
H. 16785 [Voice] 11/24/70
H. appoints conferees 11/24/70
S. appoints conferees 11/30/70
Conf. Rept. agreed to by S. 12/16/70
Conf. Rept. submitted to H., H. Rept.
91-1765 .... 12/16/70
Conf. Rept. agreed to by H. 12/17/70
Approved [Public Law 91-596] 12/29/70

2203
Hearing in S. 1/20/70
S. hearing available 6/12/70

★2208
Reptd., with amend., S. Rept. 91-855
.... 5/11/70
Passed S. as reported [Voice] 5/13/70
To H. Interior and Insular Affairs ......
.... 5/14/70
Reptd., with amend., H. Rept. 91-1403
.... 8/10/70
Passed H. as reported [Voice] 9/14/70
H. amend. agreed to by S. 9/16/70
Approved [Public Law 91-425] 9/26/70

2209
Reptd., with amend., S. Rept. 91-936
.... 6/18/70
Passed S. as reported [Voice] 6/23/70
To H. Interior and Insular Affairs .....
.... 6/24/70

★2211
Reptd., no amend., H. Rept. 91-802 ..
.... 1/27/70
Passed H., without amend. [Voice] .....
.... 2/9/70
Approved [Public Law 91-196] 2/20/70

★2224
H. hearing available (Part 1) 2/13/70
Amended on H. Floor [Voice] 9/23/70
Passed H., with amend., in lieu of
H. 17333 [Voice] 9/23/70
H. appoints conferees 9/23/70
S. appoints conferees 10/13/70
Conf. Rept. submitted to H., H. Rept.
91-1631 .... 11/25/70
Conf. Rept. agreed to by S. 11/30/70
Conf. Rept. agreed to by H. 12/1/70
Approved [Public Law 91-547] 12/14/70

2225
S. hearing available 2/13/70

2230
Hearing in S. 3/12/70

2242
S. hearing available 3/11/70

2245
Hearing in S. 5/6/70

2246
S. hearing available (Part 1) 5/27/70

2253
Reptd., no amend., S. Rept. 91-779 .....
.... 4/23/70
Indefinitely postponed by S. 4/30/70

Exhibit 68: The Current Senate Status Table in the CCH
Congressional Index, showing action on S. 2193,
the Occupational Safety and Health Act of
1970.

7. U. S. Code Congressional and Administrative News (West Publishing Company). The great value of this service, as noted above, is its publication of the *texts* of enacted public laws and of selective congressional committee reports on the more important acts. None of the previously mentioned publications in this section includes the actual texts of the documents. The bi-weekly advance sheets of *U.S.C.C.A.N.* during the congressional session and its cumulative bound volumes at the end of the session also include a legislative history table providing for each public law, the date approved, the *Statutes at Large* citation, the bill and report numbers, the committees that recommended the legislation, and the dates of consideration and passage. No reference is made to hearings.

U.S.C.C.A.N. only includes measures that have been enacted into law and thus cannot be used to determine the status of *pending* legislation.

Exhibit 69 shows the beginning of the Senate Report on the Occupational Safety and Health Act of 1970, as set out in *U.S.C.C.A.N.* Note that the report is preceded by references to steps in the passage of the legislation, including committee reports not set out here. Exhibit 70 illustrates the treatment of the Act in the legislative history table.

OCCUPATIONAL SAFETY AND HEALTH
P.L. 91–596

OCCUPATIONAL SAFETY AND HEALTH ACT OF 1970

P.L. 91–596, see page 1852

Senate Report (Labor and Public Welfare Committee) No. 91–1282,
Oct. 6, 1970 [To accompany S. 2193]

House Report (Education and Labor Committee) No. 91–1291,
July 9, 1970 [To accompany H.R. 16785]

Conference Report No. 91–1765, Dec. 16, 1970
[To accompany S. 2193]

Cong. Record Vol. 116 (1970)

DATES OF CONSIDERATION AND PASSAGE

Senate November 17, December 16, 1970

House November 24, December 17, 1970

The Senate bill was passed in lieu of the House bill. The Senate
Report and the Conference Report are set out.

SENATE REPORT NO. 91–1282

THE Committee on Labor and Public Welfare, to which was referred
the bill (S. 2193) to authorize the Secretary of Labor to set standards to
assure safe and healthful working conditions for working men and women,
to assist and encourage States to participate in efforts to assure such working conditions, to provide for research, information, education, and training in the field of occupational safety and health, and for other purposes,
having considered the same, reports favorably thereon with an amendment
(in the nature of a substitute) and recommends that the bill (as amended)
do pass.

PURPOSE

The purpose of S. 2193 is to reduce the number and severity of work-
related injuries and illnesses which, despite current efforts of employers
and government, are resulting in ever-increasing human misery and economic loss.

The bill would achieve its purpose through programs of research, education and training, and through the development and administration, by the
Secretary of Labor, of uniformly applied occupational safety and health
standards. Such standards would be developed with the assistance of the
Secretary of Health, Education and Welfare, and both their promulgation
and their enforcement would be judicially reviewable. Encouragement
is given to Federal-state cooperation, and financial assistance is authorized
to enable states, under approved plans, to take over entirely and administer
their own programs for achieving safe and healthful jobsites for the Nation's workers.

Exhibit 69: Senate Report No. 91–1282 on the Occupational Safety and Health Act, as set out in
*United States Code Congressional and Ad-
ministrative News.*

TABLE 4—LEGISLATIVE HISTORY

Public Law		84 Stat. Page	Bill No.	Report No. 91–		Comm. Reporting **		Cong.Rec.Vol. 116 (1970) Dates of Consideration and Passage	
No.91–	Date App.			House	Senate	House	Senate	House	Senate
572	Dec. 24	1504	S. 2108	1472 1667	1004	IFC (H.R. 19318)	LPW	Nov. 16 Dec. 8	July 14 Dec. 10
573	Dec. 24	1508	S. 1499	1711	391	PW	PW	Dec. 10	Sept. 5
574	Dec. 24	1508	S. 3192	1703	1032	PW (H.R. 15205)	PW	Dec. 10	July 21
575	Dec. 24	1509	S. 1079	1643	1333	J	J	Dec. 7	Oct. 14
576	Dec. 24	1541	S. 1100	1701	891	PW	PW	Dec. 10	May 25
577	Dec. 24	1542	S. 3070	1605	1138 1246	Agr	AgrF J	Dec. 8	Oct. 2 Dec. 9
578	Dec. 24	1559	S. 3479	1399	867	IIA (H.R. 15978)	IIA	Sept. 14 Dec. 9	May 18 Sept. 29
579	Dec. 24	1560	H.R. 19846	1651	none	Agr	none	Dec. 7	Dec. 8
580	Dec. 24	1565	S. 4557	1677	1414	AE (H.R. 19998)	AE	Dec. 10	Dec. 9
581	Dec. 24	1566	S. 368	1544	1160	IIA	IIA	Oct. 5 Dec. 9	Sept. 16 Dec. 4, 10
582	Dec. 24	1574	H.R. 8663	1138	1417	AS	AS	June 15	Dec. 10
583	Dec. 24	1574	S. 528	1709	889	PW	PW	Dec. 10	May 22
584	Dec. 24	1575	S. 3785	1232	1606	VA	LPW	Nov. 16 Dec. 10	Sept. 25 Dec. 8
585	Dec. 24	1578	S. 1500	1712	892	PW	PW	Dec. 10	May 25
586	Dec. 24	1578	H.R. 18012	1468	1420	FA	FR	Dec. 7	Dec. 10
587	Dec. 24	1579	S. 4083	1658	1070	EL	LPW	Dec. 7	Aug. 11 Dec. 8
588	Dec. 24	1580	H.R. 13911	1448	1439	VA	F	Sept. 21	Dec. 17
589	Dec. 24	1585	S.J.Res. 236	1598	1229	HA	RA	Dec. 15	Sept. 25
590	Dec. 28	1587	H.R. 8298	520 1744	1330	IFC	C	Aug. 12 Dec. 16	Nov. 23 Dec. 16
591	Dec. 28	1588	H.R. 19402	1615	1440	Agr	AgrF	Dec. 7	Dec. 17
592	Dec. 28	1588	S.J.Res. 226	none	1213	none	J	Dec. 10	Sept. 23 Dec. 15
593	Dec. 28	1589	S.J.Res. 74	none	1207	none	J	Dec. 10	Sept. 23 Dec. 15
594	Dec. 28	1589	S.J.Res. 172	none	703	none	J	Dec. 10	Feb. 17 Dec. 15
595	Dec. 28	1589	S.J.Res. 187	none	1209	none	J	Dec. 10	Sept. 23 Dec. 15
596	Dec. 29	1590	S. 2193	1291 1765	1282	EL (H.R. 16785)	LPW	Nov. 24 Dec. 17	Nov. 17 Dec. 16

** For key to Committee abbreviations see end of Table.

Exhibit 70: The legislative history table in *U.S.C.C.A.N.*, showing its treatment of the Occupational Safety and Health Act of 1970.

8. Congressional Quarterly Weekly Report.
This weekly commercial publication summarizes
congressional activity on major pieces of legislation. The weekly issue is most useful for its coverage of news developments and background discussion of pending legislation. Its status table
(Exhibit 71) covers only selected pending proposals and its legislative history table for measures enacted into public law is less comprehensive
than that found in other services. The tables
of House and Senate votes, however, are thorough
and easy to use.

The *Congressional Quarterly Almanac,* "a com-
pendium of legislation for one session of Congress," is published annually. It cumulates many
of the tables in the Weekly Report and contains
pertinent background material of permanent value
relating to Congressional activities The enactment of the Occupational Safety and Health Act is
summarized in Exhibit 72.

9. Congressional Monitor. Similar to the official *Daily Digest,* this *daily* congressional legislative service includes summaries of each day's
scheduled activity in the committees and the actions concluded the previous day on the floor. In
addition, it contains forecasts of expected activity, brief excerpts of important congressional
documents, a weekly list of printed hearings, re-

MAJOR CURRENT LEGISLATION IN 91st CONGRESS

Compiled by Congressional Quarterly as of Dec. 30, 1970

	House	Senate
Democrats	243	58
Republicans	190	42
Vacancies	2	0

HS—Hearings Scheduled OR—Ordered Reported NA—No Action Required
HB—Hearings Begun R—Reported P—Passed
HC—Hearings Completed DB—Debate Begun C—In Conference

BILL	Most Recent Page Reference	HOUSE		SENATE		FINAL
Bank Holding Companies. Federal regulation of one-bank holding companies. (HR 6778)	2641	R 7/23/69	P 11/5/69	R 8/10/70	P 9/16/70	Cleared 12/18/70
Broker-Dealer Insurance. Protect investors from broker insolvency. (HR 19333)	2939	R 10/21/70	P 12/1/70	R 9/21/70	P 12/10/70	11/30/70 PL 91-598
Congressional Reform. Revises committee and floor procedures. (HR 17654)	2321	R 6/17/70	P 9/17/70	R 5/23/69	P 10/6/70	10/26/70 PL 91-510
Consumer Agency. Creates agency to represent consumers in Government proceedings.(HR 18214)	3002	R 7/30/70		R 10/12/70	P 12/1/70	
Consumer Relief. Permits class actions in deceptive consumer practices. (S 3201)	2640	HC		R 8/14/70		✓
Credit Reporting. Disclosure of consumer credit reporting. (Attached to HR 15073)	2613	HC	P 10/13/70	R 11/5/69	P 11/6/69	10/26/70 PL 91-508
Defense Procurement. Authorizes procurement, research funds for Defense Department.(HR 17123)	2471	R 4/24/70	P 5/6/70	R 7/14/70	P 9/1/70	10/7/70 PL 91-441
Drug Control. Revises Federal narcotics and drug laws. (HR 18583)	2724	R 9/10/70	P 9/24/70	R 12/16/69	P 1/28/70	10/27/70 PL 91-513
Electoral Reform. Constitutional amendment for direct election of President. (S J Res 1, H J Res 681)	2645	R 5/16/70	P 9/18/69	R 8/14/70	DB 9/8/70	
Emergency Home Financing. Emergency funds for home mortgage market. (S 3685)	1894	R 5/28/70	P 6/25/70	R 4/7/70	P 4/16/70	7/24/70 PL 91-351
Food Stamp Reform. Free stamps for the neediest of the poor. (HR 18582, S 2547)	2900	R 8/10/70	P 12/16/70	R 7/7/69	P 9/24/69	
Foreign Bank Accounts. Curbs evasion of U.S. laws and taxes. (HR 15073)	2613	R 3/28/70	P 5/25/70	R 8/24/70	P 9/18/70	10/26/70 PL 91-508
Foreign Trade. Establishes import quotas and extends authority to cut tariffs. (HR 18970)	2948	R 8/21/70	P 11/19/70	R 12/11/70	DB 12/16/70	
Higher Education. Extends Federal aid programs for higher education. (Misc. bills)	2727	HC		HC		
Impact Aid. Revises per-pupil funding in Federally affected areas. (HR 16307)	2642	HC		HC		
Mass Transit. Long-term financing for urban public transportation programs. (S 3154, HR 18185)	2391	R 6/30/70	P 9/29/70	R 12/22/69	P 2/3/70	10/15/70 PL 91-453
Military Sales. Extends foreign credit sales 2 years; Indochina amendments. (HR 15628)	2643	R 3/5/70	P 3/24/70	R 5/12/70	P 6/30/70	C
Mutual Funds. Tighten regulation of mutual funds. (S 2224, HR 17333)	2893	R 8/7/70	P 9/23/70	R 5/21/69	P 5/26/69	12/14/70 PL 91-547
Newspaper Preservation. Exempts from antitrust laws certain operating plans. (S 1520)	1784	R 6/15/70	P 7/8/70	R 11/18/69	P 1/30/70	7/24/70 PL 91-353
Occupational Safety. Protect health and safety of employees. (S 2193)	2889	R 7/9/70	P 11/24/70	R 10/6/70	P 11/17/70	12/29/70 PL 91-596
Omnibus Farm Bill. Price supports, production controls for major commodities. (HR 18546)	2812	R 7/23/70	P 8/5/70	R 8/28/70	P 9/15/70	11/30/70 PL 91-524

Exhibit 71: A summary of the Occupational Safety and Health Act of 1970 in the *Congressional Quarterly Weekly Report.*

MAJOR CONGRESSIONAL ACTION

PASSAGE OF JOB SAFETY BILL ENDS THREE-YEAR DISPUTE

Congress in 1970 completed action on a bill (S 2193 —PL 91-596), the Occupational Safety and Health Act, establishing a comprehensive on-the-job safety program for about 55 million industrial, farm and construction workers employed by firms engaged in interstate commerce.

Final action came when the House Dec. 17 by a 309-60 roll-call vote adopted a conference report on the bill. The Senate had adopted the report Dec. 16 by voice vote. (*Vote 242, p. 84-H*)

The legislation gave the Secretary of Labor authority to set safety and health standards for the protection of workers and created a three-member commission to enforce regulations.

Final passage marked the end of a three-year dispute between labor and business forces over how the Federal Government should adopt and enforce safety standards.

Organized labor and most liberal Democrats had wanted the Secretary to set and enforce safety standards while business interests backed by Republicans and the Administration had requested that two Presidentially appointed boards be created, one to set standards and the other to enforce them.

Labor groups contended that independent boards could become captives of the industries they were supposed to regulate. Business interests argued that due process would be violated if the Secretary were allowed to set, monitor and enforce safety rules.

The Senate Nov. 17 passed a bill which provided a compromise by giving the Secretary standards-setting authority and a three-member commission enforcement power.

The House, however, Nov. 24 adopted the Administration- and business-backed approach by establishing two independent boards.

House-Senate conferees followed the Senate version, giving the Secretary the rule-making responsibilities.

But on another key provision, conferees deleted a Senate provision allowing the Secretary to close a plant if an "imminent danger" threatened the lives of workers. House conferees insisted that the Secretary should obtain a court order before a plant could be closed.

Although the conference version drew mixed reactions from labor and business interests, final passage was assured when the Labor Department as well as some business and labor groups endorsed the bill.

Provisions

As cleared by Congress, S 2193:

Duties of Employers

• Required employers to furnish a work place free from recognized hazards that had caused or were likely to cause death or serious physical harm to employees.

Safety and Health Standards

• Required the Secretary of Labor within two years after enactment to promulgate national occupational safety standards and established Federal safety standards.
• Provided that when the Secretary of Labor wished to promulgate, revise or revoke an occupational safety and

health standard, he could appoint an ad hoc advisory committee to submit recommendations within three to nine months, but not after that period.

• Required the Secretary of Labor to schedule a hearing on objections to a proposed standard within 30 days after the last day for filing recommendations.
• Authorized the Secretary of Labor to promulgate, revise or revoke a standard within 60 days after the completion of hearings or within 60 days after the last day for filing comments.
• Provided for exemption from standards for any employer who applies to the Secretary of Labor and meets certain requirements.
• Required posting of labels or warnings to apprise employers of safety and health standards to which they are exposed.
• Provided that the Secretary of Labor should establish emergency standards when employees were exposed to grave dangers from toxic materials or new hazards.
• Permitted any person to file for judicial review of a standard within 60 days after it was promulgated.

Advisory Committee

• Established a National Advisory Committee on Occupational Safety and Health consisting of 12 members representing management, labor and occupational safety and

---

Occupational Accident Facts

"The on-the-job health and safety crisis is the worst problem confronting American workers," reported the House Committee on Education and Labor in October 1970.

The following annual statistics compiled by the Bureau of Labor Statistics (BLS) were cited by the Committee for the nation's 80 million workers:

• 14,500 killed, an average of 55 per day during a five-day work week.
• 2.2 million injured.
• 390,000 cases of occupational diseases (lung cancer, asbestosis, heart disease and others).
• 250 million man days of work lost, 10 times as many as from strikes.
• More than $1.5 billion lost in wages.
• More than an $8 billion loss to the Gross National Product.

A report submitted on contract to the Labor Department Sept. 20 by the Delphic Systems and Research Corporation concluded that the annual BLS survey of work-related accidents was "seriously restricted" by survey-sampling and data-collection procedures at state levels.

The Delphic validation of work injuries reported to the BLS by the state of California—a state with rigorous accident reporting procedures—revealed that more than 36 percent of firms reporting "no injuries" actually had employee accidents. On a national basis, the report projected approximately 200,000 disabling work injuries beyond the 2.2 million reported in 1969.

<u>Exhibit 72:</u> A summary of the Occupational Safety and Health Act of 1970 in the *Congressional Quarterly Almanac.*

[*195*]

ports and other legislative documents, and a weekly status table of active bills arranged by broad subject groups. It is not as complete a status table as those in the other services discussed here.

COMPILED LEGISLATIVE HISTORIES

The legislative histories of a few important laws have been compiled and published in book form. These compilations may include some or all of the important bills, debates, committee reports, hearings, etc. Such collections save the researcher the considerable time and trouble of compiling relevant references and documents. Some are issued commercially, e. g., Jacob Seidman's *Legislative History of Federal Income and Excess Profits Laws, 1953–1939* (Prentice-Hall, 1954) in two volumes. Others are published by government agencies, e. g., the National Labor Relations Board's excellent two volume histories of the Wagner Act, the Taft-Hartley Act, and the Labor-Management Reporting and Disclosure Act of 1959. For an example of a recent compiled legislative history, see Exhibit 73, the *Legislative History of the Occupational Safety and Health Act of 1970* prepared by the Subcommittee on Labor of the Committee on Labor and Public Welfare of the U. S. Senate.

92d Congress
1st Session }   **COMMITTEE PRINT**

LEGISLATIVE HISTORY OF THE OCCUPATIONAL SAFETY AND HEALTH ACT OF 1970
(S. 2193, P.L. 91–596)

PREPARED BY THE

SUBCOMMITTEE ON LABOR

OF THE

COMMITTEE ON LABOR AND PUBLIC WELFARE UNITED STATES SENATE

JUNE 1971

Printed for the use of the Committee on Labor and Public Welfare

Exhibit 73:   The title page of a compiled legislative history of the Occupational Safety and Health Act of 1970.

The Law Librarian's Society of Washington, D. C. issues a *Union List of Legislative Histories* (3rd ed., 1968) which lists unpublished legislative histories available in its libraries.   In addition, Microcard Editions of Information Handling Services publishes in microfacsimile the *Legislative Histories of Internal Revenue Acts* and another more general microfiche series called *Legislative History Service,* which compiles histories of the important enactments of each congressional session since the Eighty-Second Congress in 1951–2.

There is, unfortunately, no single checklist of all available compiled legislative histories.   Before beginning an extensive legislative history project, a researcher should always consult a law librarian to determine if a compiled history already exists.

STATE LEGISLATIVE HISTORY

The search for legislative history on the state level is a very difficult and frequently impossible task.   Although almost every state has a legislative journal, only a few of these actually include the transcript of the debates.   Bills are usually available from the state legislatures on request, but are not widely distributed and hence hard to locate after enactment.   Committee reports are published in only a few states and hearings even more rarely.

There are status tables or digests of current bills published in a number of states, either officially by the state or by a private publisher. One of the best sources of legislative history are the session law services published in connection with some of the annotated statutory codes. Some looseleaf services also provide coverage of current state legislation in their subject areas.

Official agencies for the recommendation and drafting of new legislation have appeared in many states. These may be independent agencies (such as some of the law revision commissions); or be attached to the judiciary (such as judicial councils); or may function as branches of the legislatures (like the legislative councils). Such groups recommend new rules or legislation and prepare drafts of bills designed to implement their proposals. Their studies are, of course, persuasive with the legislatures and their recommendations are often enacted into law. In such a case the published report of the commission or council may provide an invaluable source of legislative history of the resultant enactment. Abstracts of such reports can often be found in the *Legislative Research Checklist*, issued monthly by the Council of State Governments.

Since the available materials and tools for research in legislative history vary widely from state to state, one should become familiar with the

sources that exist in your state. Frequently the state law library or legislative reference library offers useful assistance in this area. Appendix C, below, contains a list of legal research guides for a number of states. Many of these guides include information on the state's legislative materials.

CHAPTER VI

ADMINISTRATIVE LAW

Although administrative and executive agencies have existed since the creation of our country, their real growth began with the Industrial Revolution in the late nineteenth century. At that time, the increasingly complex problems of society and economy led to an expansion of the traditional functions of executive departments and to the creation of many new administrative agencies. In this century, two World Wars and an economic depression hastened this development and brought about a tremendous proliferation of documentary output, most of which is of legal significance.

The regulatory agencies were created by Congress to carry out new economic legislation when it became apparent that Congress and the courts lacked the flexibility, expertise, time and manpower to handle this task. To do their work, the agencies were given the power to promulgate regulations and, when it appeared that these had been violated, to hold quasi-judicial hearings. Their orders, regulations and decisions have the force of law and form an important segment of legal bibliography.

Administrative agencies exist on all levels of our political system: in the federal government,

where access to regulations and decisions is relatively good; in the states, where such administrative materials are often difficult to locate; and on the local level, where published texts of regulations and decisions are virtually non-existent.

GOVERNMENT ORGANIZATION MANUAL

Research in administrative law frequently requires a preliminary understanding of the functions and structure of the agency under consideration.   The most comprehensive single source for such information is the *United States Government Manual,* an annual directory of general information about the federal government, with primary emphasis upon the executive branch and regulatory agencies.   (It also contains some information about Congress and the judiciary.)   Each executive department and agency is described with the following coverage:

1. Citations to relevant statutes creating and affecting the agency.

2. Descriptions of the functions and authority of the agency.

3. Information about subsidiary units, bureaus, and predecessor agencies.

4. Names and functions of major officials.

5. Organizational charts.

6. Sources of information available from the agency.

The *Manual* is one of the most important reference books of the federal government and is a major publication of the Federal Register System. It can often save a researcher considerable time by providing quick answers to questions which might otherwise require extensive research.

For a description of the Occupational Safety and Health Review Commission in the *Manual,* see Exhibit 74.

EMPLOYMENT

NRC's employment activities are exempt from civil service requirements and are conducted under NRC's independent merit system. However, NRC employees receive Federal Employee Benefits (retirement, group life insurance, and health benefits) on the same basis as other Federal employees. Applicants with veterans' preference are accorded the preference granted to them by the Veterans' Preference Act of 1944 (58 Stat. 387).

Recruitment is continuous and applications from individuals qualified for NRC needs are accepted whenever they are received. NRC recruits annually from colleges as appropriate to fill foreseen needs.

Employment inquiries, applications and requests from schools for participation in the recruitment program may be directed to the Director, Division of Organization and Personnel, Nuclear Regulatory Commission, Washington, D.C. 20555.

For further information, contact the Division of Organization and Personnel, Nuclear Regulatory Commission, Washington, D.C. 20555. Phone, 301–427–4430.

Approved.

LEE V. GOSSICK,
Executive Director for Operations.

OCCUPATIONAL SAFETY AND HEALTH REVIEW COMMISSION

1825 K Street NW., Washington, D.C. 20006
Phone, 202–634–7943

Chairman	FRANK R. BARNAKO.
Chief Legal Counsel	W. SCOTT RAILTON.
Commissioner	ROBERT D. MORAN.
Chief Legal Counsel	JAMES E. WELDON.
Commissioner	TIMOTHY F. CLEARY.
Chief Legal Counsel	PAUL A. TENNEY.

ADMINISTRATIVE LAW JUDGES

CHARLES K. CHAPLIN, *Chief Judge.*
EDWARD V. ALFIERI.
DEE C. BLYTH.
PAUL L. BRADY.
WILLIAM E. BRENNAN.
JUDD P. BRENTON.
ROBERT N. BURCHMORE.
JAMES D. BURROUGHS.
JOYCE CAPPS.
JOHN A. CARLSON.
JOSEPH L. CHALK.
JOSEPH CHODES.
JAMES A. CRONIN, JR.
RICHARD DEBENNEDETTO.

JEROME C. DITORE.
PAUL E. DIXON.
THOMAS J. DONEGAN.
DONALD K. DUVALL.
SEYMOUR FIER.
FOSTER FURCOLO.
ABRAHAM M. GOLD.
SIDNEY J. GOLDSTEIN.
DAVID H. HARRIS.
HAROLD A. KENNEDY.
DAVID J. KNIGHT.
JOHN J. LARKIN.
LOUIS C. LAVECCHIA.
HENRY F. MARTIN, JR.
JERRY W. MITCHELL.

JOHN J. MORRIS.
JAMES P. O'CONNELL.
DAVID G. ORINGER.
HENRY K. OSTERMAN.
GEORGE W. OTTO.
JOHN S. PATTON.
VERNON G. RIEHL.
LOUIS J. RUBIN.
ERWIN L. STULLER.
BENJAMIN G. USHER.
GARL J. WATKINS.
ROBERT P. WEIL.
ALAN M. WIENMAN.
BEN D. WORCESTER.
FRANK B. ZINN.

EXECUTIVE STAFF

Chairman	FRANK R. BARNAKO.
Executive Director	GUY T. MOORE.
Chief Judge	CHARLES K. CHAPLIN.
Assistant Chief Judge	JOSEPH L. CHALK.
Counsel to the Commission	PAUL R. WALLACE.
Executive Secretary	WILLIAM S. MCLAUGHLIN.
Assistant to Executive Secretary	GLORIA W. WHITE.
Chief Review Counsel	RICHARD F. SCHIFFMANN.

Exhibit 74:   Description of the Occupational Safety and Health Review Commission in the *United States Government Manual.*

EXECUTIVE STAFF—Continued

Chairman—Continued
Director of Management Systems Division_____   JEFFREY A. MILLER.
Director of Information and Publications_____   LINDA P. DODD.

The Occupational Safety and Health Review Commission (OSHRC) is concerned with providing safe and healthful working conditions for both the employer and the employee. It adjudicates cases forwarded to it by the Department of Labor when disagreements arise over the results of safety and health inspections performed by the Department.

The Occupational Safety and Health Review Commission is an independent adjudicatory agency established by the Occupational Safety and Health Act of 1970 (84 Stat. 1590; 29 U.S.C. 651).

The act, enforced by the Secretary of Labor, is an effort to reduce the incidence of personal injuries, illnesses, and deaths among working men and women in the United States which result from their employment. The Review Commission was created to adjudicate enforcement actions initiated under the act when they are contested by employers, employees, or representatives of employees.

The principal office of the Review Commission is in Washington, D.C. There are also 10 offices where Review Commission Judges are stationed:

Review Commission Judges—Occupational Safety and Health Review Commission

Address	Phone
Atlanta, Ga. 30309	
1365 Peachtree St. NE	404-526-5197.
Boston, Mass. 02109	
147 Milk St	617-223-3757.
Chicago, Ill. 60603	
55 E. Monroe St	312-353-4634.
Dallas, Tex. 75201	
Fidelity Union Life Bldg	214-749-7171.
Denver, Colo. 80202	
1050 17th St	303-837-2281.
Hyattsville, Md. 20782	
6525 Belcrest Rd	301-436-8870.
Lawndale, Calif. 90260	
Federal Office Bldg. 2E2	213-536-6468.
New York, N.Y. 10036	
1515 Broadway	212-971-7985.
Seattle, Wash. 98101	
625 Logan Bldg	206-442-5744.
St. Louis, Mo. 63101	
1114 Market St	314-622-5071.

FUNCTIONS

The Commission's functions are strictly adjudicatory; it is, however, more of a court system than a simple tribunal, for within the Review Commission there are two levels of adjudication. All cases which require a hearing are assigned to a Review Commission Judge who will decide the case. Each such decision is subject to discretionary review by the three members of the Review Commission upon the motion of any one of the three. However, approximately 90 percent of the decisions of the Judges become final orders without any change whatsoever.

The Occupational Safety and Health Act covers virtually every employer in the country. It requires each employer to furnish to each of his employees employment and a place of employment which are free from recognized hazards that are causing or are likely to cause death or serious physical harm to his employees, and comply with occupational safety and health standards promulgated under the act.

The Secretary of Labor has promulgated a substantial number of occupational safety and health standards which, pursuant to the act, have the force and effect of law. He has also initiated a regular program of inspections in order to check upon compliance. A case for adjudication by the Commission arises when a citation is issued against an employer as the result of such an inspection and it is contested within 15 working days thereafter.

<u>Exhibit 74:</u>   Cont'd.

When a case is docketed, it is assigned for hearing to a Review Commission Judge. The hearing will ordinarily be held in the community where the alleged violation occurred or close thereto. At the hearing, the Secretary of Labor will have the burden of proving his case.

After the hearing, the Judge must issue a report, based on findings of fact, affirming, modifying, or vacating the Secretary's citation or proposed penalty, or directing other appropriate relief. His report will become a final order of the Commission 30 days thereafter unless, within such period, any Commission member directs that such report shall be reviewed by the Commission itself. When that occurs, the members of the Commission will thereafter issue their own decision on the case.

Once a case is decided, any person adversely affected or aggrieved thereby, may obtain a review of such decision in the United States Court of Appeals.

Sources of Information

To give the public and persons appearing before the Commission a better understanding of the act, and the Commission's procedures and decisions, members and officials participate as speakers or panel members before bar associations, safety councils, labor organizations, management associations, and educational, civic, and other groups. Requests for speakers or panelists may be made to the Commission's Washington office.

For further information, contact the Director of Information and Publications, Occupational Safety and Health Review Commission (OSHRC), 1825 K Street NW., Washington, D.C. 20006. Phone, 202–634–7943.

Approved.

FRANK R. BARNAKO,
Chairman.

OVERSEAS PRIVATE INVESTMENT CORPORATION

1129 Twentieth Street NW., Washington, D.C. 20527
Phone, 202–632–1804

President and Chief Executive Officer	MARSHALL T. MAYS.
Executive Vice President	DAVID GREGG III.
General Counsel	GERALD D. MORGAN, JR.
Treasurer	PAUL J. MULLER.
Vice President for Development	ERLAND H. HEGINBOTHAM.
Vice President for Insurance	GEORGE R. COOPER, JR.
Vice President for Financing	ANTHONY J. HOPE.

The Overseas Private Investment Corporation (OPIC) assists United States investors to make profitable investments in about 80 developing countries. It encourages investment projects that will help the social and economic development of these countries. At the same time it helps the U.S. balance of payments through the profits they return to this country, as well as the U.S. jobs and exports they create. OPIC offers U.S. investors assistance in finding investment opportunities, insurance to protect their investments, and loans and loan guaranties to help finance their projects.

The Overseas Private Investment Corporation was authorized as an independent agency in the executive branch pursuant to the act of December 30, 1969 (83 Stat. 805; 22 U.S.C. 2191 et seq.). The authorities were formally transferred to the Corporation by Executive Order 11579 of January 19, 1971.

OPIC is governed by an 11-member

Exhibit 74: Cont'd.

[*206*]

FEDERAL ADMINISTRATIVE
REGULATIONS

1.   Federal Register. As more and more executive and administrative orders and regulations were promulgated in the early New Deal period it became increasingly difficult to locate copies and to know which were in effect at any particular time.   There was no requirement that regulations be centrally filed, nor that they be published either as issued or in a compiled form.   Public indignation arose over the confusion, uncertainty, and inaccessibility of these legal sources.   Two important cases reached the U. S. Supreme Court where it was discovered that the administrative regulations on which they were based no longer were in effect.   Newspapers throughout the country and opponents of the government criticized it for prosecuting people under non-existent laws. This furor led in 1935 to the enactment of the Federal Register Act which established the *Federal Register* as a daily gazette for executive and administrative promulgations.   Executive orders and administrative regulations must be published in the *Federal Register* if they are to be legally effective.   A 1937 amendment to the Act created the *Code of Federal Regulations,* which arranged the effective regulations in an indexed subject compilation with provision for supplementation.

The *Federal Register,* pursuant to its authorizing legislation, contains the following documents:

(a) Presidential proclamations and executive orders of general applicability and legal effect;

(b) Such other documents as the President may determine from time to time have general applicability and legal effect;

(c) Such documents as may be required to be published by act of Congress;

(d) Other documents selected by the director of the *Federal Register.*

For the purpose of inclusion in the *Register* the following are considered to have general applicability and legal effect:

" * * * document(s) issued under proper authority prescribing a penalty or a course of conduct, conferring a right, privilege, authority, or immunity, or imposing an obligation, and relevant or applicable to the general public, the members of a class, or the persons of a locality, as distinguished from named individuals or organizations * * * " (1 C.F.R. 81.1).

For an example of a regulation published in the *Register*, see Exhibit 75 below.

Rules and Regulations

Title 29—LABOR

Chapter I—National Labor Relations Board

PART 102—RULES AND REGULATIONS, SERIES 8

Subpart I—Service and Filing of Papers

PROOF OF SERVICE

Section 102.112 is amended to read as follows:

§ 102.112 Same; by parties; proof of service.

Service of papers by a party on other parties shall be made by registered mail, or by certified mail, or in any manner provided for the service of papers in a civil action by the law of the State in which the hearing is pending. Except for charges, petitions, exceptions, briefs, and other papers for which a time for both filing and response has been otherwise established, service on all parties shall be made in the same manner as that utilized in filing the paper with the Board, or in a more expeditious manner; however, when filing with the Board is accomplished by personal service the other parties shall be promptly notified of such action by telephone, followed by service of a copy by mail or telegraph. When service is made by registered mail, or by certified mail, the return post office receipt shall be proof of service. When service is made in any manner provided by the law of a State, proof of service shall be made in accordance with such law.

This section shall become effective upon date of publication (8–13–71).

OGDEN W. FIELDS,
Executive Secretary.

[FR Doc.71–11719 Filed 8–12–71; 8:50 am]

Chapter XVII—Occupational Safety and Health Administration, Department of Labor

PART 1910—OCCUPATIONAL SAFETY AND HEALTH STANDARDS

Miscellaneous Amendments

On May 29, 1971, occupational safety and health standards were promulgated (36 F.R. 10466). Subsequent review of the standards, and comments and requests for information from the public have pointed up the need for some clarifications, corrections, and changes in effective dates of standards.

Reconsideration of "additional delay in effective date" provisions in various subparts of 29 CFR Part 1910 has shown that the scope of the provisions is too broad, and includes standards for which no delay is necessary for compliance. The purpose of some of the amendments is to limit the additional delay provisions to the specific standards that need additional time, so that the other standards may become effective sooner. On the other hand, Subpart J of Part 1910 is amended to give for the first time an additional delay to specified provisions.

Section 1910.179(b)(2) has been revised in order to give some time for the modification of existing overhead and gantry cranes, and to reflect accurately the American National Standards Institute (ANSI) standard from which the provision is derived. Similar changes have been made in § 1910.180 (crawler, locomotive, and truck cranes) and in § 1910.181 (derricks), for the same reasons.

Section 1910.217(a)(2) has been revised in order to give 36 months for the modification of presently installed mechanical power presses. The delay is given in the ANSI standard adopted in the section.

Section 1910.93 (air contaminants) has been revised in its entirety, in the interest of greater intelligibility and accuracy.

Several different dates have been changed to August 31, 1971, in order to achieve greater uniformity throughout Part 1910. Other amendments are made to correct mistakes, supply omissions, and to provide greater clarity.

Accordingly, pursuant to authority in section 6(a) and 8(g) of the Williams-Steiger Occupational Safety and Health Act of 1970 (84 Stat. 1593, 1600; 29 U.S.C. 655, 357), 29 CFR Part 1910 is hereby amended as set forth below. The provisions of 5 U.S.C. 553 concerning notice of proposed rule making, public participation therein, and delay in effective date are inapplicable by virtue of the exception to 5 U.S.C. Chapter 5 provided in section 6(a) of the Act. In addition, notice and public procedure are unnecessary because of the nature of the amendments, and impracticable, because of the need to give as much advance notice as possible of the changes before August 27, 1971, when many standards in Part 1910 become effective.

Part 1910 is amended as follows:

1. Section 1910.93 of Subpart G is revised to read as follows:

§ 1910.93 Air contaminants.

An employee's exposure to any material listed in table G–1, G–2, or G–3 of this section shall be limited in accordance with the requirements of the following paragraphs of this section.

(a) Table G–1:

(1) *Materials with names preceded by "C"—Ceiling Values.* An employee's exposure to any material in table G–1, the name of which is preceded by a "C" (e.g., C Boron trifluoride), shall at no time exceed the ceiling value given for that material in the table.

(2) *Other materials—8-hour time weighted averages.* An employee's exposure to any material in table G–1, the name of which is not preceded by "C", in any 8-hour work shift of a 40-hour work week, shall not exceed the 8-hour time weighted average given for that material in the table.

(b) Table G–2:

(1) *8-hour time weighted averages.* An employee's exposure to any material listed in table G–2, in any 8-hour work shift of a 40-hour work week, shall not exceed the 8-hour time weighted average limit given for that material in the table.

(2) *Acceptable ceiling concentrations.* An employee's exposure to a material listed in table G–2 shall not exceed at any time during an 8-hour shift the acceptable ceiling concentration limit given for the material in the table, except for a time period, and up to a concentration not exceeding the maximum duration and concentration allowed in the column under "acceptable maximum peak above the acceptable ceiling concentration for an 8-hour shift".

(3) *Example.* During an 8-hour shift, an employee may be exposed to a concentration of Benzene above 25 p.p.m. (but never above 50 p.p.m.) only for a maximum period of 10 minutes. Such exposure must be compensated by exposures to concentrations less than 10 p.p.m. so that the cumulative exposure for the entire 8-hour work shift does not exceed a weighted average of 10 p.p.m.

(c) Table G–3: An employee's exposure to any material listed in table G–3, in any 8-hour work shift of a 40-hour work week, shall not exceed the 8-hour time weighted average limit given for that material in the table.

(d) Computation formulae:

(1) (i) The cumulative exposure for an 8-hour work shift shall be computed as follows:

$$E = \frac{C_a T_a + C_b T_b + \ \ldots \ C_n T_n}{8}$$

where:

E is the equivalent exposure for the working shift.

C is the concentration during any period of time T where the concentration remains constant.

T is the duration in hours of the exposure at the concentration C.

The value of E shall not exceed the 8-hour time weighted average limit in table G–1, G–2, or G–3 for the material involved.

(ii) To illustrate the formula prescribed in subdivision (i) of this subparagraph, note that isomyl acetate has an 8-hour time weighted average limit of 100 p.p.m. (table G–1). Assume that an

Exhibit 75: Amendments to occupational safety and health standards in a daily issue of the *Federal Register.*

[*209*]

The *Federal Register* has been published continuously since March 14, 1936 and provides a chronological source, similar to a session law text, for these documents. Indexing has improved over the years until now each daily issue contains its own table of contents as well as two guides noting which regulations have been changed in that issue (List of C.F.R. Parts Affected in this Issue) and which have been changed since the beginning of the month (Cumulative List of C.F.R. Parts Affected During ———). In addition, at the end of each month, a monthly index is published along with a separate pamphlet entitled *List of C.F.R. Sections Affected* which cumulates references to all changes since the last revision of the titles in the *Code of Federal Regulations*. These lists, which are the basic finding tool for locating changes in the *Register,* are based on the titles and sections of the *Code of Federal Regulations.* Exhibit 76 shows a portion of such a list in the August 13, 1971, issue of the *Register*.

The text of material in the *Federal Register* is *prima facie* evidence of its filing. If a regulation is not published therein, it is not binding unless one can be shown to have had *actual* knowledge of the regulation. Such proof is, of course, quite difficult and the requirement effectively deters non-publication.

CONTENTS

List of CFR Parts Affected

The following numerical guide is a list of the parts of each title of the Code of Federal Regulations affected by documents published in today's issue. A cumulative list of parts affected, covering the current month to date, appears following the Notices section of each issue beginning with the second issue of the month.

A cumulative guide is published separately at the end of each month. The guide lists the parts and sections affected by documents published since January 1, 1971, and specifies how they are affected.

5 CFR			
1602	15107		

7 CFR			
PROPOSED RULES:			
210	15125		
220	15125		
245	15125		
926	15125		

9 CFR			
311	15109		
•316	15109		
317	15109		

12 CFR			
PROPOSED RULES:			
226	15130		

14 CFR			
39 (3 documents)	15109, 15110		
71 (14 documents)	15111–15114		
PROPOSED RULES:			
39	15127		
71	15127		

19 CFR		
1	15114	

21 CFR		
420	15114	

26 CFR		
PROPOSED RULES:		
1 (3 documents)	15123	

29 CFR		
102	15101	
1910	15101	

32 CFR		
46	15114	
241	15114	

41 CFR		
Ch. 14	15116	

43 CFR		
4	15116	
1840	15119	
1850	15119	
4110	15119	
9230	15120	

46 CFR		
PROPOSED RULES:		
530	15128	
545	15128	

47 CFR		
0	15120	
21	15121	
89	15121	
91	15121	
93	15121	
PROPOSED RULES:		
21	15131	
43	15131	
61	15131	
87	15131	

49 CFR		
1	15122	
1033	15122	

Exhibit 76: List of C.F.R. Parts Affected in a daily issue of the *Federal Register*.

Because of the great bulk of the *Register* and because of the poor quality of paper used, more and more libraries are purchasing a microfilm or microfiche edition of the *Register* and keeping only the annual index and *List of C.F.R. Sections Affected* in its original form as a finding tool for the microfacsimile. The *Federal Register* has a permanent reference value and consequently should be accessible in some form. Its value stems from the fact that it includes some material which never appears in its companion publication, the *Code of Federal Regulations*, and it provides the only complete history of the regulations with the text of all changes.

2. Code of Federal Regulations. In 1937, realizing the limitations of chronological publication and the need for a permanent subject compilation of current regulations, Congress established the *Code of Federal Regulations*. The regulations in the *Code* are collected from the *Federal Register* and are arranged in a subject scheme that comprises fifty titles, some of which duplicate the titles of the *U. S. Code*. Each title is divided into chapters, parts, and sections, and the citation form is to title and section, e. g., 29 *C.F.R.* § 1910 (Title 29, Section 1910). The *Code* has a general index volume providing access to the *Code*'s contents by agency name and subject.

The *Code* is kept up to date by a process of perpetual revision. Each year, the set is completely revised by the issuance of new pamphlets, containing all the regulations in force at the time of publication. The revisions of the various titles are issued on a quarterly basis—Titles 1–16 as of January 1; titles 17–27 as of April 1; titles 28–41 as of July 1; and titles 42–50 as of October 1.

Each volume contains a list of C.F.R. Sections Affected, cumulating all changes back to January 1, 1964. Lists prior to 1964 have been cumulated and published in a separate volume, *List of C.F.R. Sections Affected, 1949–1963* (G.P.O., 1966).

The *C.F.R.* pamphlets themselves do not reflect all of the changes which may have been made

during the year and which were then modified again. The *Federal Register* therefore remains the only source for obtaining *all* of the different versions which may have been in effect, even briefly, during the year. Sample pages of the *Code* are reproduced in Exhibit 77.

---

§ 1908.7   Title 29—Labor

§ 1908.7   Termination of agreement.

(a) *Termination by the parties.* Either party may terminate this agreement upon 15 days written notice to the other party.

(b) *Termination upon plan approval.* In no event shall an agreement under this part continue in effect beyond 30 days after a State's occupational safety and health plan has been approved under section 18(c) of the Act.

§ 1908.8   Exclusion.

This agreement does not restrict in any manner the authority and responsibility of the Assistant Secretary under sections 8, 9, 10, 13, and 17 of the Act.

PART 1910—OCCUPATIONAL SAFETY AND HEALTH STANDARDS

Subpart A—General

64

Exhibit 77:   Excerpts from the *Code of Federal Regulations* setting out occupational safety and health standards.

Subject Index for 29 CFR 1910—Occupational Safety and Health Standards.

➤ AUTHORITY: The provisions of this Part
1910 issued under secs. 6(a), 8(g), 84 Stat.
1593, 1598; 29 U.S.C. 655, 657, unless otherwise noted.

SOURCE: 39 FR 23502, June 27, 1974, unless
otherwise noted.

Subpart A—General

➤ § 1910.1 Purpose and scope.

(a) Section 6(a) of the Williams-
Steiger Occupational Safety and Health
Act of 1970 (84 Stat. 1593) provides that
"without regard to chapter 5 of title 5,
United States Code, or to the other subsections of this section, the Secretary
shall, as soon as practicable during the
period beginning with the effective date
of this Act and ending 2 years after such
date, by rule promulgate as an occupational safety or health standard any national consensus standard, and any established Federal standard, unless he
determines that the promulgation of
such a standard would not result in improved safety or health for specifically
designated employees." The legislative
purpose of this provision is to establish,
as rapidly as possible and without regard
to the rule-making provisions of the Administrative Procedure Act, standards
with which industries are generally familiar, and on whose adoption interested
and affected persons have already had an
opportunity to express their views. Such
standards are either (1) national consensus standards on whose adoption affected persons have reached substantial
agreement, or (2) Federal standards already established by Federal statutes or
regulations.

(b) This part carries out the directive
to the Secretary of Labor under section
6(a) of the Act. It contains occupational
safety and health standards which have
been found to be national consensus
standards or established Federal standards.

§ 1910.2 Definitions.

As used in this part, unless the context clearly requires otherwise:

(a) "Act" means the Williams-Steiger
Occupational Safety and Health Act of
1970 (84 Stat. 1590).

(b) "Assistant Secretary of Labor"
means the Assistant Secretary of Labor
for Occupational Safety and Health;

(c) "Employer" means a person engaged in a business affecting commerce
who has employees, but does not include
the United States or any State or political subdivision of a State;

(d) "Employee" means an employee of
an employer who is employed in a business of his employer which affects commerce;

(e) "Commerce" means trade, traffic,
commerce, transportation, or communication among the several States, or between a State and any place outside
thereof, or within the District of Columbia, or a possession of the United States
(other than the Trust Territory of the
Pacific Islands), or between points in the
same State but through a point outside
thereof;

(f) "Standard" means a standard
which requires conditions, or the adoption or use of one or more practices,
means, methods, operations, or processes,
reasonably necessary or appropriate to

The Finding Aids volume of the *Code* contains many parallel reference tables which enable the researcher to convert from one legal form to another. The following parallel references can be obtained in this way:

(a) **U. S. Code to C.F.R.:** This table lists those sections of the *U.S. Code* which have been cited as the authority for the rules of an administrative agency. Rules issued by the agency pursuant to that authority appear in the column headed "Code of Federal Regulations." See Exhibit 78 below.

(b) **C.F.R. to U. S. Code or Statutes at Large:** This information is provided not by a table, but by an "Authority" note at the end of each section of the *C.F.R.,* or at the beginning of a group of similar sections in the *Code.* See the "Authority" section in Exhibit 77 on p. 214.

(c) **Proclamation, executive order, or reorganization plan to C.F.R.:** These tables give parallel references from presidential documents to those sections of the *Code* which cite or utilize them. Information given includes document number, date, *Federal Register* citation, subject, and *C.F.R.* reference. Exhibit 79 shows the listing for Executive Order

11612 relating to occupational safety and health.

---

29 U. S. C. 655   **Finding Aids**

United States Code	Code of Federal Regulations
29 U. S. C. 655	29 CFR Part 1905
	Parts 1910–1912
	Part 1926
	Part 1928
	41 CFR Part 50–204
656	29 CFR Part 1908
	Part 1912
	Part 1926
657	29 CFR Parts 1901–1912a
	Parts 1950–1955
	30 CFR Part 11
	41 CFR Part 50–204
	42 CFR Parts 84–87
657g	29 CFR Part 1902
658	29 CFR Part 1903
660	29 CFR Part 1977
661	29 CFR Part 2100
	Part 2200
	Part 2300
665	29 CFR Part 1905
667	29 CFR Part 1901
	Part 1902
	Parts 1952–1955
	Part 1975
	41 CFR Part 50–204

1021 through 1022	29 CFR Part 2520
1024 through 1025	29 CFR Part 2520
1029 through 1031	29 CFR Part 2520
1030	29 CFR Part 2555
1031	29 CFR Part 2510
1051 through 1054	29 CFR Part 2530
1060	29 CFR Part 2530
1112	29 CFR Part 2550
	Part 2555
1114	29 CFR Part 1
	Part 2550
1135	29 CFR Part 2510
	Part 2520
	Part 2530
	Part 2550
	Part 2555
1241 through 1242	20 CFR Parts 900–902

106

Exhibit 78: Table in Finding Aids volume of *C.F.R.*, listing that section of the *U.S. Code* which is authority for the regulations at 29 *C.F.R.* § 1910.

Finding Aids

E. O. No.	Date	F. R. Citation	Subject
	1971 (Con.)	**36 F.R.**	
11609	July 22	13747	Delegating certain functions vested in the President to other officers of the government.
11612	July 28	13891	Occupational safety and health programs for Federal employees.
11615	Aug. 17	15727	Providing for the stabilization of prices, rents, wages, and salaries.
11616	Aug. 28	17319	Amending Executive Order No. 11491, relating to labor-management relations in the Federal service.
11623	Oct. 12	19963	Delegating to the Director of Selective Service authority to issue rules and regulations under the Military Selective Service Act.
11625	Oct. 14	19967	Prescribing additional arrangements for developing and coordinating a national program for minority business enterprise.
11627	Oct. 16	20139	Further providing for the stabilization of the economy_____
11636	Dec. 24	24901	Employee-management relations in the Foreign Service of the United States.
	1972	**37 F.R.**	
11640	Jan. 27	1213	Further providing for the stabilization of the economy_____
11644	Feb. 8	2877	Use of off-road vehicles on the public lands_____
11645	Feb. 8	2923	Authority of the Secretary of Transportation to prescribe certain regulations relating to Coast Guard housing.
11647	Feb. 10	3167	Federal Regional Councils_____

Exhibit 79: Parallel reference table in *C.F.R.*, providing reference from Executive Order to *C.F.R.* citation.

Table II—Presidential Documents

Reference	Comment
{ 5 CFR 591, Subpart C	Cited as authority.
{41 CFR Part 101–7	Cited as authority and in text.
{29 CFR 1960.1	Cited in text.
{41 CFR 101–20.109–1	Cited in text.
{18 CFR 2.90	Cited in heading and in text.
{ 154.63	Cited in text.
{32A CFR Ch. 1, ES Reg. 1	Cited as authority and in text.
{ 5 CFR 2410.1	Cited in text.
{ Part 2411	Cited as authority and in text.
{ Parts 2413, 2470, 2471	Cited as authority.
{29 CFR Part 201	Cited as authority and in text.
{ Parts 202–206	Cited as authority.
{32 CFR 516.1	Cited in text.
32 CFR Parts 1624, 1626, 1627, 1628, 1631, 1661, 1680.	Cited as authority.
{24 CFR 43.16	Cited in text.
{41 CFR 1–1.1300	Cited in text.
{ 3–1.752–2	Cited in text.
{ 18–1.332–1	Cited in text.
{18 CFR 2.90a	Cited in heading.
{ 154.63	Cited in text.
{26 CFR 301.9000–1	Cited in text.
{32A CFR Ch. 1, ES Reg. 1	Cited in text.
{46 CFR 548	Cited as authority.
{ 5 CFR 550.341	**Cited in text.**
{ **2410.1**	**Cited in text.**
{ Part 2411	**Cited as** authority and in text.
{ Parts 2413, 2470, 2471	Cited as authority.
{22 CFR Parts 14–15,801–806	Cited as authority and in text.
{29 CFR Parts 201–206	Cited as authority.
{ Part 201	Cited in text.
{ 1960.2	Cited in text.
18 CFR 154.13, 154.63	Cited in text.
{18 CFR Part 305	Cited as authority.
{36 CFR 2.34	Cited in text.
{ 4.19	Cited in text.
{ Part 295	Cited as authority.
{43 CFR Part 420	Cited as authority.
{ Part 6290	Cited as authority and in text.
{49 CFR 1.46	Cited in text.
7 CFR 22.202	Cited in text.

Exhibit 79: Right-hand continuation of above *C.F.R.* table.

(d) **U. S. Code to Presidential Documents:**
Before 1970, the five year cumulations
of Title 3 of *C.F.R.* contained a table of
statutory authorities for executive orders and proclamations which had cited
the *U. S. Code* as authority. Since 1970
this table has been discontinued.

(e) **Presidential Documents to U. S. Code:**
These tables, illustrated in Exhibit 80,
are not found in *C.F.R.*, but in the Tables
volumes of the *U. S. Code* and its two unofficial versions *U.S.C.A.* and *U.S.C.S.*
They list each executive publication by
date and indicate its statutory source in
the *U. S. Code.*

EXECUTIVE ORDERS

Date	Exec. Ord. No.	Title	Sec.	Status
1970				
June 4	11533	50 App.	2403 nt	
	11534	18	prec. 1 nt	
12	11535	26 [I.R.C. 1939]	55 nt	
		26	6103 nt	
30	11539	7	1854 nt	
July 1	11540	5	5317 nt	Elim.
	11541	31	16 nt	
2	11542	5	5317 nt	Elim.
8	11544	10	Prec. 1121 nt	
9	11545	10	1125 nt	
10	11547	42	Prec. 2711 nt	
20	11548	33	1151 nt	
28	11549	18	2152 nt	
30	11550	5	5317 nt	Elim.
Aug. 11	11551	25	Prec. 1 nt	
24	11552	5	3584 nt	
29	11554	10	5707 nt	
Sept. 4	11556	47	305 nt, 606 nt, 721 nt	
		50 App.	2271 nt, 2292 nt	
23	11560	40	486 nt	Elim.
25	11561	42	5055 nt	
Oct. 6	11564	15	1517 nt	
13	11565	3	110 nt	
Nov. 16	11567	15	1511 nt	Elim.
24	11570	39	3604 nt	
Dec. 23	11574	33	407 nt	
31	11575	42	prec. 4411 nt	Elim.
1971				
Jan. 8	11576	5	5332 nt	
		22	867 nt, 870 nt	
		38	4107 nt	
	11577	37	203 nt	
13	11578	42	1962b nt	
19	11579	22	2191 nt	
20	11581	5	5317 nt	Elim.
Feb. 11	11582	5	6103 nt	
Mar. 3	11584	26 [I.R.C. 1939]	55 nt	
		26	6103 nt	
15	11587	5	5317 nt	Elim.
Apr. 1	11589	5	3376 nt	
23	11590	18	201 nt	
		42	2000e nt	
	11591	37	301 nt	
May 6	11592	3	301 nt	
13	11593	16	470 nt	
June 5	11596	22	288 nt	
16	11598	5	3301 nt	
17	11599	21	801 nt	
29	11601	3	301 nt	
	11602	42	1857h—4 nt	Elim.
30	11603	22	2501 nt	
July 2	11604	5	5317 nt	Elim.
	11605	5	7311 nt	Elim.
19	11607	42	4712 nt	Elim.
	11608	42	3191 nt	
22	11609	3	301 nt	
		20	107 nt	
		38	111 nt	
	11610	50	1431 nt	
26	11611	26	6103 nt	
		26 [I.R.C.1939]	55 nt	
→	11612	5	7902 nt	
Aug. 2	11613	42	1962b nt	
15	11615	12	1904 nt	
26	11616	5	7301 nt	
Sept. 2	11617	12	1904 nt	
Oct. 4	11621	29	176 nt	
5	11622	29	176 nt	

427

Exhibit 80: Table in the *U.S. Code Annotated* indicating statutory authority for Executive Order 11612.

Since title numbers and section numbers of the *Code of Federal Regulations* are used in the List of C.F.R. Parts Affected of the *Federal Register* as a means of identifying subsequent changes in those sections, the *Register* is really a daily supplement to the *C.F.R.* Without the *Code* it would be virtually impossible to research federal regulations, since only it provides the current text with subject access.

In order to make a complete search for a current regulation, the researcher should follow these steps:

(a) Consult the general index volume of the *Code of Federal Regulations* to ascertain the relevant title and section of the *Code*.

(b) Locate the regulation itself in the latest revised volume of that title in the *Code*.

(c) Check the monthly pamphlets of the List of C.F.R. Sections Affected to determine if changes in the particular section have occurred since the last revision.

(d) Use the cumulative List of C.F.R. Sections Affected in the most recent issue of the *Federal Register*. This list updates the last pamphlet in (c), by indicating changes occurring within the current month.

(e) Locate the changes that have occurred by consulting the daily issues of the *Fed-*

eral Register referred to in the List of C.F.R. Sections Affected in steps (c) and (d).

3. Looseleaf Publication of Regulations. Administrative regulations on selected subjects, such as taxation, labor relations, securities, etc., also appear in commercially published looseleaf services which are dealt with in the next chapter. In that form, the regulations are well indexed and supplemented frequently, usually on a weekly basis. For that reason and also because of their integration with other relevant source material, regulations are widely used in this form. Unfortunately, however, looseleaf services are not available for every subject field.

4. Agency Publication of Regulations. The federal administrative agencies themselves often publish texts of their regulations—in either looseleaf or pamphlet form. However, these publications are not well supplemented and, although relatively inexpensive, are not widely used by lawyers or legal scholars. Information as to their availability is provided in the *Monthly Catalog of U. S. Government Publications.*

ADMINISTRATIVE DECISIONS AND RULINGS

In addition to their legislative output, administrative agencies also issue decisions and rulings in the course of their quasi-judicial functions.

Over thirty federal agencies, including the major regulatory commissions, now publish an official edition of those decisions in a form similar to that of the official state reports of court decisions. These reports are in chronological series, usually published first in an advance sheet or slip decision form and then cumulated, though not promptly, into bound volumes. They are cited like court decisions, but with only the name of the private party involved in the proceeding, e. g. General Electric Co., 18 F.T.C. 501 (1958). Depending on the agency, the volumes of decisions may include indexes, digests and tables. However, most of these aids are non-cumulative, applying only to the decisions in the volume in which they appear and so are of limited utility. The cumulative digest covering decisions of the National Labor Relations Board is an exception. Subject access to the decisions of most agencies is effectively provided only by the privately published looseleaf services.

There are unofficial publications of some administrative decisions in the following forms:

1. Many looseleaf services publish decisions of administrative agencies in their subject fields (e. g., CCH *Trade Regulation Reporter* which publishes decisions of the Federal Trade Commission). These services usually contain better indexing than the official edition, appear more promptly, and contain other useful research material, such

as relevant statutes, *court* decisions, regulations and news developments. However, in many of the services, the decisions appear only in a digested form.

2.   Some unofficial topical reporters in particular fields will include both court decisions and administrative decisions. Examples of these are the *U. S. Patents Quarterly* which contains decisions of the federal courts in patent matters, as well as selected decisions of the Commissioner of Patents and the Patent Office Board of Appeals; and *Public Utilities Reports,* which includes Federal Power Commission decisions, as well as court decisions in that field.

3.   Pike and Fischer's *Administrative Law Service* is devoted to *procedural* aspects of administrative law and contains decisions of the major regulatory agencies which have been rendered on questions of procedure. These decisions, arranged according to the sections of the Federal Administrative Procedure Act, appear first in looseleaf sheets, then in bound volumes. The service also includes a digest, an index, court decisions, and rules of practice of some agencies.

CITATORS FOR FEDERAL ADMINISTRATIVE MATERIALS

Although Shepard's does not offer citator service for administrative *regulations,* it does include

coverage of many important administrative agency *decisions*. In 1967 a separate citator was initiated for this purpose, *Shepard's United States Administrative Citations*. Previously, many of those reports were included in *Shepard's U. S. and Federal Citations*. In addition, administrative decisions in labor law are included in *Shepard's Federal Labor Law Citations*. Some other research tools noted below perform a partial citator function. In summary, the following aids are useful for this purpose:

1. **For Regulations:**
   (a) Lists of C.F.R. Parts Affected in the *Federal Register*.
   (b) Lists of Sections Affected in *C.F.R.*
   (c) Looseleaf services in some fields.
   (d) Tables of Statutes Construed in National Reporter System.
   (e) *Shepard's U. S. and Federal Citations* for those regulations which can be shepardized through their related federal statute citation.

2. **For Decisions:**
   (a) *Shepard's U.S. Administrative Citations*.
   (b) *Shepard's Federal Labor Law Citations* for N.L.R.B. decisions.

(c) *Shepard's United States Citations: Patents and Trademarks* for decisions of the Commissioner of Patents and reports of the Court of Customs and Patent Appeals.

(d) Looseleaf services (particularly in taxation).

On the state level, such citator aids are almost non-existent.

EXECUTIVE DOCUMENTS

In addition to the independent agencies and executive departments, the President of the United States also functions as a law-maker in his own right. In that capacity, he issues a variety of legally significant documents, most of which (since 1965) appear promptly in an official publication, the *Weekly Compilation of Presidential Documents*. (Exhibit 81 shows remarks of the President upon the signing of the Occupational Safety and Health Act.) In addition, such documents appear as follows:

1. **Executive Orders and Presidential Proclamations:** The line dividing executive orders from proclamations is blurred, but it may be said that orders usually involve an exercise of presidential authority related to government business, while proclamations are announcements of policy or

of matters requiring public notice. Orders and proclamations are found in the *Federal Register,* are cumulated in Title 3A of the *Code of Federal Regulations,* and selected ones appear in *U.S.C.C.A.N.* and in the supplements to *U.S.C.S.* Proclamations also appear in the *Statutes at Large.*

See Exhibit 82 for an executive order issued in connection with the Occupational Safety and Health Act of 1970.

Weekly Compilation of

PRESIDENTIAL DOCUMENTS

Week Ending Saturday, January 2, 1971

Representative L. Mendel Rivers of South Carolina

Statement by the President on the Death of the Congressman. December 28, 1970

For 30 years, Mendel Rivers served the State of South Carolina and the Nation with dignity, with distinction, and with high integrity in the Congress of the United States. Throughout his career, Congressman Rivers held unswervingly to the belief that the freedom that exists in the modern world is inextricably tied to the military strength of the United States. He fought for that belief in committee, in the Congress, in the country. No shifting national opinion, no amount of hostile criticism, deterred him from the course he deemed right for America. In his death, I have lost a friend upon whom I could rely in times of grave difficulty; South Carolina has lost one of the most distinguished men in her history; and America has lost a patriot.

United States Ambassador to Western Samoa

Announcement of Intention To Nominate Ambassador Kenneth Franzheim II To Serve Concurrently as Ambassador to Western Samoa. December 28, 1970

The President today announced his intention to nominate Kenneth Franzheim II, Ambassador to New Zealand, to serve concurrently and without additional compensation as Ambassador to Western Samoa. Ambassador Franzheim will be the first United States Ambassador to Western Samoa, which achieved its independence in January 1962.

Born in New York City, September 12, 1925, Franzheim received his B.A. (1948) from Yale University.

Upon graduation from college, he worked in various positions with oil field operations and joined Shell Oil Company in their gas contract department in 1952.

In 1953, Franzheim moved into independent oil operation and investment. He joined the board of directors of Southern National Bank in Houston in 1969. On August 4, 1969, Franzheim was appointed by President Nixon to serve as Ambassador to New Zealand.

Ambassador Franzheim is married and has four children. His legal residence is Houston, Tex.

Occupational Safety and Health Act of 1970

Remarks of the President and Secretary of Labor James D. Hodgson at the Signing Ceremony at the Department of Labor. December 29, 1970

SECRETARY HODGSON. *Mr. President, distinguished Members of the Senate and the House, leaders of organized labor, industry, administration officials, professionals in the field of safety and health, and ladies and gentlemen:*

Welcome to the Labor Department and to our signing ceremony.

Through the years, Federal legislation has been marked by some truly milestone measures in the field of worker protection. When you think back, there is the Social Security Act with its provisions to provide a cushion for various kinds of economic adversity; the National Labor Relations Act with provisions protecting organizing rights and concerted activity; then the Fair Labor Standards Act with provisions to prevent abuses in hours and wages and conditions of work.

Through all of this period there had been, it seems to us, a gap in the worker protection, namely, with regard to safety and health.

It is rather curious that more attention hadn't been paid to this subject earlier. Through the years a number of workers were killed, were injured, or fell ill due to working conditions on the job, but it has only been in

Exhibit 81:   Remarks of the President at the signing of the OSHA as published in the *Weekly Compilation of Presidential Documents.*

[*228*]

THE PRESIDENT

EXECUTIVE ORDER 11612

Occupational Safety and Health Programs for Federal Employees

The Occupational Safety and Health Act of 1970, 84 Stat. 1590, authorizes the development and enforcement of standards to assure safe and healthful working conditions for employees in the private sector. Section 19 of that Act makes each Federal agency head responsible for establishing and maintaining an effective and comprehensive occupational safety and health program which is consistent with the standards promulgated by the Secretary of Labor for businesses affecting interstate commerce.

Section 7902 of Title 5, United States Code, authorizes the President to establish by Executive Order a safety council composed of representatives of Federal agencies and of labor organizations representing employees to serve as an advisory body to the Secretary of Labor in carrying out a Federal safety program.

As the Nation's largest employer, the Federal Government has a special obligation to set an example for safe and healthful employment. It is appropriate that the Federal Government strengthen its efforts to assure safe and healthful working conditions for its own employees.

NOW, THEREFORE, by virtue of the authority vested in me by section 7902 of Title 5 of the United States Code, and as President of the United States, it is hereby ordered as follows:

ESTABLISHMENT OF OCCUPATIONAL SAFETY AND HEALTH PROGRAMS IN FEDERAL DEPARTMENTS AND AGENCIES

SECTION 1. The head of each Federal department and agency shall establish an occupational safety and health program (hereinafter referred to as a safety program) in compliance with the requirements of section 7902 of Title 5 of the United States Code and section 19(a) of the Occupational Safety and Health Act of 1970 (which Act shall hereinafter be referred to as the Safety Act). The programs shall be consistent with the standards prescribed by section 6 of the Safety Act. In providing safety programs for Federal employees, the head of each Federal department and agency shall—

(1) Designate or appoint a qualified official who shall be responsible for the management of the safety program within his agency.

(2) Establish (A) a safety policy; (B) an organization and a set of procedures, providing for appropriate consultation with employees, that will permit that policy to be implemented effectively; (C) a safety management information system; (D) goals and objectives for reducing and eliminating employee injuries and occupational illnesses; (E) periodic inspections of workplaces to ensure compliance with standards; (F) plans and procedures for evaluating the program's effectiveness; and (G) priorities with respect to the factors which cause occupational injury and illness so that appropriate countermeasures can be developed.

(3) Correct conditions that do not meet safety and health standards.

(4) Submit to the Secretary of Labor by April 1 of each year a report containing (A) the status of his agency's safety program in reducing

Exhibit 82: Executive Order 11612 on occupational safety and health, as set out in the *Federal Register*.

2. **Presidential Messages:** These communications from the President to Congress explain proposed legislation or vetoes, report on the state of the nation, and serve other functions.   Messages are found in the *Congressional Record, House* and *Senate Journals, House* and *Senate Documents,* and selectively in the advance sheets of the *U.S.C.C.A.N.*

3. **Reorganization Plans:** These plans contain presidential proposals for the reorganization of agencies and departments within the executive branch.   When submitted to Congress, the plans are published in the *Congressional Record.*   If the plans subsequently become effective, they will also appear in the *Statutes at Large,* Title 5 of the *U. S. Code,* the *Federal Register* and Title 3 of the *Code of Federal Regulations,* as well as in *U.S.C.C.A.N.*

4. **Executive Agreements:** Executive agreements reflect diplomatic arrangements made by the President with other nations, under his power to conduct foreign affairs.   Unlike treaties, these agreements do not require the advice and consent of the Senate.

Since 1950, agreements have appeared in the official bound series, *U. S. Treaties*

and Other International Agreements (*U.S.T.*). Prior to that date, they were published in the *Statutes at Large*. Two cumulative indexes to *U.S.T.* covering 1776–1949 and 1950–1970 enable a researcher to locate an agreement in these sources by number, country, subject, or date. See page 264 below.

Since 1958 an official series called *Public Papers of the Presidents* has also been published by the Federal Register Division. It contains collections of presidential documents, arranged by year, for all presidents after Franklin D. Roosevelt, and for Herbert Hoover. These volumes, which are individually indexed, contain most of the documents listed above. With the important exception of the texts of executive orders and proclamations, they cumulate the contents of the *Weekly Compilation of Presidential Documents*. So far, the papers of Presidents Hoover, Truman, Eisenhower, Kennedy, Johnson, Nixon and Ford, have been published and the project will continue to issue the state papers of future presidents. Papers of most of the earlier presidents are generally available in other editions. Currently, the Library of Congress is planning to reproduce its collections of earlier presidential papers on microfilm to facilitate public access to those documents.

ADMINISTRATIVE LAW AT THE STATE AND LOCAL LEVEL

Like the federal government, state governments have experienced in recent years an increase in the number and activity of their administrative agencies. However, as a general rule, publication of state agency rules and decisions is far less systematic than that of the federal government.

Nearly every state publishes a state manual, variously called a redbook, a register, or a legislative manual, which parallels the *United States Government Manual,* providing quick access to information about the state's government, agencies, and officials. In addition, the Council of State Governments issues *The Book of the States* which combines in one volume basic information on government operations in each of the fifty states.

Rules and regulations themselves, however, may be extremely difficult to locate. Only three-fourths of the states require that regulations be filed with an appointed official. Of this group, only fifteen issue compilations of their administrative regulations and only half of these are well-supplemented. For states without such compilations, a researcher must apply to the Secretary of State or to the particular agency for a copy of a specific regulation.

Decisions of some state agencies, especially those dealing with banking, workmen's compensation, public utilities, taxation, and insurance, may be published in official form in chronological series. Some looseleaf services, particularly in the tax field, also include decisions of state tribunals, but this practice is limited to a few subject areas.

Though no publication as comprehensive as the *Monthly Catalog of U.S. Government Publications* exists in any of the states, the *Monthly Checklist of State Publications,* issued by the Library of Congress, lists all state documents received by that library. The documents listed are arranged by state and agency, with a comprehensive annual index.

On the municipal and local level, administrative decisions are almost never published, and regulations, if published, are rarely kept up to date. One would have to request a specific regulation from a town clerk or particular agency, if it were definitely known to exist. It would be very difficult, however, to determine the existence of a particular regulation since they are not available to the public in a compiled or current text, and are rarely indexed in official files.

OPINIONS OF THE ATTORNEYS GENERAL

The opinions of the U. S. Attorney General and the attorneys general of the various states have considerable significance in legal research. These officials render formal and informal opinions of law in response to questions from their respective governments or officials. Their decisions are advisory in nature and do not have binding authority, but they are given considerable weight by the courts in interpreting statutes and regulations. Consequently they may be useful to the attorney with a similar problem or to the scholar investigating that area of law.

For the federal government, the published series of opinions is entitled *Opinions of the Attorneys General of the United States.* Opinions appear first in slip form and are then cumulated into bound volumes at a slow pace. Each volume contains its own index, and, in addition, some cumulative indexing is available. U. S. Attorney General opinions are cited in *Shepard's United States Citations, U. S. Administrative Citations,* and *Federal Citations,* and in some annotated state and federal statutory codes.

Most states also issue these opinions in bound volumes, published chronologically. In some states, the opinions are published every year, but in many there is a long time lag between issuance

and publication. The volumes are rarely preceded by slip opinions.

Each volume of state attorney general opinions usually contains an index but these rarely cumulate. Subject access to these rulings in all of the states was formerly provided by the *Digest of Opinions of the Attorneys General,* published by the Council of State Governments. Unfortunately, it ceased publication in 1969, and no other service has replaced it.

Many of Shepard's state citators use the opinions of the state's attorney general as cited material (with references thereunder to judicial decisions, etc.) and all of the state citators use those opinions as citing material for both cases and statutes.

CHAPTER VII

LOOSELEAF SERVICES

One of the unique inventions of legal bibliography has been the looseleaf service, which offers researchers an easily supplemented tool in specific subject areas, containing legal source material of various kinds, special finding aids and secondary material. These publications provide *comprehensive, unified* and *current* access to selected fields of legal literature. They have become particularly popular in public law areas where government regulation is the central focus of legal development, e. g., taxation, labor, antitrust, and regulated industries such as transportation, communication, banking, utilities, etc. Recently new services have been published in such areas of current interest as criminal law, education, environmental control, housing, poverty law, and urban law. For many lawyers and other researchers specializing in those fields, the looseleaf services are their primary sources of material. A list of most looseleaf services being published at the end of 1977 can be found in Appendix D.

The methods of organization of these tools vary according to the nature of the material, the requirements of the subject matter, and the publisher's predilection. In areas where one major

statute dominates the legal order, the service may be arranged by statutory sections or divisions (e. g., the taxation services, which are structured according to the sections of the Internal Revenue Code). Where several statutes are significant, the service may be divided into areas by the relevant statutes (e. g., labor law services which offer separate sections for the Labor Management Relations Act, the Labor Management Reporting and Disclosure Act, the Wage and Hour Act, State Laws, etc.). In other fields where common law or judicial rules predominate, or where there is a mixture of case and statutory law, the service may follow a logical arrangement of the subject matter (e. g., Trusts and Estates, or Corporations).

ADVANTAGES

The following are the major advantages of looseleaf services over separate research in each of the original primary sources. It should be noted, however, that not every service contains all of these features.

1. Primary Sources Compiled. *All* relevant law is collected in one place by a convenient, compact and coordinated presentation of primary authority, regardless of its original form of publication. By using this integrated approach to varied legal sources, the researcher on a particular topic can work largely within the confines of a

single tool.   A lawyer can have available eco-
nomically a wide range of material, which would
otherwise require vast shelf space, greater costs
and considerable searching and coordination.

A typical looseleaf service may include the following *primary* sources:

(a) Statutes, both state and federal.

(b) Decisions, not only of state and federal
     courts, but also of administrative agen-
     cies which operate in that area.

(c) Rules and regulations of those admin-
     istrative agencies, promulgated pursuant
     to their authorizing statute.

(d) Rulings of agencies on adjudicated mat-
     ters or submitted questions.

Of course, most of these authorities would be
available in their primary form of publication
(e. g. in statutory compilations like the *U. S.
Code* and similar state codes; in official and unofficial state and federal court reporters; in the
Federal Register, the *Code of Federal Regulations* and state administrative compilations; and
in the reporters of administrative agency decisions)—but, as noted above, at far greater cost
in time, space and money.   However, there may
be differences of treatment and coverage between
the usual forms of publication and the looseleaf
services.   For example, decisions appear in some
looseleaf services only in an abbreviated form;

on the other hand, some decisions, not otherwise published in official or unofficial reporters, can be found in these services. Sometimes entire classes of material are available only in a looseleaf service.

2. Secondary Material. Looseleaf services offer the following additional features, usually co-ordinated with, or cross-referenced to, the primary sources:

(a) Summaries of *proposed* legislation and regulations, along with their analysis, status and purpose.

(b) News coverage of the legal and general developments in the particular area covered.

(c) Editorial notes and comments, interpretations of the primary sources, projections of current trends, and related background material.

3. Speed. By regular supplementation, all of these materials appear promptly, frequently weekly, while there are often delays in the *official* publication of the primary sources. The looseleaf service cuts through these delays by offering prompt transmittals and an easy, economical means of updating by simply filing the new sheets into the service as they are received.

4. Integrated Coverage. The services cut across jurisdictional lines and cover their respective fields as units without regard to the source of the particular publications.

5. Indexing. Quick and detailed indexing, which coordinates the whole collection and affords convenient access at many points. A typical service may include all of the following indexes under these or similar names:

> (a) **Rapid Finder Index**—using a broad, analytical approach, it divides the whole service into major areas and provides an initial orientation to its contents.

> (b) **Basic or Topical Index**—using the catch word or topical approach, it provides more direct and specific reference to the service.

> (c) **Finding Lists**—include different types of documentary material by their official citations, enabling the researcher to locate a specific regulation, rule, order, decision or ruling directly.

> (d) **Current and Supplementary Indexes**—update the basic index and include references to the latest additions to the service.

> (e) **Tables of Cases**—not only locate these materials directly (like the Finding

Lists), but sometimes also provide a limited citator function.

COMMON FEATURES

A detailed and specific description of looseleaf services is impossible because of the variety and individuality of their form and content. Each publisher approaches the problem of arrangement in a slightly different way and the variations of subject material often require markedly different treatment as well. However, the following common features of most looseleaf services can be noted:

1. Looseleaf supplementation by expandable binders into which sheets are filed periodically (weekly in most services).

2. Detailed instructions for use of the service, which are set out at the beginning of the first volume.

3. Paragraph number arrangement and citation in preference to page references.

4. Indexes and tables as described above.

5. Current material and news developments.

6. Commentary and editorial analysis on the primary sources.

RESEARCH STEPS IN USING SERVICES

Although again it is difficult to generalize about the best procedure to be followed in working with

a looseleaf service, the following steps are typical for most cases:

1.   Analysis of one's problem into general areas of concern, noting the type of source material likely to be needed.

2.   Perusal of the instructions at the front of the applicable service, which, in three minutes, can usually provide an adequate working orientation.   This is the most neglected step and one which can save the researcher much time and trouble.

3.   Use of the service's various indexes to locate the specific material for solution of the problem—generally proceeding from the Rapid Finder Index to the Basic or Topical Index and then to the Current Material Index.   If the researcher has specific reference to a relevant document (order, regulation, ruling or bulletin), the Finding Lists can be used to locate it directly.

4.   Study of the actual texts of the relevant primary material, supplemented by the editorial explanation and secondary materials.   It should be noted that, although many services contain only digests of court or administrative decisions, some publishers will provide the *full* text of such decisions to subscribers on a complimentary basis, upon request.

5.   Up-dating the relevant sources by use of the citators and current material sections.

AN ILLUSTRATIVE SEARCH PROBLEM

The actual research aids and procedures of a typical looseleaf service are illustrated in the following exhibits. To provide a focus for examining the service, consider the problem of determining the rights of an employee who has been discharged because of his or her observance of a Saturday Sabbath. The service used here is CCH's *Employment Practices Guide*. Note that citations within the service refer to paragraph numbers, rather than page numbers.

The search begins with several subject or topical indexes which give access to most of the material in the service, including short essays summarizing various topics in the field, federal statutes and regulations, and federal judicial and administrative agency decisions. Also included in this service, but not shown in these exhibits, are state statutes and decisions. The finding lists and tables of cases give the looseleaf paragraph number of materials cited in decisions, so that they can easily be located.

242 **Topical Index**

References are to paragraph (¶) numbers.
See also Current Topical Index at page 2651.

Religious discrimination—continued
. discharge or discipline exemption
. . employer . . . 543
. . unions . . . 663
. discharges of employees . . . 1051; 1066
. District of Columbia government employees . . . 3855.201 et seq.
. educational institution exemption
. . employer . . . 545
. . general aspects . . . 535
. . sex bias . . . 535; 535.85
. election activities . . . 3310
. employee benefit plans . . . 1204
. . employer . . . 541
. . employment agencies . . . 716
. . unions . . . 661
. employee rights . . . 360; 385
. employers
. . practices outlawed . . . 345; 507; 523; 3051
. employment, interference with right of . . . 3310
. employment agencies . . . 692; 700
. . practices outlawed . . . 355; 700; 3052
. . referrals for employment . . . 706
. establishments serving the public . . . 3310
. executive agencies . . . 3855.201 et seq.
. exemptions from ban on—see specific type of exemption hereunder
. facilities for employees . . . 1120
. federal government exemption . . . 694
. . employer . . . 531
. federally assisted apprenticeship and training programs . . . 743
. federally assisted construction contracts . . . 375; 583; 591
. federally assisted highway contracts . . . 1754
. federally assisted programs or activities . . . 380; 585; 591; 3310
. gasoline stations . . . 3310
. government agency, employment by . . . 3310
. government agency exemption . . . 710; 712
. government benefits, services, programs, participation in . . . 3310
. government contractors . . . 1170
. . affirmative action programs . . . 1630; 1630.10
. . equal opportunity clause . . . 597
. . practices outlawed . . . 577; 579; 583; 585; 591
. . provisions in agreement . . . 3680
. government employees . . . 435; 1943; 2943
. . exhaustion of administrative remedies . . . 2952.15
. government policy . . . 3042; 3711
. grants-in-aid programs . . . 2792
. guidelines . . . 3970
. help-wanted advertisements . . . 507; 921; 926
. . employers . . . 523; 545; 3063
. . employment agencies . . . 720; 3063
. . government contractors . . . 591
. . job qualifications exemption . . . 720
. . unions . . . 3063
. hiring process . . . 1152; 1164
. hotels and motels . . . 3310
. Illinois guidelines . . . 22,398; 22,498
. Indian tribe exemption . . . 549; 694
. interference or intimidation . . . 1220
. interstate commerce facilities, use of . . . 3310
. job applicant rights . . . 360; 385
. job qualifications exemption . . . 523; 1262
. . apprenticeship and training programs . . . 743; 755; 3055
. . educational institutions . . . 3055
. . employer . . . 545; 3055
. . employment agencies . . . 720; 3055
. . joint labor-management committees . . . 3055
. . unions . . . 665; 3055

Religious discrimination—continued
. judicial branch of government, employees of . . . 3855.201 et seq.
. jury service . . . 3310
. legislative branch of government, employees of . . . 3855.201 et seq.
. military departments . . . 3855.201 et seq.
. motion picture theaters . . . 3310
. national security exemption
. . employer . . . 553
. . unions . . . 669
. pattern, policy or practice of employer or union . . . 1290
. post-hiring inquiries
. . validity of ruling permitting . . . 23,999.40
. pre-employment inquiries as evidence of . . . 4030
. private membership club exemption . . . 559; 694
. public school or college attendance or enrollment . . . 3310
. radio broadcasters . . . 1847
. railroads . . . 2890
. recruitment of personnel . . . 1335
. referrals to jobs . . . 1340
. refusals to hire . . . 1152; 1164
. religious observances and holidays . . . 1170
. religious organization exemption
. . employer . . . 537
. restaurants and like establishments . . . 3310
. schools . . . 3310
. . construction contract clauses . . . 20,799.62
. seniority, merit or incentive system exemption . . . 1372
. . employer . . . 539; 3058
. . employment agencies . . . 714
. . unions . . . 659
. service, supply and construction contracts . . . 370
. social and recreational activities . . . 1400
. sports arenas or stadiums . . . 3310
. state government exemption
. . employer . . . 533
. state laws—see specific states
. state or local government services or programs . . . 694; 3310
. terms, conditions and privileges of employment . . . 1412; 1416
. testing and other selection procedures . . . 1427
. transferrals of employees . . . 1482
. transportation, interference with use of modes of . . . 3310
. unemployed persons, exemption of programs for . . . 561; 673; 726; 761
. unions . . . 637; 639; 647; 1533
. . causing employer discrimination . . . 653
. . membership in . . . 1523
. . practices outlawed . . . 350; 647; 653; 3053
. . referrals for employment . . . 655
. veterans' preference . . . 551
. voting rights . . . 3310
. wage differentials . . . 1542
. wage increases . . . 1550
. wage reductions . . . 1560
. wages . . . 1573
. working conditions . . . 1590

Religious institutions
. minister's retirement age . . . 1208.837

Religious observances and holidays . . . 1170, 1170.10-1170.15
. discharges for . . . 1170; 1170.11, 1170.113; 1170.1131; 1170.14; 1170.15; 21,199.13
. discontent of other employees as factor . . . 1170; 1170.16; 1170.161
. employer's accommodation to . . . 1164

Exhibit 83: The search begins in the basic Topical Index of the service, where introductory or background material on a particular topic can be located by paragraph number. Here we find, under the entry "Religious observances and holidays," references to paragraph 1170 and various annotations thereunder.

Holidays—Vacations—Time Off

¶ 1170

Most of the problems surrounding the granting of time off from work for holidays and vacations involve the observance of religious holidays. The 1972 amendments to Title VII of the Civil Rights Act of 1964 contain a new definition of "religion" to include all aspects of religious observance and practice, as well as belief (.01). Under this definition, an employer is expected to recognize the reasonable religious needs of his employees, unless he can show that he is unable to reasonably accommodate an employee's or prospective employee's religious observance without undue hardship on the conduct of his business.

Religious Holidays and Beliefs—Sabbath Observance

While it is unlawful to refuse to hire or to discharge employees because of their religion, the principal problem involving religious discrimination arises in connection with the granting of religious holidays or permitting the observance of the Sabbath. According to EEOC guidelines, employers have an obligation to accommodate the reasonable religious needs of their employees and prospective employees when such accommodations can be made without undue hardship on the conduct of the employer's business (.03). According to the Commission, undue hardship may exist when an employee's job cannot be performed by another worker of substantially similar qualifications during the time when the employee is absent for religious reasons. Because of the sensitive nature of discharging or refusing to hire an employee or applicant on account of his religious beliefs, an employer has the burden of proving that an undue hardship renders the required accommodations to the religious needs of the employee unreasonable. The Commission has stated that it will review each case on an individual basis in an effort to seek an equitable application of its religious discrimination guidelines.

Similarly, government agencies are required by regulation to make reasonable accommodations to the religious needs of applicants and federal government employees, including the observance of the Sabbath on days other than Sunday, when those accommodations can be made without undue interference with the business of the agency or with the rights of other applicants and employees (.031). Government contractors and subcontractors are also prohibited from discrimination on the basis of religion (.02).

An employer established that its accommodation to the religious belief of a process engineer by allowing him time off during the winter months would have involved an undue hardship on the conduct of its business since the responsibilities of the process engineer required that he be available on a 24-hour, seven-day-a-week basis (.10). Similarly, an employer would suffer undue hardship where it was not practical for him to find a replacement for the employee, a Seventh-Day Adventist, who did not work on Saturdays during the harvest season (.11). In the absence of evidence presented by the employer, however, that its accommodation to an employee's religious beliefs, generally requiring time off for observance of Sabbaths or other religious holidays, would involve an undue hardship on the conduct of its business, discharge of the employee for observance of such holidays constituted religious discrimination (.13-.15). Another factor considered in determining whether or not an employer discriminated on a religious basis was whether its accommodation to the

---

Exhibit 84: Paragraph 1170 contains a background summary which provides an overview of the topic and citations to other relevant material in the service.

[245]

religious beliefs of an employee created discontent among the other employees (.16).

Refusal to allow a nurse in a hospital to wear a religious head covering, in lieu of the usual nurse's cap, forced the nurse to choose between her job and her religious conviction and this, in effect, constituted constructive discharge of the nurse when she resigned rather than make an exception to her belief (.20). Recognition of a Sunday Sabbath for certain employees who worked overtime and refusal to allow overtime work to an employee whose Sabbath was Saturday constituted unlawful discrimination by the employer (.30). Sometimes union contract provisions entered into the situation and relieved the employer (including the government as employer) of the need to accommodate to the employees' religious beliefs (.40). This was true even as to a union provision for the employee to seek his own replacement. Hence, where the employee did not find his own replacement for the time when he would be off due to religious beliefs, the employer was held to have made reasonable accommodations to such beliefs (.50).

Equal Pay for Equal Work

There can be no wage differential by employers as to vacation or holiday pay to employees of either sex if the work of both sexes is subject to the equal pay standard and the differential is not shown to come within any exception to such standard (.032). Thus, covered male and female employees performing equal work must receive equal pay for holidays not worked (.62). The same is true as to vacation pay, so that an employer violated the equal pay provisions by giving vacation pay to covered employees of only one sex (.60). Such equality, however, was not required between women employees who took six-month pregnancy leaves of absence and other employees who worked a full year (.61).

Age Discrimination in Employment

It is unlawful for an employer to discriminate against any individual because of such individual's age with respect to vacations and holidays (.033). Vacation rights based upon length of service, however, with age being no factor for consideration therein, are not violative of the age discrimination ban (.65).

Racial and National Origin Discrimination

Vacation rights of a Spanish-surnamed American employee, based upon seniority and in accordance with collective bargaining agreement provisions, did not violate the ban against national origin discrimination (.75). Time off with pay to Negro workers to observe the funeral of a slain Negro leader did not constitute racial discrimination by an employer who was willing to grant all employees (Negro and white) the same time off (.80).

.01 **Laws.**—*Civil Rights Act of 1964, Title VII*, 42 U.S.C. 2000e(j), ¶ 3048A.

.02 **Executive Orders.**—*Executive Order 11246 on Government Contractors and Subcontractors*, 3 CFR 339, Sec. 202, ¶ 3680.

.03 **Regulations.**—*EEOC, Religious Discrimination Guidelines*, 29 CFR 1605.1, ¶ 3970.

.031 *Civil Service Commission, Equal Federal Employment Opportunity*, 5 CFR 713.204(f), ¶ 3855.204(f).

.032 *Wage-Hour Division, Interpretative Bulletin on Equal Pay for Equal Work Under FLSA*, 29 CFR 800.116(c), ¶ 4750.116(c).

.033 *Wage-Hour Division, Interpretative Bulletin on Age Discrimination in Employment*, 29 CFR 860.50(c), ¶ 4770.50(c).

.10 **Undue hardship to employer.**—Reasonable cause did not exist to support belief that employer had engaged in job bias on basis of religion by refusing to hire for position of process engineer applicant whose religious beliefs required him to be absent from work

¶ 1170   ©**1972, Commerce Clearing House, Inc.**

Exhibit 85: Index to "Current Items" covers the most recent material of the four subject indexes in this service (Exhibit 83, Topical Index, was the first or basic index of this kind). "Current Items" provides access to the latest court and agency decisions.

Conclusion

The charge against Respondent State Commissioner of Education is dismissed for lack of jurisdiction.

There is no reasonable cause to believe that Respondent Board of Education discriminated against Charging Party on the basis of sex.

[¶ 6500]   FAILURE TO ACCOMMODATE EMPLOYEE'S RELIGIOUS NEEDS WAS BIAS

Decision of the Equal Employment Opportunity Commission, Decision No. 76-104, April 2, 1976.

Title VII—Civil Rights Act of 1964

Religious Discrimination—Lumber and Building Supply Company—Discharged Employee—Failure to Accommodate Religious Need.—By an employer failing to sustain the burden of proving that an undue hardship existed which prevented it from accommodating the religious needs of its employee not to work on the Saturday Sabbath, there was reasonable cause to believe the employer engaged in an unlawful employment practice in violation of the Act, as amended, by discriminating against claimant because of his religion.

Back reference.—¶ 1164.

Full Text of EEOC Decision

Summary of Charge

Charging Party alleges that Respondent has engaged in an unlawful employment practice in violation of Title VII of the Civil Rights Act of 1964, as amended, by discharging him because of his religion.

Jurisdiction

Respondent is a lumber and building supply facility engaging in interstate commerce, and is an employer within the meaning of 701(b) of the Civil Rights Act of 1964, as amended. The charge was timely filed and deferred within the time limitations as prescribed by Title VII, and all other jurisdictional requirements have been met.

Summary of Investigation

The record discloses that the facts are that Charging Party was employed by Respondent as a salesman in 1964. It is unclear when Charging Party adopted his religious philosophy, but he became a Christian and began the study of the scriptures. Although Charging Party belonged to no established religion which worshiped on Saturday he attended the Free Will Baptist Church of God which held services on Saturdays and Sundays.

It appears that Charging Party's convictions about Sabbath work became more and more rigid as he became convinced that Saturday was to be observed as a day of rest. At this junction he informed his supervisor that he no longer wanted Thursdays off, but instead wanted Saturdays off to observe the Sabbath. Respondent's manager never questioned the sincerity of Charging Party's religious conviction, instead he informed

him that he had the alternative to either work on Saturdays or his absence would be construed as a resignation. No attempt of any kind was made to accommodate Charging Party in order for him to have Saturdays off. Charging Party did not work on the following Saturday, and when he returned to work on the next Monday, he was considered as having resigned effective his last working day. Respondent never claimed that Charging Party's absence would cause an undue hardship on the conduct of its business.

Respondent's manager asserted in an interview with this Commission's representative that Charging Party would have been accommodated if he were either a Seventh Day Adventist or Jewish, while at the same time unequivocally emphasizing that he had previously accommodated another employee who was a member of the Seventh Day Adventist Church.

The question Respondent seems to be raising here is whether Charging Party's conviction regarding Sabbath work qualifies as an expression of a "religion" within the protection of Title VII. The Supreme Court's construction of Section 6(j) of the Universal Military Training and Service Act is instructive. In *United States v. Seeger*, 380 U. S. 163 (1965), the Court's principal statement of its test for determining whether a conscientious objector's beliefs are religious within the meaning of Section 6(j) was as follows (380 U. S. at 176):

A sincere and meaningful belief which occupies in the life of its possessor a place parallel to that filled by the God of those admittedly qualifying for the exemption comes within the statutory definition.

Exhibit 86: This service contains decisions of the relevant administrative agency in full text. Here is a decision of the Equal Employment Opportunity Commission on the problem being researched. This paragraph reference was given in the "Current Items" index above. Note the back reference to ¶ 1164 which contains another background summary on this problem. (See Exhibit 87 below.)

The Court also held that "intensely personal" convictions which some might find "incomprehensible" or "incorrect" come within the meaning of "religious belief" in the Training and Service Act. *Welsh v. United States*, 90 S. Ct. 1792, 1796 (1970), citing 380 U. S. at 186-187. If "religion" were construed more narrowly for Title VII purposes than it is in the context of Section 6(j), then Title VII's proscription of religious discrimination would conflict with the First Amendment's Establishment Clause.

There is no contention that Charging Party's beliefs are not deeply and sincerely held religious convictions. See C. D. 71-779, CCH EEOC Decisions (1973) ¶ 6180.

These beliefs are therefore entitled to protection under the 1964 Civil Rights Act, as amended.

We also disagree with Respondent's view that Charging Party had to be of a particular faith before any attempt at accommodation is necessary. In an amendment to the Civil Rights Act of 1964, effective March 1972, Congress determined the meaning of what is the meaning of "religion" in the act, by incorporating this Commission's guidelines into the federal statute. See *Commission's Guidelines on Religious Discrimination*, 29 C. F. R. 16051. The following provision was added to Section 701:

(j) The term "religion" includes all aspects of religious observance and practice, as well as belief, unless an employer demonstrates that he is unable to reasonably accommodate to an employee's or prospective employee's religious observance or practice without undue hardship on the conduct of the employer's business.

The gravamen of the statute clearly states that Congress did not intend that employees of one religion be given preference over another. Where an employee's religious belief meets the standard set forth by the Supreme Court in *Seeger*, supra, that belief is protected by Title VII. If there is a conflict between the requirements of his protected religious belief and of his work schedule, the employer is obligated to accommodate the employee unless such accommodation would impose an undue hardship on the employer. See, *Cummins v. Parker Seal Co.*, (6th Cir. 1975) 9 EPD ¶ 10,171. Further, the employer has the burden of proving that an undue hardship renders the required accommodation to the religious need of the employee unreasonable. See *Commissions Guidelines On Religious Discrimination*, 29 C. F. R. 1605.1(c).

We do not know what kind of accommodation could have been made had the employer made a good faith effort in this direction: other employers in similar situations have arranged shift-exchanges with other employees, have gotten along with one less person on the shift, or have hired part-time help. The record shows that Respondent had hired part-time help on Saturdays in situations similar to the Charging Party's to cover a busy day.[1] It does not appear, however, that Respondent gave serious thought to any of these alternatives here.

We must conclude that where similarly placed persons of different religious beliefs are accorded dissimilar treatment, the Commission must find, in the absence of other evidence, that religion was a factor in the disparate treatment. Further, Respondent has not met the burden of proving that an undue hardship exists in rendering the required accommodation to the religious needs of Charging Party. Absent such evidence, we find Charging Party's constructive discharge constituted discrimination against him because of his religion within the meaning of Section 703(a) of Title VII.

Conclusion

There is reasonable cause to believe that Respondent engaged in an unlawful employment practice in violation of Title VII of the Civil Rights Act, as amended, by discharging Charging Party because of his religion.

---

[1] As courts have recently noted, "The regulation does not preclude some cost to the employer any more than it precludes some degree of inconvenience to effect a reasonable accommodation." *Hardison v. TWA*, — F. 2d — (10th Cir. 1975) 10 EPD ¶ 10,554; *Ward v. Allegheny Ludlum Steel Corp.*, 397 F. Supp. 375 (W. D. Pa. 1975) 10 EPD ¶ 10,327.

¶ 6500

Exhibit 86: Cont'd. Note references in the decision to other decisions in this service and to administrative regulations or guidelines in *C.F.R.* The latter are set forth in Exhibit 90 below.

Ch. 7 *LOOSELEAF SERVICES*

Ricans applied, their chances of consideration for employment were nil.

EEOC Decision, Case No. CC AT 7-2-112, June 30, 1969.

.88 **Concerted activities.**—Employer discriminatorily denied employment to two Negro carpenters because of their engagement in protected concerted activities as evidenced by employer's knowledge that they were seeking employment not only for themselves but for other Negroes. Fact that employer hired two Negro carpenters at later date did not establish that employer's earlier refusal to hire these employees was not due to racial discrimination.

Mason & Hanger-Silas Mason Co., 1969 CCH NLRB ¶21,323, 179 NLRB (No. 71).

.90 **State agency.**—Employer effectively discontinued his racially discriminatory practices of hiring directly employees needed and necessary in operation of his plant when he commenced by contract hiring of employees through state agency.

Irvin v. Mohawk Rubber Co. (DC, Ark.; 1970) 2 EPD ¶10,152, 308 F.Supp. 152.

Religion Discrimination
¶1164

Federal law makes it unlawful to refuse to hire employees because of their religion (.01). The principal problems involving religious discrimination arise in connection with observation of Sabbaths and granting of religious holidays (see ¶1170).

Under the 1972 amendments to Title VII of the Civil Rights Act of 1964, "religion" was defined to include all aspects of religious observance and practice as well as belief (.011). The effect of this new definition was that, unless an employer demonstrates that he is unable to reasonably accommodate to an employee's or prospective employee's religious observance without undue hardship on the conduct of his business, he will be deemed to have violated the law. Employers are expected to make reasonable accommodations for employees whose "religion" may include observances, practices and beliefs, such as Sabbath observance, which may differ from the employer's or potential employer's requirements regarding standards, schedules, or other business-related employment conditions.

The exemption from the ban on religious discrimination given to religious corporations and societies, which was formerly restricted to employees working in religious activities, was broadened by the 1972 amendments to Title VII to cover all secular activities of these institutions (.012). This means that these institutions may now employ individuals of a particular religion in all their activities, instead of only in their religious activities.

Under EEOC guidelines employers have an obligation to accommodate the reasonable religious needs of their employees and prospective employees when such accommodations can be made without undue hardship on the conduct of the employer's business (.03). Under these rules, undue hardship may exist when an employee's job cannot be performed by another worker of substantially similar qualifications during the time when the employee is absent for religious reasons. Because of the sensitive nature of refusing to hire an applicant on account of his religious beliefs, an employer has the burden of proving that an undue hardship renders the required accommodation to the religious needs of an employee as unreasonable. The Commission will review each case on an individual basis in an effort to seek an equitable application of its guidelines.

.01 **Laws.**—*Civil Rights Act of 1964, Title VII,* 42 U.S.C. 2000e-2(a)(1), ¶3051(a)(1).

.011 *Civil Rights Act of 1964, Title VII,* 42 U.S.C. 2000e(j), ¶3048A.

.012 *Civil Rights Act of 1964, Title VII,* 42 U. S. C. 2000e-1, ¶3049A.

.03 **Regulations.**—*EEOC,. Religious Discrimination Guidelines,* 29 CFR 1605.1, ¶3970.

Exhibit 87: Background summary, cited in previous exhibit, refers to relevant statutes and regulations.

pursuant to this section, the head of the Federal department or agency shall file with the committees of the House and Senate having legislative jurisdiction over the program or activity involved a full written report of the circumstances and the grounds for such action. No such action shall become effective until thirty days have elapsed after the filing of such report. [July 2, 1964, P. L. 88-352, Title VI, § 602, 78 Stat. 252, 42 U. S. C. § 2000d-1.]

[¶ 3023] JUDICIAL REVIEW—ADMINISTRATIVE
PROCEDURE ACT

Sec. 603. Any department or agency action taken pursuant to section 2000d-1 of this title shall be subject to such judicial review as may otherwise be provided by law for similar action taken by such department or agency on other grounds. In the case of action, not otherwise subject to judicial review, terminating or refusing to grant or to continue financial assistance upon a finding of failure to comply with a requirement imposed pursuant to section 2000d-1 of this title, any person aggrieved (including any State or political subdivision thereof and any agency of either) may obtain judicial review of such action in accordance with section 1009 of Title 5, and such action shall not be deemed committed to unreviewable agency discretion within the meaning of that section. [July 2, 1964, P. L. 88-352, Title VI, § 603, 78 Stat. 253, 42 U. S. C. § 2000d-2.]

[¶ 3024] ADMINISTRATIVE ACTION—FEDERALLY
FINANCED ASSISTANCE—EMPLOY-
MENT AS PRIMARY OBJECTIVE

Sec. 604. Nothing contained in this subchapter [Title] shall be construed to authorize action under this subchapter [Title] by any department or agency with respect to any employment practice of any employer, employment agency, or labor organization except where a primary objective of the Federal financial assistance is to provide employment. [July 2, 1964, P. L. 880352, Title VI, § 604, 78 Stat. 253, 42 U. S. C. § 2000d-3.]

[¶ 3025] FEDERALLY FINANCED ASSISTANCE
—INSURANCE AND GUAR-
ANTY PROGRAMS

Sec. 605. Nothing in this subchapter [Title] shall add to or detract from any existing authority with respect to any program or activity under which Federal financial assistance is extended by way of a contract of insurance or guaranty. [July 2, 1964, P. L. 88-352, Title VI, § 605, 78 Stat. 253, 42 U. S. C. § 2000d-4.]

→ Title VII—Equal Employment Opportunity

[¶ 3040] DEFINITIONS

Sec. 701. For the purposes of this title—

[¶ 3041] [Person]

(a) The term "person" includes one or more individuals, governments, governmental agencies, political subdivisions, labor unions, partnerships, associations, corporations, legal representatives, mutual companies, joint-stock companies, trusts, unincorporated organizations, trustees, trustees in bankruptcy, or receivers. [As amended March 24, 1972, P. L. 92-261, Title VII, 86 Stat. 103, 42 U. S. C. § 2000e(a).]

[¶ 3042] [Employer]

(b) The term "employer" means a person engaged in an industry affecting commerce who has fifteen or more employees for each working day in each of twenty or more calendar weeks in the current or preceding calendar year, and any agent of such a person, but such term does not include (1) the United States, a corporation wholly owned by the Government of the United States, an Indian tribe, or any department or agency of the District of Columbia subject by statute to procedures of the competitive service (as defined in section 2102 of Title 5 of

¶ 3023 © 1974, Commerce Clearing House, Inc.

Exhibit 88: Here paragraphs containing relevant statutes are set forth. These documents were referred to in the earlier background summary and in the E.E.O.C. decision.

office in any State or political subdivision of any State by the qualified voters thereof, or any person chosen by such officer to be on such officer's personal staff, or an appointee on the policy making level or an immediate adviser with respect to the exercise of the constitutional or legal powers of the office. The exemption set forth in the preceding sentence shall not include employees subject to the civil service laws of a State government, governmental agency or political subdivision. [As amended March 24, 1972, P. L. 92-261, Title VII, 86 Stat. 103, 42 U. S. C. § 2000e(f).]

[¶ 3046]   [Commerce]

(g) The term "commerce" means trade, traffic, commerce, transportation, transmission, or communication among the several States; or between a State and any place outside thereof; or within the District of Columbia, or a possession of the United States; or between points in the same State but through a point outside thereof. [As amended July 2, 1964, P. L. 88-352, Title VII, 78 Stat. 253, 42 U. S. C. § 2000e(g).]

[¶ 3047]   [Industry Affecting Commerce]

(h) The term "industry affecting commerce" means any activity, business, or industry in commerce or in which a labor dispute would hinder or obstruct commerce or the free flow of commerce and includes any activity or industry "affecting commerce" within the meaning of the Labor-Management Reporting and Disclosure Act of 1959 and further includes any governmental industry, business, or activity. [As amended March 24, 1972, P. L. 92-261, Title VII, 86 Stat. 103, 42 U. S. C. § 2000e(h).]

[¶ 3048]   [State]

(i) The term "State" includes a State of the United States, the District of Columbia, Puerto Rico, the Virgin Islands, American Samoa, Guam, Wake Island, the Canal Zone, and Outer Continental Shelf lands defined in the Outer Continental Shelf Lands Act. [As amended July 2, 1964, P. L. 88-352, Title VII, 78 Stat. 253, 42 U. S. C. § 2000e(i).]

[¶ 3048A]   [Religion]

(j) The term "religion" includes all aspects of religious observance and practice, as well as belief, unless an employer demonstrates that he is unable to reasonably accommodate to an employee's or prospective employee's religious observance or practice without undue hardship on the conduct of the employer's business. [As added March 24, 1972, P. L. 92-261, Title VII, 86 Stat. 103, 42 U. S. C. § 2000e(j).]

[¶ 3049]   EXEMPTION

[¶ 3049A]   [Non-Resident Aliens—Religious Institutions]

Sec. 702. This title shall not apply to an employer with respect to the employment of aliens outside any State, or to a religious corporation, association, educational institution, or society with respect to the employment of individuals of a particular religion to perform work connected with the carrying on by such corporation, association, educational institution, or society of its activties. [As amended March 24, 1972, P. L. 92-261, Title VII, 86 Stat. 103, 42 U. S. C. § 2000e-1.]

[¶ 3050]   DISCRIMINATION BECAUSE OF RACE,
COLOR, RELIGION, SEX, OR
NATIONAL ORIGIN

[¶ 3051]   [Unlawful Practices of Employers]

Sec. 703. (a) It shall be an unlawful employment practice for an employer—

(1) to fail or refuse to hire or to discharge any individual, or otherwise to discriminate against any individual with respect to his compensation, terms,

Exhibit 88: Cont'd.

conditions, or privileges of employment, because of such individual's race, color, religion, sex, or national origin; [July 2, 1964, P. L. 88-352, Title VII, 78 Stat. 255, 42 U. S. C. § 2000e-2(a)(1)] or

(2) to limit, segregate, or classify his employees or applicants for employment in any way which would deprive or tend to deprive any individual of employment opportunities or otherwise adversely affect his status as an employee, because of such individual's race, color, religion, sex, or national origin. [As amended March 24, 1972, P. L. 92-261, Title VII, 86 Stat. 109, 42 U. S. C. § 2000e-2(a)(2).]

[¶ 3052]   [Unlawful Practices of Employment Agencies]

(b) It shall be an unlawful employment practice for an employment agency to fail or refuse to refer for employment, or otherwise to discriminate against, any individual because of his race, color, religion, sex, or national origin, or to classify or refer for employment any individual on the basis of his race, color, religion, sex, or national origin. [July 2, 1964, P. L. 88-352, Title VII, 78 Stat. 255, 42 U. S. C. § 2000e-2(b).]

[¶ 3053]   [Unlawful Practices of Labor Organizations]

(c) It shall be an unlawful employment practice for a labor organization—

(1) to exclude or to expel from its membership, or otherwise to discriminate against, any individual because of his race, color, religion, sex, or national origin [July 2, 1964, P. L. 88-352, Title VII, 78 Stat. 255, 42 U. S. C. § 2000e-2(c)(1)];

(2) to limit, segregate, or classify its membership or applicants for membership, or to classify or fail or refuse to refer for employment any individual, in any way which would deprive or tend to deprive any individual of employment opportunities, or would limit such employment opportunities or otherwise adversely affect his status as an employee or as an applicant for employment, because of such individual's race, color, religion, sex, or national origin; [As amended March 24, 1972, P. L. 92-261, Title VII, 86 Stat. 109, 42 U. S. C. § 2000e-2(c)(2)] or

(3) to cause or attempt to cause an employer to discriminate against an individual in violation of this section. [July 2, 1964, P. L. 88-352, Title VII, 78 Stat. 255, 42 U. S. C. § 2000e-2(c)(3).]

[¶ 3054]   [Apprenticeship Programs]

(d) It shall be an unlawful employment practice for any employer, labor organization, or joint labor-management committee controlling apprenticeship or other training or retraining, including on-the-job training programs to discriminate against any individual because of his race, color, religion, sex, or national origin in admission to, or employment in, any program established to provide apprenticeship or other training. [July 2, 1964, P. L. 88-352, Title VII, 78 Stat. 255, 42 U. S. C. § 2000e-2(d).]

[¶ 3055]   [Religion, Sex or National Origin as
                    Occupational Qualification]

(e) Notwithstanding any other provision of this title, (1) it shall not be an unlawful employment practice for an employer to hire and employ employees, for an employment agency to classify, or refer for employment any individual, for a labor organization to classify its membership or to classify or refer for employment any individual, or for an employer, labor organization, or joint labor-management committee controlling apprenticeship or other training or retraining programs to admit or employ any individual in any such program, on the basis of his religion, sex, or national origin in those certain instances where religion, sex, or national origin is a bona fide occupational qualification reasonably necessary to the normal operation of that particular business or enterprise, and (2) it shall not be an unlawful employment practice for a school, college, university, or other educational institution or institution of learning to hire and employ employees of a particular religion if such school, college, university, or other edu-

Exhibit 88:   Cont'd.

Chapter XIV—Equal Employment Opportunity Commission—Continued

29 CFR Sec.	Par.
1601.25	4070.25
1601.25a	4070.25a
1601.25b	4070.25b
1601.25c	4070.25c
1601.26	4070.26
1601.27	4070.27
1601.28	4070.28
1601.29	4070.29
1601.30	4070.30
1601.31	4070.31
1601.32	4070.32
1601.33	4070.33
1601.50	4070.50
1601.51	4070.51
1601.52	4070.52
1601.53	4070.53
1601.54	4070.54
1601.55	4070.55
1601.56	4070.56
1601.57	4070.57
1601.58	4070.58
1601.59	4070.59

PART 1602

29 CFR Sec.	Par.
1602.1	4050.01
1602.2	4050.02
1602.3	4050.03
1602.4	4050.04
1602.5	4050.05
1602.6	4050.06
1602.7	4050.07
1602.8	4050.08
1602.9	4050.09
1602.10	4050.10
1602.11	4050.11
1602.12	4050.12
1602.13	4050.13
1602.14	4050.14
1602.15	4050.15
1602.16	4050.16
1602.17	4050.17
1602.18	4050.18
1602.19	4050.19
1602.20	4050.20
1602.21	4050.21
1602.22	4050.22
1602.23	4050.23
1602.24	4050.24
1602.25	4050.25
1602.26	4050.26
1602.27	4050.27
1602.28	4050.28
1602.29	4050.29
1602.30	4050.30

29 CFR Sec.	Par.
1602.31	4050.31
1602.32	4050.32
1602.33	4050.33
1602.34	4050.34
1602.35	4050.35
1602.36	4050.36
1602.37	4050.37
1602.38	4050.38
1602.39	4050.39
1602.40	4050.40
1602.41	4050.41
1602.42	4050.42
1602.43	4050.43
1602.44	4050.44
1602.45	4050.45
1602.46	4050.46
1602.47	4050.47
1602.48	4050.48
1602.49	4050.49
1602.50	4050.50
1602.51	4050.51
1602.52	4050.52
1602.53	4050.53
1602.54	4050.54
1602.55	4050.55

PART 1604

29 CFR Sec.	Par.
1604.1	3950.01
1604.2	3950.02
1604.3	3950.03
1604.4	3950.04
1604.5	3950.05
1604.6	3950.06
1604.7	3950.07
1604.31	3950.31

PART 1605

29 CFR Sec.	Par.
1605.1	3970

PART 1606

29 CFR Sec.	Par.
1606.1	3990

PART 1607

29 CFR Sec.	Par.
1607.1	4010.1
1607.2	4010.2
1607.3	4010.3
1607.4	4010.4
1607.5	4010.5

29 CFR Sec.	Par.
1607.6	4010.6
1607.7	4010.7
1607.8	4010.8
1607.9	4010.9
1607.10	4010.10
1607.11	4010.11
1607.12	4010.12
1607.13	4010.13
1607.14	4010.14

PART 1610

29 CFR Sec.	Par.
1610.1	4110.01
1610.2	4110.02
1610.3	4110.03
1610.4	4110.04
1610.5	4110.05
1610.6	4110.06
1610.7	4110.07
1610.8	4110.08
1610.9	4110.09
1610.10	4110.10
1610.11	4110.11
1610.13	4110.13
1610.14	4110.14
1610.15	4110.15
1610.16	4110.16
1610.17	4110.17
1610.18	4110.18
1610.19	4110.19
1610.20	4110.20
1610.21	4110.21
1610.30	4110.30
1610.32	4110.32
1610.34	4110.34
1610.36	4110.36

PART 1611

29 CFR Sec.	Par.
1611.1	4111.1
1611.2	4111.2
1611.3	4111.3
1611.4	4111.4
1611.5	4111.5
1611.6	4111.6
1611.7	4111.7
1611.8	4111.8
1611.9	4111.9
1611.10	4111.10
1611.11	4111.11
1611.12	4111.12
1611.13	4111.3
1611.14	4111.14

TITLE 31—MONEY AND FINANCE: TREASURY

Chapter 1—Monetary Offices, Dept. of the Treas.

PART 51

31 CFR Sec.	Par.
51.50	4620.50
51.51	4620.51
51.52	4620.52
51.53	4620.53
51.54	4620.54
51.55	4620.55
51.56	4620.56
51.57	4620.57
51.58	4620.58
51.59	4620.59
51.60	4620.60
51.61	4620.61
51.62	4620.62

Exhibit 89: Finding lists enable the researcher to locate regulations and other documents within the service by references to their paragraph numbers. Here the E.E.O.C. Guidelines, referred to in the E.E.O.C. decision in Exhibit 86, can be located in ¶ 3970.

Equal Employment Opportunity Commission

Religious Discrimination Guidelines

¶ 3970

The following guidelines on religious discrimination were signed July 10, 1967, effective immediately. They replace prior guidelines,[1] issued June 15, 1966 (31 F. R. 8370), and were codified and published in the Federal Register July 13, 1967 (32 F. R. 10298) as Title 29—Labor, Chapter XIV—Equal Employment Opportunity Commission, Part 1605—Guidelines on Discrimination Because of Religion.

Section 1605.1 Observance of Sabbath and other religious holidays.—(a) Several complaints filed with the Commission have raised the question whether it is discrimination on account of religion to discharge or refuse to hire employees who regularly observe Friday evening and Saturday, or some other day of the week, as the Sabbath or who observe certain special religious holidays during the year and, as a consequence, do not work on such days.

(b) The Commission believes that the duty not to discriminate on religious grounds, required by section 703(a)(1) of the Civil Rights Act of 1964, includes an obligation on the part of the employer to make reasonable accommodations to the religious needs of employees and prospective employees where such accommodations can be made without undue hardship on the conduct of the employer's business. Such undue hardship, for example, may exist where the employee's needed work cannot be performed by another employee of substantially similar qualifications during the period of absence of the Sabbath observer.

(c) Because of the particularly sensitive nature of discharging or refusing to hire an employee or applicant on account of his religious beliefs, the employer has the burden of proving that an undue hardship renders the required accommodations to

[1] Prior to amendment, Section 1605.1 read as follows:

"**Section 1605.1 Observance of Sabbath and religious holidays.**—(a)(1) Several complaints filed with the Commission have raised the question whether it is discrimination on account of religion to discharge or to refuse to hire a person whose religious observances require that he take time off during the employer's regular work week. These complaints arise in a variety of contexts, but typically involve employees who regularly observe Saturdays as the Sabbath or who observe certain special holidays during the year.

"(2) The Commission believes that the duty not to discriminate on religious grounds includes an obligation on the part of the employer to accommodate the reasonable religious needs of employees and, in some cases, prospective employees where such accommodation can be made without serious inconvenience to the conduct of the business.

"(3) However, the Commission believes that an employer is free under Title VII to establish a normal work week (including paid holidays) generally applicable to all employees, notwithstanding that this schedule may not operate with uniformity in its effect upon the religious observances of his employees. For example, an employer who is closed for business on Sunday does not discriminate merely because he requires that all his employees be available for work on Saturday.

"Likewise, an employer who closes his business on Christmas or Good Friday is not thereby obligated to give time off with pay to Jewish employees for Rosh Hashanah or Yom Kippur:

"(b) While the question of what accommodation by the employer may reasonably be required must be decided on the peculiar facts of each case, the following guidelines may prove helpful.

"(1) An employer may permit absences from work on religious holidays, with or without pay, but must treat all religions with substantial uniformity in this respect. However, the closing of a business on one religious holiday creates no obligation to permit time off from work on another.

"(2) An employer, to the extent he can do so without serious inconvenience to the conduct of his business should make a reasonable accommodation to the needs of his employees and applicants for employment in connection with special religious holiday observances.

"(3) The employer may prescribe the normal work week and foreseeable overtime requirements, and, absent an intent on the part of the employer to discriminate on religious grounds, a job applicant or employee who accepted the job knowing or having reason to believe that such requirements would conflict with his religious obligations is not entitled to demand any alterations in such requirements to accommodate his religious needs.

"(4) Where an employee has previously been employed on a schedule which does not conflict with his religious obligations, and it becomes necessary to alter his work schedule, the employer should attempt to achieve an accommodation so as to avoid a conflict. However, an employer is not compelled to make such an accommodation at the expense of serious inconvenience to the conduct of his business or disproportionate allocation of unfavorable work assignments to other employees."

the religious needs of the employee unreasonable.

(d) The Commission will review each case on an individual basis in an effort to seek an equitable application of these guidelines to the variety of situations which arise due to the varied religious practices of the American people.

Exhibit 90: ¶ 3970, shown here, contains the E.E.O.C. Guidelines, referred to above.

2514 **Current Items to Cumulative Index** NA 6-76
See also Cumulative Indexes at pages 2531 and 2551.

From Compilation
Paragraph No.
To New Development
Paragraph No.

Restaurant's decision to replace all waiters with waitresses was sex bias (NY SCt App
Div) 10,188

1170   Ban of pay for Good Friday holiday stayed pending appeal (Cal Ct App) 5 EPD
¶ 8553.—Aff'd (Cal Ct App) 9 EPD ¶ 10,003.—Aff'd (Cal S Ct) 10,891

→   Discharge of employee was not religious bias where employer made reasonable attempt
to accommodate religious needs (CA-10) 10,621
    .10   Airline's failure to accommodate Sabbath justified by hardship and union rules
(DC Mo) 8 EPD ¶ 9546.—Rev'd (CA-8) 10,554
    .40   Union failure to accommodate Sabbath justified by seniority rules (DC Mo) 8
EPD ¶ 9546.—Aff'd on other issues (CA-8) 10,554
→   .50   Applicant had right to job if religious needs not an undue hardship (CA-6) 5 EPD
¶ 8013.—Decision on the merits (DC Tenn) 7 EPD ¶ 9206.—Rev'd on this issue
(CA-6) 10 EPD ¶ 10,373.—Full court hearing on this issue denied (CA-6) 10,759

1180   Female overtime law violates sex bias bans, extension to males rejected (DC Ark) 10,675
   State female overtime laws invalid due to conflict with federal law—extension to males
rejected (Ark Ct) 10,675
    .32   No evidence supported conclusion that Negro laborer was denied overtime
opportunities because of his race (EEOC) 6472

1201   Racial bias in promotions indicated by results of subsequently instituted affirmative
action plan (DC Ohio) 9 EPD ¶ 10,019.—Aff'd (CA-6) 10,741

1208   Railroad law allowing earlier female retirement constitutional and not in conflict with
Title VII (DC Pa) 10,857
   Retirement plan which penalized males more heavily than females for early retirement
was sex biased (EEOC) 6471

1210   Agreement allowing forced retirement at age 52 illegal (W-H Opinion Letter) 5366
   Early retirement under bona fide labor pact not age bias (DC Mich) 10,702

1230   Biased seniority practices warrant relief from layoff (DC Miss) 10,784
   Layoff and recall policy was sex biased (EEOC) 6464
   Layoff of Negro foreman under subjective standards was race bias (DC Ohio) 8 EPD
¶ 9523.—Aff'd (CA-6) 10,688
   School employees hired under affirmative action programs not entitled to preferential
treatment in event of layoffs 5375
   State layoff preference for longer seniority and veterans constitutional (CA-2) 10,834
    .12   Effect of past bias shown in recall from layoff (CA-7) 8 EPD ¶ 9658.—Cert den
(US S Ct) 10,925
    .12   Processing of layoff grievances barred by conciliation agreement (DC Miss) 10,556
    .12   Proportionate layoff of women under conciliation, rather than union, agreement
(DC Miss) 10,556

1240   Demotion and bias charges of nominal director dismissed as unsupported (DC Ohio) ... 10,926
    .40   No race bias despite few Negro supervisors in paper mill (DC Ala) 6 EPD
¶ 8912.—Rev'd & rem'd (CA-5) 10,880

1250   Back pay and seniority for female flight attendants dismissed under no-marriage rule
(DC Cal) 10,933
   Discharge of white female married to black victim of racial bias (Mich Cir Ct) 10,763
   Lower seniority justified wife's discharge under ban on employment of spouses (DC Mo)
9 EPD ¶ 9982.—Aff'd (CA-8) 10,498
   Policy of not hiring spouse of employee who works for company was sex discrimination
(EEOC) 6492
   Requiring married females to use husband's name on personnel records was reasonable
(DC Tenn) 10,548

1268   Age was occupational qualification for hiring as bus driver (DC Fla) 4 EPD ¶ 7795.—
Aff'd (CA-5) 10,916
   Factual basis needed for belief that age is occupational qualification (DC Fla) 4 EPD
¶ 7795.—Aff'd (CA-5) 10,916

1290   .20   Exclusion of Negroes from jobs as welders and fabricators constitutes pattern and
practice of bias (DC NC) 10,916

1295   Fire and police height rule biased and not justified by business necessity (DC Cal) 10,492
   Height requirements for police department biased against females (DC Ill) 10,597
   Rejection of blind teacher violated Rehabilitation Act (DC Pa) 10,823

1300   Apprenticeship affirmative action not unlawful reverse bias (DC Tenn) 10,846
   Black fireman promotion under affirmative action plan vacated—no showing of bias
(DC Cal) 10,804
   Preferential hiring order for fire and fire national origin bias (DC Cal) 10,818
   School employees hired under affirmative action programs not entitled to preferential
treatment in event of layoffs 5375

1310   Denial of benefits for pregnancy barred as sex bias (DC Miss) 10,784
   Denial of pregnancy leave and termination was sex bias (DC NC) 10,651
   Denial of reemployment to teacher following pregnancy was bias (DC SC) 10,652
   Denial of sick leave for maternity purposes was sex bias (DC NC) 10,651
   Denial of sickness disability benefits for pregnancy related disability was sex bias
(EEOC) 6462
   Discriminatory reinstatement policy following maternity leave was sex bias (EEOC) 6461
   Failure to rehire pregnant teacher because of impending interruption was sex bias (DC
SC) 10,652
   Fixed date maternity leave for school teachers was sex bias (EEOC) 6463
   Fixed maternity leave dates and sick benefit denial for pregnancy sex bias (EEOC) 6487

Exhibit 91: By using this table, "Current Items to Cumulative Index," one gets references from an
earlier background paragraph (¶ 1170, shown
in Exhibit 84 above) to new material on the
same subject. Note how the reference to the
case in ¶ 1170.50 serves as a citator by locating
later court proceedings in the same case.

6588　　　**Employment Practices Decisions**　　101　2-76
　　　　　　　Williams v. Southern Union Gas Co.

— Footnotes —

[1] See *Waters v. Heublein, Inc.,* 8 EPD ¶ 9522 (N.D.Cal. 1974).

[2] It has been previously ruled that there is no independent cause of action against Heublein. See fn. 1, *supra*.

[3] See Exhibit A to affidavit of EEOC officer Brenda Brush filed August 14, 1973.

[4] This situation may change if it is later determined that subclasses are necessary.

[5] Since plaintiff's complaint alleges continuous violations of the law by United Vintners, she may represent a class of present and future employees. However, some past employees cannot be represented because of their failure to file charges with the EEOC. *Wetzel v. Liberty Mutual Insurance Co.,* [9 EPD ¶ 9931] 508 F.2d 239, 246 (3rd Cir. 1975), *cert. denied,* [9 EPD ¶ 10,176] 421 U.S. 1011 (1975) *(Wetzel I).* (Another case involving the same parties, *Wetzel II,* reported at [9 EPD ¶ 9942] 511 F.2d 199 [3rd Cir. 1975] will be heard by the Supreme Court. 421 U.S. 987 (1975). The class action issues in *Wetzel I* are not involved in *Wetzel II.*)

However, no exact cutoff date can be established because some past employees nominally excluded from the class by the time limitations of 42 U.S.C. § 2000e-5(e) [§ 2000e-5(d) when plaintiff filed her EEOC charges] may be able to avoid operation of that limitation because of their specific individual circumstances. See *Reeb v. Economic Opportunity Atlanta, Inc.,* [10 EPD ¶ 10,358] 516 F.2d 924 (5th Cir. 1975).

Consequently, for present purposes, inclusion of all past employees in the class is acceptable. If plaintiff prevails on her class claims, other individuals must then prove that they are members of the class and entitled to relief. *Baxter v. Savannah Sugar Refining Corp.,* [7 EPD ¶ 9426] 495 F.2d 437, 443-444 (5th Cir. 1974), *cert. denied,* [8 EPD ¶ 9789] 419 U.S. 1033 (1974). Any statute of limitations problems can be resolved at that time. As a woman and a former employee of United Vintners, plaintiff has standing to represent the proposed class. *See, e.g., Long v. Sapp,* [8 EPD ¶ 9712] 502 F.2d 34, 42-43 (5th Cir. 1974).

[6] See fn. 3, *supra.*

[7] It is thus unnecessary to rely on past employees who may be barred by the statute of limitations from participating in the case, fn. 5, *supra,* to establish a class large enough to satisfy Rule 23(a)(1).

[8] Appendix to Plaintiff's Memorandum in Support of Class Certification Motion, p. A-4.

[9] Defendant asserts that only one other woman employee of United Vintners has filed such a charge. Defendant's Memorandum in Support of Motion to Strike the Class, p. 10.

[10] It is thus unnecessary to evaluate this class claim in terms of the other requirements of Rule 23. If plaintiff can correct the defect outlined above, the Court will consider the matter further.

[11] Similarly, there is no requirement that all questions of law and fact be common to the class. The existence of some common questions is sufficient. *Like v. Carter,* 448 F.2d 798, 802 (8th Cir. 1971), *cert. denied,* 405 U.S. 1045 (1972).

[¶ 10,621] Larry J. Williams, Plaintiff-Appellant, Cross-Appellee v. Southern Union Gas Company, Defendant-Appellee, Cross-Appellant, United States Equal Employment Opportunity Commission, *Amicus Curiae,* Newspaper Agency Corporation, *Amicus Curiae* in the CrossAppeal.

United States Court of Appeals, Tenth Circuit. Nos. 75-1104 and 75-1105. January 21, 1976.

On Appeal from United States District Court, District of New Mexico. Affirmed.

Title VII—Civil Rights Act of 1964

Court Action—Timeliness.—The statutory period of 180 days allotted the EEOC for efforts to reach a voluntary settlement of employment discrimination claims does not place a time limit on complainants for bringing court action. The complainant has 90 days in which to initiate court action after receipt of the EEOC notice of right to sue, which need not be issued on expiration of the 100 day period.

Back reference.—¶ 2420.

Court Action—Timeliness—EEOC Notice.—An EEOC notice advising a job bias claimant of the failure of conciliation efforts and of his right to request a notice of right to sue did not start running of the time period for bringing an action in court. Since the court action was brought within 90 days of receipt of the notice of right to sue, it was not to be dismissed as untimely.

Back reference.—¶ 2420.

Religious Discrimination—Saturday Sabbath—Reasonable Accommodation.—A federal trial court properly determined that an employee observing Saturdays as Sabbath days was lawfully discharged for not working on a Saturday. The employer's business required service to the public 24 hours a day, seven days per week, and the requirement of work on Saturday was occasioned by an emergency to which the employee may have contributed by taking off the preceding Wednesday for a religious holiday. Considering that the employer had a duty to serve the consuming public and to adhere to employment practices

¶ 10,621　　　　　　　©1976, Commerce Clearing House, Inc.

Exhibit 92:　One of the new developments cited in the last Exhibit is the U.S. Court of Appeals decision shown here in full text.

Cases Cited "11 EPD ¶...."   **6589**
Williams v. Southern Union Gas Co.

that were fair to other employees, he was properly held to have acted reasonably. 42 U.S.C. Sec. 2000e-5(f)(1).

Back reference.—¶ 1170.

Robert J. Laughlin (Ralph K. Helge, on brief), for Plaintiff-Appellant and Cross-Appellee.

Owen M. Lopez (Jeffrey R. Brannen, Montgomery, Federici, Andrews, Hannahs & Buell, on brief), for Defendant-Appellee and Cross-Appellant.

Charles L. Reischel, Assistant General Counsel (Julia P. Cooper, Acting General Counsel, Joseph T. Eddins, Associate General Counsel, Beatrice Rosenberg, Assistant General Counsel, on brief), for Equal Employment Opportunity Commission. *Amicus Curiae.*

James S. Lowrie and Edward J. McDonough (Jones, Waldo, Holbrook & McDonough), on brief, for Newspaper Agency Corporation, *Amicus Curiae.*

Before HOLLOWAY, MCWILLIAMS and BARRETT, Circuit Judges.

[*Statement of Case*]

MCWILLIAMS, C.J.: This is a Civil Rights case based on a claim of unlawful job discharge. From July 1962 until October 3, 1970, Larry Williams was employed by the Southern Union Gas Company, initially as a dehydrator repairman's helper and later as a production repairman. On October 3, 1970, a Saturday, Williams was fired by Southern Union when he refused to report for work. Williams was at that time a member of the Worldwide Church of God. One of the tenets of this church is that its members should not work on the Sabbath, and Sabbath for this church is from sundown Friday to sundown Saturday. The reason given by Williams for not reporting for work on Saturday, October 3, 1970, was that his religion forbade working on the Sabbath.

On March 26, 1971, Williams filed a complaint with the Equal Employment Opportunity Commission alleging that Southern Union in firing him had discriminated against him because of his religion and in so doing had engaged in unlawful employment practices in violation of Title VII of the Civil Rights Act of 1964. On May 30, 1973, the Commission sent a letter to Williams advising him that compliance efforts had been unsuccessful and that he could bring a private action if he so desired. More specifically, this letter of May 30, 1973, advised Williams that if he decided to sue he should request a "Right-to-Sue" letter from the Commission and that he would have 90 days from the time the "Right-to-Sue" letter was received within which to bring an action against Southern Union. Williams did request such a letter, and on December 6, 1973, the "Right-to-Sue" letter was issued. Williams

instituted the present action under 42 U.S.C. § 2000(e), as amended, on March 6, 1974. On trial the trial court found for Southern Union and entered judgment dismissing the action "on the merits." Williams now appeals.

By separate appeal Southern Union seeks review of the trial court's ruling that it had subject matter jurisdiction. In this regard it is Southern Union's position that the suit was not timely brought. The background facts must be developed in some detail.

[*Background Facts*]

When Williams went to work for Southern Union in 1962 he was informed that it was a company policy that all employees should be available for work seven days a week, 24 hours per day. Southern Union felt this was necessary inasmuch as it was a public utility and as such was obligated to provide continuous and uninterrupted natural gas service to the general public. It was also Southern Union's policy, however, to schedule its employees for only five days of work each week, eight hours per day. Williams in 1962 did not belong to any church and hence was under no prohibition, religious or otherwise, from working any day in the week.

During the fall of 1969 Williams became a member of the Worldwide Church of God. He informed his supervisor of his conversion and advised him that he would no longer be able to work between Friday at sundown and Saturday at sundown. The supervisor, one Al Dean, explained that it would be difficult to promise that Williams would never be called on to work on a Saturday, but that he would do what he could. Coincidentally, or otherwise, at the time of his conversion Williams'

Employment Practices   **¶ 10,621**

TOPICAL REPORTERS

Most of the looseleaf services which publish the full text of decisions also issue them in bound volume series for permanent retention. These decisions will have a continuing reference value and are to be retained despite changes in the rest of the service. In many cases, these unofficial reporters duplicate official editions (e. g., the CCH —*N.L.R.B. Decisions* and the BNA *Labor Relations Reference Manual* both include material which can be found in the official *Decisions of the National Labor Relations Board*). However, these reporters include better indexing and finding devices than the official editions, are issued more quickly, and are tied into the other research features of their looseleaf services.

CHAPTER VIII

U. S. TREATIES

Treaties are formal agreements between countries, and have legal significance for both domestic and international purposes. When they are made between two governments, treaties are called *bilateral;* when entered into by more than two governments, they are called *multilateral.* Since Article VI of our Constitution provides that they shall be the supreme law of the land and shall bind all judges, treaties have the same legal effect and status as statutes. Thus, treaties can supersede prior statutes and statutes can revoke prior treaties, as the Seneca Indians of New York discovered sadly a few years ago when their lands, secured to them for over 200 years by treaty, were taken from them pursuant to a later statute.

The treaties of the United States are published in a variety of forms—official and unofficial, national and international, current and retrospective. There are a number of useful finding tools and aids available for research in treaties, but the bibliography of this literature is somewhat complex. Most of the various publications described herein include treaties, which require ratification by the Senate, and executive agreements, which generally do not require Senate approval. Execu-

tive agreements may, however, be submitted to the Senate for approval if the President so decides.

An understanding of treaty publications generally may be facilitated by a review of the following critical dates in the progress of a treaty from signing to adoption:

1. Date of Signing. The date on which the treaty is actually signed by the 1epresentatives of the U. S. and the other country is ordinarily used in citations. It is so cited by the Department of State and lawyers generally, and is also the form of listing in *Shepard's Citations*. It is not, however, the treaty's effective date, nor the date on which it becomes the "law of the land".

2. Date of Approval by Senate. The date on which the Senate "consents" to the treaty by a two-thirds vote of those present.

3. Date of Ratification by the President.

4. Effective Date of Treaty. Unless the treaty provides otherwise, this is usually the date on which the President ratifies the treaty, or on which ratifications are exchanged with the other signatory.

5. Date of Proclamation. The date on which the President proclaims the treaty, following which it is usually published.

CURRENT PUBLICATION OF U. S. TREATIES AND EXECUTIVE AGREEMENTS

The following are the most common forms of treaty publication:

1. Press Releases of Department of State. These are usually issued on the date of signing.

2. Department of State Bulletin. This weekly periodical is an authoritative source of treaty information and sometimes contains the text of treaties shortly after signing. It also carries information concerning negotiations, congressional action, ratification, and other developments in the progress of the treaty from signing to proclamation.

3. Senate Executive Documents. A treaty is transmitted to the Senate for its consideration in this form. These publications usually include transmittal messages from the President and the Secretary of State. Sometimes Senate Executive Documents are initially confidential and are not available for distribution or listed in the *Monthly Catalog of U. S. Government Publications* until the Senate lifts its injunction of secrecy. They receive an *alphabetical* designation and are cited by that letter and by the number of the Congress and session in which they are trans-

mitted. They may be pending before the Senate for many sessions before approval, but still retain their original citation. Senate Executive Documents should be distinguished from Senate Executive Reports which contain the report of the Senate Committee on Foreign Relations on the treaty and receive a *numerical* designation. A useful bibliography of these documents and reports has been published by the Tarlton Law Library of the University of Texas: *Checklist of Senate Executive Documents and Reports.* * * *1947–1970* (December 1970), compiled by Mariana G. Mabry.

4. Slip Treaty Form. These publications are usually the first widely disseminated official publication and comprise the *Treaties and Other International Acts Series* (*T.I.A.S.*) which began in 1945, as a successor to two separate series called Treaty Series (1908–1945) and Executive Agreement Series (1929–1945). It is a pamphlet form of publication, similar to the statutory slip law. The slip treaties are cumulated and bound into the annual volumes of *United States Treaties and Other International Agreements*, but there is often a considerable delay between the effective date of a treaty and the publication of its slip form.

5. U. S. Treaties and Other International Agreements. Since 1949 when the publication of treaties in the *Statutes at Large* was discontinued, this series (*U.S.T.*) has become the permanent

form of official treaty publication. These volumes cumulate the *T.I.A.S.* pamphlets in the same way that the *Statutes at Large* collect the slip laws. *U.S.T.* includes both treaties and executive agreements, and provides the English language text first, followed by the texts in any other official languages of the compact. Several volumes are issued every year and each is indexed by subject and country. There are now two commercially published cumulative indexes providing access to this material by *T.I.A.S.* number, date, country and subject: Kavass and Sprudzs, *U.S.T. Cumulative Index 1950–1970,* in four volumes (Hein, 1973) and Kavass and Michael, *United States Treaties and Other International Agreements Cumulative Index 1776–1949,* also in four volumes (Hein, 1975). These two indexes fill a long-existing need in American treaty research.

6. Unofficial Publications. There are some unofficial sources for U. S. treaties, but they are selective and do not offer the complete coverage of *T.I.A.S.* and *U.S.T. International Legal Materials,* published bi-monthly since 1962 by the American Society of International Law, contains the texts of treaties of major significance and sometimes provides drafts before final agreement. Although selective, it is considerably faster than most of the other publications described in this section and is particularly useful for that reason. Prior to its inception, similar material was issued

in the *Supplement* to the *American Journal of International Law.* *U.S.C.A.* and *U.S.C.S.,* like the *U.S.Code* itself, publish a few important treaties which substantially affect related *Code* provisions (e. g., the Universal Copyright Convention in Title 17). *U.S.C.C.A.N.* also publishes selected treaties after their ratification. CCH *Tax Treaties* is a looseleaf service which publishes treaties relating to federal taxation.

7. United Nations Treaty Series (U.N.T.S.). Since 1946 this series has published all treaties registered with the United Nations by member nations (including the U. S.) and some filed by non-members. It succeeds the old *League of Nations Treaty Series* (*L.N.T.S.*) which was published on a similar basis from 1920 to 1946. The treaties appear in their original languages *and* in English and French translations. Cumulative indexes originally appeared for each one hundred volumes published and more recently for every fifty volumes. The series is the most comprehensive treaty collection and already contains over 800 volumes, with thirty to forty new volumes being published each year. Unfortunately, there is a time lag of approximately four years in its publication of treaties and six to seven years in its publication of indexes. For retrospective cumulative indexing to *U.N.T.S.* and *L.N.T.S.,* see P. Rohn, *World Treaty Index,* at page 275 below.

[*265*]

8. Organization of American States Treaty.
Some individual countries and several regional
organizations publish their own treaty series.
The *Organization of American States Treaty
Series,* beginning in 1957 as the successor to the
Pan American Union Treaty Series, contains the
texts of multilateral treaties entered into by its
members, including the United States. It includes
the official treaty texts in English, Spanish, Portu-
guese and French.

RETROSPECTIVE COLLECTIONS
OF U. S. TREATIES

For research in treaties of the past, the following historical sources are generally used:

1. Indian Treaties. Volume 7 of the *Statutes at
Large* included a collection of Indian treaties for
the years 1778–1842. Thereafter, Indian treaties
continued to appear with other treaties in the regular volumes of the *Statutes at Large.* The best
compilations of Indian treaties (and statutes) —
are Kappler, *Indian Affairs, Laws and Treaties*
(U.S.G.P.O., 1904–1941, 5 vols.), Felix Cohen's
Handbook of Federal Indian Law (U.S.G.P.O.,
1945) and *Federal Indian Law* (U.S.G.P.O., 1958).

2. Statutes at Large. Volume 8 of the *Statutes at Large* published a compilation of treaties
entered into between 1778 and 1845; and thereafter, until 1949, treaties appeared regularly in the

individual volumes of *Statutes*. Volume 18 includes a collection of treaties in force as of 1873 and was published in connection with the *Revised Statutes* of 1873. Beginning in 1931 executive international agreements were also included. In 1949 their publication in the *Statutes at Large* was discontinued and the *U.S.T.* took over the publication of both treaties and agreements. The last volume of the *Statutes at Large* to include treaties (vol. 64) also included a complete listing of all treaties appearing in the *Statutes,* arranged by country.

3. Bevans' Treaties and Other International Agreements of the United States of America 1776–1949 (U.S.G.P.O., 1968–75). This retrospective compilation of American treaties brings together in a convenient form all treaties and other international agreements entered into by the United States from 1776 to 1949. The set consists of thirteen volumes, the first four of which contain multilateral treaties (arranged chronologically by date of signature) and the balance, bilateral treaties (arranged alphabetically by countries). Cumulative analytical indexes are included as volume 13. *Bevans* is now the definitive retrospective compilation of United States treaties, superseding its predecessors, *Malloy* and *Miller* (see below).

4. Malloy's Treaties, Conventions, International Acts, Protocols, and Agreements Between

the **U. S. A. and Other Powers** (U.S.G.P.O., 1910–1938, 4 vols.) and **Miller's Treaties and Other International Acts of the U. S. A.** (U.S.G.P.O., 1931–1948, 8 vols.)   These two sets covering the years, 1776–1937, and 1776–1863, respectively, were the major retrospective collections of U. S. treaties. They have now been superseded by *Bevans* and are of interest primarily for tracing references to them in texts which pre-date *Bevans*.

5.   **Unperfected Treaties of the United States of America 1776–1976** (Oceana, 1976——), edited by Christian Wiktor. This new compilation contains all *unperfected* U.S. treaties, i. e., those which, for one reason or another, did not become effective. It includes legislative history and analysis of each treaty. The work is projected to include five or six volumes, with indexes.

6.   **League of Nations Treaty Series.** Although not a member of the League, U. S. treaties appeared in this series during its publication from 1920 to 1946. It is now discontinued, having been succeeded by the *United Nations Treaty Series,* as noted above, but it is still the best collection for the period covered.

7.   **Consolidated Treaty Series** (Oceana, 1969——), edited by Clive Parry. This useful compilation will include all treaties between national states from 1641 to 1918. It is designed to provide a complete compilation of treaties (including

those of the United States) up to the beginning of the *League of Nations Treaty Series.* The series is now projected for approximately two hundred volumes and indexes will be provided at its completion.

8. Major Peace Treaties of Modern History 1648–1967, edited by Fred L. Israel ·(Chelsea, 1967). This four volume compilation of peace treaties provides English translations, where necessary. The arrangement is chronological with a subject index included.

FINDING TOOLS

Because of the chronological publication of treaties and the necessity for some means of subject access to them, the following finding tools are generally used:

1. Treaties in Force. The most important current index to United States treaties in force is this annual publication of the Department of State, which has been issued since 1950. It is revised annually to include only treaties *in force,* but gives citations to earlier forms of such treaties where appropriate. It offers citations to all of the major treaty publications, including *Statutes at Large, T.I.A.S., U.S.T., Bevans, League of Nations Treaty Series,* and *U.N. Treaty Series.* The first part of the index lists bilateral treaties alphabetically by country and then subdivides them

by subject. The second section lists multilateral treaties alphabetically by subject. This index is usually the starting point for searching current treaties. Its two sections are illustrated in Exhibit 93 below. *Treaties in Force* is supplemented between its annual revisions by the "Treaty Information" section of the weekly *Department of State Bulletin,* as illustrated in Exhibit 94 below.

UNION OF SOVIET SOCIALIST REPUBLICS

AGRICULTURE

Agreement on cooperation in the field of agriculture. Signed at Washington June 19, 1973; entered into force June 19, 1973.
24 UST 1439; TIAS 7650.

ARMS LIMITATION

Treaty on the limitation of anti-ballistic missile systems. Signed at Moscow May 26, 1972; entered into force October 3, 1972.
23 UST 3435; TIAS 7503.

Interim agreement on certain measures with respect to the limitation of strategic offensive arms with protocol. Signed at Moscow May 26, 1972; entered into force October 3, 1972.
23 UST 3462; TIAS 7504.

Memorandum of understanding regarding the establishment of a Standing Consultative Commission. Signed at Geneva December 21, 1972; entered into force December 21, 1972.
24 UST 238; TIAS 7545.

Protocol establishing and approving regulations governing procedures and other matters of the Standing Consultative Commission with regulations. Signed at Geneva May 30, 1973; entered into force May 30, 1973.
24 UST 1124; TIAS 7637.

Basic principles of negotiation on the further limitation of strategic offensive arms. Signed at Washington June 21, 1973; entered into force June 21, 1973.
24 UST 1472; TIAS 7653.

ATOMIC ENERGY

Agreement on scientific and technical cooperation in the field of peaceful uses of atomic energy. Signed at Washington June 21, 1973; entered into force June 21, 1973.
24 UST 1486; TIAS 7655.

AVIATION

Civil air transport agreement with exchange of notes. Signed at Washington November 4, 1966; entered into force November 4, 1966.
17 UST 1909; TIAS 6135; 675 UNTS 3.

Amendment:
December 4 and 22, 1975.

SOUTHEAST ASIA TREATY ORGANIZATION (SEATO) (See under DEFENSE)

SPACE (See also ASTRONAUTS)

Treaty on principles governing the activities of states in the exploration and use of outer space, including the moon and other celestial bodies. Done at Washington, London, and Moscow January 27, 1967; entered into force for the United States October 10, 1967.
18 UST 2410; TIAS 6347; 610 UNTS 205.
Ratification, accession or notification of succession deposited by:

Argentina	Madagascar 1
Australia	Mali
Austria	Mauritius
Barbados	Mexico
Belgium	Mongolia
Brazil 1	Morocco
Bulgaria	Nepal
Burma	Netherlands 4
[Byelorussian Soviet Socialist Rep.] 2	New Zealand
Canada	Niger
China, Rep.	Nigeria
Cyprus	Norway
Czechoslovakia	Pakistan
Denmark	Poland
Dominican Rep.	Romania
Ecuador	San Marino
Egypt	Sierra Leone
El Salvador	South Africa
Fiji	Spain
Finland	Sweden
France	Switzerland
German Dem. Rep.	Syrian Arab Rep.
Germany, Fed. Rep. 3	Thailand
Greece	Tonga
Hungary	Tunisia
Iceland	Turkey
Iraq	Uganda
Ireland	[Ukrainian Soviet Socialist Rep.] 2
Italy	Union of Soviet Socialist Reps.
Jamaica	United Kingdom 5
Japan	United States
Korea	Upper Volta
Kuwait	Uruguay
Laos	Venezuela
Lebanon	Zambia
Libya	

1 With a statement.
2 With reference to the reported signature and deposit of ratification at Moscow by the Byelorussian Soviet Socialist Republic and the Ukrainian Soviet Socialist Republic, the Government of the United States considers those two constituent republics as already covered by the signature and deposit of ratification by the Union of Soviet Socialist Republics.
3 Applicable to Land Berlin.
4 Extended to the Netherlands Antilles.

Exhibit 93: *Treaties in Force.* Bilateral treaties on the left (arranged by country and then subject); multilateral treaties on the right (listed by subject).

Current Actions

MULTILATERAL

Agriculture

Agreement establishing the International Fund for Agricultural Development (IFAD). Done at Rome June 13, 1976. [1]
Signatures: Venezuela, January 4, 1977; Switzerland, January 24, 1977; Italy, Somalia, January 26, 1977; Tunisia, January 27, 1977; Pakistan, January 28, 1977.

Antarctica

Recommendations relating to the furtherance of the principles and objectives of the Antarctic treaty of December 1, 1959 (TIAS 4780). Adopted at Oslo June 20, 1975. [1]
Notification of approval: Belgium, January 21, 1977, for recommendations VIII-3, VIII-6-VIII-14.

Copyright

Universal copyright convention, as revised. Done at Paris July 24, 1971. Entered into force July 10, 1974. TIAS 7868.
Accession deposited: Bahamas, September 27, 1976.

Cultural Property

Convention on the means of prohibiting and preventing the illicit import, export and transfer of ownership of cultural property. Done at Paris November 14, 1970. Entered into force April 24, 1972. [2]
Acceptance deposited: Saudi Arabia, September 8, 1976.
Ratification deposited: Bolivia, October 4, 1976.

Diplomatic Relations

Optional protocol to the Vienna convention on diplomatic relations concerning the compulsory settlement of disputes. Done at Vienna April 18, 1961. Entered into force April 24, 1964; for the United States December 13, 1972. TIAS 7502.
Ratification deposited: Korea, January 25, 1977.

Expositions

Protocol revising the convention of November 22, 1928, relating to international expositions, with appendix and annex. Done at Paris November 30, 1972. [1]
Ratification deposited: Romania, May 12, 1976. [3]

Gas

Protocol for the prohibition of the use in war of asphyxiating, poisonous or other gases, and of bacteriological methods of warfare. Done at Geneva June 7, 1925. Entered into force February 8, 1928; for the United States April 10, 1975. TIAS 8061.
Accession deposited: Qatar, September 16, 1976.

Health

Amendments to articles 35 and 55 of the Constitution of the World Health Organization of July 22, 1946, as amended (TIAS 1808, 4643, 8086). Adopted at Geneva May 22, 1973. [1]
Acceptances deposited: Comoros, Surinam, January 27, 1977.

Oil Pollution

Amendments to the international convention for the prevention of pollution of the sea by oil, 1954, as amended (TIAS 4900, 6109). Adopted at London October 21, 1969.
Acceptances deposited: Dominican Republic, January 14, 1977; Nigeria, January 19, 1977.
Enters into force: January 20, 1978.

Space

Convention on international liability for damage caused by space objects. Done at Washington, London, and Moscow March 29, 1972. Entered into force September 1, 1972; for the United States October 9, 1973. TIAS 7762.
Ratification deposited: Finland, February 1, 1977.

Terrorism—Protection of Diplomats

Convention on the prevention and punishment of crimes against internationally protected persons, including diplomatic agents. Done at New York December 14, 1973. Enters into force February 20, 1977.
Ratifications deposited: Federal Republic of Germany, January 25, 1977; Tunisia, January 21, 1977.
Accession deposited: Chile, January 21, 1977.

United Nations

Charter of the United Nations and Statute of the International Court of Justice. Signed at San Francisco June 26, 1945. Entered into force October 24, 1945. 59 Stat. 1031.
Admission to membership: Angola, December 1, 1976; Western Samoa, December 15, 1976.

World Heritage

Convention concerning the protection of the world cultural and natural heritage. Done at Paris November 23, 1972. Entered into force December 17, 1975. TIAS 8226.
Ratification deposited: Bolivia, October 4, 1976.

BILATERAL

Australia

Agreement relating to the limitation of meat imports from Australia during calendar year 1977. Effected by exchange of notes at Washington December 14, 1976, and January 18, 1977. Entered into force January 18, 1977.

---

[1] Not in force.
[2] Not in force for the United States.
[3] With reservation.

Exhibit 94: "Treaty Information" section of the weekly *Department of State Bulletin* showing current actions on various multilateral and bilateral treaties.

2. U.S.T. Cumulative Index 1950–1970 and **United States Treaties and Other International Agreements Cumulative Index 1776–1949,** as noted above, now index all U. S. treaties up to 1970.

3. Multilateral Treaties in Respect of Which the Secretary General Performs Depositary Functions (United Nations, Office of Legal Affairs). This useful compilation supersedes the *United Nations Status of Multilateral Conventions*. It consists of an annually revised, comprehensive list of multilateral treaties arranged by subject with current information as to their status, signatories, ratifications, accessions, etc. It also includes coverage of League of Nations multilateral treaties, but is otherwise limited to treaties for which the U. N. Secretary General acts as depository. The listings are arranged by subject, and, in addition to basic information on each treaty, includes any reservations imposed by the signatories. Exhibit 95 below illustrates the format of this finding tool.

11. Convention on the Prevention and Punishment of Crimes against Internationally Protected Persons, including Diplomatic Agents

Adopted by the General Assembly of the United Nations on 14 December 1973[1]

Not yet in force (see article 17).

TEXT: Annex to General Assembly resolution 3166 (XXVIII) of 14 December 1973.

State	Signature		Ratification, accession (a)	
AUSTRALIA	30 December	1974		
BULGARIA	27 June	1974	18 July	1974
BYELORUSSIAN SOVIET SOCIALIST REPUBLIC	11 June	1974		
CANADA	26 June	1974		
CYPRUS			24 December	1975 a
CZECHOSLOVAKIA	11 October	1974	30 June	1975
DENMARK	10 May	1974	1 July	1975[2]
ECUADOR	27 August	1974	12 March	1975
FINLAND	10 May	1974		
GERMAN DEMOCRATIC REPUBLIC	23 May	1974		
GERMANY, FEDERAL REPUBLIC OF	15 August	1974		
GHANA			25 April	1975 a
GUATEMALA	12 December	1974		
HUNGARY	6 November	1974	26 March	1975
ICELAND	10 May	1974		
ITALY	30 December	1974		
LIBERIA			30 September	1975 a
MONGOLIA	23 August	1974	8 August	1975
NICARAGUA	29 October	1974	10 March	1975
NORWAY	10 May	1974		
PARAGUAY	25 October	1974	24 November	1975
POLAND	7 June	1974		
ROMANIA	27 December	1974		
RWANDA	15 October	1974		
SWEDEN	10 May	1974	1 July	1975
TUNISIA	15 May	1974		
UKRAINIAN SSR	18 June	1974		
UNION OF SOVIET SOCIALIST REPUBLICS	7 June	1974		
UNITED KINGDOM	13 December	1974		
UNITED STATES OF AMERICA	28 December	1973		
YUGOSLAVIA	17 December	1974		

[1] Resolution 3166 (XXVIII) of 14 December 1973. For the text of the resolution, see *Official Records of the General Assembly, Twenty-eighth Session, Supplement No. 30* (A/9030). The Convention was opened for signature at New York on 14 December 1973.
[2] With the following declaration: Until further decision, the Convention shall not apply to the Faroe Islands or Greenland.

Declarations and Reservations

BULGARIA

Declaration made upon signature and renewed upon ratification:

Bulgaria does not consider itself bound by the provisions of article 13, paragraph 1, of the Convention, under which any dispute between two or more States Parties concerning the interpretation or application of the Convention shall, at the request of one of them, be submitted to arbitration or to the International Court of Justice, and states that, in each individual case, the consent of all parties to such a dispute is necessary for submission of the dispute to arbitration or to the International Court of Justice.

BYELORUSSIAN SOVIET SOCIALIST REPUBLIC

Upon signature:

The Byelorussian Soviet Socialist Republic does not consider itself bound by the provisions of article 13, paragraph 1, of the Convention, under which any dispute between two or more States Parties concerning

---

Exhibit 95: *Multilateral Treaties in Respect of Which the Secretary-General Performs Depository Functions: with information on a convention for the protection of diplomats, including signatories, date of signature, ratifications, and texts of declarations and reservations.*

4. Status of Inter-American Treaties and Conventions (Organization of American States). This annual status table offers substantially the same data on O.A.S. treaties as does the United Nations service described above.

5. Indexes to the United Nations Treaty Series. These indexes cover many more treaties than those of the United States. As noted above, they now cumulate every fifty volumes and are useful for research in the *United Nations Treaty Series,* despite the substantial delay in their publication. The researcher should note that these indexes are not limited to treaties in force and may refer to treaties which have been modified or renounced.

6. World Treaty Index, compiled by Peter H. Rohn (ABC-Clio, 1974). This five volume set indexes the *United Nations* and *League of Nations Treaty Series,* and many other series of treaties made since 1920. It provides access by the parties to the treaty, subject, date, and the name of any international organization involved.

7. Index to Multilateral Treaties (Harvard Law School Library, 1965, with three annual supplements to 1966). This chronological list of multilateral treaties covers the period from 1596 to 1963, with guides by subject, region, place and date of agreement, etc. Unfortunately, this useful index has not been kept up to date.

8. Computer Services. Although neither *LEXIS* or *WESTLAW* provide direct or comprehensive access to treaties, a number of computer projects are being developed which may improve treaty research in the future. Rohn's *World Treaty Index* stems from a computerized retrieval system for treaties directed by Professor Rohn at the University of Washington. The U. S. Air Force project *FLITE* has been building a large data base of international agreements for full text searching. The United Nations has been developing a computer-assisted index of international documents, including treaties, for several years. The Queens University Treaty Project in Canada has been compiling British and Commonwealth treaties for computer retrieval and may facilitate future development of a broader system for treaty research.

GUIDES TO THE LEGISLATIVE HISTORY OF TREATIES

Congressional deliberations and actions on pending treaties, like the legislative histories of statutes, are often the subject of legal research. The following finding tools aid in locating relevant material:

1. CCH Congressional Index. This looseleaf service, discussed above in Chapter V, includes among its other features a table of treaties pending before the Senate. It is one of the most valu-

able status tables for determining actions taken on pending treaties and their present status, regardless of when they were introduced. Treaty listings include references to Executive Reports of the Senate Foreign Relations Committee, hearings, ratifications, etc. The treaties are listed chronologically by the session of transmittal and designated by their executive letter. The table is shown in Exhibit 96, below:

---

88 9-22-76   **Treaties**   **1639**

Executive C—Income Taxes—International Convention—Israel

  Convention with respect to taxes on income.
  Injunction on secrecy removed February 11, 1976.
  In Foreign Relations Committee February 11, 1976.

Executive D—Income Taxes—International Convention—Egypt

  Convention for the avoidance of double taxation and the prevention of fiscal evasion with respect to taxes on income.
  Injunction on secrecy removed February 11, 1976.
  In Foreign Relations Committee February 11, 1976.

Executive E—Foreign Affairs—Friendship and Cooperation—Spain

  The treaty provides for the course of the U.S.-Spanish Defense Relationship and assistance for the modernization of the Spanish military.
  Injunction on secrecy removed February 18, 1976.
  In Foreign Relations Committee February 11, 1976.
  Hearing 3/15/76.
  Reported (Ex. Rept. 94-25), May 20, 1976.
  Ratified by S., June 21, 1976.

Executive F—Law Enforcement—Investigations—Mutual Assistance

  The Treaty with the Swiss Confederation on Mutual Assistance in Criminal Matters is aimed at obtaining information and evidence needed for criminal investigations and prosecutions, especially from Swiss banks.
  Injunction of secrecy removed February 18, 1976.
  In S. Foreign Relations Committee February 18, 1976.
  Ratified by S., June 21, 1976.

Congressional Index—1975-1976

Exhibit 96: An entry from the CCH *Congressional Index* table of treaties pending before the Senate.

2.   Calendar of the Senate Foreign Relations Committee.   This official status table of business before the Senate committee is perhaps the best list of pending treaties with actions taken thereon, but has been less accessible than the CCH service.   Its information on hearings is particularly useful.

3.   Congressional Information Service.   This important legislative history service, described above at page 183, includes coverage of treaties. These appear in the subject index, documents lists and in the summaries of actions by committee.

4.   Congressional Quarterly.   This publication which is devoted to congressional activity generally, also includes useful information on treaties.   In addition to occasional special reports on major treaties, the *Weekly Report* of *C.Q.* includes the actual text of important documents, chronologies, summaries of debates and messages, and general information about current treaties.   The indexes to the *Weekly Reports* offer leads to current information and documents on pending treaties.

5.   Congressional Record Indexes.   In the fortnightly indexes to the *Congressional Record* and in the bound volume index for each session there is a listing of treaty actions and discussions appearing in the *Record*.   These references appear under the heading "Treaties" in the alphabetical subject index and also occasionally under the

name of a particular treaty or its subject matter. The *Congressional Record* indexes are not very convenient for current use, but they are helpful for retrospective research into a particular treaty's legislative history. However, they only cover material in the *Record,* which is not the only source of legislative history of treaties.

6. Lists of Treaties Submitted to the Senate. The Department of State has issued treaty lists of different kinds, among which are the following three lists of treaties submitted to the Senate:

> *List of Treaties Submitted to Senate, 1789–1931, which have not gone into force* (Publication No. 382, 1932).

> *List of Treaties Submitted to the Senate, 1789–1934* (Publication No. 765, 1935).

> *Treaties Submitted to the Senate, 1935–1944* (Publication No. 2311, 1945).

Although long out of date, these publications are still used, particularly in historical studies of legislative action on treaties.

EXTRINSIC AIDS IN TREATY RESEARCH

The study of treaties often involves their history and interpretation, for which the following external sources may offer useful information:

1. Citators. The interpretation of treaties by courts provides authoritative material for the re-

searcher who seeks information on the meaning or effect of a treaty. Citations to such decisions can be found in:

(a) **Shepard's United States Citations—Statutes Edition.** This citator is limited to *federal* court decisions, but includes all cases mentioning the treaty in addition to those actually interpreting it. For treaties up to 1949, listing is by date of signing rather than by *Statutes at Large* citation. After 1950 a special section was set up listing treaties by their treaty series citation. Shepard's also includes modifications of the cited treaty by later legislation or a subsequent treaty change.

(b) **Shepard's Citations for various states.** There are similar listings of state court decisions citing U. S. treaties in the statutes volume of every state Shepard's citator. Many more judicial interpretations of U. S. treaties occur in the *state* courts than in the federal courts.

(c) **U. S. Code Service.** In a special volume of *Annotations to Uncodified Laws & Treaties,* this edition of the *United States Code* includes citations to both state and federal judicial decisions interpreting U. S. treaties.

2. Digests of International Law. There have been a number of encyclopedic digests of international law which include material on treaties and their judicial interpretation, analytical and historic notes, and other scholarly comments. The current and now most important of these works is Whiteman's *Digest of International Law* (1963–1973), described below. The whole series includes:

(a) Cadwalader, John L. *Digest of the Published Opinions of the Attorney General and of Leading Decisions of the Federal Courts, with Reference to International Law, Treaties and Kindred Subjects* (1877).

(b) Wharton, Francis. *A Digest of the International Law of the United States* (1886 in 3 volumes and 2nd ed. in 1887 with appendix). Continued and expanded Cadwalader's *Digest.*

(c) Moore, John Bassett. *A Digest of International Law* (1906 in 8 volumes). Largely superseded Wharton.

(d) Hackworth, Green H. *Digest of International Law* (1940–44 in 8 volumes). Based on material which developed since Moore, but does not completely supersede it.

(e) Whiteman, Marjorie M. *Digest of International Law* (U.S.G.P.O., 1963–1973, in

15 vols.). This digest is now the current official statement of American international law practice, but does not entirely replace Hackworth.

(f) *Digest of the United States Practice in International Law* (U.S.G.P.O., 1973 to date). These annual volumes, prepared by the Office of the Legal Advisor in the Department of State, are designed to supplement the Whiteman *Digest.*

(g) *Restatement of the Law. Foreign Relations Law of the United States* (American Law Institute, 1965). Similar to the other *Restatements,* this is an unofficial but well reputed summary of American law and practice in this field. The *Restatement of Conflict of Laws* (A.L.I., 1971, 2 vols.) covers private international law.

3. Documentary Compilations. There are several useful collections of documentary materials in the international law field which include sources for treaty research. Most of the documents contained in these compilations are available in other primary forms of publication, but they may be more conveniently accessible through these editions.

(a) *Reports of the Committee on Foreign Relations, 1789–1901* (U.S.G.P.O., Sen.

Doc. 231, 56th Congress, 2d Session, 8 vols.). This set is a handy compilation of important source material for research in the legislative history of U. S. treaties. It is an exhaustive collection of regular committee reports, executive reports and documents. There is a cumulative index in the last volume. Unfortunately, the work has not been continued beyond 1901.

(b) *American International Law Cases, 1783–1968* (Oceana, 1971–), edited initially by Francis Deak and continued by Frank S. Ruddy. This reprint collection of American federal and state court decisions relating to international law, includes annotations to relevant treaties.

(c) *Foreign Relations of the United States* (U.S.G.P.O., 1861 to date). This continuing series of official papers is prepared by the Historical Office of the U. S. Department of State and includes considerable material relating to treaties, their negotiation and adoption. Unfortunately, there is a time lag of twenty to twenty-five years between issuance of these documents and their publication. The weekly *Department of State Bulletin,* as noted above, is a useful current source for selected documents. From

1959 to 1969, the State Department published an annual cumulation, *American Foreign Policy: Current Documents,* updating, for the years 1956 to 1967, two earlier compilations which were also prepared by the State Department: *A Decade of American Foreign Policy: Basic Documents, 1941–1949* (U.S.G.P.O., 1950) and *American Foreign Policy, 1950–1955: Basic Documents,* 2 vols. (U.S.G.P.O., 1957).

(d) *American Foreign Relations, A Documentary Record* (beginning in 1976, with coverage of 1971), continuing the series *Documents on American Foreign Relations.* This annual compilation was published from 1938 to 1951 by the World Peace Foundation and since then by the Council on Foreign Relations. It includes material on treaties and is similar in coverage to the now discontinued *American Foreign Policy: Current Documents,* above.

(e) *International Legal Materials* (American Society of International Law, 1962–date). As noted above, this bi-monthly compilation includes drafts and final texts of many treaties, as well as other documentation relating to them. It continues a similar compilation which ap-

peared as the *Supplement* to the *American Journal of International Law.*

Additional publications from foreign and international sources, relating to international law and, incidentally, to treaties, are described in Chapter X below.

CHAPTER IX
SECONDARY MATERIALS

Most of the materials discussed so far have been primary sources of law, that is, documents with actual legal effect (reports, statutes, regulations, treaties, etc.) or their related bibliographic apparatus (digests, indexes, citators, etc.). Primary materials may have mandatory or persuasive authority (or no authority at all) depending on their source, official status and inherent quality, the jurisdiction and tribunal in which they are presented, and their legal and factual relevance to a particular problem. We now examine the vast literature of unofficial, non-authoritative, *secondary* materials consisting of encyclopedias, treatises, periodicals and related publications. These range from scholarly writings of the highest repute and lasting influence, through a varied spectrum, down to hack work of low quality and fortunately short life. When creatively and effectively exploited, the best of the secondary materials may directly affect the development of the law. Many scholarly articles have shaped law reform and stimulated new legislation (e. g., Erwin Griswold's article, "Government in Ignorance of the Law—A Plea for Better Publication of Executive Legislation", appearing in the *Harvard Law Review* in 1934, which had considerable in-

fluence in bringing about the passage of the Federal Register Act of 1935).

Secondary materials also perform other more mundane functions in legal research. They serve as search books or finding tools which aid the researcher in locating relevant primary sources and authorities. They can refresh the reader's recollection of a well settled, but neglected area, or provide an introduction to the law in a new or developing field. Handbooks and manuals provide the forms and guidelines for the operational details of daily law practice. From other sources, lawyers or scholars can construct or buttress legal arguments and enhance the effectiveness of their advocacy. Some works may describe the non-legal context or historical background of a legally significant event or state of affairs, while others illuminate the possible effects and social consequences of proposed legal action. The creative insights of some published writings can reveal trends and patterns in unsettled areas and detect incipient strains and shifts in apparently settled law.

Although secondary materials are as old as legal research, they have been used and cited more frequently in recent years by both lawyers and judges to bring non-legal scholarship to bear on legal problems. A greater interest in the social and economic consequences of particular legal actions has led to interdisciplinary cooperation be-

tween law and the other social sciences. The development of social and experimental schools of jurisprudence further enhanced this interest in materials which are available only in secondary sources. The extension of legal concern into many new areas of human activity and the growing willingness of the courts to re-examine and revise traditional notions have increased the importance of secondary materials. Judicial and legislative history of recent years contains a scholarly documentation far more eclectic than the strictly legal references of the older literature.

The means of access to secondary sources vary widely. Some, like the encyclopedias, *Restatements of Law*, and treatises, are in effect self-indexing. Periodicals are accessible through separate tools, such as the *Index to Legal Periodicals*. Separately published books and non-serial publications can be identified and retrieved through several bibliographic guides (e. g. *Law Books in Print*) and, of course, the card catalogs of many libraries.

LEGAL ENCYCLOPEDIAS

Although legal encyclopedias are avidly used by law students and many lawyers, they are considered by many to be neither very scholarly nor authoritative. Among academics, they lack the prestige of general encyclopedias like the older *Britannicas* or the *Encyclopedia of the Social*

Sciences. If, however, they are not used as authority in their own right, but rather as finding tools to the primary sources of authority, they can be helpful aids to legal research. Although their use requires caution, they need not be totally avoided, as some law professors would suggest. In any case, encyclopedias are widely used (and often misused), particularly where comprehensive law libraries are not available. Because of their convenience and the apparent completeness of their predigested research, they will undoubtedly continue to flourish.

The two main legal encyclopedias are *Corpus Juris Secundum,* published by the West Publishing Company, and *American Jurisprudence 2nd,* published by Lawyers' Co-operative Publishing Company. Both employ an alphabetical arrangement of broad legal topics similar to those of the digests and provide indexing both to the entire set and to individual topics. The articles are prepared by editorial writers of each publisher and not by independent legal scholars. The legal propositions and discussions in the main body of text are supported by extensive footnotes containing hundreds of citations to relevant and not so relevant judicial decisions. These footnotes give the encyclopedias their value as search books, described more fully in Chapter III above.

Although encyclopedias are often quoted for axiomatic statements of broadly accepted law,

they lack the careful analysis and fine distinctions of a good treatise. Both *C.J.S.* and *Am.Jur.* (as they are called) are supplemented by annual pocket parts and completely revised every generation, but they are still often slow to reflect subtle changes in the law and significant trends which might be apparent to the alert scholar. Other shortcomings include both gaps and overlapping between articles; overgeneralization and oversimplification; neglect of statutory law and almost complete reliance on case law. This last factor results in a grossly misleading view of American law, in which statutes bulk quite large.

Not surprisingly, each encyclopedia emphasizes the sister publications of its respective publisher. *Corpus Juris Secundum* purports to cite in its footnotes all of the significant decisions found in the West digests, while *American Jurisprudence* provides similar leads in its references to the numerous annotations of *A.L.R.* Illustrations of the format of these encyclopedias are shown above in Exhibits 33 and 34 at pages 93, 94. Both West and Lawyers Co-op also publish several state encyclopedias which follow roughly the same pattern as their national publications. In addition, there are a number of topical encyclopedias covering specific subjects in depth, appealing to practitioners and researchers in those particular areas.

Words and Phrases, also described and illustrated in Chapter III, can be mentioned here as an encyclopedic collection of legally significant words and phrases. These are arranged alphabetically, with numerous constructions, interpretations and definitions culled from the cases reported in the National Reporter System and West's federal reporters. If one's research focuses on the meaning of a particular word or phrase, this set is a very useful source of judicial interpretations. It is kept up to date by annual pocket parts, as well as by tables of words and phrases appearing in the advance sheets and bound volumes of the West reporters. A sample page is illustrated in Exhibit 35 at page 96 above.

TEXTS AND TREATISES

In addition to the encyclopedias, there are thousands of texts and treatises dealing with the many topics of substantive and procedural law. These include multi volume topical encyclopedias and detailed surveys, as well as short monographs on limited aspects of single topics.

Legal treatises appeared shortly after the earliest English reports in the twelfth century *Plea Rolls.* They summarized the developing law of the English courts and statutes and contributed their own analysis and influence to this development. One of the first and most durable of these treatises was that of Henry Bracton which ap-

peared around 1250. Bracton stated his intent
most felicitously in the following language, which
describes as well the purpose of many later serious
commentators (as translated by Pound and Pluck-
nett in their *Readings in the History of the Common Law,* Lawyers Co-op, 3rd ed., 1927, pp. 127–
8):

> "Since, however, laws and customs of this
> kind are often abusively perverted by the
> foolish and unlearned (who ascend the judg-
> ment-seat before they have learnt the laws),
> and those who are involved in doubts and con-
> jectures are very frequently led astray by
> their elders, who decide causes rather accord-
> ing to their own pleasure than by the author-
> ity of the laws, I, Henry de Bracton, have,
> for the instruction, at least of the younger
> generation, undertaken the task of diligently
> examining the ancient judgments of righteous
> men, not without much loss of sleep and la-
> bour, and by reducing their acts, counsels,
> and answers, and whatever thereof I have
> found noteworthy into one summary, I have
> brought it into order under titles and para-
> graphs (without prejudice against any better
> system) to be commended to perpetual mem-
> ory by the aid of writing; requesting the
> reader, if he should find anything superfluous
> or erroneously stated in this work, to correct
> and amend it, or to pass it over with eyes half

closed, since to retain everything in memory, and to make no mistakes, is an attribute of God rather than man."

Legal texts and treatises, like encyclopedias, lack authority and legal effect and are never *binding* on courts. Some of them, however, are written by scholars of outstanding reputation and prestige and hence engender considerable judicial respect. Other texts make no pretense at scholarly analysis but offer convenient guides by which practitioners can familiarize themselves with particular fields of law. These practice books often contain sample forms, checklists and how-to-do-it advice. The inclusion of tables of cases and other research aids can facilitate the use of treatises as finding tools. Among the varied types of texts, the following groups can be noted:

1. Scholarly surveys of particular fields in depth (e. g., *Wigmore on Evidence,* Moore's *Federal Practice, Corbin on Contracts).*

2. Hornbooks, student texts and treatise abridgements (e. g., *Prosser on Torts, Simpson on Contracts).*

3. Practitioners' handbooks in particular fields.

4. Procedural manuals (e. g., Carmody-Wait *Cyclopedia of New York Practice 2d* and Goodrich-Amram *Standard Pennsylvania Practice).*

5. Specialized monographs on more or less narrow topics.

6. Comprehensive commentaries, histories and works of jurisprudence (e. g., Blackstone's *Commentaries,* Pound's *Jurisprudence,* Holdsworth's *History of English Law*).

These works may be supplemented by looseleaf inserts, pocket parts or bound additions. *Some* form of up-dating is usually essential however, and works which are not supplemented lose their value as to current law coverage very quickly. The bypaths of legal bibliography are cluttered with the debris of out-dated and unrevised texts. The everchanging nature of law requires a literature capable of reflecting that change promptly and accurately.

It is often difficult for the researcher to evaluate texts, but the following considerations may aid selection from among the many available: the purpose of the particular publication; the reputation of the author and publisher and the standing of their previous books; the organization, scope and depth of research in this work; its scholarly apparatus (footnotes, tables, bibliography, etc.); the adequacy of supplementation and present timeliness; and how it has been reviewed.

RESTATEMENTS OF THE LAW

Some of the most important commentaries on American law are to be found in the series of *Restatements* prepared under the auspices of the American Law Institute and published by West. These surveys of particular legal subjects were designed:

> "To present an orderly restatement of the general common law of the United States, including in that term not only the law developed solely by judicial decision, but also law that has grown from the application by the courts of statutes that were generally enacted and were in force for many years."

They cover many, but not all, of the important fields: contracts, torts, agency, trusts, conflict of laws, judgments, property, security, and restitution. *The Foreign Relations Law of the United States,* also published in this series, was referred to in Chapter VIII, Treaties. In most cases a second edition of the *Restatement* has been published or is being prepared to reflect new developments or later thinking. While these revisions are being considered and debated, tentative drafts are distributed and are of considerable interest to scholars and researchers.

The *Restatements* are divided into sections, each of which contains a "black letter" general

statement of law, followed by an explanatory
comment on the general principles, and then illustrated by examples of particular cases and variations on the general proposition. A general index volume is provided for all of the *Restatements*, as well as individual indexes for each subject. A glossary of terms defines the significant
words appearing in the *Restatements*.

A series called *Restatement in the Courts* provides annotations to court decisions and legal periodical articles (in the usual West abstracting format) which have applied or interpreted the various sections of each *Restatement*. These volumes
are updated, but with a time lag of several years.
Separate volumes of annotations of court decisions
citing or applying the various *Restatement* sections were previously provided for many of the
states, but are no longer kept up to date.

Shepard's for some time included the *Restatements* as cited material in the supplements to several of their state citators. In 1976, however, this
service was improved by the publication of a separate Shepard's citator for the *Restatements*. This
work covers all of the *Restatements* and lists citations to all reported decisions and leading law
reviews which have mentioned *Restatement* sections. Pamphlet supplementation is projected.

Although they are not official and are not binding, the *Restatements* are persuasive in the courts
—perhaps more so than any other secondary ma-

terial. . Their authors, advisors and discussants are well known scholars and include outstanding members of the judiciary. Although some of the reporters reflected what they thought the law ought to be rather than what the law was, by and large these volumes are considered among the authoritative works of American legal scholarship.

Model codes have also been prepared by the American Law Institute. These include the widely adopted *Uniform Commercial Code* and the *Model Penal Code* which has influenced criminal law reform on the federal and state levels.

PERIODICALS

American legal periodicals parallel in quality and variety the other secondary materials. They have been said to reflect "the law as it was, as it is, as it is tending, and as it ought to be". Periodicals are issued by law schools, bar associations, private publishers, and other groups. Their source is often indicative of their quality and point of view, the most scholarly being the student-edited law school reviews, which are published by every major law school as a training ground for their best students. These contain articles by established scholars, student comments and case notes, which reflect change and innovation in the law, as well as describe historical developments, and mirror the current state of the law.

[*297*]

Outstanding articles in the best reviews are often persuasive in the courts and are occasionally cited in judicial opinions.

1. Types of Periodicals. Examples of the varied types of legal periodicals include the following:

(a) Law school reviews published by almost every accredited school.

(b) Specialized scholarly journals like *Law and Contemporary Problems, Journal of Family Law, Tax Law Review* and *American Journal of Legal History.*

(c) Bar association journals, including those national in scope like the *American Bar Association Journal*; statewide like the *Pennsylvania Bar Association Quarterly* and *New York State Bar Bulletin*; local like the Philadelphia Bar Association's *Shingle* and the *Record of the Association of the Bar of the City of New York;* and those of professionally specialized bar groups like the *I.C.C. Practitioners' Journal* and the *Journal of the Patent Office Society.*

(d) Commercial journals in specialized fields like CCH's *Insurance Law Journal, Labor Law Journal,* etc.

(e) Legal newspapers in many large cities, such as the *New York Law Journal, Philadelphia Legal Intelligencer,* etc.

2. Periodical Indexes. Access to this huge periodical literature is provided by the following indexes, most of which are similar to those in other fields:

(a) Jones-Chipman *Index to Periodical Literature* (1803–1937)

(b) *Index to Legal Periodicals* (1926 to date) —Three year cumulations, annual supplements, monthly advance sheets (except for September).

—Indexes by author and subject, case name, and book reviews.

—Scope: Approximately 385 Anglo-American periodicals.

(c) *Index to Foreign Legal Periodicals and Collections of Essays* (1960 to date)

—Quarterly pamphlets, annual volumes and three year cumulations.

—Coverage: Articles and book reviews and, since 1963, collections of essays, bibliographies, biographies and *festschriften.*

—Subject and author indexes, geographic index and book review index.

—Scope: Approximately 350 periodicals.

(d) *Harvard Current* and *Annual Legal Bibliography*

—Monthly pamphlets (except for July–September) and annual volumes (the latter containing many more entries than the monthly issues).

—Coverage: Periodicals, monographs, collections of essays (American and foreign).

—Classified arrangement by legal system, subject, and country.

—Scope: More than 2500 periodicals and 8,000 monographic works annually, from both common law and civil law jurisdictions.

(e) *Index to Periodical Articles Related to Law*

—Quarterly with annual cumulations and ten year cumulation (1970).

—Coverage: Journals not included in the *Index to Legal Periodicals* or the *Index to Foreign Legal Periodicals*.

(f) *Current Index to Legal Periodicals* (University of Washington Law Library and *Washington Law Review*)

—Weekly subject guide to the contents of law school reviews and other major legal periodicals.

(g) *Index to Canadian Legal Periodical Literature*

—Issued six times a year, with annual cumulations, and one cumulation for the period 1961–1970.

—Indexes by subject, author, case name, and a book review index.

—Scope: Over 60 periodicals.

(h) Periodical digests

—CCH *Federal Tax Articles* (looseleaf format, with monthly supplementation).

—*Law Review Digest* (bimonthly).

3. Periodical Citator. Shepard's Citations publishes the *Shepard's Law Review Citations,* a compilation of citations to articles in 140 law reviews and legal periodicals. This citator, with its supplements, permits the user to determine where any article published since 1947 has been cited in later articles from 1957 to date, or in state or federal decisions.

OTHER MATERIALS

There are a number of other specialized types of secondary material which should also be noted:

1. Directories of practicing lawyers are published, which are based on professional specialization, geographical area, or bar association membership. The most comprehensive of these is *Martindale-Hubbell* which provides a national listing of lawyers in all states, most cities and many

towns. The first five volumes of *Martindale-Hubbell* provide classified listings, as well as fuller descriptions of those who care to purchase space beyond a simple one line entry. In addition, the sixth volume of the directory includes court calendars and brief digests of the law of every state and many foreign countries on specific legal topics. These are usually prepared by outstanding practitioners in the area and often provide references to the primary sources on which they are based. Although they are no substitute for actual research in the authoritative sources and cannot support a definitive judgment, they are useful for a brief statement of law on a particular point or for a reference from which further research can be undertaken.

   2. Records and Briefs. The printed records and briefs of the parties in cases before appellate courts are distributed to a limited number of libraries around the country for research use. The records and briefs of the Supreme Court of the United States, in their official form, go to approximately twenty-seven libraries around the country, while many more libraries subscribe to microform editions. A microfilm edition of the U. S. Supreme Court records and briefs from 1832 to 1925 (with hardcopy indexes) is also commercially available. Records and briefs of the various U. S. Courts of Appeals have a more limited distribution. Records and briefs of the appellate courts .

in most states are also distributed to local law libraries in those areas.

These materials have a permanent value in that they enable attorneys and other legal researchers to study in detail the arguments and facts of significant cases decided by these courts. These documents are usually retrievable by report citation or docket number of the case in which they were submitted. The researcher typically begins with an interest in a case or decision and then seeks this additional source of material on the case. There is no direct subject approach to appellate records and briefs.

The record consists of a transcript of all proceedings below, including the trial testimony, as well as all of the previous legal papers, documents, opinions and judgments. The briefs consist of the written arguments and authorities cited by the attorneys for the respective parties.

3. Form Books. Because of the recurrence of similar problems in the course of legal practice, a literature of form books has developed which contains sample forms of commonly used legal documents and instruments. These can be consulted by attorneys and used as the basis for the preparation of similar papers in later situations. Forms can be found in great multi-volumed collections covering different types of proceedings and subjects and as singly printed forms for a particular transaction or purpose which can be purchased

at a legal stationery store. Handbooks or manuals of practice in particular subject areas frequently contain sample forms, and compilations of statutory forms are often issued in conjunction with state statutory codes. Annotated form books are also published and include citations to cases in which the particular forms have actually been litigated and upheld on appeal.

4. Bar Associations issue legal materials of various kinds including the following types of publications:

> (a) Newsletters and periodicals containing reports on association activities, articles on legal topics, and notices of recent developments.
>
> (b) Annual proceedings or yearbooks of meetings and committee reports.
>
> (c) Handbooks or manuals for the continuing legal education of practitioners.
>
> (d) Comments or special reports on proposed legislation or important developments in law.

5. Dictionaries. Law dictionaries come in a variety of sizes and contain many useful features in addition to definitions. *Black's* (West, revised 4th ed., 1968) and *Balletine* (Lawyers Co-op, 3d ed., 1969) are the most popular, although some still prefer the older, more scholarly *Bouvier's Law Dictionary* (West, 3d revision by Francis

Rawle, 8th ed., 3 vols., 1914). *Cochran's Law Lexicon* (W. H. Anderson, 5th ed., 1973) offers a pocket-size format. Most legal dictionaries include coverage of legal maxims, which are otherwise often elusive, and *Black's* provides an extensive appendix of abbreviations. *Ballentine* may be useful for its aids to correct pronunciation.

There are many, many other types of secondary materials, but these are perhaps the most important.

CHAPTER X
INTERNATIONAL LAW

Although this is primarily a manual of *American* legal bibliography, some mention should be made of the main sources of international law and of research aids and procedures in this field. With the increased contact among nations and the growing impact of international law on the American legal system, the researcher needs some familiarity with the basic materials and bibliographic problems. Obviously the subject deserves fuller coverage than can be given in this sketchy outline, but even this brief treatment may be of some help for a beginning orientation.

INTRODUCTION

International law is the law governing relations between nations—it is to be distinguished from foreign law, which refers to the domestic law of nations other than our own. Foreign law will be treated briefly in Chapter XI which follows. Simply stated, international law deals with the external relations of nations, while foreign law refers to the internal law governing matters *within* a particular country. There is a further significant distinction in this field between public international law and private international law.

The latter (in this country frequently called conflict of laws) determines where and by whose law controversies involving the law of more than one jurisdiction are to be resolved, as well as how foreign judgments are enforced.

Public international law can be viewed as those rules, procedures and customs which regulate the conduct of nations in their relations with each other. Its literature is derived from the following sources:

    (a) Treaties, covenants and agreements between nations.

    (b) Traditional law of nations, as established by customary practice and generally accepted principles of international law.

    (c) International adjudications, tribunals and arbitrations.

    (d) Classic commentaries and digests on international law.

    (e) Law developed by international organizations and reflected in their documentation.

    (f) Law of foreign relations (including diplomatic and consular law).

    (g) Municipal (i. e., domestic or internal) law of individual states relating to international matters.

The published forms of most of these sources can be found within the broad bibliographic cate-

gories already discussed. Treatises, periodicals, casebooks, encyclopedias, looseleaf services, treaty compilations, and digests are available for basic research in international law. The specialized literature of international organizations requires special attention, however.

RESEARCH STEPS IN INTERNATIONAL LAW

A researcher facing a problem in international law can begin in any one of a variety of sources. If the problem deals with a particular area (e. g., an international organization's activities, a treaty, foreign relations of a particular country, etc.), one can proceed directly to the relevant documentation in that field. For a general problem, without immediate references to specifically identifiable sources, recourse to the following materials is suggested:

1. Reference Works. To obtain an overview of an area of international law, one can consult a general treatise, such as L. Oppenheim's *International Law*, edited in two volumes by H. Lauterpacht (Longmans, Green, 8th ed., 1955); J. L. Brierly, *The Law of Nations* (Oxford U. Press, 6th ed., 1963); G. Schwarzenberger, *International Law* (Stevens, vol. 1, 1957; vol. 2, 1968); and, by the same author, *Manual of International Law* (Stevens, 6th ed., 1976). Digests of international law for particular countries are also helpful in this

regard. See, for example, the various American digests of international law, described in Chapter VIII, U.S. Treaties, at pages 281–282 above. Many other general treatises exist, and can be located by using the bibliographies listed in the next section.

2. Yearbooks. Yearbooks of international organizations and annuals on the international law practice of particular countries are a valuable source of information on current international developments and the activities of the organization or country covered by the yearbook. They can also help locate further sources, particularly documents published by the organization or country itself. The *Yearbook of the United Nations* is a leading example of these annual publications. Other important yearbooks are listed at pages 315–316, below.

3. Treaties. When they apply to a particular problem, international agreements are an essential research source in this field. Extended treat ment of treaty collections, indexes, and other treaty material can be found in Chapter VIII, above, and will not be discussed here.

4. International Organizations. Because of the increasingly active role of international organizations in promulgating and administering international law, documents issued by these bodies are frequently important both as sources in their

own right and as material illuminating other sources. An introduction to their literature is provided by T. D. Dimitrov, *Documents of International Organisations: A Bibliographic Handbook* (International University Publications, 1973). A more complete list of bibliographic guides is set forth on pages 312–314, below.

5. International Adjudications and Arbitrations. Adjudications and arbitrations by some international bodies are recognized as authoritative in interpreting international law and resolving international disputes, although they sometimes lack effective enforcement procedures. The published opinions of such tribunals (particularly those of the International Court of Justice) may be relevant in treaty interpretation, and in defining the customary and general law of nations. Information on the publications of the I.C.J. and other international and regional organization tribunals can be found on pages 326–331, below. Sources for the decisions of international arbitrations are also summarized below.

6. Municipal or Domestic Law. This body of internal national law dealing with international law problems, is in part statutory, and in part judicial in nature. It can be found in the usual primary published sources for each country, as well as in special compilations. Decisions of courts all over the world are collected in the series *International Law Reports,* the present title

of a continuing series begun in 1919 and edited by E. Lauterpacht (Butterworth). Deak, *American International Law Cases, 1783–1968* (see page 283 above) collects American decisions, and similar series are available for Great Britain, the Commonwealth and other countries.

7. Foreign Relations Law. Documents of their foreign relations, published by individual countries, along with digests and annuals of their international practice, are useful in revealing both official policies of a general nature and specific handling of particular problems. *Foreign Relations of the United States,* as the series is now called (1861–date), is an example of such a collection. Many nations publish such series, and separate collections of documents relating to specific topics or periods also exist. Most can be found through the bibliographies listed below.

8. Secondary Materials. Many specialized treatises and periodical articles by scholars can provide further research leads and help in understanding the background, current state and future direction of law in this field. Bibliographies and periodical indexes for locating these sources are indicated below.

REFERENCE BIBLIOGRAPHIES

A complete survey of reference sources in international law is beyond the scope and purpose of

this *Nutshell*.   In addition to the few basic treatises cited in paragraph 1 above, and the American sources referred to in Chapter VIII, U.S.
Treaties, above, the researcher is directed to the
following bibliographies for references to particular problems under consideration.   Unfortunately,
most of these bibliographies are not being updated, and hence are primarily useful for retrospective searches:

1. **Retrospective Bibliographies**

    (a) I. Delupis, *Bibliography of International
    Law* (Bowker, 1975).

    (b) J. Robinson, *International Law and
    Organization, General Sources of In-
    formation* (Sijthoff, 1967).

    (c) Association of American Law Schools,
    Law Books Recommended for Libraries
    (Fred B. Rothman & Co., 1967–1970, 6
    vols. looseleaf, with supplements).   Par-
    ticularly "International Law," List no.
    46 (1968).

    (d) Harvard Law School Library, *Catalog of
    International Law and Relations,* in 20
    volumes (1965–1967).

    (e) G. Schwarzenberger, *Manual of Interna-
    tional Law* (Stevens, 6th ed., 1976), con-
    tains an extensive bibliography of books
    and periodical articles.

2. Current Bibliographies. A variety of bibliographies, being published on a current and continuing basis, are available in the field of international law. These can be employed effectively to supplement the retrospective bibliographies cited above and provide subject access to current monographs and/or articles:

(a) *American Journal of International Law* (Quarterly). The bibliographic section of each issue is an invaluable source of information on current publications.

(b) *International Organization* (Quarterly). Each issue contains a useful bibliography on international organizations.

(c) *Current Bibliography of Articles on Public International Law* (Max Planck Institute, Heidelberg). This new bibliography, begun in 1976, is projected for semi-annual publication and world-wide coverage.

(d) *Foreign Affairs Bibliography* (Russell & Russell, 1933–date). Issued for ten year periods, the last volume, covering 1962–1972, was published in 1976. A fifty year cumulation, *Foreign Affairs 50 Year Bibliography: An Evaluation of Significant Books on International Relations 1920–1970,* edited by B. Dexter (Bowker, 1972) is also available.

(e) Jacobstein & Pimsleur, *Law Books in Print,* 4 vols. (Glanville, 1976 revision). Includes references to international law books in English by author, title and subject. Updated by *Law Books Published,* quarterly.

(f) Periodical indexes, such as *Index to Legal Periodicals, Index to Foreign Legal Periodicals* and *Harvard Annual Legal Bibliography,* include coverage of international law and foreign relations. (See Chapter IX above for details.)

INTERNATIONAL ORGANIZATIONS

Today, international organizations such as the United Nations and its many affiliated organizations, and regional organizations such as the European Communities, the Council of Europe, the Organization of African Unity, the Organization of American States, etc., are major sources of international law. Research in their documents and in the general literature about them is becoming increasingly frequent in American law libraries.

There are several useful basic references on international organizations generally. These include D. W. Bowett, *The Law of International Institutions* (Stevens, 3d ed., 1975); H. G. Schermers, *International Institutional Law,* 3 vols. (Sij-

thoff, 1972–1974); A. J. Peaslee, *International Governmental Organizations, Constitutional Documents* * * * (Nijhoff, 3d rev. ed., 1974); and the now somewhat outdated, R. C. Lawson, *International Regional Organizations* (Praeger, 1962).

In beginning work on a current problem dealing with an international organization or its activities, it is often desirable to begin with the yearbook of that organization, particularly if the primary documents of the organization are not easily accessible. These yearbooks review the activities of the organization during the preceding year and frequently provide general directory information. The existence of a relevant yearbook can be ascertained from the *Yearbook of International Organizations* which provides data on most international organizations. If a yearbook has been located, its index will provide access to pertinent information. These volumes also have a permanent reference value, since research can be carried out retrospectively in their review sections, and citations to primary sources and documents can be found in them. Among the most useful are the following:

    (a) *Yearbook of International Organizations* (Brussels, Union of International Associations, 1951 to date, published every two years in English).

(b) *Yearbook of the United Nations* (United Nations, 1946–7 to date).

(c) *Yearbook on Human Rights* (United Nations, 1946 to date).

(d) *Yearbook of the European Convention on Human Rights* (Nijhoff, for the European Commission and European Court of Human Rights, 1959, covering 1955, to date).

(e) *Yearbook of the International Court of Justice* (1946)–7 to date).

(f) *United Nations Juridical Yearbook* (United Nations, 1965 to date).

(g) *Yearbook of the International Law Commission* (United Nations, 1949 to date).

(h) *European Yearbook* (*Annuaire Européen*)—published under the auspices of the Council of Europe annually at the Hague, 1955 to date, with coverage of several European organizations.

(i) *Everyman's United Nations*—an invaluable basic reference tool on all phases of the U.N. and related organizations—similar to the *U.S. Government Manual,* but not issued annually (United Nations, Basic volume covering 1945–1965, published 1968; Supplement for 1966–1970, published 1971).

1. Bibliographic Guides to the United Nations.
The publications of the United Nations are probably the most important materials in the field of
international organizations and, because of their
rapid growth and diverse sources, they are the
most complex.   There is one general index for
United Nations documents, UNDEX (described
below) and separate indexes for the main bodies
(such as the General Assembly, the Security
Council, and the Economic and Social Council)
and for many of the affiliated organizations (e. g.,
the I.L.O., F.A.O., I.C.A.O., etc.).   The following
indexes and guides are particularly useful in locating specific documents or developing research
leads:

> (a) *UNDEX,* successor to *United Nations
> Documents Index* (1950 to date).   This
> is the single most important finding tool
> for U. N. documents.   Prior to 1973, the
> *Index* was published in two parts.   Part
> I was a monthly subject index with a
> cumulative annual index and checklist,
> listing all documents and publications,
> except restricted and internal papers.
> Part II was a checklist arranged by agen-
> cy and various separate publication
> series.   In 1974, a *Cumulative Index,
> Volumes 1–13, 1950–1962* was published
> for the *Index.*   A second cumulation,
> covering 1963–1973, is in preparation.

Beginning in 1974, the *Index* was succeeded by the *UNDEX*. This new index appears in three series, each being published ten times a year, as follows:

Series A: a subject index to U. N. documents;

Series B: a country index to the documents; and

Series C: a descriptive bibliographic listing of all documents, except those which are restricted or for internal use.

Exhibits 97 and 98 below illustrate the subject index of Series A and the descriptive listing of Series C, respectively.

SUBJECT INDEX

Subject	Type of document	Author	Date of issue	Symbol
INTERNATIONAL RELATIONS: role of UN; strengthening See/See also SPECIAL COMMITTEE ON THE CHARTER OF THE UNITED NATIONS AND ON THE STRENGTHENING OF THE ROLE OF THE ORGANIZATION				
INTERNATIONAL SECURITY: strengthening; Declaration 1970; implementation	MEETING RECORDS		751212	A/PV.2439
"	MISC DOCUMENTS		751224	A/31/41
"	"		760203	A/31/47
"	"		760210	A/31/49
INTERNATIONAL TERRORISM See/See also MIDDLE EAST SITUATION: terrorist activities				
INTERNATIONAL TERRORISM: prevention; measures	DECISIONS		751215	A/PV.2441
"	MEETING RECORDS		751215	A/PV.2441

INTERNATIONAL TRADE
See/See also
  AFRICA: international trade
  DEVELOPING COUNTRIES: agricultural trade
  FOOD: international trade
  STEEL: international trade
  UNITED NATIONS COMMISSION ON INTERNATIONAL TRADE LAW
  UNITED NATIONS CONFERENCE ON TRADE AND DEVELOPMENT				

INTERNATIONAL TRADE: general agreement; special intergovernmental committee; establishment	MEETING RECORDS		751215	A/PV.2441
"	VOTING		751215	A/PV.2441
INTERNATIONAL WOMEN'S YEAR (1975): programme	MEETING RECORDS		751215	A/PV.2441
"	MISC DOCUMENTS		751217	A/10506
"	VOTING		751215	A/PV.2441
INVESTMENTS COMMITTEE: composition 1976	RESOLUTIONS		760123	A/RES/3492
INVESTMENTS COMMITTEE: members; appointment; confirmation	DECISIONS		751215	A/PV.2440
"	MEETING RECORDS		751215	A/PV.2440
"	RESOLUTIONS		760123	A/RES/3492
"	VOTING		761215	A/PV.2440

Exhibit 97: A sample page from *UNDEX*, Series A, the official subject index to U.N. documents.

General Assembly   A/10034 <u>to</u> 10105

<u>*General Series*</u> (continued)

A/10034. <u>Resolutions</u> [and <u>decisions</u>] adopted by the General Assembly during its 30th session, 19 Sep - 17 Dec 1975. (To be issued as GAOR, 30th sess., Suppl. No. 34).

A/10035. Programme budget for the biennium 1974-1975. Agenda item 95 (XXX). Budget and programme performance of the United Nations for the biennium 1974-1975. <u>Report</u> of the Secretary-General. 13 Nov 1975. 438 p., tables, including annexes.

--/Add. 1. 4 Nov 1975. 48 p.

A/10079/Corr. 1. 6 Jun 1975. 1 p.

--/Add. 1. Office of the United Nations Disaster Relief Co-ordinator. Agenda item 63 (XXX). <u>Report</u> of the Secretary-General. 22 Oct 1975. 6 p., including annex.

A/10080/Add. 1. Implementation of the Declaration on the Granting of Independence to Colonial Countries and Peoples by the specialized agencies and the international institutions associated with the United Nations. Agenda item 91 (XXX). <u>Report</u> of the Secretary-General. 18 Jun 1975. 11 p.
  Transmits replies from international organizations.

--/Add. 2-4. 21 Jul - 2 Sep 1975. [46] p.
  Transmit replies from international organizations.

A/10081. Review of the intergovernmental and expert machinery dealing with the formulation, review and approval of programmes and budgets. Agenda item 97 (XXX). Joint Inspection Unit. Agenda item 99 (XXX). Report on medium-term planning in the United Nations system. <u>Observations</u> of the Advisory Committee on Administrative and Budgetary Questions. 1 Jul 1975. 7 p.

A/10088. International Women's Year, including the proposals and recommendations of the World Conference of the International Women's Year. Agenda item 75 (XXX). Status and role of women in society, with special reference to the need for achieving equal rights for women and to women's contribution to the attainment of the goals of the Second United Nations Development Decade, to the struggle against colonialism, racism and racial discrimination and to the strengthening of international peace and of co-operation between States. Agenda item 76 (XXX). <u>Note verbale</u> dated 16 Apr 1975 from the Permanent Mission of Bulgaria to the United Nations addressed to the Secretary-General. 5 Jun 1975. [36] p., including annex.

■<u>*General Series*</u> (continued)

A/10094/Add. 1. ... Contribution made by individual organizations. International Telecommunication Union. 17 Jun 1975. 2 p.

A/10099. International Women's Year, including the proposals and recommendations of the World Conference of the International Women's Year. Agenda item 75 (XXX). Status and role of women in society, with special reference to the need for achieving equal rights for women and to women's contribution to the attainment of the goals of the Second United Nations Development Decade, to the struggle against colonialism, racism and racial discrimination and to the strengthening of international peace and of co-operation between States. Agenda item 76 (XXX). <u>Note verbale</u> dated 28 May 1975 from the Permanent Mission of Hungary to the United Nations addressed to the Secretary-General. 3 Jun 1975. [5] p., including annex.
  Annex contains statement by Mr. Antal Apró, Speaker of the National Assembly of the Hungarian People's Republic.

A/10100. Annotated preliminary <u>list</u> of items to be included in the provisional agenda of the 30th regular session of the General Assembly. 13 Jun 1975. [210] p., including annexes.

--/Add. 1. Annotated draft <u>agenda</u> of the 30th regular session of the General Assembly. 16 Sep 1975. 55 p.

A/10102. Report of the <u>Ad Hoc</u> Committee on the Charter of the United Nations. Agenda item 113 (XXX). <u>Letter</u> dated 31 May 1975 from the Permanent Representative of the USSR to the United Nations addressed to the Secretary-General. 2 Jun 1975. [2] p., including annex.

--/Corr. 1. 4 Jun 1975. 1 p.
  Russian only.

A/10103 (S/11708). Policies of <u>apartheid</u> of the Government of South Africa. Agenda item 53 (XXX). <u>Letter</u> dated 29 May 1975 from the Chairman of the Special Committee against <u>Apartheid</u> to the Secretary-General. 3 Jun 1975. 10 p., including annex.

A/10105. Report of the Economic and Social Council. Agenda item 12 (XXX). Economic, financial and technical assistance to the Government of Guinea-Bissau. <u>Report</u> of the Secretary-General. 13 Jun 1975. 2 p.

<u>Exhibit 98:</u> A sample page from *UNDEX*, Series C, the official descriptive listing of U.N. documents, here covering General Assembly publications.

(b) *Checklists of United Nations Documents* (1946–49). This is a special series listing documents of all U. N. organs, issued prior to the *United Nations Documents Index*, with subject indexes.

(c) *Catalog of U. N. Publications,* formerly called *United Nations Publications* (1967, with periodic supplements and revisions). Although basically a sales catalog, it is also a useful and comprehensive guide to U. N. publications. There are also similar catalogs issued for other international organizations.

(d) T. D. Dimitrov, *Documents of International Organisations: A Bibliographic Handbook* (International University Publications, 1973).

(e) B. Brimmer, et al. *A Guide to the Use of United Nations Documents* (Oceana, 1962) and H. Winston, *Publications of the United Nations Systems* (Bowker, 1972). Detailed and sometimes bewildering, these, and Dimitrov (cited above) are the basic guides to U. N. documentary sources.

Preceding the United Nations, the League of Nations had a similar literary output and bibli-

ographic organization. The most useful tools explaining its documentary materials are:

(a) H. Aufricht, *Guide to League of Nations Publications* (Columbia University Press, 1951; reprinted by AMS Press, 1966).

(b) A. C. Breycha-Vauthier, *Sources of Information: A Handbook on Publications of the League of Nations* (Columbia University Press, 1939).

(c) E. A. Reno, Jr., ed., *League of Nations Documents 1919–1946*, 3 vols. (Research Publications, 1973–1975).

2. Documentation and Distribution Systems. International organizations often issue their documents in different forms for distribution. The forms of United Nations' publications are typical of this pattern. They include the following:

(a) **Mimeographed Document Series.** Most international organizations issue their documents initially in a provisional mimeographed form. It is in this series that they receive their identifying document numbers to which most publications cite. These documents comprise the most comprehensive and current set, and a large proportion of them are not reproduced in any other form. Unfortunately, the mimeographed series are generally received only in the largest research libraries.

(b) **Official Records.** This series (much of which appears first in the mimeographed set) includes the corrected and final versions of documents which are designated as part of the official record of the particular organization or body. Records of debates and documents relevant to agenda items are included (reports of commissions, resolutions, etc.).

(c) **Sales Publications.** This series of documents includes those judged to be of wide public interest. They are available by subscription or individually and are given individual sales numbers for identification. They are usually printed, but occasionally appear in other processed form.

Depository libraries have been designated to assure a wide distribution and use of the organization's documents. Such libraries contain all of the materials in (a), (b) and (c), except restricted and limited distribution material Unofficial commercially published microform editions of U.N. documents are now available and being acquired by many libraries.

3. Special Indexes to U. N. Bodies. In many instances, indexes to the publications of specific U. N. bodies are more effective finding tools than the rather diffuse and cumbersome *UNDEX*. Examples of such specialized indexes are the *In-*

dex to Resolutions of the General Assembly 1946–1970 (1972) and the *Index to Resolutions of the Security Council 1946–1970* (1972). Resolutions of the General Assembly and other major bodies of the U. N. are published separately as supplementary volumes to the Official Records for each session. These cumulative indexes provide convenient subject access to what are some of the most heavily used U. N. documents. Part 2 of the *Index to Resolutions of the General Assembly* is a subject index and is illustrated in Exhibit 99 below. A commercial reprint series of these resolutions has recently been issued: *United Nations Resolutions,* edited by D. J. Djonovich (Oceana, 1973 to date), with cumulative indexes in each volume.

Although beyond the scope of this work, it must be noted that there are many regional organizations of nations throughout the world which contain similar deliberative bodies, promulgate resolutions and propose covenants, and in some cases maintain tribunals. Their publications must be included in the research sources of international law. Most of these groups issue occasional catalogs and bibliographies of their documentation and some publish periodic indexes of their publications.

SUBJECT INDEX

Exhibit 99: Sample page from *Index to Resolutions of the
General Assembly 1946–1970* (1972).

ADJUDICATIONS AND ARBITRATIONS

1.   International Court of Justice. Of particular interest in legal research are the publications of the International Court of Justice, which succeeded the Permanent Court of International Justice of the League of Nations. The I.C.J. meets at the Hague to settle legal controversies between countries and to resolve a limited number of other cases involving serious questions of international law. The publications of the I.C.J. include the following.

  (a) *Reports of Judgments, Advisory Opinions and Orders.* (issued individually in advance sheets and then in bound volumes, with both English and French texts).

  (b) *Pleadings, Oral Arguments, Documents* (issued as above).

  (c) *Yearbook of the I.C.J.:*

    "Contains information on the composition of the Court (with biography of each Judge) * * * jurisdiction of the Court in contentious and advisory proceedings * * * it lists the states and others who are entitled to appear before the Court and matters dealt with by the Court since 1946 together with summary of judgments and advisory opinions

given during the course of the year
* * * digests of the decisions relating
to the application of the Statute and
Rules, a bibliography of works published
on the Court and relevant extracts from
treaties, agreements and conventions
governing the jurisdiction of the Court".
Published in French and English editions.

(d) *Rules of the Court* (published as Series
D, although designation of Series A, B,
and C is no longer used).

A similar, but somewhat more elaborate official publication scheme existed for Permanent
Court of International Justice, which was affiliated with the League of Nations and functioned as
the World Court between the two World Wars.
An unofficial compilation of P.C.I.J. decisions was
published as *World Court Reports*, edited by
Manley O. Hudson in four volumes covering 1922
to 1942 (Carnegie Endowment of International
Justice, 1934–1943).

There are also several unofficial series of reporters for the present International Court of Justice: *Case Law of the International Court*, edited
initially by Edward Hambro and continued by
Arthur W. Rovine (Sijthoff, 1961–date) and K.
Marek, *Digest of the Decisions of the International
Court* (Nijhoff, Vol. 1, 1974, on the P.C.I.J.; Vol.
2, on the I.C.J., not yet published) and E. Lauter-

pacht, *International Law Reports,* cited above
(Butterworth, 1919–date) which includes P.C.I.J.
and I.C.J. decisions, as well as selected decisions
of national courts on international law, with
several consolidated indexes.

2. Regional Organization Courts. Although a
complete survey of the courts of the various
regional organizations is impossible here, two such
tribunals can be mentioned for illustrative purposes. The Court of Justice of the European Communities publishes its decisions in several official
languages. An English edition, *Reports of Cases
Before the Court,* was started in 1973, in connection with the United Kingdom's membership in
the Community. Retrospective publication of
earlier cases is in progress in that series. Several unofficial, commercial publishers also provide those decisions as part of larger services.

The European Court of Human Rights was
created by most Western European countries under the European Convention of Human Rights of
November 4, 1950. The Court issues two publication series covering its cases: Series A, *Judgments and Decisions,* and Series B, *Pleadings, Oral
Arguments and Documents.* The Convention is
unusual in having established a system for the
international protection of the rights of individuals. Through the European Commission on Human Rights and, in some cases, through the
European Court of Human Rights, a citizen can

seek redress against the acts of his or her own government. The Commission itself began publication in 1975 of its own series, *Decisions and Reports*.

3. Arbitrations. The settlement of disputes between nations by arbitration has produced publications which constitute another important research source in international law. The awards of the Permanent Court of Arbitration and the International Commission of Inquiry, both established by the Hague International Peace Conference of 1907, were published in the *Hague Court Reports*, edited by James B. Scott (Oxford University Press, 1916; 1932). This set was continued by the United Nations in its series, *Reports of International Arbitral Awards* (1948–date). The initial coverage is retrospective in part. The awards now appear in English or French with bi-lingual headnotes. The set includes agreements reached by mediation or conciliation, as well as awards resulting from contested arbitrations.

A still useful historical compilation of arbitrations involving the United States is J. B. Moore's * * * *International Arbitrations,* 6 vols. (Washington, U.S.G.P.O., 1898) and the documentation of several major arbitrations have been published separately. There is also a growing literature on international claim settlement which is of interest in this area (e. g. Lillich &

Weston, *International Claims: Their Settlement by Lump Sum Agreements,* 2 vols., University Press of Virginia, 1975).

Although there is considerable research interest in international arbitrations between private parties, there has been little reporting of these awards. Some coverage is provided in *International Legal Materials* (American Society of International Law), cited above. A new service, *International Commercial Arbitrations,* edited by C. M. Schmitthoff in 2 vols. (Oceana, 1974, loose-leaf) offers a selective collection of conventions, uniform laws, enactments and arbitration rules "dealing with the settlement of international commercial disputes"—but, alas, not the awards themselves.

4. Domestic Adjudications. Judicial decisions of the courts of individual countries on matters of international law are a valuable source of research information and are accessible through the reporters and case-finders for each country. This jurisprudence is also summarized in the yearbooks, periodicals and digests of international law published in many countries. In addition, several specialized reporters, as noted above, have been issued for such cases by Oceana Publications (*American International Law Cases, 1783–1968; British International Law Cases;* and *Commonwealth International Law Cases*). E. Lauterpacht's indispensable *International Law Reports*

(cited above) includes decisions, not only of international and regional organization courts and arbitration tribunals, but also selective decisions of national courts from many countries.

*   *   *

The confining limits of this manual are felt most intensely in areas like international law and foreign law, each of which requires a Nutshell of its own. Reference to the relevant chapters in *How to Find the Law* (West, 7th ed., 1976) is recommended for fuller treatment.

CHAPTER XI

FOREIGN LAW: COMMON AND CIVIL

Foreign law, as considered in this Chapter, consists of the domestic law of countries other than the United States. For the most part, those countries can be divided into two groups—those comprising the common law system and those of the civil law system. Each system has its own history, its own fundamental principles and procedures, and forms of publication for its legal sources. The treatment of foreign law here will therefore be divided by the two systems, with the primary focus of the common law system on English materials. The literature of most foreign legal systems parallels our own, but often with significant differences. Most countries will have court reports, statutes, administrative decrees and decisions, finding tools, encyclopedias, treatises and periodicals, but their relative status as authority and their forms of publications may differ widely from those of the United States.

There are several basic differences between the common and civil law systems, although the two systems have in recent years influenced each other and their unique characteristics have become much less absolute. It should also be noted that

there is considerable variation between the law, procedures and publications of individual countries within each system. The civil law system is still marked by a primary emphasis on legislation, which constitute the basic legal norms. Judicial decisions are generally not considered primary sources of law and may be less authoritative than important commentaries on the codes by leading scholars. The codes themselves are original statutes which form a comprehensive statement of the law on their subject, as distinguished from the so-called codes of common law countries, which are usually alphabetically arranged subject compilations of previously enacted specific statutes. There are other crucial differences in terminology, in procedure and remedies, and in the status and role of judges, prosecutors, juries and even lawyers themselves.

The common law system includes the law of the United States, England and those countries which have adopted the basic structure of the English common law. This includes most of the Commonwealth of Nations and a few other jurisdictions which have directly or indirectly followed the common law structure and its basic approach. The forms of publication and research procedures under the common law most closely resemble those of the United States.

The civil law system is characterized by the tradition of the European codes and exists in the

countries of continental Western Europe, Latin America, and those parts of Africa and Asia which historically were not subject to English rule. The publications of civil law, shaped largely by the primacy of its codes, differ considerably from those of the common law. The socialist countries of Eastern Europe must be considered part of the civil law system, although they have incorporated into it significant conceptual and procedural changes. There are other countries which do not fit clearly into either system, but are strongly influenced by Roman law, customary law, or traditional religious systems, particularly Hindu or Moslem law. Their legal publications tend to differ most markedly from those in this country and are the least familiar to American law.

Although the law of civil law countries has in the past not been an important part of the practice of the average American lawyer and its sources rarely appear in most small law library collections, today civil law has become a more frequent concern of the legal profession. The law of other common law countries, particularly that of England, has always been of much greater interest in American legal research. Expanded foreign communication, travel and trade, however, have made the law of many other countries increasingly significant to life in this country and frequently relevant to legal proceedings in our

courts. Business transactions between Americans and the citizens, companies and governments of foreign countries have given rise to many legal problems involving the law of other countries. More and more American attorneys are required to prove the law of a foreign country in American court proceedings and many American legal scholars are now using foreign law as a basis for comparing and analyzing our own system. Foreign law sources are essential to the growing study of comparative law, by which the differences and similarities of law in different countries and systems are analyzed.

Whether one is pursuing comparative study of another country's law for academic or scholarly purposes, or preparing for a problem in law practice, it is necessary to have some knowledge of the published sources of law and of the research procedures for their use. This Chapter is designed as an introduction for that purpose. It deals first with English law as illustrative of common law countries generally, and then discusses research in the sources available for countries of the civil law system.

THE COMMON LAW: ENGLISH SOURCES

Among all of the foreign legal systems, the one which is closest to our own is that of England. English law and tradition still have a special relevance in this country by virtue of our common

Anglo-American legal development. The American colonies inherited the English common law and a legal tradition of statutes, cases, customs, and attitudes. Although, since then, American law has developed quite separately, we still share a heritage which often gives English law a persuasive value in our courts not generally afforded to the law of other countries. In general, English legal scholarship, legislation and judicial decisions are frequently of interest here.

Although common law countries with federal systems, such as Canada and Australia, offer different research problems, this description will be limited to English sources. For an introduction to research in Canadian law, see M. A. Banks, *Using a Law Library, A Guide for Students and Lawyers in the Common Law Provinces of Canada* (Carswell, 2d ed., 1974) and for Australia, see E. Campbell and D. MacDougall, *Legal Research: Materials and Methods* (The Law Book Company, 1967).

The following is a brief outline of the main sources and forms of publication of English legal materials.

1. English Statutes. The standard historical collection of English statutes is the *Statutes of the Realm*, covering 1225 to 1713 in 10 vols. (1810–1822), with alphabetical and chronological indexes. Several other collections, all arranged

chronologically, were published during the 19th century under the title, *Statutes at Large*. The contents and coverage of these compilations and later statutory publications are more fully described in *Guide to Law Reports and Statutes* (Sweet & Maxwell, 4th ed., 1962). The *current* forms of published statutes are as follows:

(a) **Slip laws,** issued by Her Majesty's Stationery Office (H.M.S.O.).

(b) **Session laws:**

   1. *Public General Acts and Measures* (H.M.S.O.), published since 1831. An annual chronological compilation of slip laws, now issued in two volumes with a non-cumulating subject index. This compilation also appears in the same form in the *Law Reports* series, described below.

   2. *Current Law Statutes Annotated* (Sweet & Maxwell). A commercial annual session law compilation, chronologically arranged, with annotations.

   3. *Butterworth's Annotated Legislation Series* (Butterworth). A *selective* annotated session law service.

(c) **Compiled statutes:**

   1. *Halsbury's Statutes of England* (Butterworth, 3rd ed., 1968–1975).

An unofficial, well-indexed encyclopedic arrangement of acts in force, supplemented with annual bound volumes and looseleaf service. This is the most convenient subject compilation of English statutes and includes footnote annotations to judicial decisions.

2. *Statutes Revised, 1235–1948* (H.M. S.O., 3rd ed., 1950). This official chronological arrangement of statutes, supplemented annually by a volume of amending acts, is badly out of date and difficult to use.

3. *Statutes in Force, Official Revised Edition* (H.M.S.O., 1972– ——). This official compilation is designed to replace the 3rd ed. of the *Statutes Revised* and is projected for completion in 1980. Each act is issued in a separate pamphlet for inclusion in looseleaf volumes by broad subject categories. A primitive form of publication as compared to *Halsbury's Statutes* or the *U.S.Code,* it will be updated by revised pamphlets as necessary.

2. Statutory Indexes. The various session law compilations generally contain their own indexes

and, in addition, the following compiled indexes
are available for English statutes:

- (a) *Chronological Table of Statutes* (H.M.
  S.O.). Covers 1235 to date; cumulated
  and revised annually.

- (b) *Index to the Statutes in Force* (H.M.
  S.O.). This companion volume to the
  Chronological Table of Statutes, above, is
  cumulated and revised annually and provides an excellent subject index to English statutes.

- (c) *Halsbury's Statutes of England* (Butterworth). Includes a consolidated index
  and individual volume indexes. The general index is revised annually.

- (d) *Statutes of the Realm* and *Statutes at
  Large.* Alphabetical and chronological
  indexes for historical research only.

3. Early Law Reports. As described above in
Chapter II (at pages 12 13), English law reporting has had a long and varied history. The
recording of decisions began with the pleas rolls,
then developed into the Yearbooks, and next
into the nominative reporters. The many nominative reports were cumulated into the *English
Reports, Full Reprint,* covering 1378 to 1865 (W.
Green, 1900–1930, in 176 vols.; reprinted by Fred
B. Rothman & Stevens & Sons). This invaluable
set contains about 100,000 of the most important

decisions, originally published in some 275 nominative reporters. The volumes are arranged by courts, star-paged to the original reporter, and made accessible by a two volume alphabetical table of cases. A similar compilation, the *Revised Reports,* covering 1785 to 1865 (Sweet & Maxwell and Little, Brown, 1891–1917, in 149 vols.) partially duplicates the *Full Reprint*, but adds many other reporters not in the latter. A microform collection of early reports not included in either of these compilations has been issued commercially by Trans-Media Corporation.

4. Current Law Reporting. For decisions since those published in the *English Reports, Full Reprint* (i. e., since 1865), the following reporters are used:

> (a) *Law Reports* (Incorporated Council of Law Reporting for England and Wales, 1865 to date). These current series have semi-official status and authority; they include four specialized reporters which cover:
>
> Appeal Cases (from the House of Lords and the Privy Council);
>
> Queen's Bench Division;
>
> Chancery Division; and
>
> Family Division (prior to 1972, called Probate, Divorce and Admiralty Division)

(b) *Weekly Law Reports* (Incorporated Council of Law Reporting for England and Wales, 1953 to date). Most complete of all current English law reporters, it includes many decisions not appearing in the *Law Reports* series.

(c) *All England Law Reports* (Butterworth, 1936 to date). Contains more decisions than the *Law Reports,* but not always with complete text.

(d) Special subject and topical reporters, similar to such specialized American reports, are currently being published in many fields.

(e) Several reporters published in conjunction with legal periodicals are now discontinued, but still cited for early cases. These include, among others: *Law Journal Reports* (1832–1949); *Law Times Reports* (1859–1947); and *Times Law Reports* (1884–1952).

5. Finding Tools.

(a) *Current Law* and *Current Law Yearbook* (Sweet & Maxwell). This comprehensive research service includes a case digest and citator, statutory digest and citator, and a limited index to British legal periodicals and texts. Issued in monthly pamphlets, annual bound vol-

[*341*]

umes and periodic consolidations, it is the most effective citator for English law. Separate editions are also published for Canada and Scotland.

(b) *English and Empire Digest* (Butterworth, 3rd ed., 1971– ——). This most comprehensive and popular English case digest is now being published in a new "green band" edition, replacing the 2d or "blue band" edition. The arrangement is similar to American digests and it includes references to cases from other commonwealth countries. It is well indexed and supplemented, although its use during the transition from the 2d to 3d edition can be confusing.

(c) *Mews' Digest of English Case Law* (Sweet & Maxwell, 2d ed., 1925–28, with supplements). The necessity of referring to two 10 year supplements (1925–35 and 1936–45) and individual annual supplements since 1945, makes this digest less useful than the *English and Empire Digest*.

(d) *Halsbury's Laws of England* (Butterworth, 3rd ed., 1952–1962). Despite its title, this is a general legal encyclopedia, with references to case law, statutes, and administrative sources. It is well indexed, offers tables of cases and statutes

cited, and provides cumulative annual supplements and a current looseleaf service.   A 4th edition is currently being published (1973– ——), with temporary indexing and supplementation.

(e) *Halsbury's Statutes of England* (Butterworth).   See 1(c) above, at pages 337–338.

(f) *Law Reports Digest* (Incorporated Council of Law Reporting * * *).   This companion publication to the *Law Reports* began in 1892 and consists of a series of cumulations of little current use.   However, its *Consolidated Index* has continued as an updated subject index and digest to the *Law Reports,* with a table of cases reported, and citators for cases, statutes, and statutory instruments.   The *Index* appears currently in monthly advance sheets, annual cumulations, and five and ten year consolidations.

6. English Citators. There is no equivalent of Shepard's citators for English legal bibliography, but the following tools, described above, offer the best citator service and can be used effectively for that purpose.   See Exhibits 100 and 101 below for illustrations of the *Current Law* statutory and case citators.

(a) **Statutory citators:**

    1.   *Current Law Statutes Citator*

    2.   *Halsbury's Statutes of England*

    3.   *Law Reports Consolidated Index*

(b) **Case citators:**

    1.   *Current Law Case Citator*

    2.   *English and Empire Digest*

    3.   *Law Reports Consolidated Index*

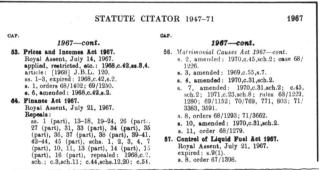

Exhibit 100: A sample page from the *Current Law Statute Citator 1947–1971* (1972).

Adams v. National Bank of Greece S.A. Darling v. National Bank of Greece
    S.A. [1961] A.C. 255; [1960] 3 W.L.R. 8; 104 S.J. 489; [1960]
    2 All E.R. 421; [24 M.L.R. 701; 104 S.J. 737; 9 I.C.L.Q. 695],
    H.L.; reversing [1960] 1 Q.B. 64; [1959] 2 W.L.R. 800; 103 S.J.
    431; [1959] 2 All E.R. 362; [26 Sol. 241; 22 M.L.R. 556; 228 L.T.
    269]; [1959] C.L.Y. 476, 487, C.A.; affirming [1958] 2 Q.B. 59;
    [1958] 2 W.L.R. 588; 102 S.J. 251; [1958] 2 All E.R. 3; [7 I.C.L.Q.
    613; 21 M.L.R. 425, 429; 26 Sol. 32]; [1958] C.L.Y. 492 ....
                                         Digested, 60/477: Considered, 69/1733
—— v. Naylor [1944] K.B. 750 .... *Followed, 57/2368*
—— v. —— [1946] A.C. 543 .... *Applied, 1651, 7254; 53/2826*
—— v. Railway Executive (1952) 96 S.J. 361 .... *Reported, 52/1580*
—— v. Richardson & Starling [1969] 1 W.L.R. 1645; 113 S.J. 282, 832;
    [1969] 2 All E.R. 1221, C.A. Petition for leave to appeal to the
    House of Lords refused .... *Digested, 69/1875*
—— v. Rowley Regis Borough Council (1962) 106 S.J. 551; 60 L.G.R.
    518; 183 E.G. 15; [126 J.P.J. 523], D.C. .... *Digested, 63/1620: Followed, 64/1667*
—— v. Southerden [1925] P. 177 .... *Applied, 11000*
—— v. Spencer (James) & Co., 1951 S.L.T. 223; affirming 1951 S.C. 175;
    1951 S.L.T. 62 .... *Digested, 2538*
—— v. Sunday Pictorial Newspapers [1951] 1 K.B. 354; 66 T.L.R. (Pt. 2)
    771; 94 S.J. 741; [1951] 1 All E.R. 865, C.A. .... *Digested, 7715*
—— v. Union Cinemas [1939] 3 All E.R. 136 .... *Considered, 69/1235*
—— v. Valentine [1975] R.T.R. 563; [1975] Crim.L.R. 238, D.C. .... *Digested, 75/2968*
—— v. War Office [1955] 1 W.L.R. 1116; 99 S.J. 746; [1955] 3 All E.R.
    245 .... *Digested. 55/2110*
—— v. Watson (S. J.) & Co. (1967) 117 New L.J. 130 .... *Digested, 67/2667*
—— v. Wright (John) & Sons (Blackwall) [1972] I.C.R. 463; [1972]
    I.T.R. 191, N.I.R.C. .... *Digested, 73/1093*
Adams (Durham) v. Trust Houses [1960] 1 Lloyd's Rep. 380 ....
                                         Digested, 60/1560: Dictum applied, 68/172
Adams (J.) (Casings) v. Sprung (Henry) & Co., *The Guardian*, November 8,
    1961, C.A. .... *Digested, 61/8024*
Adams and Kensington Vestry, Re (1884) 27 Ch.D. 394 .... *Digested, 57/1962*
Adams & Wade v. Minister of Housing and Local Government (1965) 18 P.
    & C.R. 60 .... *Digested, 67/3880: Applied, 71/11500*
Adams Bruce v. Frozen Products [1953] N.Z.L.R. 63 .... *Digested, 53/244*
Adams Furniture Co. v. Johar Investments (1961) 26 D.L.R. (2d) 380 .... *Digested, 61/4805*
Adams (Henry William Allen), Re the Estate of, Bank of Ireland Trustee
    Co. v. Adams (Charlotte Margaret Lothian), Hutchings (Carol) and
    Parker (Betty Melian) [1967] I.R. 424 .... *Digested, 69/3653*
Adams S.S. Co. v. London Assurance Corporation [1914] 3 K.B. 1256 .... *Applied, 7664*
Adamson v. Att.-Gen. [1933] A.C. 257 .... *Distinguished, 55/754; 61/6116; 63/550.*
                                         Applied, 56/2381: Considered, 66/3407
—— v. Ayr Engineering and Constructional Co. [1963] 1 Lloyd's Rep. 117 . . *Digested, 63/2389*
—— v. Bickle Bros. (January 21, 1957), unreported .... *Reported, 57/2426*
—— v. Jarvis (1827) 4 Bing. 66 .... *Applied, 55/984*
—— v. Knight; Hollingsworth v. Knight, LVC/631-635/1959 [1960] J.P.L.
    652; 176 E.G. 385, Lands Tribunal .... *Digested, 60/2669*
—— v. Secretary of State for Air (1953) 4 P. & C.R. 87, Lands Tribunal .. *Digested, 53/650*
—— v. Smith (Arthur M.) (Hull) (1967) 2 K.I.R. 302, Industrial Tribunal *Digested, 67/1450*
Adamson (D. M.) (Appeal), Re, 1972 No. J. 41, Rd. Haulage App.Div. .. *Digested, 73/3407*
Adamson (T. H.) & Sons v. Liverpool and London and Globe Insurance
    Co. [1953] 2 Lloyd's Rep. 355; [104 L.J. 133] .... *Digested, 53/1803*
Adan Haji Jama v. R. [1948] A.C. 225; [1948] L.J.R. 1503, P.C. ...... *Digested, 2364*
Adart Displays v. Letraset, *The Times*, September 29, 1966 .... *Digested, 66/12130*
Adcock v. Loveridge, *The Times*, June 21, 1956 .... *Reported, 56/5902*
—— v. Wilson [1969] 2 A.C. 326; [1968] 2 W.L.R. 914; 132 J.P. 234;
    112 S.J. 213; [1968] 1 All E.R. 929; [84 L.Q.R. 297], H.L.: affirm-
    ing [1967] 2 Q.B. 683; [1967] 2 W.L.R. 1189; 131 J.P. 292; 111
    S.J. 294; [1967] 1 All E.R. 1028; [1967] C.L.Y. 1760, D.C. ...... *Digested, 68/1712*
Addams v. Carter (1862) 6 L.T. 130 .... *Overruled, 70/894*
Addie (R.) & Sons (Collieries) v. Dumbreck [1929] A.C. 358; [116 S.J. 706]
              Distinguished. 6681, 6692. 55/1850: Applied, 6739, 6746; 52/2386; 60/2137:
              Test applied, 64/2516: Considered, 63/2337: 71/7793; 72/2367:
              Reconsidered, 72/2344: Not followed, 74/2574: Referred to, 75/2341
Addington Community Association v. Croydon Borough Council and Gudgion,
    LVC/1013/1965 [1967] J.P.L. 406; 13 R.R.C. 126; 202 E.G. 647,
    Lands Tribunal .... *Digested, 67/3352*
Addington Smallholders, Re. *See* Surrey Garden Village Trust, Re.

18

Exhibit 101: A sample page from the *Current Law Case
Citator 1947-1975* (1976).

7. Administrative Law. English administrative regulations, formerly called *Statutory Rules and Orders,* are now known as *Statutory Instruments,* and are issued by governmental ministeries or agencies as subordinate legislation under statutory authority. They are published in the following official and unofficial forms and some appear also in looseleaf services on specialized subjects:

(a) *Statutory Rules and Orders and Statutory Instruments, Revised to December 31, 1948,* in a 3rd ed. of 25 vols. (H.M.S.O., 1949–1952). This is the official subject compilation of permanent rules of general application and includes a general subject index, tables and a looseleaf supplement. It is also updated by annual volumes called *Statutory Instruments.* Subject access to the *Statutory Instruments* is provided by the biennial *Index to Government Orders,* which indicates those instruments still in force, and contains a table of statutes under which the orders have been issued.

(b) *Halsbury's Statutory Instrument,* 24 vols. (Butterworth, 1951–52). This useful unofficial subject arrangement of instruments is a companion set to Halsbury's Statutes of England. It is updated by replacement volumes, as needed, and a

cumulative looseleaf supplement. The compilation includes a frequently revised index volume.

8. Bibliographies of English Law. As noted above, there are no comprehensive handbooks or treatises on English legal bibliography. The following bibliographies, however, are helpful for research in English law:

(a) *A Legal Bibliography of the British Commonwealth of Nations* (Sweet & Maxwell, 2d ed., 1955–1964, 7 vols.)

(b) *Guide to Law Reports and Statutes* (Sweet & Maxwell, 4th ed., 1963).

(c) *A Bibliographic Guide to the Law of the United Kingdom,* etc., edited by A. G. Chloros (Institute of Advanced Legal Studies, 2d ed., 1973).

(d) Beale, Joseph H. *Bibliography of Early English Law Books.* (Harvard University Press, 1926, Supplement, 1943).

(e) Maxwell, Wm. Harold. *A Complete List of British & Colonial Law Reports & Legal Periodicals* * * * (Carswell, 3rd ed., 1937).

(f) *Where to Look for Your Law* (Sweet & Maxwell, revised periodically, last edition: 14th, 1962).

Despite their basic similarity of form, there are significant differences between the tools and meth-

ods of legal research in English sources and our
own legal bibliography. Therefore, the fuller discussion in the first edition of Price & Bitner, *Effective Legal Research* is recommended here, as
elsewhere, for more detailed information.

CIVIL LAW

Bibliographic guides and general introductions
are available in English for the law of many civil
law countries, but foreign legal literature, outside
of common law countries, remains an impenetra-
ble mystery to most American legal researchers.
Part of the bibliographic problem in dealing with
foreign law stems of course from differences in
language.   Foreign legal dictionaries exist for
many languages and they are collected in the
major law libraries, but it is impossible to com-
prehend the law of an unfamiliar country in an
unfamiliar language with only the aid of a legal
dictionary. 'Translations and summaries of foreign law in English may be quite helpful, but research in translated texts of legal materials is no
substitute for study of the original documents.
Where a lack of facility with the original language precludes that, recourse to practitioners
trained in the foreign legal system is frequently
required and may, in any event, be necessary to
adequately handle the interests of a client faced
with a problem involving foreign law. The use of
translations can, however, provide some familiar-

ity with the basic concepts and issues of the foreign law problem and facilitate other approaches.

CIVIL LAW TOOLS IN ENGLISH

Research in English language materials on civil law should begin with the many bibliographic guides which are available for references to specific publications on the country and subject involved in your problem. These may cover both primary and secondary materials, but tend to focus on the latter. The use of encyclopedias and treatises is also helpful for background analysis of the legal system and subjects being studied. Then research in English translations and summaries of law can be undertaken. Periodical articles can provide discussion of specific problems, comparative analysis, or leads to other sources.

1. Bibliographic Guides. Some guides are general legal bibliographies providing coverage of all subjects and jurisdictions. Others are specialized bibliographic surveys of the law of a particular region or country, or of a particular subject.

(a) General bibliographic guides.

(1) *Law Books Recommended for Libraries* (Fred B. Rothman & Co., 1967–1970, 6 vols.) and its *Supplements* (Rothman, 1974–75). Published under the auspices of the Association of American Law Schools, this

looseleaf compilation of bibliographies on a wide variety of legal subjects combines the attributes of both general and specialized guides. Volume 5 is devoted entirely to the subject of foreign law while sections in other volumes of the set are devoted to the law of specific areas, such as Africa, Asia, Latin America, and Russia.

(2) Szladits, Charles. *A Bibliography on Foreign and Comparative Law. Books and Articles in English* (Oceana). This excellent tool consists of one basic volume published in 1955, supplemented by periodic cumulations, and is updated regularly in the *American Journal of Comparative Law.*

(3) Jacobstein, J. M. and M. G. Pimsleur. *Law Books in Print* (Glanville Publishers, Inc., 1976, 4 vols.), updated quarterly by *Law Books Published* (Glanville). The most recent edition of *Law Books in Print* is a four volume set listing law books in English in print as of 1974. These volumes, arranged by author/title, subject, and publishers, include some foreign and comparative law titles.

(4) UNESCO, *Register of Legal Documentation in the World* (2d ed., 1957). This is a country-by-country survey of the important legal sources throughout the world. Although out of date, it is still useful.

(5) Harvard's *Current* and *Annual Legal Bibliography* (Harvard Law School Library, 1961 to date). Issued since 1961, these bibliographies index articles and books from all nations as received in the Harvard Law School Library. Both *Current Legal Bibliography,* published monthly, and *Annual Legal Bibliography* are arranged by subject with separate divisions for common and civil law jurisdictions.

(b) **Specialized guides.**

As noted earlier, bibliographic guides exist for specific regions, countries, and subjects. The scope of this publication does not permit a comprehensive listing of such guides. For such a list, one may consult Chapter 15, Foreign and Comparative Law, in *How to Find the Law* (West, 7th ed., 1976). A few examples for Western Europe include: *Bibliography of Translations of Codes and Other Laws of Private Law* (Council of Europe, 1975); P. Graulich, et al., *Guide to Foreign Legal Materials: Belgium, Luxemburg, Netherlands* (Oceana, 1968); and C. Szladits, *Guide to Foreign Legal Materials: French, German, Swiss* ,(Oceana, 1959).

2. Encyclopedias and Treatises. The most extensive survey in English of the law of various nations is the *International Encyclopedia of Com-*

parative Law.   When completed, this work will consist of seventeen volumes, providing background material on the legal systems of many countries and detailed information on specific legal topics, such as contracts, torts, and civil procedure.

A more concise overview of the comparative laws of many countries can be found in general treatises of foreign law, such as Rene David and J. Brierley, *Major Legal Systems in the World Today* (Stevens, 1968).   Some casebooks useful as introductions to foreign law are Henry De-Vries, *Civil Law and the Anglo-American Lawyer* (Oceana, 1976), Rudolf Schlesinger, *Comparative Law* (3rd ed., Foundation Press, 1970) and Arthur von Mehren, *Civil Law System* (2d ed. in preparation, Little, Brown).

3.   Translations and Summaries of Foreign Law.   The growing literature on foreign law includes many translations of actual laws, as well as discussions of law on different subjects for various foreign countries.   For the simplest information, English summaries of the major areas of law of many countries appear annually in the sixth volume (*Law Digests*) of the *Martindale-Hubbell Law Directory*, arranged first by country and then by subject.

Several commercially published series for foreign laws in translation are also available, prominent among which are *Digest of Commercial Laws*

of the World sponsored by the National Association of Credit Management (Oceana, 1966–1975, five volumes in six, looseleaf); *American Series of Foreign Penal Codes*, compiled by the Comparative Criminal Law Project of the New York University School of Law (Fred B. Rothman & Co., various dates); and a series of looseleaf volumes published by the Foreign Tax Law Association on the commercial laws and income tax laws of many countries.

Similar publications have also been issued by official bodies, such as the Organization of American States (*A Statement of the Laws of* * * * *in Matters Affecting Business*, covering various Latin American countries) and the U. S. Bureau of Labor Statistics (*Labor Law and Practice in* * * *, covering countries throughout the world).

In addition, several American accounting firms have been publishing series of brief guides to foreign tax and commercial law in English (e. g., Price, Waterhouse & Co., Arthur Andersen & Co., Ernst & Ernst, and Peat, Marwick & Mitchell). These are available from the issuing firm, sometimes on a complimentary basis.

A useful compilation of the constitutions of the countries of the world is A. J. Peaslee, *Constitutions of Nations* (Martinus Nijhoff, Vol. 1, rev. 4th ed., 1974; vols. 2–4, rev. 3rd ed., 1965–1970). Another useful compilation is *Constitutions of the*

Countries of the World edited by Albert Blaustein
and G. H. Flanz (Oceana, 1971–1975, 14 vols.,
looseleaf). A supplementary series edited by
Albert Blaustein and Eric Blaustein is *Constitutions of Dependencies and Special Sovereignties*
(Oceana, 1975–1976, 4 vols., looseleaf).

4. Periodical Guides. For periodical literature
on foreign law, the following aids are helpful:

(a) Periodical indexes such as the *Index to
Foreign Legal Periodicals, Index to Legal Periodicals*, and Harvard's *Current*
and *Annual Legal Bibliography,* all of
which are discussed above and in Chapter IX.

(b) Szladits, Charles. *A Bibliography on
Foreign and Comparative Law,* described
above, also indexes periodical articles.

(c) Blaustein, Albert. *Manual on Foreign
Legal Periodicals and their Index* (Oceana, 1962) contains a list of important
foreign legal periodicals, providing for
each the country of origin, the language
in which it is written, and the subjects
which it includes.

CIVIL LAW IN ORIGINAL SOURCES

1. Basic Legal Sources

(a) **Codes.** Each country in the civil law
system will have separately published

codes, as described above. These include the basic codes (civil, criminal, commercial, civil procedure and criminal procedure) and several minor codes which are really statutory compilations on other specific subjects (e. g., taxation, labor law, family law, etc.). The codes are usually published in a simple unadorned text, in frequent editions, and also in larger editions with scholarly commentary, annotations and other aids. There is, however, no legal distinction between a code and other legislation, and the codes are amended or repealed by ordinary statutes.

(b) **Collections of Laws.** Laws, decrees and administrative orders are typically published in comprehensive official gazettes, often appearing daily. In some countries, cumulative indexing is unfortunately infrequent. As a result, research is often carried on in periodicals which contain legislative sections, or in looseleaf services, where indexing is more effective.

(c) **Collections of Decisions.** Since there are far fewer reported judicial decisions in civil law countries, there are fewer reporters of such decisions. Both official and commercial series do exist, however,

[*355*]

the latter often being part of larger periodical or looseleaf services.

2. Secondary Materials. As noted above, legal commentaries and treatises may have considerable weight as persuasive authority under the civil law system.   The range of text material, however, as in common law countries, is quite broad, both with respect to subject and quality. There are comprehensive scholarly treatises, highly specialized monographs on narrow topics, pragmatic manuals and guides for the practitioner, and simplified texts for students and more popular use.   For those with the necessary language skills, these works can offer considerable help in legal research.   Information about the foreign language literature available on specific topics can be found in legal bibliographies and guides published for particular countries (e. g., Szladits' *Guide to Foreign Legal Materials: French, German, Swiss*, cited above).   The Harvard *Current* and *Annual Legal Bibliography* offers extensive coverage of treatises and monographs, arranged by subject and country.   The introductory volumes of the *International Encyclopedia of Comparative Law* (see above) contain not only sections on "Sources of Law," but also on "Selective Bibliography," which include major treatises for many individual countries.

The literature of foreign periodicals is equally varied and frequently helpful for the treatment

of specific legal problems. In addition to such English language journals as the *American Journal of Comparative Law* and the *International and Comparative Law Quarterly*, which specialize in foreign and comparative law, there are numerous journals both in English and foreign languages dealing with the law of particular civil law countries and regions. The bulk of the civil law periodical literature is of course in foreign languages. In the major civil law countries, many legal periodicals focus on specific subjects, in addition to those offering general coverage. Access to foreign language periodical articles is primarily available through the Harvard *Current* and *Annual Legal Bibliography* and the *Index to Foreign Legal Periodicals* (cited above), both of which also cover *festschriften* and other collections of essays

Foreign legal encyclopedias, particularly in France, are generally of much higher quality and reputation than those in this country. Although they are still basically guides to authority, their articles are written by leading experts and are usually very reliable.

3. Research Steps. Since the best research approach to a specific legal problem will vary from country to country and depend on the subject under consideration and the published sources available for that jurisdiction, it is impossible to offer one effective model procedure.

Background reading in an encyclopedia or loose-leaf service, if available, is always helpful, both for its introductory value and as a lead to further sources. Failing that, a treatise or relevant periodical articles may serve the same purpose. The leading general French periodicals, e. g., *Recueil Dalloz Sirey* and *La Semaine Juridique*, are particularly useful in offering legislative texts and judicial decisions, along with their scholarly articles.

Inevitably, however, the researcher must consult the relevant code (preferably in an edition with good commentary) or other statutes, and then refer to administrative decrees or orders which may have been promulgated on the particular problem. Judicial and administrative decisions interpreting the legislative norms must also be studied. In the absence of citators, the current authority of decisions can be determined through digests or indexes to collections of decisions, if available, or from references in recent treatises and articles.

It should be emphasized, however, that the above order will not apply to every civil law country. In many countries, research will typically begin with the code itself, but almost never, as in the United States, with a review of judicial decisions.

4. Research Aids. Citation forms for foreign legal materials can be very confusing for Ameri-

can lawyers. Fortunately, the *Uniform System of Citation* (the now familiar *bluebook*) includes in its latest edition citation information for ten major civil law countries and for the basic Roman law sources. Its coverage is quite limited, but still helpful.

The extensive use of abbreviations adds another difficulty to foreign law research. The following guides in English, compiled by A. Sprudsz and published by Oceana Publications, can be consulted: *Benelux Abbreviations and Symbols: Law and Related Subjects* (1971); *Foreign Law Abbreviations: French* (1967); and *Italian Abbreviations and Symbols: Law and Related Subjects* (1969). For Germany, only a guide in German is available: H. Kirchner, *Abkuerzungsverzeichnis der Rechtssprache* (2d ed., 1968).

POSTSCRIPT

It is the author's hope that this *Nutshell* will be accepted for no more than what it is—the briefest of introductions to:

"The lawless science of our law,
That codeless myriad of precedent,
That wilderness of single instances."
　　　—Tennyson, *Aylmer's Field.*

The author concludes with this caveat from an earlier but no less cautious compiler:

"Learned Homer sometime sleepeth, and the fastest foote sometime slyppeth, the wysest tongue may catch a tryp, and the wariest penne commit a fault, errour is as naturall, as the correction thereof commendable. Wherefore that which remaineth is, I commit my selfe and my labour to thy good lyking, if thou lyke it, commend it, and vse it, if thou dyslike it, amend it."
　　　—William Averell, Preface to
　　　Foure notable Histories (1590).

Appendix A

CONTENTS OF REPORTERS IN THE NATIONAL REPORTER SYSTEM AND DATES OF INCEPTION

Atlantic Reporter (1886 to date): Includes decisions beginning with the designated volumes of the following major state reports: 53 Connecticut; 12 Delaware (7 Houston); 6 Delaware Chancery; 77 Maine; 63 Maryland; 63 New Hampshire; 47 New Jersey Law; 40 New Jersey Equity; 108 Pennsylvania State; 102 Pennsylvania Superior; 15 Rhode Island; 58 Vermont.

North Eastern Reporter (1885 to date): 112 Illinois; 284 Illinois Appellate; 102 Indiana; 1 Indiana Appellate; 139 Massachusetts; 99 New York; 43 Ohio State; 20 Ohio Appellate.

North Western Reporter (1879 to date): 1 Dakota; 51 Iowa; 41 Michigan; 26 Minnesota; 8 Nebraska; 1 North Dakota; 1 South Dakota; 46 Wisconsin.

Pacific Reporter (1884 to date): 1 Arizona; 64 California; 1 California Appellate; 7 Colorado; 1 Colorado Appellate; 2 Idaho; 30 Kansas; 1 Kansas Appellate; 4 Montana; 17 Nevada; 3 New Mexico; 1 Oklahoma; 1 Oklahoma Criminal Appeals; 11 Oregon; 3 Utah; 1 Washington; 2 Washington Territory; 3 Wyoming.

South Eastern Reporter (1887 to date): 77 Georgia; 1 Georgia Appellate; 96 North Carolina; 25 South Carolina; 82 Virginia; 29 West Virginia.

APPENDIX A

South Western Reporter (1887 to date): 47 Arkansas; 84 Kentucky; 8 Kentucky Law Reporter; 1 Kentucky Decisions; 89 Missouri; 93 Missouri Appellate; 85 Tennessee; 16 Tennessee Appellate; 66 Texas; 21 Texas Appellate; 1 Texas Civil Appeals; 31 Texas Criminal Reports.

Southern Reporter (1887 to date): 80 Alabama; 1 Alabama Appellate; 22 Florida; 104 Louisiana; 39 Louisiana Annotated; 9 Louisiana Appellate; 64 Mississippi.

California Reporter (1960 to date): 53 California 2d; 176 California Appellate 2d.

New York Supplement (1888 to date): 1 New York (1 Comstock); 1 Appellate Division; 1 Miscellaneous; and containing many other now discontinued lower court reporters, plus numerous decisions, not otherwise reported. Since February 1963, however, coverage is virtually the same as that of the three official reporters, *New York, Appellate Division* and *Miscellaneous Reports*.

Appendix B

CURRENT STATUS OF MAJOR OFFICIAL
STATE REPORTS

(This listing does not include *unofficial* reporters unless they have received official recognition or are generally used in place of discontinued official reporters. See the *bluebook* (pp. 104–142) for a fuller listing of current state reports (with abbreviations) and Price & Bitner, *Effective Legal Research* (1st ed., Appendix I) for earlier reports.)

Alabama: *Alabama Reports* (1840–date), published by West since vol. 200 (1916); *Alabama Appellate Court Reports* (1910–date) published by West, since vol. 16 (1920).

Alaska: *Alaska Reports* (1869–1958) discontinued with vol. 17 (1958). Current official source is West's *Alaska Reporter,* a state edition of the *Pacific Reporter.*

Arizona: *Arizona Reports* (1866–date) published by West since vol. 64 (1945); *Arizona Appeals Reports* (1965–date) published by West since vol. 1.

Arkansas: *Arkansas Reports* (1837–date).

California: *California Reports* (1850–date); *California Appellate Reports* (1906 to date).

Colorado: *Colorado Reports* (1864–date).

APPENDIX B

Connecticut: *Connecticut Reports* (1817–date); *Connecticut Supplement* (1935–date); *Connecticut Circuit Court Reports* (1961–1970), discontinued with vol. 6 (1977).

Delaware: *Delaware Reports* (1832–1866) discontinued with vol. 59 (1966). Current official source is West's *Delaware Reporter,* a state edition of the *Atlantic Reporter.*

Florida: *Florida Reports* (1846–1948) discontinued with vol. 160 (1948). Current official source is West's *Florida Cases,* a state edition of the *Southern Reporter. Florida Supplement* (1952–date).

Georgia: *Georgia Reports* (1846–date); *Georgia Appeals Reports* (1807–date).

Hawaii: *Hawaii Reports* (1847–date).

Idaho: *Idaho Reports* (1866–date), published by West since vol. 67 (1946) without apparent change in status.

Illinois: *Illinois Reports* (Vol. 11, 1850–date); *Illinois Appellate Court Reports* (1877–date); *Illinois Court of Claims Reports* (1889–date).

Indiana: *Indiana Reports* (1848–date); *Indiana Appellate Court Reports* (1890–date), since 1972 called *Indiana Court of Appeals Reports.*

Iowa: *Iowa Reports* (1855–1968) discontinued with vol. 261 (1968). Cur-

rent official source is the *North Western Reporter*, which has been designated as the official reporter in Iowa.

Kansas: *Kansas Reports* (1862–date).

Kentucky: *Kentucky Reports* (Vol. 78, 1879–1951) discontinued with vol. 314 (1951). Current source is West's *Kentucky Decisions*, a state edition of the *South Western Reporter*.

Louisiana: *Louisiana Reports* (Vol. 104, 1901–1972) published by West since vol. 109 (1902); discontinued with vol. 263 (1972). Current source (unofficial) is West's *Louisiana Cases*, a state edition of the *Southern Reporter*.

Maine: *Maine Reports* (1820–1965) discontinued with vol. 161 (1965). Current official source is West's *Maine Reporter*, a state edition of the *Atlantic Reporter*.

Maryland: *Maryland Reports* (1851–date); *Maryland Appellate Reports* (1962–date).

Massachusetts: *Massachusetts Reports* (1804–date); *Massachusetts Appeals Court Reports* (1976–date); *Massachusetts Appellate Decisions* (1941–date).

Michigan: *Michigan Reports* (1847–date); *Michigan Appeals Reports* (1965–date).

Minnesota: *Minnesota Reports* (1851–date).

Mississippi: *Mississippi Reports* (1818–1966) discontinued with vol. 254 (1966). Current official source is West's *Mississippi Cases,* a state edition of the *Southern Reporter.*

Missouri: *Missouri Reports* (1821–1956) discontinued with vol. 365 (1956). Current official source is West's *Missouri Cases,* a state edition of the *South Western Reporter. Missouri Appeal Reports* (1876–1952) discontinued with vol. 241 (1952).

Montana: *Montana Reports* (1868–date).

Nebraska: *Nebraska Reports* (1860–date).

Nevada: *Nevada Reports* (1865–date).

New Hampshire: *New Hampshire Reports* (1816–date).

New Jersey: *New Jersey Law Reports* (1790–1948, vol. 137) and *New Jersey Equity Reports* (1830–1948, vol. 142) combined and continued by *New Jersey Reports* (1948–date), published by West since vol. 53 (1968); *New Jersey Superior Court Reports* (1948–date), published by West since vol. 103 (1968).

New Mexico: *New Mexico Reports* (1852–date), published by West since vol. 36 (1933).

New York: *New York Reports* (1847–date); *Appellate Division Reports* (1896–

date); *Miscellaneous Reports* (1892–date).

North Carolina: *North Carolina Reports* (1778–date); *North Carolina Court of Appeals Reports* (1968–date).

North Dakota: *North Dakota Reports* (1890–1953) discontinued with vol. 79 (1953). Current source (unofficial) is *North Western Reporter.*

Ohio: *Ohio Reports* (1821–1852) succeeded by *Ohio State Reports* (1852–date); *Ohio Appellate Reports* (1913–date); *Ohio Miscellaneous* (1965–date).

Oklahoma: *Oklahoma Reports* (1890–1953) discontinued with vol. 208 (1953); *Oklahoma Criminal Reports* (1908–1953) discontinued with vol. 97 (1953). Current official source is West's *Oklahoma Decisions,* a state edition of the *Pacific Reporter.*

Oregon: *Oregon Reports* (1853–date); *Oregon Reports, Court of Appeal* (1969–date); *Oregon Tax Reporter* (1962–date).

Pennsylvania: *Pennsylvania State Reports* (1845–date); *Pennsylvania Superior Court Reports* (1895–date); *Pennsylvania Commonwealth Court Reports* (1970–date); *Pennsylvania District and County Reports* (1922–date).

Puerto Rico: *Puerto Rico Reports* (1899–date); *Decisiones de Puerto Rico* (1899–date).

Rhode Island: *Rhode Island Reports* (1828–date).

South Carolina: *South Carolina Reports* (1868–date).

South Dakota: *South Dakota Reports* (1890–date).

Tennessee: *Tennessee Reports* (1791–1971) discontinued with vol. 225 (1971); *Tennessee Appeals Reports* (1925–1971) discontinued with vol. 63 (1971). Current official source is West's *Tennessee Decisions,* a state edition of the *South Western Reporter.*

Texas: *Texas Reports* (1846–1963) discontinued with vol. 163 (1963); *Texas Criminal Reports* (1876–1963) discontinued with vol. 172 (1963). Current source (unofficial) is West's *Texas Cases,* a state edition of the *South Western Reporter.*

Utah: *Utah Reports* (1855–1974) published by West from vol. 1, 2d series—vol. 30, 2d series (1953–1974) and then discontinued. Current source (unofficial) is West's *Utah Reporter,* a state edition of *Pacific Reporter.*

Vermont: *Vermont Reports* (1826–date).

Virgin Islands: *Virgin Islands Reports* (1917–date).

Virginia: *Virginia Reports* (1790–date).

STATE REPORTS

Washington: *Washington Territory Reports* (1854–1888); *Washington Reports* (1899 to date); *Washington Appellate Reports* (1969–date).

West Virginia: *West Virginia Reports* (1864–date); *West Virginia Court of Claims Report* (1942–date).

Wisconsin: *Wisconsin Reports* (1853–date).

Wyoming: *Wyoming Reports* (1870–1959) discontinued with vol. 80 (1959). Current official source is West's *Wyoming Reporter,* a state edition of the *Pacific Reporter.*

*

Appendix C

LIST OF STATE RESEARCH GUIDES

STATE	GUIDE
California	Myron Fink, *Research in California Law* (Dennis, 2d ed., 1964).
	Dan Henke, *California Law Guide,* (Parker & Sons Publications, 2d ed., 1976).
Florida	Harriett French, *Research in Florida Law* (Oceana, 2d ed., 1965).
Illinois	Bernita Davies, *Research in Illinois Law* (Oceana, 1954).
Louisiana	Kate Wallach, *Louisiana Legal Research Manual* (LSU Law School, Institute of Continuing Legal Education, 1972).
Michigan	Richard Beer, *An Annotated Guide to the Legal Literature of Michigan* (Fitzsimmons Sales, 1973).
New Mexico	Arie Poldervaart, *Manual for Effective New Mexico Legal Research* (University of New Mexico Press, 1955).
North Carolina	Igor Kavass, *Guide to North Carolina Legal Research* (Hein, 1973).
Pennsylvania	Erwin Surrency, *Research in Pennsylvania Law* (Oceana, 2d ed., 1965).

South Carolina	Robin Mills and Jon Schultz, *South Carolina Legal Research Methods* (Hein, 1976).
Texas	Marian Boner, *A Reference Guide to Texas Law and Legal History: Sources and Documentation* (University of Texas Press, 1976).
	Leon Lebowitz, *Legal Bibliography and Research: An Outlined Manual on the Use of Law Books for Practice in the Texas and Federal Courts* (Austin, Texas, 2d rev. ed., 1957).
Wisconsin	William Knudson, *Wisconsin Legal Research Guide* (University of Wisconsin—Extension Department of Law, 2d ed., 1972).

Appendix D

Selective List of Looseleaf Services

The following is a selective list of looseleaf services which are useful in legal research. It does not purport to include all such publications, and it should be used with caution since new services are issued from time to time and others cease publication. The basic criteria for inclusion were frequent supplementation (at least monthly) and publication of primary documents (either abstracts or full texts). The many services which are published for various foreign countries and those in fields of international law are not included except for an illustrative sampling in the fields of international taxation and international trade law.

A list of publishers and their abbreviations precedes the listing of services.

Publishers of Looseleaf Services

Abbreviation	Publisher
BNA	Bureau of National Affairs
Bender	Matthew Bender & Company
CCH	Commerce Clearing House
CIS	Congressional Information Service
Callaghan	Callaghan & Company
ELI	Environmental Law Institute

APPENDIX D

Abbreviation	Publisher
IBP	Institute for Business Planning
IBFD	International Bureau of Fiscal Documentation
L.E.	L.E. Publishers
Oceana	Oceana Publications
P–H	Prentice-Hall
PLEI	Public Law Education Institute
PLR	Professional Liability Reporter (San Francisco)
P & F	Pike & Fischer
RIA	Research Institute of America
Sweet & Maxwell	Sweet & Maxwell (London)

Looseleaf Services by Subject

ACCOUNTING
Accountancy Law Reporter (CCH)

ADMINISTRATIVE LAW
Pike & Fischer Administrative Law (P & F)

ANTITRUST, see TRADE REGULATION

AVIATION
Aviation Law Reporter (CCH)

BANKING
Banking (Control of Banking; Federal Aids to Financing) (P–H)
Federal Banking Law Reporter (CCH)

BANKRUPTCY
Bankruptcy Law Reporter (CCH)

LOOSELEAF SERVICES

CARRIERS
Federal Carriers Reporter (CCH)
State Motor Carrier Guide (CCH)

CHEMICAL AND TOXIC SUBSTANCES, see ENVIRONMENT

COMMERCIAL LAW AND CONSUMERISM
Consumer and Commercial Credit—Installment Sales Service (P–H)
Consumer Credit Guide (CCH)
Secured Transactions Guide (CCH)
Uniform Commercial Code Reporting Service (Callaghan)

COMMUNICATIONS
Communications Service (P–H)
Media Law Reporter (BNA)
Radio Regulation (P & F)

COMPENSATION, see PENSION AND COMPENSATION

CONSUMER ISSUES, see COMMERCIAL LAW AND CONSUMERISM; PRODUCTS LIABILITY

COPYRIGHT, see PATENT AND COPYRIGHT

CORPORATIONS
Corporation Law Guide (CCH)
Corporation Service (P–H)
Professional Corporation Guide (P–H)

CRIMINAL LAW
Criminal Law, edited by Duane Nedrud (L.E.)
Criminal Law Reporter (BNA)

EDUCATION AND FOUNDATIONS
College and University Reporter (CCH)
Private Foundations Reporter (CCH)

ENERGY
    Energy Controls (P–H)
    Energy Management and Federal Energy Guide-
        lines (CCH)
    Energy Users Report (BNA)
    Nuclear Regulation Reporter (CCH)

ENVIRONMENT
    Chemical Regulation Reporter (BNA)
    Environment Reporter (BNA)
    Environmental Law Reporter (ELI)
    International Environment Guide (BNA)
    Noise Regulation Reporter (BNA)
    Pollution Control Guide (CCH)

ESTATES—WILLS—TRUSTS
    Estate Planning (IBP)
    Inheritance, Estate and Gift Taxes (CCH)
    Inheritance Taxes (P–H)
    Successful Estate Planning Ideas and Methods
        (P–H)
    Tax Management—Estates, Gifts, and Trusts
        (BNA)
    Wills, Estates and Trusts (P–H)

FAIR EMPLOYMENT, see LABOR AND EM-
PLOYMENT RELATIONS

FAMILY LAW
    Family Law Reporter (BNA)

FOOD, DRUG AND MEDICAL
    Food, Drug, Cosmetic Law Reporter (CCH)
    Medical Devices Reporter (CCH)

FOREIGN TAXATION, see TAXATION, INTER-
NATIONAL AND FOREIGN

LOOSELEAF SERVICES

FOUNDATIONS, see EDUCATION AND FOUNDA-
TIONS

GOVERNMENT CONTRACTS
    Contract Appeals Decisions (CCH)
    Federal Contracts Report (BNA)
    Government Contracts Reporter (CCH)

HOUSING, see URBAN PROBLEMS

INSURANCE
    Automobile Law Reporter (CCH)
    Benefits Review Board Service (Bender)
    Insurance Guide (P–H)
    Insurance Law Reporter (CCH)
    Unemployment Insurance Reporter (CCH)
    Workmen's Compensation Law Reporter (CCH)

INTERNATIONAL TAXATION, see TAXATION,
INTERNATIONAL AND FOREIGN

INTERNATIONAL TRADE, see TRADE, INTER-
NATIONAL

LABOR AND EMPLOYMENT RELATIONS, see also
INSURANCE; OCCUPATIONAL SAFETY AND
HEALTH; PENSION AND COMPENSATION
    Collective Bargaining Negotiations and Contracts
      (BNA)
    Construction Labor Report (BNA)
    Employment Practices Guide (CCH)
    Government Employee Relations Report (BNA)
    Industrial Relations Guide (P–H)
    Labor Arbitration Awards (CCH)
    Labor Law Reporter—Labor Relations—Wages-
      Hours (CCH)
    Labor Relations Guide (P–H)

LABOR AND EMPLOYMENT RELATIONS—Continued

Labor Relations Reporter (BNA)
—Labor-Management Relations
—State Laws
—Fair Employment Practice
—Wages and Hours
—Labor Arbitration

Public Personnel Administration—Labor-Management Relations (P–H)

Wage-Hour Guide (P–H)

LEGISLATION

Advance Session Laws Reporter (CCH)
Congressional Index (CCH)
Congressional Information Service/Index (CIS)

LIQUOR CONTROL

Liquor Control Law Reporter (CCH)

MALPRACTICE

Professional Liability Reporter: Malpractice Decisions & Developments (PLR)

MEDICARE AND MEDICAID

Medicare and Medicaid Guide (CCH)

MILITARY LAW

Military Law Reporter (PLEI)

PATENT AND COPYRIGHT

Patent, Trademark & Copyright Journal (BNA)
United States Patent Quarterly (BNA)

PENSION AND COMPENSATION

Federal Pension Law Service (Bender)
Pay Planning Program (IBP)
Pension and Profit Sharing (P–H)
Pension Coordinator (RIA)

LOOSELEAF SERVICES

PENSION AND COMPENSATION —Continued
    Pension Plan Guide (CCH)
    Pension Reporter (BNA)
    Plan Administrator's Compliance Manual (P–H)

POVERTY
    Poverty Law Reporter (CCH)

PRODUCTS LIABILITY
    Consumer Product Safety Guide (CCH)
    Federal Consumer Product Safety (Bender)
    Product Safety and Liability Reporter (BNA)
    Products Liability Reporter (CCH)

PROFIT SHARING, see PENSION AND COMPEN-
SATION

PUBLIC UTILITIES
    Federal Power Service (Bender)
    Utilities Law Reporter (CCH)

OCCUPATIONAL SAFETY AND HEALTH
    Employment Safety and Health Guide (CCH)
    Occupational Safety and Health Reporter (BNA)

SECURITIES
    Blue Sky Law Reporter (CCH)
    Commodity Futures Law Reporter (CCH)
    Executive Disclosure Guide—SEC Compliance (CCH)
    Federal Securities Law Reporter (CCH)
    Mutual Funds Guide (CCH)
    SEC Compliance—Financial Reporting and Forms (P–H)
    Securities Regulation and Law Report (BNA)
    Securities Regulation Service and Guide (P–H)

SUPREME COURT
    U.S. Supreme Court Bulletin (CCH)
    United States Law Week (BNA)

APPENDIX D

TAXATION
All-State Sales Tax Reporter (CCH)
Capital Adjustments (P–H)
Cumulative Changes (P–H)
Federal Excise Tax Reporter (CCH)
Federal Taxes Citator (P–H)
Federal Taxes—IRS Letter Rulings (CCH)
Federal Taxes—Private Letter Rulings (P–H)
Federal Taxes Service (P–H)
Oil and Gas—Natural Resources Taxes (P–H)
Property Tax Service (P–H)
Sales Tax Service (P–H)
Standard Federal Tax Reporter (CCH)
State and Local Taxes (P–H)
State Income Taxes Service (P–H)
State Tax Guide (CCH)
State Tax Reporter (CCH)
Tax Coordinator (RIA)
Tax Court Reporter (CCH)
Tax Court Service (P–H)
Tax-Exempt Organizations (P–H)
Tax Guide (RIA)
Tax Ideas (P–H)
Tax Management (BNA)
—U.S. Income
—Primary Sources
Tax Planning (IBP)

TAXATION, INTERNATIONAL AND FOREIGN
African Tax Systems (IBFD)
Corporate Taxation in Latin America (IBFD)
European Taxation (IBFD)
Foreign Tax and Trade Briefs, edited by Walter
Diamond (Bender)

TAXATION. INTERNATIONAL AND FOREIGN
—Continued

Guides to European Taxation (IBFD)
—Taxation of Patent Royalties, Dividends, Interest in Europe
—Taxation of Companies in Europe
—Corporate Taxation in the Common Market
—Taxation of Private Investment Income
—Value Added Taxation in Europe

Income Taxes World-Wide (CCH)

Tax Havens of the World, edited by Walter Diamond (Bender)

Tax Management—Foreign Income (BNA)

Tax Treaties (CCH)

Tax Treaties/Excise Taxes (P–H)

U.S. Taxation of International Operations (P–H)

TRADE, INTERNATIONAL

Balance of Payments Reporter (CCH)

Common Market Reporter (CCH)

Digest of Commercial Laws of the World (Oceana)

Encyclopedia of European Community Law (Sweet & Maxwell; Bender)
—United Kingdom Sources
—European Community Treaties

Investment Laws of the World (Oceana)

International Trade Reporter's Export Shipping Manual (BNA)

International Trade Reporter's U.S. Export Weekly (BNA)

TRADE REGULATION

Antitrust and Trade Regulation Reporter (BNA)

Trade Regulation Reporter (CCH)

TRUSTS, see ESTATES—WILLS—TRUSTS

URBAN PROBLEMS
    Equal Opportunity in Housing (P–H)
    Housing and Development Reporter (BNA)
    Urban Affairs Reporter (CCH)

WILLS, see ESTATES—WILLS—TRUSTS

WORKMEN'S COMPENSATION, see INSURANCE

INDEX

References are to Pages

INDEX

INDEX

INDEX

INDEX

References are to Pages

INDEX

INDEX

INDEX

INDEX

INDEX

References are to Pages

INDEX

INDEX

References are to Pages

INDEX

INDEX

References are to Pages

HOUSE REPORTS
See Congressional Committee Reports

INDEX

References are to Pages

INDEX

LAW REPORTS
See Court Reports

LAW REPORTS (English), 13, 340–341

LAW REPORTS DIGEST (English), 343

LAW REVIEW DIGEST, 301

LAWS
See Legislation; Statutes

LAWYERS' DIRECTORIES
See Directories

LAWYERS' EDITION, 23–28, 31, 90–91, 100
Advance sheets, 31
Annotation history table, 90
  Exhibit, 91
Exhibits, 24–28, 91

*LAWYERS' EDITION (2d SERIES) LATER CASE SER-
  VICE*, 23

LAWYERS' REPORTS ANNOTATED, 57

LEAGUE OF NATIONS, 321–322
Bibliographic guides, 322

LEAGUE OF NATIONS TREATY SERIES, 265, 268, 269,
  273, 275

LEGAL ABBREVIATIONS
See Abbreviations

LEGAL BIBLIOGRAPHY
See Bibliography

*LEGAL BIBLIOGRAPHY OF THE BRITISH COMMON-
  WEALTH OF NATIONS* (Sweet and Maxwell), 347

LEGAL CITATIONS
See Citations

LEGAL DICTIONARIES
See Dictionaries

INDEX

INDEX

INDEX

INDEX

INDEX

SHEPARD'S CITATIONS—Continued
Parallel tables, 60–63
Periodicals, 301
Popular name tables, 60, 144, 147
Restatements of the Law, 296
State constitutions, 135–136
State statutes, 149, 153, 157–159
Supplementation, 99
Treaties, 261, 280

SIMPLE RESOLUTIONS, 114

SLIP DECISIONS, 30, 56
State, 56
United States Supreme Court, 30

SLIP LAWS, 109, 117–118, 136, 145–146, 162, 337
English law, 337

SLIP TREATIES, 263

STAR PAGING OF UNOFFICIAL REPORTS, 19–20
Exhibit, 20

STARE DECISIS, 2, 10–11, 64

STATE BLUE AND WHITE BOOKS, 62–63

STATE CONSTITUTIONS, 134–135

STATE COURT REPORTS, 35–37, 54–58, 238, 363–369
(Appendix B)
See also, *American Law Reports; National Reporter System*
Current status of official reports, Appendix B, 363–369
Discontinued, 54–55

STATE LAW INDEX, 147

STATE LEGISLATIVE HISTORY, 198–200

STATE REPORTS
See State Court Reports

INDEX

References are to Pages

INDEX

INDEX

INDEX

References are to Pages

INDEX

INDEX

References are to Pages

INDEX

INDEX

References are to Pages